RECIPES BY THE
ALABAMA
LIONS

LIONS CLUB · ALL IN
FUND RAISING ACTIVITY

LIONS
L
CLUB
®

This cookbook is a collection of our favorite recipes
which are not necessarily original recipes.

Published by: Favorite Recipes® Press
P.O. Box 305142
Nashville, TN 37230

Printed in the United States of America
First Printing: 1990, 15,000 copies

Library of Congress Number: 90-41798
ISBN: 0-87197-284-0

Contents

LIONS IN THE KITCHEN

Selected Recipes from
The Huntsville Lions Club and Lions Clubs of Alabama

The Lions Club is a service organization dedicated to helping people in need from all walks of life. Lions are very active in sight conservation, diabetes and drug awareness as well as numerous local projects. The Lions motto, "We Serve," is very fitting for the Lions organization. Lions give many hours of their time and talent in service to others.

The Lions Club began in 1917 in Chicago, Illinois when Melvin Jones became concerned with the betterment of the community and the world at large. The first Lions organizational meeting was held June 7, 1917. In October of the same year, representatives from 22 clubs from 9 states gathered at a national convention held in Dallas, Texas. The purpose of this meeting was to define what Lionism was to become.

Over the years, new clubs began to emerge all over the United States. In 1920, the Lions Club took on the name "International," when a club was formed in Windsor, Ontario. Today there are clubs in more than 160 countries and geographical areas worldwide.

We of the Huntsville Lions Club wish to express our sincere appreciation to all those who helped make this cookbook a reality. We want to thank all Lions and Lioness Clubs throughout the state of Alabama and all family, friends and relatives for their kind support and contributions. Each recipe is treasured and has been husband-tested. We are especially appreciative of your purchases. Your generous contribution will enable the Lions tradition of service to continue.

Appetizers and Beverages

 **A**PPETIZERS

ASPARAGUS ROLL-UPS

Day-old bread slices
Softened butter
Parmesan cheese

1 can asparagus spears, drained

Trim crusts from bread. Roll slices flat. Spread with butter. Sprinkle with Parmesan cheese. Place 1 asparagus spear on each slice bread. Roll up; secure with toothpicks. Place on baking sheet. Bake at 400 degrees for 10 minutes or until lightly browned. Yield: 6 to 8 servings.

BACON MARMALADE ROUNDS

4 cups shredded Cheddar cheese
8 ounces cream cheese, softened
3 egg yolks, slightly beaten

1/2 cup orange marmalade
Melba rounds
8 ounces bacon, crisp-fried, crumbled

Combine Cheddar cheese, cream cheese and egg yolks in bowl; mix well. Blend in marmalade. Spread on Melba rounds. Top with crumbled bacon. Place on broiler pan. Broil until hot and bubbly. Yield: 3 dozen.

CHEESY CRISPS

2 cups shredded cheese
1 cup margarine, softened

2 cups flour
2 cups crisp rice cereal

Combine cheese and margarine in bowl; mix well. Stir in flour and cereal. Shape into small balls. Place 2 inches apart on greased baking sheet. Flatten with fork. Bake at 375 degrees for 10 minutes or until lightly browned. Yield: 6 to 8 dozen.

CHEESE STRAWS

1/2 cup butter or
  margarine, softened
16 ounces sharp cheese,
  shredded

2 cups flour
1/2 teaspoon salt
Dash of red pepper

Cream butter and cheese in mixer bowl until light and fluffy. Add flour, salt and red pepper; mix well. Roll 1/4 inch thick on lightly floured surface. Cut into 2-inch strips. Place on lightly greased baking sheet. Bake at 400 degrees for 10 minutes or until lightly browned. Yield: 5 to 6 dozen.

CHICKEN ALMOND SWIRLS

1 8-ounce can crescent
  rolls
1 5-ounce can chicken
  spread
1 tablespoon mayonnaise

1 tablespoon chopped
  toasted almonds
1/2 teaspoon lemon juice
Seasoned salt to taste

Unroll crescent roll dough. Separate into 4 rectangles; seal perforations. Combine chicken spread, mayonnaise, almonds, lemon juice and seasoned salt in bowl; mix well. Spread on rectangles. Roll each rectangle as for jelly roll. Cut each into 8 slices. Place cut side down on greased baking sheet. Bake at 375 degrees for 12 to 15 minutes or until golden brown. Yield: 32 servings.

PARTY CHICKEN WINGS

3 pounds chicken wing
  drumettes
1/2 cup butter, softened
1 cup soy sauce

1 cup packed brown
  sugar
3/4 cup water

Place drumettes in 9x13-inch baking dish. Combine butter, soy sauce, brown sugar and water in saucepan; mix well. Cook over low heat until brown sugar is dissolved, stirring frequently. Pour over drumettes. Marinate, covered, in refrigerator for 2 hours. Drain. Bake at 350 degrees for 1 hour. Yield: 2 to 3 dozen.

SOUTHERN STUFFED EGGS

6 hard-boiled eggs
2 tablespoons
  mayonnaise
1 tablespoon sweet
  pickle relish

1 teaspoon prepared
  mustard

Peel eggs; cut into halves lengthwise. Mash yolks in bowl. Add mayonnaise, relish and mustard; mix well. Spoon into egg whites. Place on serving platter. Chill until serving time. Garnish with paprika, pimento strips or green bell pepper strips. Add bacon bits, chopped apple, salmon or crab meat to egg yolk mixture if desired. Yield: 12 servings.

CRISP YOGURT-FRUIT TIDBITS

1 banana, cut into 1-inch
  pieces
1 11-ounce can
  mandarin oranges,
  drained

1 8-ounce can pineapple
  chunks, drained
8 ounces lemon yogurt
4 cups crushed sugar-
  frosted cornflakes

Dip fruit pieces into yogurt. Coat with crushed cereal. Place in waxed paper-lined freezer container. Spear with cocktail toothpicks. Freeze until firm. Place on serving platter. Serve frozen. Yield: 1 to 2 dozen.

HAM ROLL-UPS

8 ounces cream cheese,
  softened
1/2 cup chopped nuts

1 tablespoon mayonnaise
1 teaspoon garlic salt
8 slices ham

Combine cream cheese, nuts, mayonnaise and garlic salt in bowl; mix well. Spread on ham slices. Roll up; secure with toothpicks. Chill, covered, overnight. Cut into 1/2-inch slices. Yield: 2 to 3 dozen.

MINIATURE MEATBALLS

1½ pounds ground beef
½ cup dry bread crumbs
1 egg, slightly beaten
¼ cup milk
¼ teaspoon cloves

Onion salt and celery salt
to taste
1 8-ounce bottle of chili
sauce
1 10-ounce jar grape jelly

Combine ground beef, bread crumbs, egg, milk and seasonings in bowl; mix well. Shape into small balls. Brown on all sides in a small amount of oil in skillet; drain. Combine chili sauce and jelly in saucepan. Cook over low heat until heated through, stirring frequently. Add meatballs. Simmer for 45 minutes. Serve in chafing dish. Yield: 10 servings.

SAUSAGE BALLS

1 pound hot sausage
3½ cups baking mix

10 ounces cheese,
shredded

Combine sausage, baking mix and cheese in bowl; mix well. Shape into small balls. Place on ungreased baking sheet. Bake at 350 degrees for 15 to 20 minutes or until cooked through. Yield: 2 to 3 dozen.

SPINACH-STUFFED MUSHROOMS

20 large mushrooms
1 10-ounce package
frozen chopped spinach,
thawed, drained
¼ cup chopped onion
⅓ cup plain low-fat yogurt
¼ cup Parmesan cheese
¼ cup shredded low-fat
Cheddar cheese

¼ cup shredded low-fat
Monterey Jack cheese
¼ teaspoon garlic powder
¼ teaspoon oregano
¼ teaspoon salt
1 tablespoon Sherry
1 tablespoon Parmesan
cheese

Clean mushrooms with damp paper towels. Remove and mince stems. Place caps on paper towel-lined microwave-safe plate. Combine mushroom stems with next 10 ingredients in bowl; mix well. Spoon into mushroom caps. Sprinkle with remaining 1 tablespoon Parmesan cheese. Microwave on High for 4 to 5 minutes or until heated through, turning every minute. Yield: 20 servings.

POPOVER PIZZA

1 pound ground beef
1/2 cup minced onion
1 8-ounce can tomato
  sauce
1/2 cup water
1 teaspoon salt
1/2 teaspoon oregano
1/4 teaspoon pepper
1/4 teaspoon basil
1/8 teaspoon garlic powder

1 4-ounce can sliced
  mushrooms, drained
1/4 cup Parmesan cheese
2 cups shredded
  mozzarella cheese
2 eggs, beaten
1 tablespoon oil
1 cup milk
1 cup flour
1/2 teaspoon salt

Brown ground beef in skillet, stirring until crumbly; drain. Add onion, tomato sauce, water, 1 teaspoon salt, oregano, pepper, basil, garlic powder, mushrooms and Parmesan cheese; mix well. Bring to a boil, stirring frequently. Spoon into greased 9x13-inch baking dish. Top with mozzarella cheese. Bake at 400 degrees for 5 minutes. Beat eggs and oil in mixer bowl until foamy. Stir in milk, flour and remaining 1/2 teaspoon salt. Beat for 2 minutes or until smooth. Pour over ground beef mixture. Bake for 30 minutes or until puffed and golden brown. Cut into squares. Yield: 4 to 5 dozen.

TORTILLA APPETIZERS

1/2 pound ground beef
1/4 cup taco sauce
3 flour tortillas
3/4 cup shredded
  Monterey Jack cheese
3/4 cup shredded Cheddar
  cheese

3 tablespoons chopped
  green onions
3 tablespoons chopped
  green chilies

Brown ground beef in skillet, stirring until crumbly; drain. Stir in taco sauce. Place tortillas on ungreased baking sheet. Bake at 350 degrees for 5 minutes or until crisp. Spoon ground beef mixture onto tortillas. Top with cheeses, green onions and chilies. Bake for 5 minutes or until cheese is melted. Cut each tortilla into 6 wedges. Yield: 1 1/2 dozen.

SAVORY STUFFING BALLS

1 cup butter	1 teaspoon salt
2 cups chopped onion	1/2 teaspoon pepper
1 cup chopped celery	12 cups dry bread cubes
1/4 cup chopped fresh	1 egg, slightly beaten
parsley	1 10-ounce can chicken
1 tablespoon sage	broth
1 teaspoon thyme	

Melt butter in skillet over medium heat. Add onion. Sauté for 10 minutes or until tender. Stir in celery and seasonings. Cook for 5 minutes longer, stirring frequently. Add bread cubes; mix well. Stir in egg and 3/4 cup chicken broth. Shape into twenty-four 1 1/2-inch balls. Place in shallow greased baking dish. Pour remaining chicken broth over stuffing balls. Bake at 375 degrees for 20 to 25 minutes or until lightly browned. Yield: 2 dozen.

TWO-CHEESE ONION DIP

1 cup cream-style cottage	1 3-ounce can French-
cheese	fried onions, crushed
4 ounces bleu cheese	Paprika
1/3 cup light cream	Minced parsley

Combine cottage cheese, bleu cheese and light cream in blender container. Process until smooth. Spoon into serving dish. Stir in crushed onions. Sprinkle with paprika and parsley. Serve with potato chips and crisp crackers. Yield: 2 cups.

CHILI CON QUESO

1 16-ounce can chili	2 to 3 green chilies,
without beans	chopped
1 pound Velveeta cheese,	2 green onions, chopped
cut into cubes	

Combine chili, Velveeta cheese, chilies and green onions in 2-quart baking dish; mix well. Bake at 350 degrees for 45 minutes. Serve with corn chips. May prepare ahead and freeze. Reheat to serving temperature. Yield: 4 to 5 cups.

HOT CRAB DIP

1 cup low-fat ricotta
  cheese
1 clove of garlic, minced
2 ounces tofu
2 tablespoons Sherry

1 teaspoon prepared
  mustard
1 teaspoon freshly
  squeezed lemon juice
8 ounces crab meat

    Combine cheese, garlic, tofu, Sherry, prepared mustard and lemon juice in blender container. Process until smooth. Pour into saucepan. Stir in crab meat. Cook over low heat until heated through, stirring frequently. Yield: 2 to 3 cups.

CUCUMBER DIP

3 ounces cream cheese,
  softened
2 tablespoons
  mayonnaise
1 tablespoon grated
  cucumber

1/8 teaspoon
  Worcestershire sauce
1/8 teaspoon paprika
1/8 teaspoon salt
1/8 teaspoon celery salt
1/8 teaspoon onion salt

    Blend cream cheese and mayonnaise in bowl. Stir in cucumber and seasonings. Chill until serving time.
Yield: 1 cup.

DILL DIP

2/3 cup sour cream
1/3 cup mayonnaise
1 tablespoon minced
  onion

1 teaspoon seasoned salt
1 tablespoon parsley
1 tablespoon dillweed

    Combine sour cream, mayonnaise, onion, seasoned salt, parsley and dillweed in bowl; mix well. Serve with bite-sized fresh vegetables. Yield: 1 cup.

A Lion Tip

Mix 1 can of drained minced clams with 1 package dry vegetable soup mix and 2 cups sour cream for an easy dip.

MUSHROOM CAVIAR

¼ cup minced onion
1 tablespoon butter
12 ounces mushrooms, finely chopped

1 tablespoon lemon juice
½ tablespoon Worcestershire sauce
Salt and pepper to taste

Sauté onion in butter in skillet until golden brown. Stir in mushrooms. Sauté for 5 minutes longer. Add lemon juice, Worcestershire sauce, salt and pepper; mix well. Chill until serving time. Serve with Melba toast. Yield: 1½ cups.

SUPER NACHOS

1 pound ground beef
2 large cans refried beans
1 can chopped green chilies, drained

1½ to 2 cups shredded Cheddar cheese
1 cup guacamole

Brown ground beef in skillet, stirring until crumbly; drain. Spread beans on microwave-safe platter. Spoon ground beef over beans. Sprinkle with chilies and Cheddar cheese. Microwave for 3 to 5 minutes or until heated through. Top with guacamole. Serve with nacho chips. Yield: 10 servings.

CHUNKY SALSA

1 35-ounce can tomatoes
2 tablespoons olive oil
1 cup coarsely chopped onion
1 cup coarsely chopped green bell pepper
1 tablespoon lime juice

2 tablespoons Tabasco sauce
½ teaspoon salt
2 tablespoons chopped fresh cilantro

Drain tomatoes, reserving ½ cup juice. Chop tomatoes coarsely. Heat olive oil in heavy saucepan over high heat. Sauté onion and green pepper in hot oil for 5 minutes or until tender, stirring frequently. Stir in tomatoes and reserved juice. Bring to a boil; reduce heat. Simmer for 6 to 8 minutes or until slightly thickened, stirring frequently. Stir in lime juice, Tabasco sauce and salt. Cool to lukewarm. Stir in cilantro. Spoon into jars. Store in refrigerator. Will keep for 5 days. Serve with tortilla chips. Yield: 3 to 4 cups.

HOT SHRIMP DIP

1 roll garlic cheese, cut up
1 can frozen shrimp
  soup, thawed
1 small can shrimp

1 small can chopped
  mushrooms
Worcestershire sauce and
  lemon juice to taste

Combine cheese, shrimp soup, shrimp, mushrooms, Worcestershire sauce and lemon juice in double boiler; mix well. Heat over hot water until cheese is melted, stirring frequently. Cook over simmering water for 5 minutes, stirring occasionally. Yield: 2 to 2½ cups.

SHRIMPLY DIVINE

1 cup sour cream
3 ounces cream cheese,
  softened
1 envelope Italian salad
  dressing mix

2 teaspoons lemon juice
½ cup chopped cooked
  shrimp

Cream sour cream and cream cheese in mixer bowl until light and fluffy. Stir in salad dressing mix and lemon juice. Add shrimp; mix well. Chill, covered, for 1 hour. Yield: 2 cups.

SPINACH DIP

1 10-ounce package
  frozen chopped spinach,
  thawed, drained
1 cup mayonnaise
1 bunch green onions,
  minced

½ cup chopped fresh
  parsley
1 teaspoon dill
1 teaspoon salt
1 teaspoon pepper

Combine spinach, mayonnaise, green onions, parsley, dill, salt and pepper in bowl; mix well. Chill, covered, until serving time. Serve with bite-sized fresh vegetables. Yield: 2 to 3 cups.

PARTY SPINACH DIP

1 10-ounce package
   frozen chopped spinach,
   thawed, drained
2 cups sour cream

1 cup mayonnaise
1 envelope vegetable
   soup mix

Combine all ingredients in bowl; mix well. Chill, covered, for 2 hours. Yield: 4 cups.

TUNA PARTY DIP

2 7-ounce cans tuna in
   vegetable oil, drained
1 envelope onion soup
   mix

2 cups sour cream
1 teaspoon Tabasco
   sauce

Combine tuna, soup mix, sour cream and Tabasco sauce in bowl; mix well. Chill, covered, until serving time. Serve with crackers or potato chips. Yield: 3 cups.

VEGETABLE DIP

2 cups sour cream
2 cups mayonnaise
2 tablespoons Beau
   Monde seasoning

1 tablespoon dillseed
1 teaspoon dried minced
   onion

Combine all ingredients in blender. Process until smooth. Pour into serving dish. Chill, covered, overnight. Yield: 4 cups.

HOLIDAY CHEESE RING

1 pound sharp Cheddar
   cheese, shredded
3/4 cup mayonnaise
1 cup chopped pecans
1 onion, grated

1 clove of garlic, pressed
1/2 teaspoon Tabasco
   sauce
1 cup strawberry
   preserves

Combine first 6 ingredients in bowl; mix well. Press into lightly greased ring mold. Chill, covered, overnight. Unmold onto serving plate. Fill center with preserves. Serve with crackers. Yield: 10 servings.

SANTA'S CHEESE BALL

12 ounces sharp Cheddar cheese, shredded
3 ounces cream cheese, softened
1 pimento, chopped
1 clove of garlic, minced
3/4 cup chopped pecans

1 teaspoon Worcestershire sauce
1/4 teaspoon salt
1/4 teaspoon cayenne pepper
1/4 cup chopped pecans
Paprika

Combine Cheddar cheese, cream cheese, pimento, garlic, 3/4 cup pecans, Worcestershire sauce, salt and cayenne pepper in mixer bowl; mix well. Shape into large ball. Roll in remaining 1/4 cup pecans. Sprinkle with paprika. Chill, wrapped in plastic wrap, for 24 hours. May prepare ahead and freeze. Yield: 10 servings.

FRESH VEGETABLE CHEESE BALL

8 ounces Neufchâtel cheese, softened
2 cups shredded low-fat mild Cheddar cheese
1/4 cup finely chopped broccoli flowerets

1/3 cup shredded carrot
2 tablespoons chopped green onions
1/2 teaspoon dillweed
1/2 tablespoon coarsely ground pepper

Combine cheeses, broccoli, carrot, green onions and dillweed in mixer bowl; mix well. Chill, covered, for several hours. Shape into large ball. Roll in pepper. Serve with crackers. Yield: 6 to 8 servings.

CHICKEN LIVER PÂTÉ

1 6-ounce can pitted black olives
1/2 cup chicken broth
1 pound chicken livers
2 envelopes unflavored gelatin
1/2 cup chicken broth
1/4 cup buttermilk
2 tablespoons parsley flakes

1 tablespoon prepared mustard
1 teaspoon onion powder
1/2 teaspoon salt
1/8 teaspoon white pepper
1/8 teaspoon nutmeg
1/8 teaspoon thyme
2 tablespoons Brandy (optional)

Drain olives, reserving ½ cup liquid. Combine reserved liquid, ½ cup chicken broth and chicken livers in saucepan. Bring to a boil over medium heat, stirring occasionally. Reduce heat. Simmer for 5 to 8 minutes or until livers are tender, stirring frequently. Sprinkle gelatin over remaining ½ cup chicken broth in blender container. Add chicken livers and cooking liquid, buttermilk, parsley, prepared mustard, onion powder, salt, white pepper, nutmeg, thyme and Brandy. Process until smooth. Pour into 1-quart mold. Chill, covered, for 4 to 5 hours or until firm. Unmold onto serving plate. Yield: 6 to 8 servings.

LIVERWURST PARTY SPREAD

4 to 5 teaspoons butter or margarine
3 tablespoons minced onion
4 to 5 teaspoons chives
2 4½-ounce cans liverwurst spread
¼ cup cream cheese, softened
3 slices crisp-fried bacon, crumbled
1 envelope unflavored gelatin
2 tablespoons cold water
3 tablespoons dry Sherry

Melt butter in small skillet over medium heat. Add onion. Sauté until tender. Stir in chives. Combine with liverwurst spread, cream cheese and bacon in bowl; mix well. Soften gelatin in cold water in small saucepan. Add Sherry. Heat over medium heat until gelatin dissolves, stirring constantly. Stir into liverwurst mixture. Press into 2-cup mold. Chill, covered, for 1 to 3 hours or until firm. Unmold onto serving plate. Garnish with herb sprigs. Serve with crackers. Yield: 1½ cups.

QUICK MEXICAN SPREAD

8 ounces Neufchâtel cheese, softened
1 4-ounce can chopped green chilies, drained

Combine cheese and chilies in bowl; mix well. Chill, covered, until serving time. Serve with tortilla chips or spread over warm tortillas or corn bread. Yield: 1 cup.

LEMON ZEST ALMONDS

1/3 cup sugar
1 tablespoon grated
  lemon rind

2 cups whole almonds
1 egg white, slightly
  beaten

Combine sugar and lemon rind in bowl; mix well. Toss almonds in egg white then in sugar mixture to coat well. Spread almonds in single layer on baking sheet. Bake at 350 degrees for 12 to 15 minutes or until sugar is lightly browned and almonds are toasted, stirring occasionally. Cool. Store in airtight container. Yield: 2 cups.

HARVEST MIX

16 ounces dry roasted
  peanuts
1 8-ounce package
  "M & M's" Plain
  Chocolate Candies

1 small package candy
  corn
1/2 cup raisins

Combine peanuts, candies and raisins in large bowl; mix well. Store in airtight container. Yield: 4 to 5 cups.

NUTS AND BOLTS AND SCREWS

2 cups margarine
1 pound pecans
1 large package Cheerios
1 package wheat Chex
1 medium package
  pretzel sticks

2 tablespoons salt
1 tablespoon garlic salt
1 tablespoon
  Worcestershire sauce

Melt margarine in large roasting pan. Add pecans, cereals, pretzels, salt, garlic salt and Worcestershire sauce; mix well. Bake at 200 degrees for 1 hour, stirring every 15 minutes. Yield: 25 to 30 cups.

OYSTER CRACKERS

1 10-ounce package oyster crackers	²/₃ cup oil
1 envelope buttermilk ranch-style salad dressing mix	1 teaspoon dillweed
	1 teaspoon lemon pepper
	¹/₂ teaspoon garlic salt

Place crackers in tightly sealed plastic bag. Combine salad dressing mix, oil, dillweed, lemon pepper and garlic salt in bowl; mix well. Add to crackers; shake well. Store in airtight container. Yield: 3 to 4 cups.

SUGARED WALNUTS

1¹/₂ cups sugar	¹/₂ teaspoon vanilla extract
¹/₂ cup water	3 cups walnuts
¹/₄ cup honey	

Combine sugar, water and honey in saucepan; mix well. Bring to a boil. Cook to 234 degrees on candy thermometer, soft-ball stage, stirring constantly. Beat in vanilla. Add walnuts. Stir until candy coating is creamy and walnuts begin to separate. Spread on waxed paper to cool. Break into bite-sized pieces. Store in airtight container. Yield: 3 cups.

BAKED FINGER SANDWICHES

1 large loaf coarse-textured bread, sliced	1 envelope onion soup mix
1 cup margarine, softened	

Trim crusts from bread. Combine margarine and soup mix in bowl; mix well. Spread on half the bread slices. Top with remaining slices. Cut each sandwich into 3 strips. Place on baking sheet. Bake at 350 degrees for 10 minutes or until lightly browned. Serve warm. Yield: 2 to 3 dozen.

SAVORY THREE-CHEESE SANDWICH SPREAD

2/3 cup ricotta cheese
1/2 cup shredded Cheddar
cheese
1/2 cup shredded Swiss
cheese
1/4 cup minced green
onions

1 teaspoon prepared
mustard
1/8 teaspoon pepper
1 tablespoon (about) milk

Combine cheeses, green onions, prepared mustard and pepper in bowl; mix well. Add enough milk to make of spreading consistency. Chill, covered, until serving time. Serve on French or whole grain bread or with crackers or fresh vegetable sticks. May substitute other shredded cheeses for Swiss and Cheddar such as mozzarella or Monterey Jack. Yield: 1 1/2 cups.

CHICKEN TEA SANDWICH SPREAD

1 cup finely chopped
cooked chicken
1/2 cup finely chopped
walnuts or pecans

2 teaspoons Dijon
mustard
Mayonnaise

Combine chicken, walnuts and mustard in bowl; mix well. Add enough mayonnaise to make of spreading consistency. Chill, covered, until serving time. Yield: 1 1/2 cups.

CHICKEN SWISSWICHES

10 slices white bread
1 1/2 cups chopped
cooked chicken or
turkey
1/2 cup shredded Swiss
cheese

1/4 cup chopped celery
1/3 cup mayonnaise
2 cups chopped cooked
fresh asparagus
1/4 cup butter or
margarine, softened

Combine first 4 ingredients in bowl; mix well. Stir in asparagus gently. Spread on 5 bread slices. Top with remaining bread. Spread half the butter on 1 side of each sandwich. Place buttered side down on griddle. Spread remaining butter on sandwiches. Bake on griddle at 375 degrees for 4 to 6 minutes or until cheese is melted and bread is golden brown, turning once. Cut into quarters. Yield: 20 servings.

HAM ROLLS

2 packages party rolls
1 cup margarine, softened
1 small onion, grated
3 tablespoons poppy seed
3 tablespoons Dijon
  mustard
1 tablespoon
  Worcestershire sauce

8 ounces sliced cooked
  ham
1 cup shredded Swiss
  cheese
1 cup shredded Cheddar
  cheese

Cut rolls into halves horizontally. Combine margarine, onion, poppy seed, mustard and Worcestershire sauce in bowl; mix well. Spread over cut surfaces of rolls. Place ham slices on bottom halves. Sprinkle with cheeses. Replace top halves. Wrap in foil; place on baking sheet. Bake at 400 degrees for 10 to 12 minutes or until heated through. Cool. Cut into bite-sized pieces. Yield: 2 to 4 dozen.

TRIPLE RIBBON SANDWICHES

2 4$\frac{1}{2}$-ounce cans
  deviled ham
$\frac{1}{4}$ cup mayonnaise
2 tablespoons chopped
  onion
$\frac{1}{4}$ cup finely chopped
  walnuts
$\frac{1}{4}$ teaspoon dry mustard
6 thin slices white bread
6 thin slices pumpernickel
  bread

1 4-ounce can chunky
  chicken spread
3 ounces cream cheese,
  softened
$\frac{1}{2}$ cup raisins
$\frac{1}{2}$ cup finely chopped
  celery
6 thin slices whole wheat
  bread

Combine ham, mayonnaise, onion, walnuts and dry mustard in bowl; mix well. Spread on white bread slices. Top with pumpernickel slices. Combine chicken spread, cream cheese, raisins and celery in bowl; mix well. Spread on pumpernickel slices. Top with whole wheat slices. Wrap each sandwich in plastic wrap. Chill for several hours. Trim crusts with serrated knife. Cut each sandwich into 4 triangles. Yield: 2 dozen.

PIGS-IN-A-BLANKET

4 8-count cans crescent
rolls

2 packages miniature hot
dogs

Separate roll dough into triangles. Cut each into 3 small triangles. Wrap 1 triangle around each hot dog. Place on baking sheet sprayed with nonstick cooking spray. Bake at 375 degrees for 10 to 12 minutes or until lightly browned. Yield: 8 dozen.

BROILED TUNAWICH

1 6-ounce can tuna,
drained
1/4 cup finely chopped
onion
2 tablespoons chopped
seeded cucumber
1/4 cup mayonnaise

1/4 teaspoon dillweed
2 English muffins, split,
toasted
4 slices tomato
4 1-ounce slices
Cheddar cheese

Combine tuna, onion, cucumber, mayonnaise and dillweed in bowl; mix well. Spread on cut sides of muffin halves. Top with tomato slices. Place on ungreased baking sheet. Broil 4 to 6 inches from heat source for 4 to 5 minutes or until tomato is heated through. Top with cheese slices. Broil for 1 to 2 minutes longer or until cheese is melted. Yield: 4 servings.

SUNNY GARDEN SALAD SANDWICH

2 slices 7-grain bread
2 teaspoons prepared
mustard
Spinach or romaine
lettuce leaves
1 very thin slice red onion

2 very thin slices tomato
1 hard-boiled egg, sliced
1/2 cup alfalfa sprouts
1 1/2 tablespoons creamy
garlic salad dressing

Spread 1 side of 1 bread slice with mustard. Top with spinach or lettuce leaves. Layer with onion, tomato, egg, alfalfa sprouts and salad dressing. Top with remaining bread slice. Yield: 1 serving.

BEVERAGES

APPLE BRANDY

2 cups chopped red
  apples
3 3-inch sticks cinnamon
2 tablespoons water

$2^{1}/_{2}$ cups sugar
2 cups Brandy
3 cups dry white wine

Combine apples, cinnamon sticks and water in sauce-pan. Cook, covered, over medium heat for 10 minutes. Add sugar; stir until dissolved. Cool. Combine apple mixture, Brandy and wine in large airtight glass container. Store in cool dark place for 3 weeks, shaking container every 3 days. Strain through double thickness of cheesecloth. Pour liquid into glass bottle; cover tightly. Store in cool dark place for 2 weeks. Yield: $1^{1}/_{2}$ quarts.

CRANBERRY LIQUEUR

2 cups sugar
1 cup water
3 cups coarsely chopped
  fresh cranberries

1 teaspoon grated orange
  rind
3 cups vodka

Combine sugar and water in medium saucepan. Bring to a boil. Simmer until sugar is dissolved, stirring constantly. Add cranberries and orange rind. Cool. Combine cranberry mixture and vodka in large airtight glass container. Store in cool dark place for 4 weeks, shaking container every 3 days. Strain cranberry mixture through sieve, pressing cranberries against sieve to remove as much liquid as possible. Strain through double thickness of cheesecloth. Repeat straining process until liquid is clear. Pour liquid into glass bottle; cover tightly. Store in cool dark place for 2 weeks. Yield: 1 quart.

A Lion Tip

Add a small amount of grenadine syrup to lemonade for pink lemonade.

CRÈME DE MENTHE

1 1/2 cups sugar
2 cups boiling water
1/2 ounce peppermint
  extract

Green food coloring
1 pint vodka

Dissolve sugar in water. Cool. Add peppermint extract, food coloring and vodka. Store in airtight container for 30 days. May substitute 2 drops of oil of peppermint for peppermint extract. Yield: 1 quart.

COFFEE LIQUEUR

2 ounces instant coffee
2 cups boiling water
4 cups sugar

1 vanilla bean, cut into
  halves
2 cups (or more) Brandy

Combine coffee powder, water and sugar in bowl; stir until dissolved. Cool. Place vanilla bean half in each of two 4/5-quart bottles. Pour 1 cup Brandy into each bottle. Add coffee mixture. Fill to top with Brandy. Store, covered, in cool dark place for 4 weeks. May substitute vodka for Brandy. Yield: 2 fifths.

EGGNOG

6 eggs, separated
Pinch of soda
2 ounces rum
1 cup sugar
1 cup milk

2 cups whipping cream
2 cups whiskey
1 pint vanilla ice cream
Nutmeg

Beat egg whites in large mixer bowl until soft peaks form. Beat egg yolks in small mixer bowl. Add yolks, soda, rum and sugar to egg whites, beating until very stiff peaks form. Add milk, whipping cream and whiskey; mix well. Chill in airtight container overnight. Add ice cream; beat until smooth. Ladle into punch cups. Garnish with nutmeg. Yield: 12 servings.

ORANGE CRANBERRY LIQUEUR

Zest and juice of 1 orange　　**2 cups vodka**
2 cups coarsely chopped　　　**2 cups sugar**
fresh cranberries

　　Slice orange zest into thin strips. Place zest, orange juice, cranberries, vodka and sugar in airtight glass container. Refrigerate for 1 month, shaking container occasionally. Strain through double thickness of cheesecloth. Store in airtight glass container in refrigerator. Yield: 3 cups.

PEAR LIQUEUR

3 pears　　　　　　　**1 3-inch stick cinnamon**
2 whole cloves　　　　**1 cup sugar**
2 whole allspice　　　**2 cups vodka**

　　Cut pears into 1/2-inch strips. Combine with cloves, allspice, cinnamon stick, sugar and vodka in airtight glass container. Store in cool dark place for 2 weeks, shaking container every 2 days. Strain through double thickness of cheesecloth. Pour liquid into glass bottle; cover tightly. Store in cool dark place for 2 weeks. Yield: 2 1/2 cups.

TROPICAL BANANA PUNCH

4 large bananas, mashed　　**3 cups pineapple juice**
Juice of 2 lemons　　　　　**6 cups water**
2 cups frozen orange　　　　**4 cups sugar**
juice concentrate,　　　　　**2 liters ginger ale**
thawed

　　Combine bananas, lemon juice, orange juice concentrate, pineapple juice, water and sugar in freezer container. Freeze until firm. Let stand at room temperature until slushy. Spoon into punch bowl. Add ginger ale just before serving. Yield: 50 servings.

BLACKBERRY NECTAR

1 gallon mashed fresh
  blackberries
1 quart boiling water

2¹/₂ ounces tartaric acid
Sugar

    Combine berries and water in large container. Let stand for 6 hours. Strain through double thickness of cheesecloth. Measure juice. Place in large storage container. Add 2 cups sugar for each cup juice. Add tartaric acid; stir until sugar is dissolved. Store in refrigerator. Place 2 tablespoons nectar in tall glass. Add ice and water to fill. Yield: 1 gallon.

MOCK CHAMPAGNE PUNCH

1 quart white grape juice   1 quart ginger ale

    Combine grape juice and ginger ale in airtight container. Chill in refrigerator. Serve in champagne glasses. Yield: 2 quarts.

COFFEE AND CREAM PUNCH

2 quarts strong coffee,
  chilled
¹/₂ gallon vanilla ice
  cream, softened

¹/₂ gallon vanilla ice milk,
  softened
2 liters ginger ale, chilled

    Combine coffee, ice cream and ice milk in punch bowl; mix until almost smooth. Stir in ginger ale. Serve in punch cups. Yield: 30 servings.

A Lion Tip

For an elegant touch, serve a mixture of tomato juice and clam juice seasoned with onion, salt and pepper in demitasse cups.

DON PARDO COOLER

1 6-ounce can frozen
limeade concentrate,
thawed
1 6-ounce can frozen
lemonade concentrate,
thawed
1 6-ounce can frozen
orange juice concentrate,
thawed

Dry white wine, chilled
Carbonated water, chilled
Orange, lemon or lime
slices

Combine limeade concentrate, lemonade concentrate and orange juice concentrate in airtight container. Store in refrigerator; will keep for up to 2 weeks. Combine 3 tablespoons concentrate mixture with 1 cup white wine and 1 cup carbonated water in tall glasses. Add ice. Garnish with citrus slices. Yield: 12 servings.

PINEAPPLE SHERBET DRINK

1 gallon pineapple
sherbet, softened
Juice and grated rind of
10 lemons
1 46-ounce can
pineapple-grapefruit
juice

1 quart ginger ale
1/4 teaspoon almond
extract

Combine sherbet, lemon juice and rind in mixer bowl; mix well. Spoon into ice cube trays; freeze until firm. Place in tall glasses. Add mixture of pineapple-grapefruit juice, ginger ale and almond extract. Yield: 2 gallons.

SANGRIA WINE PUNCH

1 lime, sliced
1 lemon, sliced
2 oranges, sliced
1 quart Burgundy

1/2 cup Triple Sec
1 liter 7-Up
2 cups Champagne

Combine fruit slices with wine and Triple Sec in airtight container; mix well. Chill for 3 hours. Pour into punch bowl. Add 7-Up and Champagne just before serving. Yield: 10 cups.

YELLOW FRUIT PUNCH

Juice of 6 dozen oranges
Juice of 1½ lemons
1   46-ounce can
   pineapple juice

1   46-ounce can
   grapefruit juice
12 cups sugar

Combine juices; divide equally among six 1-gallon containers. Add 2 cups sugar to each gallon. Fill containers with water; mix well. Add yellow food coloring if desired. Chill until serving time. Pour into punch bowl. Yield: 150 servings.

ULTIMATE CHOCOLATE MALT

¼ cup chocolate syrup
¼ cup chocolate malted
   milk powder

½ cup milk
1 quart chocolate ice
   cream, softened

Combine chocolate syrup, malted milk powder and milk in blender container. Process on High for 10 seconds. Add ice cream. Process until smooth. Pour into glasses. May substitute chocolate milk for milk. Yield: four ½-cup servings.

HAWAIIAN MILK SHAKE

1 cup pineapple juice,
   chilled
2 tablespoons orange
   juice
1 tablespoon lemon juice

3 tablespoons sugar
⅓ cup crushed ice
2 cups milk
6 scoops vanilla ice
   cream

Combine pineapple juice, orange juice, lemon juice and sugar in blender container. Process on High for 20 seconds or until sugar is dissolved. Add crushed ice and milk. Process on High until blended. Pour into serving glasses. Add 1 scoop ice cream to each glass. Serve at once. Yield: 6 servings.

HOLIDAY HOT FRUIT PUNCH

6 cups apple juice
1 3-inch stick cinnamon
1 teaspoon nutmeg
1/2 cup sugar
2 46-ounce cans
   pineapple juice

1 46-ounce can orange
   juice
2 oranges
Whole cloves

Combine apple juice, cinnamon stick and nutmeg in large saucepan. Simmer for 20 minutes. Add sugar, pineapple juice and orange juice; mix well. Stud oranges with cloves; add to apple mixture. Heat to serving temperature; do not boil. Yield: 25 servings.

HOT MULLED CIDER

1/2 cup packed brown
   sugar
1/4 teaspoon salt
2 quarts cider

1 teaspoon whole cloves
1 teaspoon whole allspice
1 3-inch stick cinnamon
Dash of nutmeg

Combine brown sugar, salt and cider in large saucepan. Place cloves and allspice in tea ball; add spice ball and cinnamon stick to cider mixture. Bring to a boil; reduce heat. Simmer, covered for 20 minutes. Remove spices. Yield: 16 servings.

HOT MULLARD PUNCH

4 cups cranberry juice
   cocktail
2 cups unsweetened
   pineapple juice
1/2 cup sugar
1 1/2 cups water

1/4 teaspoon cloves
1/4 teaspoon allspice
1/4 teaspoon cinnamon
1/8 teaspoon nutmeg
1/2 cup rum (optional)

Combine cranberry juice, pineapple juice, sugar, water, cloves, allspice, cinnamon and nutmeg in large saucepan. Heat to serving temperature over medium heat. Add rum. Yield: 8 servings.

HOT CHOCOLATE MIX

1 8-quart package
   instant dry milk powder
1 2-pound package
   instant cocoa mix
1 8-ounce package dry
   coffee creamer
1/2 cup confectioners'
   sugar

Combine dry milk powder, cocoa mix, coffee creamer and confectioners' sugar in large bowl; mix well. Store in airtight container. Add 2 to 3 tablespoons mix to 1 cup hot water. Yield: 2 pounds.

INSTANT RUSSIAN TEA

18 ounces orange instant
   breakfast drink mix
1 cup low-calorie instant
   dry tea powder
1 tablespoon cinnamon
1 teaspoon cloves

Combine breakfast drink mix, tea powder, cinnamon and cloves in large bowl; mix well. Store in airtight container. Dissolve desired amount of mixture in hot water in mug. Yield: 1 1/4 pound.

A Lion Tip

Entertain your friends or just give yourself a treat with a "tea break."

- There are only 3 kinds of tea, but over 3,000 different varieties.
- Black tea leaves are fermented, then heated and dried.
- Green tea leaves are not fermented.
- Oolong tea leaves are fermented for only a short time.
- Orange Pekoe is not a kind of tea. It refers to the size of the tea leaf. "Pekoe" indicates a larger leaf than "orange pekoe."

Salads

FRUIT SALADS

AMBROSIA BOWL

4 large oranges
1 13-ounce can frozen
pineapple chunks,
thawed
2 tablespoons Cointreau,
white rum or orange
juice

4 medium bananas
1/4 cup confectioners'
sugar
1 3-ounce can coconut
6 maraschino cherries

Peel oranges; remove white membrane. Cut oranges crosswise into 1/8-inch thick slices. Drain pineapple, reserving juice. Combine reserved pineapple juice and Cointreau in bowl; mix well. Cut bananas diagonally into 1/8-inch thick slices. Layer half the orange slices, 2 tablespoons confectioners' sugar, half the banana slices and half the pineapple chunks in glass serving bowl. Sprinkle with half the coconut. Repeat layering. Pour Cointreau mixture over layers. Sprinkle with remaining coconut; top with maraschino cherries. Chill for several hours. Yield: 10 servings.

AMBROSIA MEDLEY

1 cup fresh pineapple
cubes
1 banana, sliced
1 cup fresh strawberry
halves
2 tablespoons
confectioners' sugar

1/2 cup coconut
1/4 cup orange juice
2 tablespoons orange-
flavored liqueur or
orange juice

Layer pineapple, banana, strawberry halves, confectioners' sugar and coconut 1/2 at a time in medium serving bowl or dessert dishes. Combine orange juice and liqueur in small bowl; mix well. Pour over layers. Chill until serving time. Orange-flavored liqueurs that may be used are Triple Sec, Curaçao and Cointreau. Grand Marnier, which contains Cognac, may also be used. Yield: 5 servings.

APPLE FRUIT SALAD

2 tart apples, chopped
5 maraschino cherries, chopped
1/3 cup raisins
1/4 cup coarsely chopped walnuts
1 teaspoon milk
1 tablespoon mayonnaise
Pinch of salt
4 large lettuce leaves

Combine apples, cherries, raisins and walnuts in bowl; mix well. Blend milk, mayonnaise and salt in small bowl. Pour over fruit; toss gently. Spoon onto lettuce-lined salad plates. Yield: 4 servings.

CINNAMON AND APPLE SALAD

1 cup water
1 cup sugar
1 cup red hot cinnamon candies
6 small apples, peeled, cored
1 cup cottage cheese
1/2 cup chopped walnuts
2 tablespoons mayonnaise
Lettuce

Heat water, sugar and cinnamon candies in saucepan over low heat until candies are dissolved, stirring constantly. Add apples. Cook, covered, until apples are tender but not broken, turning once. Apples should become bright red. Place on plate gently. Chill. Combine cottage cheese, walnuts and mayonnaise in bowl; mix well. Spoon into apples. Arrange on lettuce-lined salad plates. Serve with additional mayonnaise if desired. Yield: 6 servings.

 A Lion Tip

For easy fruit salads, fill the hollows of peach halves with blueberries and serve with honey-yogurt or roll cored pears in mayonnaise and finely chopped walnuts.

CITRUS AND APPLE SALAD WITH LEMON AND HONEY DRESSING

Salad greens
1/2 cup chopped celery
2 apples, cut into thin
  wedges
1 cucumber, peeled,
  thinly sliced
4 oranges, sliced
  crosswise
1 grapefruit, peeled,
  sectioned
1/2 cup oil
1/3 cup fresh lemon juice

1 tablespoon honey
1 teaspoon dry mustard
1/4 teaspoon salt
Dash of pepper
1/2 teaspoon paprika
1 teaspoon
  Worcestershire sauce
1/4 cup fresh or frozen
  chopped chives
1/2 cup croutons
1/3 cup crumbled bleu
  cheese

Line salad bowl with greens. Arrange celery, apples, cucumber, oranges and grapefruit in prepared bowl. Combine oil, lemon juice, honey, dry mustard, salt, pepper, paprika, Worcestershire sauce and chives in bowl; mix well. Pour enough salad dressing over salad to moisten. Add croutons and bleu cheese; toss lightly. Yield: 6 to 8 servings.

BLUEBERRY DREAM SALAD

1 3-ounce package
  black raspberry gelatin
2 envelopes whipped
  topping mix
1 can crushed pineapple,
  drained

1 can blueberries, drained
1 cup chopped pecans
1 cup miniature
  marshmallows

Prepare gelatin using package directions. Chill until set. Prepare whipped topping mix using package directions in large mixer bowl. Beat in gelatin. Fold in pineapple, blueberries, pecans and marshmallows. Spoon into salad bowl. Chill until serving time. Yield: 4 servings.

SUMMERTIME BLUEBERRY SALAD

2 3-ounce packages
grape gelatin
2 cups boiling water
1 can blueberry pie filling
1 can crushed pineapple
8 ounces cream cheese,
softened

2 cups sour cream
1/2 cup confectioners'
sugar
1 teaspoon vanilla extract
Chopped pecans
(optional)

Dissolve gelatin in boiling water in serving bowl. Stir in pie filling and pineapple. Chill until firm. Blend cream cheese, sour cream, confectioners' sugar and vanilla in bowl. Spread over top of gelatin mixture. Sprinkle with pecans. Yield: 8 servings.

BREATH O' SPRING

1 large can crushed
pineapple
1 6-ounce package
peach gelatin

2 cups buttermilk
12 ounces whipped
topping
1/2 cup chopped pecans

Place undrained pineapple in saucepan. Bring to a boil, stirring constantly. Add gelatin, stirring until dissolved. Cool. Stir in buttermilk. Fold in whipped topping and pecans. Pour into 9x13-inch dish. Chill for several hours. Sprinkle with additional pecans if desired. Yield: 15 servings.

FROZEN CHERRY SALAD

1 21-ounce can cherry
pie filling
1 15-ounce can crushed
pineapple
12 ounces whipped
topping

1 14-ounce can
sweetened condensed
milk
2 tablespoons lemon juice
(optional)

Combine pie filling, pineapple, whipped topping, sweetened condensed milk and lemon juice in bowl; mix well. Spoon into 9x13-inch dish. Freeze until firm. Cut into squares. Garnish with chopped pecans if desired. Yield: 15 servings.

CRANBERRY SALAD

1 16-ounce can whole
   cranberry sauce
1 3-ounce package
   raspberry gelatin
1 cup boiling water
1 teaspoon lemon juice

¹/₄ teaspoon salt
¹/₂ cup mayonnaise
1 apple or orange,
   peeled, chopped
¹/₄ cup chopped walnuts

Heat cranberry sauce; strain into mixer bowl, reserving cranberries. Dissolve gelatin in mixture of strained liquid and boiling water. Add lemon juice and salt; mix well. Chill until thick enough to mound lightly when dropped from spoon. Beat in mayonnaise until light and fluffy. Fold in cranberries, apple and walnuts. Chill until set. Yield: 4 servings.

OUR FAVORITE HOLIDAY CRANBERRY SALAD

1 3-ounce package
   cherry gelatin
1 cup boiling water
³/₄ cup sugar
1 tablespoon lemon juice
1 cup ground cranberries

Grated rind of 1 orange
1 cup drained crushed
   pineapple
¹/₂ cup shredded carrots
¹/₂ cup chopped pecans
¹/₂ cup chopped apples

Dissolve gelatin in boiling water in large bowl. Add sugar, stirring until dissolved. Add remaining ingredients; mix well. Chill until set, stirring occasionally to mix well. Yield: 4 servings.

FROZEN CRANBERRY SALAD

3 tablespoons sugar
8 ounces cream cheese,
   softened
2 tablespoons
   mayonnaise
¹/₂ cup chopped pecans
   (optional)

1 16-ounce can whole
   cranberry sauce
1 small can crushed
   pineapple, drained
8 ounces whipped
   topping

Cream first 3 ingredients in large mixer bowl until light and fluffy. Add pecans, cranberry sauce and pineapple; mix well. Fold in whipped topping. Spoon into large mold or paper-lined muffin cups. Freeze until firm. Yield: 12 servings.

FROSTY FRUIT LOAF

1 30-ounce can fruit
cocktail
1 envelope unflavored
gelatin
1/2 cup mayonnaise
1/2 cup light corn syrup

1 10-ounce package
frozen sweetened
strawberries, thawed,
crushed
1 cup plain yogurt

Drain fruit cocktail, reserving 1/2 cup juice. Sprinkle gelatin over reserved juice in saucepan. Cook over low heat until dissolved, stirring constantly. Add mayonnaise; beat well. Stir in corn syrup and strawberries. Chill until mixture mounds slightly when dropped from spoon. Fold in fruit cocktail and yogurt. Spoon into 5x9-inch loaf pan. Freeze, covered, until firm. Yield: 8 servings.

GREEN FRUIT COMPOTE

2 tablespoons lime juice
2 tablespoons honey
1 cup seedless green
grapes

2 kiwifruit, peeled, cut
into bite-sized pieces
2 pears, cut into 1/2-inch
pieces

Combine lime juice and honey in medium bowl; mix well. Add grapes, kiwifruit and pears; toss lightly. Spoon into individual serving dishes. Chill until serving time. Yield: 4 servings.

HONEY AND CREAM FRUIT SALAD

3 ounces cream cheese,
softened
1/4 cup honey
3 tablespoons prepared
mustard

1/4 cup orange juice
1 cup whipped topping
Assorted fresh fruit, cut
into bite-sized pieces

Beat cream cheese, honey, mustard and orange juice in mixer bowl until smooth. Fold in whipped topping. Arrange fruit on salad plates. Top with whipped topping mixture. Yield: 12 servings.

FRUIT SAMPLER WITH YOGURT SAUCE

4 large navel oranges
2 cups plain or vanilla
  yogurt
3 tablespoons honey
1 large Red Delicious
  apple, sliced

1 ripe Bartlett pear, sliced
2 kiwifruit, peeled, sliced
1/4 pound seedless red
  grapes, in small
  clusters

Grate enough rind from 1 orange to measure 1 teaspoon; set aside. Squeeze juice from orange; discard peel. Cut remaining 3 oranges in half crosswise. Section carefully using grapefruit knife; reserve shells. Combine yogurt, honey and grated orange rind in bowl; mix well. Chill, covered, in refrigerator for several minutes. Dip apple and pear slices into orange juice. Fill orange shells with yogurt sauce; place on salad plates or large platter. Arrange orange, apple, pear and kiwifruit slices and grape clusters around orange shells. Garnish with lemon, citrus or mint leaves. Yield: 6 servings.

QUICK CUKE AND FRUIT TOSS

1 cup seedless green
  grapes
1 cup seedless red grapes
1 cup chopped apple
1 cup chopped peeled
  cucumber

1/4 to 1/2 cup chopped nuts
1/2 cup sour cream
1 tablespoon sugar
1 tablespoon chopped
  fresh parsley

Combine grapes, apple, cucumber and nuts in serving bowl; toss gently. Combine sour cream and sugar in small bowl; mix well. Spoon over fruit; toss lightly. Sprinkle with parsley. Yield: 6 servings.

SMOKEY MOUNTAIN FRUIT SALAD

1   11-ounce can mandarin
  oranges, drained
1   8-ounce can pineapple
  chunks
1   8-ounce can sliced
  beets, drained
2 tart red apples, chopped

1 banana, sliced
1 tablespoon lemon juice
Shredded lettuce
1 tablespoon sugar
1/4 cup chopped peanuts
1/4 cup mayonnaise
2 tablespoons milk

Combine mandarin oranges, undrained pineapple, beets, apples and banana in bowl. Add lemon juice; toss gently. Let stand for 10 minutes; drain. Arrange on lettuce-lined platter. Sprinkle with sugar and peanuts. Mix mayonnaise and milk in small bowl until smooth. Drizzle over fruit mixture. Yield: 4 servings.

HEAVENLY HASH

2 cups whipping cream, whipped
1 medium can crushed pineapple, drained
3 or 4 bananas, thinly sliced

1 8-ounce jar maraschino cherries, drained
1 teaspoon vanilla extract
2 tablespoons sugar

Combine whipped cream, pineapple, bananas, cherries, vanilla and sugar in serving bowl; toss lightly. Chill. Garnish with fruit if desired. Yield: 10 to 12 servings.

JUBILEE SALAD

1 3-ounce package cherry gelatin
1¼ cups boiling water
1 21-ounce can cherry pie filling
1 3-ounce package orange-pineapple gelatin
1 cup boiling water

1 8-ounce can crushed pineapple
⅓ cup mayonnaise or mayonnaise-type salad dressing
1 cup whipped topping
¼ cup chopped pecans
Salad greens

Dissolve cherry gelatin in 1¼ cups boiling water in bowl. Stir in pie filling. Pour into 6½-cup mold or dish. Chill for 1 hour or until firm. Dissolve orange-pineapple gelatin in 1 cup boiling water in bowl. Stir in undrained pineapple. Chill for 30 minutes or until partially set. Mix mayonnaise and whipped topping in large bowl until smooth. Stir in pineapple mixture gradually. Fold in pecans. Spoon over cherry layer. Chill until firm. Unmold onto serving plate lined with salad greens. Yield: 12 servings.

ORANGE SHERBET SALAD

1 11-ounce can
mandarin oranges,
drained
1 6-ounce package
orange gelatin
1 cup boiling water

1 pint orange sherbet
8 ounces whipped
topping
1 large can crushed
pineapple, drained

Cut mandarin oranges into bite-sized pieces. Dissolve gelatin in boiling water in large bowl. Add sherbet, stirring until melted. Fold in whipped topping. Add pineapple and oranges; mix well. Spoon into serving dish or mold. Chill until firm. Yield: 4 servings.

OVERNIGHT SALAD

2 cans mandarin
oranges, drained
1 cup sour cream
1 cup coconut
1 cup miniature
marshmallows

1 cup drained pineapple
tidbits
1 can fruit cocktail,
drained

Combine oranges, sour cream, coconut, marshmallows, pineapple and fruit cocktail in bowl; mix well. Chill for 24 hours or longer before serving. Yield: 4 servings.

ANYTIME CONFETTI PINEAPPLE GELATIN

2 3-ounce packages
lemon gelatin
2 cups boiling water
1/2 cup cold water
1 20-ounce can crushed
pineapple
1 cup shredded carrots

1/4 cup chopped green
bell pepper
1/4 cup chopped pimento
or red bell pepper
1/4 cup vinegar
2 tablespoons lemon juice
1 teaspoon dillweed

Dissolve gelatin in boiling water in medium bowl. Add 1/2 cup cold water, undrained pineapple, carrots, green pepper, pimento, vinegar, lemon juice and dillweed; mix well. Pour into 2-quart mold. Chill for 4 hours or until set. Unmold onto serving plate. Yield: 8 servings.

PINEAPPLE DELIGHT CONGEALED SALAD

1 3-ounce package lime gelatin
1 3-ounce package lemon gelatin
1½ cups boiling water
2 cups cream-style cottage cheese

1 20-ounce can crushed pineapple
1 cup mayonnaise
Juice of ½ lemon
½ teaspoon prepared horseradish

Dissolve lime and lemon gelatins in boiling water in medium bowl. Add cottage cheese, pineapple, mayonnaise, lemon juice and horseradish; mix well. Pour into mold. Chill until firm. Unmold onto serving plate. The horseradish is very important, but it does not predominate in taste.
Yield: 10 to 12 servings.

RASPBERRY SALAD

1 10-ounce package frozen raspberries, thawed
2 3-ounce packages raspberry gelatin
2 cups boiling water

1 pint vanilla ice cream
1 6-ounce can frozen lemonade concentrate, thawed
½ cup chopped pecans

Drain raspberries, reserving juice. Dissolve gelatin in boiling water in medium bowl. Add vanilla ice cream, stirring until softened. Stir in lemonade and reserved raspberry juice. Chill until partially set. Stir in raspberries and pecans. Pour into 6-cup ring mold or 6 individual molds. Chill until set. Unmold onto serving platter or salad plates. Yield: 6 servings.

A Lion Tip

For a Salad Dressing for Fruit, mix ½ cup mayonnaise, ½ cup whipped cream, 1 tablespoon maraschino cherry juice and 4 chopped cherries.

SNOWBALL SALAD

3 large cans peach halves
3 large cans pear halves
12 ounces cream cheese,
  softened

1 cup chopped pecans
Mayonnaise
2 cans grated coconut

Chill fruit; drain thoroughly. Combine cream cheese and pecans in bowl; mix well. Add enough mayonnaise to make soft mixture. Spoon into fruit halves. Roll fruit halves in coconut. Press 1 peach half and 1 pear half together to form snowball; secure with toothpicks if necessary. Place on salad plates. Yield: 20 servings.

SWISS CHEESE MOSAIC

1/2 cup dried apricots or
  peaches
1/2 cup (or more) water
1 1/2 cups shredded
  Switzerland Swiss
  (Emmentaler) cheese

1/2 cup chopped seedless
  raisins
1/2 cup chopped walnuts

Combine apricots and water in saucepan. Bring to a boil. Simmer until tender and pulpy, stirring frequently. Mash to a smooth paste consistency. Cool. Fold in cheese, raisins and walnuts. Store, covered, in refrigerator. May substitute Switzerland natural Gruyère cheese and golden seedless raisins. May add orange, apricot or peach liqueur or dry white wine for extra moisture and flavor. Yield: 6 to 8 servings.

A Lion Tip

Combine cantaloupe and honeydew balls with strawberries and blueberries for a refreshing and colorful fruit salad. Serve in hollowed-out cantaloupe shells.

THANKSGIVING FRUIT SALAD

1 cup pineapple juice
1 egg, beaten
1 cup sugar
1 tablespoon flour
Dash of salt
4 apples, sliced
4 bananas, sliced

4 oranges, sliced
4 peaches, sliced
Grapes
Blueberries
Pineapple chunks
Cherries

Combine pineapple juice, egg, sugar, flour and salt in large saucepan; mix well. Simmer until thickened, stirring constantly. Cool. Stir in apples, bananas, oranges, peaches, grapes, blueberries, pineapple and cherries; toss gently. Spoon into serving dish. Chill for 24 hours before serving. Yield: 8 servings.

SNICKERS SALAD

4 medium apples,
   chopped
3 cups miniature
   marshmallows

2 2-ounce Snickers
   candy bars, chopped
9 ounces whipped
   topping

Combine apples and marshmallows in salad bowl; mix well. Add candy; mix well. Fold in whipped topping. Chill until serving time. Yield: 8 servings.

STRAWBERRY PURÉE OVER FRUIT

1 cup sliced strawberries
1/4 cup cream Sherry or
   orange juice
3 tablespoons sugar

1 large banana, sliced
1 8-ounce can pineapple
   chunks, drained

Combine strawberries, Sherry and sugar in blender container. Process until blended. Arrange banana slices and pineapple chunks in dessert dishes or stemmed glasses. Top with strawberry mixture. Chill until serving time. Garnish with fresh strawberries or pineapple wedges. May substitute 1 cup fresh pineapple cubes for canned pineapple chunks. Yield: 4 servings.

STRAWBERRY SALAD

1 6-ounce package
strawberry gelatin
1 cup boiling water
2 10-ounce packages
frozen strawberries,
thawed

1 8-ounce can crushed
pineapple, drained
3 bananas, mashed
1 cup chopped nuts
2 cups sour cream

Dissolve gelatin in boiling water in 2-quart bowl. Stir in strawberries, pineapple, bananas and nuts. Pour ½ of the gelatin mixture into 9-inch square dish. Chill until firm. Spread with sour cream. Top with remaining gelatin mixture. Chill until firm. Yield: 10 to 12 servings.

STRAWBERRY PRETZEL SALAD

2⅔ cups crushed pretzels
¾ cup melted margarine
3 to 4 tablespoons sugar
8 ounces cream cheese,
softened
1 cup confectioners'
sugar

8 ounces whipped
topping
1 6-ounce package
strawberry gelatin
2 cups boiling water
20 ounces frozen
strawberries, drained

Combine pretzels, margarine and sugar in bowl; mix well. Press into 9x13-inch baking dish. Bake at 400 degrees for 8 minutes. Cool completely. Beat cream cheese, confectioners' sugar and whipped topping in mixer bowl until smooth. Spread over baked layer. Dissolve gelatin in boiling water in bowl. Add strawberries; mix well. Chill slightly. Pour over cream cheese layer. Chill until firm. Yield: 12 to 15 servings.

WALDORF SALAD

Sugar to taste
1 cup light cream
1 to 2 tablespoons
vinegar

1½ cups chopped apples
¼ teaspoon salt
1 cup chopped celery
½ to 1 cup chopped nuts

Combine sugar and cream in small bowl; mix well. Add vinegar; mix well. Combine apples, salt, celery and nuts in salad bowl. Pour cream mixture over apple mixture; toss lightly. Yield: 4 servings.

BEEF AND KIDNEY BEAN SALAD

2 cups cooked beef strips
1 20-ounce can kidney
  beans, drained
1 cup chopped celery
1/4 cup chopped onion
2 hard-boiled eggs,
  chopped

2 tablespoons sliced
  sweet pickle
1/4 cup mayonnaise
1 tablespoon chili sauce
1 teaspoon salt
1 head lettuce

Combine beef, beans, celery, onion, eggs, pickle, mayonnaise, chili sauce and salt in bowl; toss lightly. Chill, covered, for 30 minutes. Spoon into lettuce cups on salad plates. Yield: 8 servings.

BEEF AND MACARONI SALAD COPENHAGEN

2 cups uncooked elbow
  macaroni
1 10-ounce package
  frozen peas
1/2 cup mayonnaise
1 envelope sour cream
  sauce mix

3/4 cup milk
1 teaspoon dillweed
1 to 2 cups chopped
  cooked beef
Lettuce

Cook macaroni using package directions, adding peas during last 5 minutes of cooking time; drain. Place in large bowl. Chill. Combine mayonnaise, sour cream sauce mix, milk and dillweed in bowl. Mix until smooth. Let stand for 10 minutes. Pour over chilled macaroni and peas. Add beef; toss lightly. Serve on lettuce-lined serving plates. May substitute ham for beef. Yield: 4 to 6 servings.

A Lion Tip

For a summer-fresh salad dressing, try using a little fresh lemon juice with a dash of your favorite herb. It makes a great calorie-wise sauce for chicken, vegetables and fish.

BREEZY FIESTA BEEF SALAD

8 ounces 1¼-inch thick
boneless beef top
sirloin steak
½ cup picante sauce
1½ teaspoons cornstarch
1 tablespoon oil
1 teaspoon cumin
½ teaspoon garlic salt
¼ teaspoon pepper

2 or 3 ripe avocados
Lime juice
2 or 3 ruby red
grapefruit, sectioned
Red leaf lettuce
½ cup sliced black olives
Chopped fresh cilantro
Fiesta Dressing

Slice steak into ⅛-inch thick strips. Combine picante sauce and cornstarch in large bowl, stirring until smooth. Add steak strips; mix well. Pour into plastic bag or dish, sealing plastic bag or covering dish. Marinate in refrigerator for 20 minutes, stirring occasionally. Place oil and cumin in 7x11-inch glass baking dish. Add beef with marinade; mix well. Cover with waxed paper. Microwave on Medium for 9 to 11 minutes or until beef is slightly pink, stirring twice; drain. Stir in garlic salt and pepper. Peel and slice avocados; brush with lime juice. Arrange avocado slices and grapefruit sections pinwheel-fashion on lettuce-lined salad plates. Arrange beef mixture in center of pinwheels. Sprinkle with olives and cilantro. Serve with Fiesta Dressing. Yield: 6 servings.

Fiesta Dressing

½ cup sour cream or
plain yogurt
½ cup picante sauce
½ cup chopped seeded
tomato

2 tablespoons chopped
green onions
1 tablespoon chopped
fresh cilantro
Hot pepper sauce to taste

Combine sour cream, picante sauce, tomato, green onions, cilantro and pepper sauce in bowl; mix well. Chill in refrigerator until ready to use.

GINGERED BEEF SALAD

1 small onion
3 whole cloves
1 3-pound boneless
  beef round roast,
  trimmed
4 cups water
1 cup dry red wine
1 large clove of garlic,
  cut into halves
6 ounces uncooked long
  grain and wild rice
1½ cups cooked green
  peas

½ cup chopped celery
½ cup sliced green
  onions
⅛ cup chopped red
  onion
⅓ cup chopped red bell
  pepper
Ginger Dressing
Romaine lettuce
2 hard-boiled eggs, cut
  into quarters

Stud onion with cloves. Place roast in large saucepan. Add onion, water, wine and garlic; mix well. Bring to a boil; reduce heat. Simmer for 2½ hours or until roast is tender. Remove roast to large bowl. Chill, covered, until cool. Cut into bite-sized pieces. Prepare rice using package directions. Add rice, peas, celery, green onions, red onion and red pepper to roast in bowl; mix well. Add Ginger Dressing; toss lightly. Spoon into lettuce-lined serving dish. Garnish with parsley sprigs and curls of tomato peel. Serve warm or at room temperature. Yield: 10 to 12 servings.

Ginger Dressing

¼ cup oil
2 tablespoons red wine
  vinegar
1 teaspoon Dijon mustard

¼ teaspoon salt
1 teaspoon ginger
½ teaspoon pepper

Combine oil, vinegar, mustard, salt, ginger and pepper in blender container. Process until blended. Pour into small jar. Chill for several hours.

DELI ROAST BEEF AND POTATO SALAD

1 8-ounce package
  frozen potato wedges
  with skins
2 tablespoons sour cream
2 tablespoons Italian
  salad dressing
Lettuce
6 ounces thinly sliced
  roast beef

1 medium tomato, cut
  into wedges
12 cucumber slices
1/2 small red onion, sliced
1 7-ounce can artichoke
  hearts, drained, cut into
  halves

Arrange potato wedges on baking sheet. Bake at 450 degrees for 20 to 25 minutes or until light brown and crisp. Mix sour cream and salad dressing in bowl until blended. Line 2 serving plates with lettuce. Arrange beef, tomato, cucumber, onion and artichoke hearts on lettuce. Add hot potato wedges just before serving. Serve with individual servings of sour cream mixture. May substitute ham or turkey for roast beef. Yield: 2 servings.

HAM AND EGG SALAD

3 slices bread
1 tablespoon olive oil
1 clove of garlic, cut into
  halves
1/2 pound cooked ham
1 head romaine lettuce
4 hard-boiled eggs, cut
  into quarters

1/2 pint cherry tomatoes
2 tablespoons lemon juice
1 teaspoon anchovy paste
1/4 teaspoon salt
1/8 teaspoon pepper
6 tablespoons olive oil
2 tablespoons Parmesan
  cheese

Brush both sides of bread with 1 tablespoon olive oil. Place on baking sheet. Bake at 350 degrees for 5 minutes on each side or until toasted. Rub with garlic. Cut into 1/2-inch croutons. Cut ham into matchsticks. Tear lettuce into bite-sized pieces; place in salad bowl. Top with eggs, ham, tomatoes and croutons. Combine lemon juice, anchovy paste, salt and pepper in small jar with lid. Seal. Shake well. Add remaining 6 tablespoons olive oil; shake well. Pour over salad; toss gently. Sprinkle with Parmesan cheese. Yield: 4 servings.

ITALIAN HAM AND PASTA SALAD

3 ounces spaghetti
1/2 cup mayonnaise-type
  salad dressing
1/3 cup Parmesan cheese
1/4 cup chopped parsley
2 tablespoons milk

1 cup ham or salami
  strips
1 cup sliced carrots
1 cup sliced zucchini
1/4 cup sliced black olives

Break spaghetti into thirds. Cook using package directions. Combine salad dressing, Parmesan cheese, parsley and milk in salad bowl; mix well. Add spaghetti, ham, carrots, zucchini and olives; toss lightly. Chill for several hours to overnight. May add additional salad dressing just before serving. Garnish with additional Parmesan cheese if desired. Yield: 4 servings.

POLYNESIAN HAM AND PINEAPPLE

1 cup mayonnaise
1 tablespoon honey
2 teaspoons prepared
  mustard
2 small pineapples, cut
  into halves lengthwise
1/3 cup raisins

1 17-ounce can apricot
  halves, drained,cut into
  halves
2 cups chopped cooked
  ham
1/2 cup slivered blanched
  almonds, toasted

Combine mayonnaise, honey and mustard in small bowl; mix well. Hollow out pineapple halves, leaving 1/2-inch shell intact. Reserve shells. Remove core; cut pineapple into chunks. Combine pineapple chunks, raisins, apricots, ham and 1/4 cup almonds in bowl; mix well. Spoon into reserved shells; drizzle with mayonnaise mixture. Sprinkle with remaining 1/4 cup almonds. May substitute one 20-ounce can pineapple chunks for fresh pineapple and serve in individual salad bowls. Yield: 4 servings.

A Lion Tip

Chop leftover ham, beef and chicken and add to salad greens for an elegant and easy chef salad.

SELECT DELI SALAD

8 ounces uncooked
rainbow rotini
1 9-ounce package
frozen artichoke hearts,
cooked, drained
1 5-ounce stick
pepperoni, sliced
1 cup sliced fresh
cauliflowerets
1 cup small fresh
broccoli flowerets

1 cup chopped Monterey
Jack cheese
1/2 cup sliced green
onions
3/4 cup vegetable or olive
oil
1/4 cup red wine vinegar
1/2 teaspoon Italian
seasoning (optional)

Cook rotini using package directions; drain. Combine rotini, artichoke hearts, pepperoni, cauliflower, broccoli, cheese, green onions, oil, vinegar and Italian seasoning in salad bowl; toss to mix. Chill, covered, for several hours. Toss gently just before serving. Store in refrigerator.
Yield: 6 to 8 servings.

CHINESE CHICKEN SALAD

1 1/2 cups julienne
cooked chicken breast
2 cups julienne, seeded
peeled cucumber
1 cup fresh mung bean
sprouts
3/4 cup sliced red radishes
3 tablespoons reduced-
sodium soy sauce
2 tablespoons sesame oil

2 tablespoons fresh
lemon juice
1 1/2 tablespoons prepared
hot mustard
Napa cabbage or red
cabbage leaves
2 green onions, thinly
sliced
1/2 cup blanched trimmed
fresh snow peas

Combine chicken, cucumber, bean sprouts and radishes in medium bowl; mix well. Mix soy sauce, sesame oil, lemon juice and mustard in small measuring cup with wire whisk. Pour over chicken mixture; toss gently. Spoon onto cabbage-lined salad plates. Sprinkle with green onions. Arrange snow peas in spiral design around chicken mixture. Yield: 2 servings.

CHICKEN FRUIT SALAD

3 cups coarsely chopped
  cooked chicken
3/4 cup chopped celery
3/4 cup seeded grape
  halves
1 20-ounce can
  pineapple chunks

1 11-ounce can
  mandarin oranges
1/4 cup mayonnaise-type
  salad dressing
1/8 teaspoon salt
Lettuce leaves

Combine chicken, celery, grapes, pineapple and mandarin oranges in bowl; toss gently. Combine salad dressing and salt in small bowl; mix well. Add to chicken mixture; toss gently. Spoon onto lettuce-lined salad plates. Yield: 6 servings.

ROASTED PEPPER AND CHICKEN SALAD

2 large green bell peppers
2 large red bell peppers
2 large yellow bell
  peppers
3 tablespoons sliced
  green onions
2 tablespoons olive oil
1 tablespoon lime juice
2 teaspoons white wine
  Worcestershire sauce
1/4 teaspoon coarsely
  ground black pepper

1/8 teaspoon garlic powder
3 whole chicken breasts,
  split, boned and skinned
Hickory-flavored salt to
  taste
Olive oil
6 English muffins, split,
  toasted and buttered
Chopped walnuts

Place peppers on rack in broiler pan. Broil 6 inches from heat source until charred on all sides turning as needed. Place in paper bag; seal. Let stand for 10 minutes. Peel peppers. Cut into strips lengthwise, reserving pepper liquid. Place pepper strips and liquid in saucepan. Combine next 6 ingredients in bowl; mix well. Pour over pepper strips. Cook over medium heat until heated through, stirring frequently. Sprinkle chicken breasts with hickory-flavored salt. Arrange on rack in broiler pan. Drizzle with small amount of olive oil. Broil 6 inches from heat source for 5 to 6 minutes on each side or until tender. Cut into strips. Place 2 muffin halves on each serving plate. Top with chicken strips. Spoon pepper mixture over chicken. Sprinkle with walnuts. Yield: 6 servings.

THAI CHICKEN SALAD

1/4 cup fresh lime juice
3 tablespoons bottled
fish sauce
2 tablespoons oil
5 teaspoons sugar
1 tablespoon chopped
mint leaves
2 cloves of garlic, minced
1/2 teaspoon salt
1 broiler-fryer chicken,
cooked, boned and
skinned

1 cucumber, peeled,
seeded and shredded
2 cups fresh bean sprouts
2 fresh green chilies,
seeded, shredded
1/2 small red onion, thinly
sliced into rings
1 tablespoon shredded
fresh ginger
1/2 cup chopped fresh
cilantro
1/4 cup chopped peanuts

Mix lime juice, fish sauce, oil, sugar, mint leaves, garlic and salt in small bowl until sugar dissolves. Cut chicken into thin shreds. Combine chicken and cucumber in large salad bowl; toss gently. Combine bean sprouts, chilies, onion and ginger in medium bowl; mix well. Add to chicken mixture. Add lime juice mixture and cilantro; toss gently. Sprinkle with peanuts. Yield: 4 to 6 servings.

FISH AND ASPARAGUS SALAD

1 1/2 pounds tile or firm-
fleshed fish
1 pound cooked peeled
shrimp
1/3 cup extra virgin olive
oil
3/4 cup imported small
black olives

2 tablespoons capers,
drained, chopped
Juice of 1 lemon
1 1/2 teaspoons oregano
Salt and pepper to taste
1 pound asparagus
16 cherry tomato halves

Poach or steam fish; cool. Flake into large pieces. Combine with shrimp, olive oil, olives, capers, lemon juice, oregano, salt and pepper in bowl; toss lightly. Let stand, covered, at room temperature for 1 hour. Cook asparagus in a small amount of boiling water in saucepan until tender-crisp; drain and cool. Add asparagus and tomatoes to fish mixture; toss lightly. Adjust seasonings. Serve immediately. Yield: 6 to 8 servings.

ELEGANT SEAFOOD SALAD

6 cups water
1 teaspoon salt
1 pound medium shrimp,
  peeled, deveined
1 pound bay scallops,
  rinsed
1/4 cup mayonnaise
1/4 cup catsup
2 tablespoons oil
1 tablespoon lemon juice
1 tablespoon Dijon
  mustard
1/4 teaspoon salt
5 drops of hot pepper
  sauce
1 1/2 cups crab meat
2 cups frozen LeSueur
  peas, thawed
2 green onions, cut into
  1/2-inch pieces
Salt and pepper to taste
5 cups torn romaine
  lettuce
2 thin slices tomato
2 thin slices kiwifruit

Bring water and 1 teaspoon salt in large saucepan to a boil. Add shrimp. Cook for 1 minute. Add scallops. Bring just to the boiling point; drain and chill. Combine mayonnaise and next 6 ingredients in small bowl; mix well. Chill, covered, until serving time. Combine shrimp, scallops, crab meat, peas and green onions in bowl; toss gently. Add salt and pepper to taste and chilled salad dressing; toss lightly. Spoon into lettuce-lined salad bowl. Top with tomato and kiwifruit. Yield: 6 servings.

MOLDED SHRIMP SALAD

1 12-ounce package
  frozen shrimp, thawed
1 can tomato soup
24 ounces cream cheese,
  softened
1 1/2 envelopes unflavored
  gelatin
1/2 cup cold water
1 1/4 cups chopped celery
1/4 cup chopped green
  bell pepper
1/2 onion, finely chopped

Coat large mold lightly with mayonnaise. Cook shrimp using package directions; drain. Cool. Heat soup and cream cheese in medium saucepan until cream cheese is melted, stirring constantly. Beat until smooth. Soften gelatin in cold water. Add to soup mixture; mix until dissolved. Let stand for 10 to 15 minutes or until cooled. Add celery, green pepper and onion; mix well. Pour into prepared mold. Chill until set. Unmold onto serving plate. Yield: 8 servings.

LEMONY WHEAT AND BARLEY SALAD

1 1/2 cups boiling water
1/2 cup bulgur
3 cups water
1/2 cup barley
2 scallions, cut into thin
strips

1 tomato, chopped
1/3 cup fresh lemon juice
3/4 cup chopped parsley
1/4 cup olive oil
Salt and pepper to taste

Pour boiling water over bulgur in medium bowl. Let stand at room temperature for 1 1/2 hours or until softened; drain. Combine 3 cups water and barley in saucepan. Bring to a boil, stirring constantly. Simmer, covered, for 30 minutes or until tender; drain. Add to bulgur; mix well. Add scallions, tomato, lemon juice, parsley, oil, salt and pepper; mix well. Chill for 30 minutes before serving. Yield: 4 servings.

HOT NOODLE SALAD

2 cups uncooked medium
noodles
3 slices bacon
1/4 cup chopped onion
1 tablespoon sugar
1 tablespoon flour
1/4 teaspoon salt

1/8 teaspoon dry mustard
1/2 cup water
1/4 cup vinegar
1 cup sliced celery
2 tablespoons chopped
parsley

Cook noodles using package directions; drain. Cook bacon in large skillet until crisp; drain, reserving 1 tablespoon drippings. Crumble bacon; set aside. Sauté onion in bacon drippings in skillet until tender. Stir in sugar, flour, salt and dry mustard. Add water and vinegar; mix well. Cook until thickened and bubbly, stirring constantly. Cook for 1 minute longer. Stir in noodles, celery and parsley. Spoon into salad bowl; sprinkle with bacon. Yield: 4 to 6 servings.

PARM-A-SALAD

2 cups uncooked elbow
macaroni
1 cup chopped tomato
3/4 cup sliced celery
1/2 cup Parmesan cheese
1/3 cup chopped onion

1/3 cup chopped dill
pickles
1 teaspoon prepared
mustard
Dash of pepper
3/4 cup mayonnaise

Cook macaroni using package directions; drain. Combine macaroni, tomato, celery, Parmesan cheese, onion, dill pickles, prepared mustard and pepper in salad bowl; toss lightly. Add mayonnaise; mix well. Chill for several hours. May add additional mayonnaise. Sprinkle with additional Parmesan cheese if desired. Yield: 6 servings.

PASTA SALAD

3 cups cooked pasta
twists
1 cup salami strips
1 cup cherry tomato
quarters
1 cup julienne cheese
1/2 cup thinly sliced celery
1/2 cup chopped purple
onion
1/2 cup green bell pepper
strips
1/3 cup sliced black olives

1/3 cup pimento strips
1/2 cup bottled Italian
salad dressing
2 tablespoons chopped
parsley
1 small clove of garlic,
minced
1/2 teaspoon salt
1/4 teaspoon sugar
1/8 teaspoon coarsely
ground pepper
Crisp lettuce leaves

Combine pasta, salami, tomato, cheese, celery, onion, green pepper, olives and pimento in large bowl; toss lightly. Combine salad dressing, parsley, garlic, salt, sugar and pepper in measuring cup; mix well. Pour over pasta mixture; toss to mix. Chill, covered, for several hours. Spoon onto lettuce-lined salad plates. Yield: 6 servings.

SPAGHETTI SALAD

1 8-ounce package
  spaghetti
1 medium green bell
  pepper, finely chopped
8 ounces cheese, cut into
  small cubes
Salt to taste
1 can finely chopped
  pimento, drained

1 bottle of sliced stuffed
  olives
1 tablespoon celery seed
1/4 cup Parmesan cheese
Mayonnaise
4 hard-boiled eggs,
  chopped

Cook spaghetti using package directions; drain. Rinse with cold water. Combine with green pepper, cheese cubes, salt, pimento, olives, celery seed and Parmesan cheese in salad bowl; mix well. Add enough mayonnaise to moisten. Add eggs; toss lightly. Yield: 4 servings.

 # VEGETABLE SALADS

EASY BEAN SALAD

1 can French-style green
  beans, drained
1 can Chinese
  vegetables, drained
1 can English peas,
  drained

1 cup chopped onion
1 cup chopped celery
1/2 cup sugar
1/2 cup vinegar
Salt and pepper to taste

Combine green beans, Chinese vegetables and peas in salad bowl. Add onion and celery; mix well. Mix sugar and vinegar in small bowl. Pour over vegetables; toss to mix. Marinate in refrigerator overnight. Yield: 6 servings.

 ### A Lion Tip

Bottled salad dressings make a delicious marinade for salad vegetables.

BEET SALAD WITH WALNUT DRESSING

4 teaspoons red wine
  vinegar
3/4 teaspoon salt
1/4 teaspoon pepper
1/4 cup oil

2/3 pound fresh beets,
  peeled, shredded
1/4 cup chopped walnuts
Salad greens

Combine vinegar, salt and pepper in covered jar. Shake until salt dissolves. Add oil; shake until blended. Pour over beets in salad bowl. Add walnuts just before serving; toss to mix. Spoon onto salad plates lined with salad greens. Yield: 4 servings.

BEET SALAD

1 3-ounce package
  lemon gelatin
1 cup boiling water
3/4 cup beet juice
1 tablespoon vinegar

1 tablespoon horseradish
1/2 cup chopped celery
1 large can diced beets,
  drained

Dissolve gelatin in boiling water in bowl. Add beet juice, vinegar, horseradish, celery and beets; mix well. Pour into serving dish. Chill until set. Yield: 4 servings.

BROCCOLI SALAD

1 cup mayonnaise
2 tablespoons apple cider
  vinegar
1/2 cup sugar
1 package fresh broccoli
  flowerets
1/2 cup chopped pecans

1/2 cup chopped apples
1/2 cup raisins
1/2 cup chopped purple
  onion
12 slices crisp-fried
  bacon, crumbled

Mix mayonnaise, vinegar and sugar in small bowl. Chill overnight. Combine broccoli, pecans, apples, raisins and onion in salad bowl; toss lightly. Pour chilled salad dressing over salad; toss to mix. Sprinkle with bacon. Yield: 4 servings.

GUACAMOLE BOWL WITH AVOCADO DRESSING

1/2 head romaine lettuce
1/2 medium head iceberg lettuce, torn
2 medium tomatoes, cut into wedges
1/2 cup sliced black olives
1/4 cup sliced green onions
1 cup corn chips
1 ripe avocado, peeled, sliced
1 ripe avocado, peeled, seeded

1 tablespoon lemon juice
1/2 cup sour cream
1/3 cup oil
1 clove of garlic, crushed
1/2 teaspoon sugar
1/2 teaspoon chili powder
1/4 teaspoon salt
1/4 teaspoon hot pepper sauce
1/2 cup shredded Cheddar cheese

Line salad bowl with romaine leaves. Top with iceberg lettuce. Add tomatoes, olives, green onions, corn chips and avocado slices. Mash remaining avocado in small mixer bowl. Beat until smooth. Add lemon juice, sour cream, oil, garlic, sugar, chili powder, salt and hot pepper sauce; beat well. Pour over salad; toss gently. Sprinkle with cheese.
Yield: 4 to 5 servings.

GREEK SALAD

1/3 cup olive oil
3 tablespoons wine vinegar
1/8 teaspoon salt
Dash of freshly ground pepper
Dash of dry mustard
1 head Bibb lettuce, torn

2 medium tomatoes, cut into 1/2-inch wedges
8 to 10 Greek or black olives
3 ounces feta cheese, crumbled
Freshly ground pepper to taste

Combine olive oil, vinegar, salt, dash of pepper and dry mustard in small covered jar; shake well to mix. Chill until serving time. Arrange lettuce, tomato wedges and olives on salad plates; sprinkle with cheese. Drizzle with salad dressing; sprinkle with pepper to taste. Yield: 4 servings.

SPRING GREEN SALAD

1/4 cup olive oil
2 tablespoons lemon juice
1/4 teaspoon sugar
1/8 teaspoon dry mustard
1 small clove of garlic,
 minced
1 egg yolk
1 small cucumber, sliced

4 cups assorted torn
 salad greens
2 medium tomatoes, cut
 into eighths
1 small green bell pepper,
 sliced
Croutons

Combine olive oil, lemon juice, sugar, dry mustard, garlic and egg yolk in small covered jar. Shake well to mix. Chill until serving time. Combine cucumber, salad greens, tomatoes and green pepper in large salad bowl; toss lightly. Drizzle with salad dressing; top with croutons just before serving.
Yield: 4 servings.

MIXED GREEN SALAD

2 tablespoons red wine
 vinegar
1/4 teaspoon minced garlic
1 tablespoon Dijon
 mustard
6 tablespoons oil
Salt and freshly ground
 pepper to taste

1 small red onion, thinly
 sliced
3 cups chopped
 watercress
4 cups chopped red leaf
 lettuce
3 cups chopped Belgian
 endive

Combine vinegar, garlic and mustard in small bowl; beat well. Add oil, salt and pepper; blend with wire whisk. Place onion slices, watercress, leaf lettuce and endive in salad bowl; toss lightly. Drizzle with salad dressing; toss to mix.
Yield: 4 to 6 servings.

A Lion Tip

Lend variety to your salads by adding romaine, escarole, endive, chicory, watercress, spinach or celery tops. Darker greens have higher vitamin and mineral content.

COUNTRY LETTUCE SALAD

2/3 cup evaporated milk
2 tablespoons sugar
1 tablespoon cider
 vinegar
1 teaspoon salt

1/8 teaspoon pepper
1/2 head iceberg lettuce,
 torn
1 large carrot, shredded

Mix evaporated milk with sugar, vinegar, salt and pepper in salad bowl. Top with lettuce and carrot; toss to coat. Yield: 4 servings.

ELEVEN-LAYER SALAD

4 cups chopped iceberg
 lettuce
2 to 3 cups chopped
 parsley
8 hard-boiled eggs,
 chopped
2 green or red bell
 peppers, sliced
1 10-ounce package
 frozen green peas

2 cups shredded carrots
1 6-ounce can colossal
 pitted black olives,
 drained, sliced
2 cups sliced radishes
2 cups shredded sharp
 Cheddar cheese
1 cup chopped red onion
Green Salad Dressing

Place lettuce in large deep salad bowl. Reserve 2 tablespoons parsley. Layer remaining parsley, eggs, green or red peppers, peas, carrots, olives, radishes, cheese and onion over lettuce. Spoon Green Salad Dressing over top; sprinkle with reserved parsley. Chill, covered, for 6 hours to overnight. Yield: 15 servings.

Green Salad Dressing

2 cups mayonnaise
1/2 cup minced parsley
1 teaspoon basil

1 teaspoon dillweed
1 tablespoon sugar
1/2 cup sour cream

Mix mayonnaise, parsley, basil, dillweed, sugar and sour cream in small bowl until smooth.

FAVORITE LAYERED GREEN SALAD

1 small head lettuce,
  finely shredded
1 cup chopped onion
2 stalks celery, finely
  chopped
1 8-ounce can sliced
  water chestnuts, drained
1 10-ounce package
  frozen green peas

2 cups mayonnaise
1 teaspoon sugar
1/2 teaspoon salt
1/4 teaspoon pepper
8 ounces mozzarella
  cheese, shredded
1/2 cup Parmesan cheese

Layer lettuce, onion, celery, water chestnuts and peas in 9x13-inch dish. Spread with mayonnaise. Sprinkle with mixture of sugar, salt and pepper. Sprinkle with mozzarella cheese and Parmesan cheese. Chill for 8 hours or longer. Yield: 15 servings.

ENGLISH PEA SALAD

1 head cabbage, shredded
1 head lettuce, shredded
1 large can English peas,
  drained

1 large onion, chopped
Mayonnaise
Parmesan cheese

Layer half the cabbage, lettuce, peas and onion in large salad bowl. Spread with thin layer of mayonnaise; sprinkle with Parmesan cheese. Repeat layers. Chill overnight. Recipe may be increased or decreased. Delicious with chicken and dressing, with ham or served alone. Yield: 10 to 12 servings.

A Lion Tip

Make Thousand Island Salad Dressing by combining half a small bottle of catsup or chili sauce, 3 cups mayonnaise, 2 tablespoons prepared mustard, 1 cup sweet pickle relish and enough relish juice to make of desired consistency.

MARINATED VEGETABLE SALAD

1 can small whole green
  beans, drained
1 can tiny green peas,
  drained
1 green bell pepper,
  chopped
1 onion, chopped
1 cup chopped celery

1 can water chestnuts,
  chopped
1 can red kidney beans
1 1/2 cups water
1 cup apple vinegar
1/2 cup oil
1 cup sugar
Salt and pepper to taste

Combine green beans, peas, green pepper, onion, celery, water chestnuts and kidney beans in bowl; mix well. Combine water, vinegar, oil, sugar, salt and pepper in small bowl, stirring until sugar dissolves. Pour over vegetables. Marinate in cool place for 24 hours; drain. Spoon onto lettuce-lined salad plate. Top with favorite mayonnaise salad dressing. May be served as salad or vegetable. Yield: 10 to 12 servings.

ROASTED PEPPER AND SNOW PEA SALAD

2 red bell peppers
12 ounces snow peas
Salt to taste
1 small red onion
1 tablespoon Dijon
  mustard
2 tablespoons red wine
  vinegar

1/2 teaspoon cumin
Freshly ground pepper to
  taste
1/4 cup olive oil
1/4 cup finely chopped
  parsley

Place red peppers on rack in broiler pan. Broil 6 inches from heat source until skin is charred on all sides. Cool. Cut into halves; core. Remove and discard charred skin. Cut peppers lengthwise into thin strips. Place in salad bowl. Place snow peas in salted water to cover in saucepan. Bring to a boil. Boil for 2 minutes; drain in sieve. Rinse with cold water; drain. Add to salad bowl. Cut onion into halves; cut each half into thin slices. Add to salad bowl. Combine mustard, vinegar and cumin in small bowl; mix well. Stir in salt and pepper to taste. Beat in oil gradually with wire whisk. Stir in parsley. Pour over vegetables; toss to mix. Yield: 4 servings.

LOW-CALORIE PERFECTION SALAD

1 tablespoon unflavored
  gelatin
2 tablespoons cold water
1 cup boiling water
3/4 cup unsweetened
  pineapple juice
2 tablespoons sugar
1 teaspoon salt

Dash of pepper
1/4 cup vinegar
3/4 cup shredded cabbage
3/4 cup chopped celery
1 tablespoon chopped
  green bell pepper
10 small stuffed olives,
  chopped

Soften gelatin in cold water for 5 minutes. Add to boiling water in medium bowl, stirring until gelatin is dissolved. Add pineapple juice, sugar, salt and pepper; mix well. Chill until partially set. Mix vinegar, cabbage, celery, green pepper and olives in bowl. Fold into gelatin mixture. Pour into 6 individual molds. Chill until firm. Unmold onto salad plates. May substitute 1 small package sugar-free lime gelatin for unflavored gelatin and sugar. Yield: 6 servings.

GREAT AMERICAN POTATO SALAD

1 cup mayonnaise-type
  salad dressing
1 teaspoon prepared
  mustard
1/2 teaspoon celery seed
1/2 teaspoon salt
1/8 teaspoon pepper
4 cups cubed cooked
  potatoes
2 cups broccoli flowerets

4 ounces sharp Cheddar
  cheese, cut into cubes
1 cup 2-inch strips ham
2 hard-boiled eggs,
  chopped
1/2 cup sliced celery
1/2 cup chopped onion
1/2 cup chopped sweet
  pickles

Combine salad dressing, mustard, celery seed, salt and pepper in large salad bowl; mix well. Add potatoes, broccoli, cheese, ham, eggs, celery, onion and pickles; toss lightly. Chill in refrigerator. Add additional salad dressing just before serving if desired. Yield: 6 servings.

GERMAN POTATO SALAD

1½ pounds russet
  potatoes
Salt to taste
⅓ cup oil
⅓ cup cider vinegar
2 teaspoons sugar
½ teaspoon salt

½ teaspoon dry mustard
⅛ teaspoon pepper
4 slices crisp-fried bacon,
  crumbled
2 tablespoons chopped
  chives or green onions
Chive blossoms

Place potatoes in 1 inch boiling salted water in large saucepan. Cook, covered, for 20 to 30 minutes or until just tender; drain. Peel; slice ¼ inch thick. Place in large salad bowl. Combine oil, vinegar, sugar, ½ teaspoon salt, dry mustard and pepper in small bowl; mix well. Pour over warm potatoes; toss gently. Chill for several hours to overnight. Sprinkle with bacon and chives. Garnish with chive blossoms. Yield: 4 to 6 servings.

FRESH APPLE SLAW

4½ cups thinly sliced red
  apples
3 cups finely shredded
  green cabbage
1 cup sour cream

3 tablespoons lemon juice
1 tablespoon sugar
¾ teaspoon salt
⅛ teaspoon pepper
1 tablespoon poppy seed

Combine apples and cabbage in salad bowl; mix well. Combine sour cream, lemon juice, sugar, salt, pepper and poppy seed in small bowl; mix well. Pour over apples and cabbage mixture; toss lightly to mix well. Chill for 1 hour or longer before serving. Yield: 6 to 8 servings.

DUTCH SLAW

2 cups white vinegar
2 cups sugar
2 cups water
1 tablespoon celery seed
2 pounds cabbage,
  chopped

1 white onion, chopped
2 green bell peppers,
  chopped
1 3-ounce jar chopped
  pimento, drained
1 tablespoon salt

Combine vinegar, sugar, water and celery seed in small saucepan; mix well. Cook until sugar dissolves, stirring constantly. Cool. Combine cabbage, onion, peppers and pimento in salad bowl. Sprinkle with salt; toss lightly. Pour vinegar mixture over top. Chill, covered, for 24 hours. Toss before serving. Yield: 12 servings.

HOT SWEET AND SOUR COLESLAW

2 tablespoons butter
2 tablespoons flour
1 tablespoon sugar
1 teaspoon salt
Dash of pepper
1/4 teaspoon dry mustard
3 tablespoons cider
vinegar

1 cup evaporated milk
4 cups coarsely shredded
cabbage
1 medium onion, thinly
sliced
1/2 cup chopped green
bell pepper

Melt butter in large saucepan; remove from heat. Add flour, sugar, salt, pepper and dry mustard; stir until smooth. Stir in vinegar and evaporated milk gradually. Cook over medium heat until thickened, stirring constantly. Add cabbage, onion and green pepper; toss lightly to mix. Cook over medium heat for 2 to 3 minutes or until vegetables are slightly heated, stirring constantly. Yield: 4 to 5 servings.

L. A. SLAW

2 cups shredded white
cabbage
2 cups shredded red
cabbage
1 cup shredded carrots
1/2 cup chopped green
bell pepper
1/2 cup chopped red bell
pepper

4 green onions, thinly
sliced
3/4 cup tarragon vinegar
1/4 cup sugar
1 tablespoon Dijon
mustard
Salt and pepper to taste
3/4 cup olive oil

Combine first 6 ingredients in salad bowl; mix well. Combine vinegar, sugar, mustard, salt and pepper in small bowl; mix well. Whisk in olive oil gradually until salad dressing thickens. Pour over vegetables; toss lightly. Chill until serving time. Yield: 6 servings.

SIX-PEPPER SLAW

1 red bell pepper
1 orange bell pepper
1 green bell pepper
1 purple bell pepper
1 yellow bell pepper
1 red onion
1 fresh jalapeño pepper, seeded, minced
2 tablespoons tarragon vinegar
1 tablespoon Dijon mustard
2 teaspoons sugar
1 teaspoon salt
1/4 teaspoon Tabasco sauce
Freshly ground pepper to taste
1 cup vegetable oil
2 tablespoons peanut oil
1 tablespoon caraway seed, toasted, crushed
2 teaspoons grated lime rind

Core and seed red, orange, green, purple and yellow peppers. Cut julienne-style. Place in large salad bowl. Cut onion lengthwise into thin strips. Add to pepper strips; toss lightly. Combine jalapeño pepper, vinegar, mustard, sugar, salt, Tabasco sauce and ground pepper in small bowl; mix well. Whisk in vegetable oil and peanut oil gradually until thick. Pour over vegetables; toss to mix. Sprinkle with caraway seed and lime rind; toss gently. Chill, covered, for 3 hours or longer. Toss lightly before serving. Yield: 6 servings.

COLORFUL PINEAPPLE SLAW

4 cups shredded cabbage
1   8-ounce can pineapple tidbits, drained
1 cup shredded Cheddar cheese
1/2 cup sliced stuffed olives
1/4 cup chopped onion
1/3 cup chopped drained pimento
1/4 cup mayonnaise
1 tablespoon lemon juice
1/8 teaspoon pepper
1/4 cup whipping cream, whipped

Combine cabbage, pineapple, cheese, olives, onion and pimento in salad bowl; mix well. Chill for 1 hour or longer. Combine mayonnaise, lemon juice and pepper in small bowl; mix well. Fold in whipped cream. Pour over cabbage mixture just before serving, tossing gently to coat. Yield: 6 to 8 servings.

REFRIGERATOR SLAW

1 large head cabbage, shredded
1 large onion, chopped
1 medium green bell pepper, chopped
1 medium red bell pepper, chopped
1 large carrot, shredded
2 cups sugar
1 cup vinegar
1 teaspoon salt
1 teaspoon celery seed
1 teaspoon mustard seed

Combine cabbage, onion, green pepper, red pepper and carrot in large salad bowl. Add sugar; mix well. Pour vinegar over vegetables. Sprinkle with salt, celery seed and mustard seed; mix well. Let stand for 15 minutes; mix well. May store, covered, in refrigerator for up to 14 days. Yield: 6 to 8 servings.

MEXICALI COLESLAW

4 cups shredded cabbage
1 12-ounce can Mexicorn
1/2 cup finely chopped onion
1/2 cup American cheese cubes
1/4 cup sliced black olives
1 cup mayonnaise
2 tablespoons sugar
1 tablespoon prepared mustard
1 tablespoon vinegar
1/2 teaspoon celery seed

Combine cabbage, Mexicorn, onion, cheese and olives in salad bowl; mix well. Combine mayonnaise, sugar, mustard, vinegar and celery seed in small bowl; mix well. Pour over cabbage mixture; toss lightly. Chill, covered, for 2 hours or longer. Yield: 6 to 8 servings.

 A Lion Tip

Dress up bottled French salad dressing by adding ripe olives, chopped green pepper, sieved hard-cooked egg and chopped chives. For herb dressing, add parsley, thyme and oregano. For Roquefort dressing, add Roquefort cheese and Worcestershire sauce.

COLESLAW SOUFFLÉ

1 8-ounce can crushed
  pineapple
1 3-ounce package
  orange gelatin
3/4 cup boiling water
3/4 cup mayonnaise
1 cup shredded carrots

1 cup finely shredded
  cabbage
1/2 cup raisins
1/2 cup chopped walnuts
3 egg whites, stiffly
  beaten

Fold 22-inch piece of foil in half lengthwise. Tape firmly around 1-quart soufflé dish. Drain pineapple, reserving juice. Dissolve gelatin in boiling water in bowl. Add reserved juice; mix well. Beat in mayonnaise. Pour into 5x9-inch loaf pan. Freeze for 20 minutes or until partially set. Pour into large mixer bowl; beat until fluffy. Stir in pineapple, carrot, cabbage, raisins and walnuts. Fold in egg whites. Spoon into prepared soufflé dish. Chill until set. Remove foil. Yield: 6 servings.

APPLE SPINACH SALAD

5 to 6 cups packed
  spinach leaves
2 to 3 cups salad greens
1/2 cup thinly sliced celery
1/4 cup sliced green
  onions

1/2 cup chopped walnuts
1 or 2 Red Delicious
  apples, sliced
Sesame Dressing

Tear spinach and salad greens into small pieces. Place in salad bowl. Add celery, green onions and walnuts; mix well. Add apples. Drizzle with Sesame Dressing just before serving; toss lightly. Yield: 4 to 5 servings.

Sesame Dressing

1/4 cup white wine vinegar
3 tablespoons oil
2 tablespoons sugar
1/4 teaspoon salt

1 tablespoon toasted
  sesame seed
Dash of hot pepper sauce

Combine vinegar, oil, sugar and salt in small bowl; mix until sugar dissolves. Add sesame seed and hot pepper sauce; mix well.

RED AND GREEN HOLIDAY SALAD

8 ounces fresh spinach
1 red bell pepper
2 tablespoons vinegar
1/2 teaspoon salt

1/4 teaspoon pepper
6 tablespoons olive oil
1/4 cup crumbled bleu
cheese

Wash and stem spinach; drain. Tear into bite-sized pieces. Place in salad bowl. Cut red pepper into strips; add to spinach. Combine vinegar, salt and pepper in covered jar. Shake well. Add oil; shake well. Add bleu cheese. Pour over salad; toss lightly. Yield: 4 servings.

SPINACH SALAD WITH LEMON ZEST ALMONDS

1 bunch spinach,
washed, trimmed and
dried
1 cup crumbled blue
cheese
2 Granny Smith apples,
sliced

1/3 cup olive oil
2 tablespoons cider
vinegar
1/8 teaspoon thyme
1/8 teaspoon pepper
1 cup Lemon Zest
Almonds (page 18)

Combine spinach, bleu cheese and apples in salad bowl; toss lightly. Whisk olive oil, vinegar, thyme and pepper in small bowl. Drizzle over spinach mixture; toss to coat well. Add Lemon Zest Almonds just before serving, tossing lightly. Yield: 6 servings.

LIGHT AND LEMONY SPINACH SALAD

1/4 cup oil
2 tablespoons lemon juice
1 tablespoon chopped
fresh parsley
1 teaspoon sugar
1/4 teaspoon salt

1/8 teaspoon pepper
2 green onions, sliced
4 cups torn spinach
2 tablespoons sunflower
seed

Combine oil, lemon juice, parsley, sugar, salt, pepper and green onions in covered jar; shake well. Pour over spinach in salad bowl; toss gently. Sprinkle sunflower seed over top. Yield: 4 servings.

SWEET POTATO AND FRUIT SALAD

3 medium sweet potatoes
or yams
2 oranges
1/2 cup seedless grape
halves
1/3 cup golden raisins
1/4 cup thinly sliced celery
1/4 cup chopped walnuts

1 teaspoon grated orange
rind
3 ounces cream cheese,
softened
2 tablespoons honey
2 to 4 tablespoons
orange juice

Scrub sweet potatoes. Place in water to cover in large saucepan. Bring to a boil. Boil for 25 minutes or just until tender; drain. Cool. Peel; cut into 3/4-inch cubes. Peel and section oranges; place in large salad bowl. Add sweet potatoes, grape halves, raisins, celery and walnuts; toss lightly. Combine orange rind, cream cheese, honey and 2 tablespoons orange juice in small mixer bowl; beat until smooth. Pour over sweet potato mixture; toss to coat. Chill, covered, until serving time. Stir in enough remaining orange juice to moisten salad if desired. Yield: 6 servings.

MARINATED TOMATOES AND CUCUMBER

4 medium tomatoes, cut
into wedges
1 cucumber, peeled, cut
into 1-inch cubes
1 1/2 teaspoons lemon
juice

1/4 cup oil
1 clove of garlic, minced
1/2 teaspoon salt
1/8 teaspoon pepper
1/2 teaspoon oregano

Place tomatoes and cucumber in salad bowl; toss lightly. Combine lemon juice, oil, garlic, salt, pepper and oregano in small bowl; mix well. Pour over vegetables; mix gently. Chill for several hours, stirring occasionally. Yield: 8 servings.

Meats

BEEF

BRISKET WITH MUSTARD SAUCE

¼ cup coarsely ground
  pepper
1 teaspoon ginger
1 3 to 5-pound boneless
  beef brisket
⅔ cup soy sauce
1 teaspoon paprika
½ cup vinegar
1 clove of garlic, crushed

1 tablespoon tomato
  paste
½ cup mayonnaise
2 tablespoons prepared
  mustard
½ cup whipping cream,
  whipped
Salt to taste

Combine pepper and ginger in small bowl; mix well. Sprinkle evenly on waxed paper. Place beef over pepper mixture; press down firmly. Turn beef over. Press pepper mixture firmly into beef with heel of hand, coating both sides evenly until all the pepper mixture is used. Combine soy sauce, paprika, vinegar, garlic and tomato paste in bowl; mix well. Place beef in shallow baking dish. Pour marinade over beef. Marinate, covered, in refrigerator overnight, turning occasionally to marinate both sides. Remove beef; discard marinade. Wrap tightly in foil. Place in baking dish. Bake at 300 degrees for 3 hours or until very tender. Fold mayonnaise and mustard into whipped cream. Stir in salt. Garnish with parsley flakes or snipped chives. Serve with beef and thinly sliced rye bread. Yield: 12 to 20 servings.

BURGUNDY AND MUSHROOM ROAST

1 cup Burgundy
1 envelope onion soup
  mix
1 can mushrooms,
  drained

1 can cream of mushroom
  soup
1 beef roast

Combine wine, onion soup mix, mushrooms and cream of mushroom soup in bowl; mix well. Place roast in baking dish. Pour wine mixture over roast. Bake, covered, at 300 degrees for 3 hours, basting occasionally with pan juices. Yield: 8 servings.

CROCK•POT POT ROAST

1 onion, chopped
2 cloves of garlic,
  chopped
1   4-pound rump roast
2 teaspoons salt
1/4 teaspoon pepper

1/2 teaspoon rosemary
1/2 teaspoon thyme
3/4 cup red wine
3 tablespoons flour
1/4 cup water

Sprinkle onion and garlic in Crock•Pot. Place roast over onion and garlic; sprinkle with salt, pepper, rosemary and thyme. Pour in wine. Cook, covered, on High for 5 hours. Remove roast to serving plate. Measure 2 cups cooking liquid. Pour into saucepan. Mix flour and water in small bowl until smooth. Stir into liquid. Bring to a boil, stirring constantly; reduce heat. Simmer for 10 minutes, stirring frequently. Slice roast; serve with gravy. Yield: 8 to 10 servings.

GARLIC POT ROAST

4 cloves of garlic
1   3 to 4-pound rolled
  beef roast
1 tablespoon oil
1 onion, chopped

3 cloves of garlic,
  chopped
1 cup red wine
1 cup beef stock
Salt and pepper to taste

Cut 4 cloves of garlic into thin slivers. Cut small slits in roast; place slivers of garlic in slits. Brown roast in hot oil in large saucepan, turning to brown all sides. Remove to plate. Sauté onion and remaining 3 cloves of garlic in pan drippings in saucepan until golden brown. Add roast, wine, beef stock, salt and pepper. Bring to a boil; reduce heat. Simmer, covered, for 2 1/2 hours or until roast is tender, turning occasionally. Remove roast to serving plate; cover with foil to keep warm. Skim cooking liquid. Bring to a boil. Cook until reduced to 1 1/2 cups. Serve with roast. Yield: 8 servings.

 A Lion Tip

Wine and tomatoes used as cooking liquid for cheaper cuts of meat act to break down tough fibers and tenderize them.

ROAST FILET OF BEEF IN RED WINE SAUCE

1   1¾-pound center-cut
filet of beef, trimmed, tied
Salt and freshly ground
pepper to taste
1 tablespoon oil
2 tablespoons finely
chopped shallots

1 cup dry red wine
2 sprigs of fresh thyme or
½ teaspoon dried thyme
1 small bay leaf
½ cup fresh or canned
beef broth
2 tablespoons butter

Sprinkle beef on all sides with salt and pepper; rub with oil. Place in small shallow roasting pan. Bake at 450 degrees for 25 minutes, turning 1 or 2 times. Remove beef to warm platter; cover loosely with foil to keep warm. Pour off fat from pan juices. Sauté shallots in pan juices in roasting pan until tender. Add wine, thyme and bay leaf. Cook until reduced by ½. Add broth and any additional juices that have accumulated around beef. Cook over high heat until reduced to ¾ cup. Stir in butter. Remove roast to serving platter. Strain sauce; pour over roast. Slice cross grain and serve. Yield: 8 servings.

BROILED SIRLOIN STEAK WITH GARLIC SAUCE

3 tablespoons butter
1 teaspoon garlic powder
3 tablespoons
Worcestershire sauce

½ cup steak sauce
1   2½-pound sirloin steak

Melt butter in saucepan over low heat. Add garlic powder, Worcestershire sauce and steak sauce; mix well. Bring just to the boiling point, stirring constantly; remove from heat. Place steak on rack in broiler pan. Brush with steak sauce mixture. Broil 3 inches from heat source for 5 minutes. Turn steak; brush with steak sauce mixture. Broil for 5 minutes longer or to desired degree of doneness. Yield: 5 servings.

LONDON BROIL

1 teaspoon salt
1/2 teaspoon pepper
1/4 teaspoon basil
1/4 teaspoon rosemary
2 cloves of garlic, pressed
1/2 medium onion,
  chopped

2 tablespoons red wine
  vinegar
1/4 cup oil
1 1 to 1 1/2-pound flank
  steak

Combine salt, pepper, basil, rosemary, garlic, onion, vinegar and oil in bowl; mix well. Place steak in shallow glass dish. Pour vinegar mixture over steak. Marinate, covered with plastic wrap, for 2 hours or longer, turning once. Remove steak, reserving marinade. Grill steak over hot coals for 15 minutes or to desired degree of doneness, turning once. Carve diagonally cross grain into thin slices. Heat reserved marinade; drizzle over steak. Yield: 4 to 6 servings.

SHERRY BAKED STEAK

1/2 cup margarine
1/2 cup Sherry

4 T-bone or sirloin steaks
Salt and pepper to taste

Melt margarine in Sherry in saucepan over low heat. Place steaks in baking pan; sprinkle with salt and pepper. Baste with Sherry mixture; cover with foil. Bake at 450 degrees for 45 minutes or to desired degree of doneness, basting frequently. Yield: 4 servings.

 A Lion Tip

When comparing the cost of different cuts of meat, consider cost per serving rather than cost per pound. A boneless roast may yield more servings than a cheaper cut with bone.

BEEF BURGUNDY

1 pound boneless beef short ribs, round steak or sirloin steak
10 new potatoes, peeled, cut into cubes
2 tablespoons margarine, softened
1/2 teaspoon salt substitute
1/2 teaspoon pepper
1 cup tiny pearl onions
1 carrot, sliced
1 clove of garlic
Dash of salt
1 cup Burgundy or dry red wine
1/2 cup water
1 teaspoon marjoram
1/2 teaspoon thyme
1 teaspoon instant beef bouillon
Pepper to taste
2 cups fresh mushroom halves
2 tablespoons flour
2 tablespoons water

Cut beef into 1-inch cubes. Place potatoes in water to cover in saucepan. Bring to a boil. Cook over medium-high heat for 20 minutes or until tender; drain and mash. Add margarine, salt substitute and 1/2 teaspoon pepper; mix well. Spray large saucepan with nonstick cooking spray. Place saucepan over medium-high heat until hot. Add beef. Cook just until light brown, stirring constantly; drain on paper towels. Wipe saucepan; spray with nonstick cooking spray. Add onions, carrot, garlic and salt; mix well. Sauté for 5 minutes. Add beef. Add wine, 1/2 cup water, marjoram, thyme, instant bouillon and pepper to taste; mix well. Reduce heat. Simmer, covered, for 45 minutes. Stir in mushrooms. Simmer, covered, for 45 minutes longer. Mix flour and 2 tablespoons water in bowl until smooth. Stir into beef mixture. Bring to a boil over medium-high heat. Cook for 1 minute or until thickened, stirring constantly. Pour into 6x10-inch baking dish. Top with potato mixture piped into lattice design. Broil 6 inches from heat source for 10 minutes or until brown. Yield: 6 servings.

 A Lion Tip

To thicken meat dishes or make smooth gravy, shake the flour and water vigorously in a covered jar until no lumps remain.

CHINESE TACOS

3/4 pound boneless tender
  beef steak
1 teaspoon cornstarch
2 teaspoons dry Sherry
1/4 cup bottled stir-fry sauce
1 clove of garlic, pressed
1/4 teaspoon crushed red
  pepper

1 tablespoon oil
1/2 cup chopped green
  onions with tops
10 taco shells
Fresh bean sprouts
Shredded Napa cabbage
Red bell pepper strips
Fresh cilantro leaves

Cut beef cross grain into thin slices; cut into thin strips. Blend cornstarch and Sherry in medium bowl. Add stir-fry sauce, garlic and crushed red pepper; mix well. Add beef; mix well. Let stand for 30 minutes. Heat oil in wok or large skillet over high heat. Add beef. Stir-fry for 1 1/2 minutes. Add green onions. Stir-fry for 30 seconds longer; remove from heat. Fill taco shells with beef mixture and desired amounts of bean sprouts, cabbage, red pepper strips and cilantro leaves. Yield: 4 to 6 servings.

ORIENTAL STEAK STRIPS

2 pounds 1-inch thick
  beef round steak
2 tablespoons oil
1/3 cup soy sauce
2 teaspoons sugar
1/4 teaspoon pepper
1 clove of garlic, minced
3 carrots, cut into strips
2 green bell peppers, cut
  into 1-inch strips

8 green onions, cut into
  1 1/2-inch pieces
8 ounces fresh
  mushrooms, cut into
  halves
1 8-ounce can water
  chestnuts
2 tablespoons cornstarch
1/4 cup water
Cooked rice

Cut steak into strips 3 to 4 inches long and 1/8 inch thick. Brown in oil in large skillet. Drain, reserving drippings. Add enough water to drippings to measure 1 cup. Combine with soy sauce, sugar, pepper and garlic in small bowl; mix well. Stir into steak. Cook, tightly covered, for 45 minutes. Add next 5 ingredients. Cook, covered, for 15 minutes longer. Mix cornstarch and 1/4 cup water until smooth. Stir into steak mixture. Cook until thickened. Serve with hot rice. May substitute venison for beef. Yield: 4 to 6 servings.

NEW ENGLAND BOILED DINNER

Corned beef or smoked
ham
1 turnip, cut into halves
2 bunches carrots, cut
into halves

6 to 8 medium potatoes,
peeled, cut into halves
1 large head cabbage,
cut into quarters

Place corned beef or ham in water to cover in large saucepan. Bring to a boil. Boil for 2 to 3 hours or until tender. Add turnip, carrots and potatoes. Boil just until vegetables are tender, stirring occasionally. Layer cabbage over vegetable mixture. Boil for 20 minutes longer. Serve from saucepan or in serving dishes. Grind leftover boiled dinner, add beets and fry for Red-Flannel Hash. Yield: 6 servings.

CORNED BEEF AND ORANGE-CANDIED VEGETABLES

1   2¹/₂ to 3¹/₂-pound
corned beef brisket
¹/₃ cup fresh orange juice
¹/₄ cup packed brown
sugar
¹/₂ teaspoon cornstarch
1 tablespoon butter,
softened

1 teaspoon grated orange
rind
1 pound carrots,
diagonally sliced ¹/₂ inch
thick
1 onion, cut into 8 wedges

Place corned beef brisket in water to cover in large saucepan. Simmer, tightly covered, for 2¹/₂ to 3¹/₂ hours or until tender. Combine orange juice, brown sugar and cornstarch in small saucepan. Bring to a boil, stirring constantly. Cook for 2 minutes or until thickened, stirring constantly; remove from heat. Stir in butter and orange rind. Cook carrots in boiling water to cover in medium saucepan for 10 minutes. Add onion. Cook until vegetables are tender; drain. Remove brisket to platter; trim. Place brisket fat side up on rack in broiler pan. Brush with 2 tablespoons orange mixture. Broil 3 to 4 inches from heat source for 3 minutes or until brisket is glazed. Pour remaining orange mixture over vegetables. Cook over medium-high heat for 1 to 2 minutes or until vegetables are glazed. Carve brisket diagonally cross grain into thin slices. Serve with candied vegetables. Yield: 12 to 14 servings.

REUBEN CASSEROLE

1 16-ounce can
sauerkraut, drained
1 12-ounce can corned
beef, flaked
2 cups shredded Swiss
cheese
1/4 cup Thousand Island
salad dressing

1/2 cup mayonnaise
2 medium tomatoes,
sliced
2 tablespoons margarine,
softened
1/4 cup pumpernickel
crumbs

Place sauerkraut in 3-quart casserole. Top with beef; sprinkle with cheese. Combine salad dressing and mayonnaise; mix well. Spread over cheese. Top with tomatoes. Toss margarine and crumbs in small bowl; sprinkle over casserole. Bake at 350 degrees for 25 to 30 minutes or until hot and bubbly. Yield: 4 servings.

VEAL SCALLOPINI

3/4 cup yellow cornmeal
1/2 teaspoon coarsely
ground pepper
4 veal scallopini,
pounded very thin
1/2 cup low-fat buttermilk
1 tablespoon margarine
2 tablespoons olive oil
1 teaspoon margarine

1/4 cup fresh lemon juice
1 tablespoon chopped
parsley
4 thin slices lemon
1/2 cup chopped, seeded
ripe tomato
1 tablespoon chopped
parsley

Mix cornmeal and pepper in shallow bowl; mix well. Dip veal in buttermilk in bowl; dredge in cornmeal mixture to coat both sides. Melt 1 tablespoon margarine in olive oil in nonstick skillet over low heat. Increase heat to medium. Sauté veal for 2 minutes on each side or until light golden brown. Do not overcook. Remove to serving platter. Drain skillet. Melt remaining 1 teaspoon margarine in skillet. Add lemon juice, 1 tablespoon parsley and lemon slices. Cook over medium heat for 1 minute, stirring 1 or 2 times. Arrange veal on serving plates. Top each with lemon slice, lemon sauce and 2 tablespoons tomato. Sprinkle with remaining 1 tablespoon parsley. Yield: 4 servings.

GROUND BEEF

CABBAGE PATCH CASSEROLE

8 ounces ground beef
1 cup chopped celery
1 medium onion, chopped
1/2 medium head
  cabbage, chopped
Salt to taste

1 tablespoon (or more)
  chili powder
1 16-ounce can red
  kidney beans
1 quart canned tomatoes

    Brown ground beef in large skillet, stirring until crumbly; drain. Add celery and onion. Cook until light brown, stirring constantly. Add remaining ingredients; mix well. Simmer until beans are tender and casserole is of desired consistency. Serve over hot corn bread squares. Yield: 2 servings.

CHILI AND BEEF CASSEROLE

2 pounds ground beef
2 15-ounce cans chili
1 pound Velveeta
  Mexican cheese,
  shredded

1 8-ounce package
  nacho chips, crushed

    Brown ground beef in skillet, stirring until crumbly; drain. Heat chili in saucepan, stirring constantly. Alternate layers of ground beef, chili, cheese and 1/2-inch layers of chips in 2-quart casserole. Bake at 350 degrees until heated through and cheese is melted. Yield: 8 servings.

GROUND BEEF COMPANY CASSEROLE

7 or 8 ounces uncooked
  medium noodles
1 to 11/2 pounds lean
  ground beef
1 cup chopped onion
1 12-ounce can whole
  kernel corn, drained
1 can cream of
  mushroom soup

1 can cream of chicken
  soup
1 cup sour cream
1 small jar salad
  pimentos, drained
3/4 teaspoon salt
1/4 teaspoon pepper
1 cup buttered crushed
  butter crackers

Cook noodles using package directions; drain. Pour into buttered 9x13-inch baking pan. Brown ground beef in large skillet, stirring until crumbly; drain. Add onion, corn, soups, sour cream, pimento, salt and pepper; mix well. Pour over noodles; sprinkle with cracker crumbs. Bake at 350 degrees for 20 to 25 minutes or until hot and bubbly. Yield: 6 servings.

PACE-SETTING ENCHILADA CASSEROLE

1¹/₂ pounds lean ground
beef
1 small onion, chopped
1 clove of garlic, minced
1¹/₂ cups picante sauce
1   10-ounce package
frozen spinach, thawed,
squeezed dry
1   8-ounce can tomato
sauce
2 medium tomatoes,
seeded, chopped

1 large red bell pepper,
chopped
1 tablespoon lime juice
1¹/₂ teaspoons salt
12 corn tortillas
1 cup sour cream
³/₄ cup shredded
Monterey Jack cheese
³/₄ cup shredded Cheddar
cheese
Shredded lettuce
¹/₂ cup sliced black olives

Brown ground beef with onion and garlic in large skillet, stirring frequently; drain. Add picante sauce, spinach, tomato sauce, tomatoes, red pepper, lime juice and salt. Simmer for 15 minutes, stirring occasionally. Arrange 6 tortillas in bottom and up sides of lightly greased 9x13-inch baking dish, overlapping as necessary. Top with half the ground beef mixture. Repeat layers. Bake at 350 degrees for 30 minutes or until hot and bubbly. Spread with sour cream; sprinkle with Monterey Jack cheese and Cheddar cheese. Let stand for 10 minutes. Cut into squares. Serve on bed of shredded lettuce; sprinkle with olives. Serve with additional picante sauce. Yield: 8 servings.

A Lion Tip

Buy ground beef in quantities. Microwave in a colander in a bowl to catch drippings. Freeze in measured portions for use in your favorite recipes.

GROUND BEEF AND NOODLE DISH

7 ounces uncooked
noodles
1 1/2 pounds ground beef
1 15-ounce jar spaghetti
sauce

6 slices bread, buttered
on both sides
1 1/2 cups shredded
Cheddar cheese

Cook noodles using package directions; drain. Place in 9x13-inch baking dish. Brown ground beef in skillet, stirring until crumbly; drain. Layer ground beef and spaghetti sauce over noodles. Crumble bread; sprinkle over spaghetti sauce. Top with cheese. Bake at 375 degrees for 30 minutes or until hot and bubbly. Yield: 6 servings.

SKILLET MACARONI AND GROUND BEEF

1 1/2 pounds ground beef
2 cups uncooked elbow
or salad macaroni
1/2 cup minced onion
1/2 cup chopped green
bell pepper
2 8-ounce cans tomato
sauce

1 cup water
1/2 teaspoon salt
1/4 teaspoon pepper
1 tablespoon (or more)
Worcestershire sauce

Brown ground beef in skillet, stirring until crumbly. Remove from skillet with slotted spoon. Cook macaroni, onion and green pepper in pan drippings until vegetables are tender, stirring frequently and adding oil if necessary to prevent sticking. Add ground beef, tomato sauce, water, salt, pepper and Worcestershire sauce; mix well. Simmer, covered, for 25 minutes or until macaroni is tender. Yield: 6 servings.

SPANISH RICE CASSEROLE

1 pound ground beef
1 16-ounce can Spanish
  rice

1 medium onion, sliced
1 cup shredded mild
  Cheddar cheese

Brown ground beef in large skillet, stirring until crumbly; drain. Add Spanish rice and onion; mix well. Cook until heated through. Pour into 2-quart casserole; sprinkle with cheese. Bake at 325 degrees for 25 to 30 minutes or until hot and bubbly. Yield: 4 servings.

TEXAS BEEF SKILLET

1 pound ground beef
3/4 cup chopped onion
1 1/2 teaspoons chili
  powder
1/2 teaspoon salt
1/2 teaspoon garlic salt
1 16-ounce can
  tomatoes, chopped
1 16-ounce can red
  kidney beans

3/4 cup uncooked quick-
  cooking rice
3/4 cup water
3 tablespoons chopped
  green bell pepper
3/4 cup shredded sharp
  American cheese
Crushed corn chips

Brown ground beef with onion in large skillet, stirring frequently; drain. Add chili powder, salt and garlic salt; mix well. Stir in undrained tomatoes, undrained beans, rice, water and green pepper. Simmer, covered, for 20 minutes, stirring occasionally. Sprinkle with cheese. Simmer, covered, for 3 minutes longer or until cheese melts. Sprinkle with crushed corn chips. Yield: 6 servings.

TAMALE CASSEROLE

1 can tamales, chopped
1 can hominy, drained
1 can cream of
mushroom soup

Shredded Cheddar
cheese

Combine tamales, hominy and soup in well-buttered casserole. Sprinkle with cheese. Bake at 350 degrees for 40 minutes. Serve with hot French bread and salad.
Yield: 2 servings.

ZESTY GROUND BEEF CASSEROLE

8 ounces uncooked egg
noodles
2 pounds ground round
1 cup chopped onion
1 cup chopped celery
1 cup chopped carrots
1/2 cup chopped green
bell pepper
1 hot pepper, chopped
2 cloves of garlic, minced
1/2 cup catsup

1 15-ounce jar meat
flavored spaghetti sauce
1 cup water
1 tablespoon sugar
2 teaspoons seasoned
salt
1 8-ounce can water
chestnuts, drained,
chopped
1/2 cup Parmesan cheese

Cook noodles using package directions; drain. Brown ground round in large skillet, stirring until crumbly; drain. Add onion, celery, carrots, green pepper, hot pepper and garlic; mix well. Sauté until vegetables are lightly browned. Add catsup, spaghetti sauce, water, sugar and seasoned salt; mix well. Simmer, covered, for 20 minutes. Stir in water chestnuts. Place noodles in 9x13-inch glass baking dish sprayed with nonstick cooking spray. Top with ground beef mixture; sprinkle with Parmesan cheese. Bake at 350 degrees for 30 minutes.
Yield: 8 to 10 servings.

BEST MEAT LOAF

2 pounds ground round
2 eggs
1 1/2 cups soft bread
  crumbs
3/4 cup catsup
1 teaspoon MSG

1/2 cup warm water
1 envelope onion soup
  mix
2 slices bacon (optional)
1 8-ounce can tomato
  sauce

Combine ground round, eggs, bread crumbs, catsup, MSG, warm water and soup mix in bowl; mix well. Pack into 5x9-inch loaf pan. Top with bacon slices and tomato sauce. Bake at 350 degrees for 1 hour. Yield: 8 servings.

HAWAIIAN BEEF LOAVES

1 envelope brown gravy
  mix
1/2 cup milk
1 teaspoon dried minced
  onion
2 eggs, slightly beaten
1 tablespoon snipped
  parsley

2 teaspoons soy sauce
1/2 teaspoon salt
Dash of pepper
1 cup soft bread crumbs
2 pounds ground beef
1 16-ounce can sweet
  and sour sauce
Hot cooked rice

Blend gravy mix and milk in large bowl. Add onion. Let stand for several minutes. Add eggs, parsley, soy sauce, salt and pepper; mix well. Stir in bread crumbs. Add ground beef; mix well. Shape into 2 loaves; place in shallow baking pan. Bake at 350 degrees for 50 minutes; drain. Pour small amount of sweet and sour sauce over loaves. Bake for 15 minutes longer. Heat remaining sweet and sour sauce in small saucepan. Serve with beef loaves and hot cooked rice. Yield: 8 servings.

MAMA'S MEAT LOAF

3/4 cup cornflakes
1/2 cup milk
1 can cream of
   mushroom soup
1 soup can milk
1 pound ground beef
1 teaspoon salt
1/8 teaspoon pepper
1/4 teaspoon celery seed

1 tablespoon dried
   parsley
1/2 teaspoon
   Worcestershire sauce
1/2 onion, finely chopped
1 egg, well beaten
1 1/2 tablespoons catsup
1 1/2 tablespoons
   barbecue sauce

Soften cornflakes in 1/2 cup milk in small bowl. Combine soup with 1 soup can milk in saucepan; mix well. Cook until heated through, stirring frequently. Combine cornflake mixture, ground beef, salt, pepper, celery seed, parsley, Worcestershire sauce, onion, egg, catsup and barbecue sauce in 2-quart casserole; mix well. Shape into loaf. Pour 1/2 of the soup mixture over loaf. Bake at 350 degrees for 15 minutes. Pour remaining soup mixture over loaf. Bake for 25 minutes longer. May substitute crushed crackers or torn bread for cornflakes. Yield: 6 servings.

GLAZED MEAT LOAF

1 pound ground chuck
2/3 cup bread crumbs
2/3 cup milk
2 eggs
1/2 teaspoon salt
1/8 teaspoon pepper
1/2 teaspoon poultry
   seasoning

1 small onion, chopped
1/4 cup catsup
3 tablespoons brown
   sugar
1 teaspoon prepared
   mustard
1/4 teaspoon nutmeg

Combine ground chuck, bread crumbs, milk, eggs, salt, pepper, poultry seasoning and onion in bowl; mix well. Spoon into 2-quart glass dish. Microwave on High for 9 minutes, turning 3 times; drain. Microwave on High for 2 minutes longer. Combine catsup, brown sugar, mustard and nutmeg in small bowl; mix well. Pour over meat loaf. Bake at 350 degrees for 45 minutes to 1 hour or until done to taste. Yield: 4 to 6 servings.

OLD-FASHIONED MEAT LOAF

1 small onion, chopped
1 clove of garlic, minced
2 eggs, slightly beaten
1¹/₂ pounds ground beef
¹/₂ cup dry bread crumbs
¹/₄ cup tomato purée

2 tablespoons chopped
  fresh parsley
1 teaspoon salt
¹/₂ teaspoon thyme
Pinch of cayenne pepper
3 slices bacon

Combine onion, garlic, eggs, ground beef, bread crumbs, tomato purée, parsley, salt, thyme and cayenne pepper in bowl; mix well. Press into 5x9-inch loaf pan; top with bacon slices. Bake at 350 degrees for 1¹/₄ hours. Let stand for 10 minutes before slicing. Yield: 12 servings.

SWEET AND SOUR MEAT LOAF

2 pounds ground beef
¹/₄ cup chopped onion
2 slices bread, crumbled
Seasoned salt and pepper
  to taste
1 egg

1 8-ounce can tomato
  sauce
3 tablespoons soy sauce
2 tablespoons lemon juice
¹/₄ cup packed brown
  sugar

Combine ground beef, onion, bread crumbs, seasoned salt, pepper, egg and ¹/₂ of the tomato sauce in bowl; mix well. Shape into loaf; place in 5x9-inch loaf pan. Combine remaining tomato sauce, soy sauce, lemon juice and brown sugar in small saucepan; mix well. Bring to a boil, stirring constantly. Pour over meat loaf. Bake at 350 degrees for 1 hour or until cooked through. Yield: 8 servings.

A Lion Tip

Enjoy the sweet, nutty flavor of wheat germ — and get a nutritious bonus — by substituting it for half the bread crumbs in meat loaf or meatballs.

BARBECUED HAMBURGERS

2/3 cup evaporated milk
1/3 cup oats
1/8 teaspoon pepper
1 pound lean ground beef
1 teaspoon salt
3 tablespoons finely
  chopped onion
1 tablespoon oil
1/2 teaspoon chili powder

1 8-ounce can tomato
  sauce
1 tablespoon vinegar
2 tablespoons water
1 teaspoon
  Worcestershire sauce
2 tablespoons brown
  sugar
1/2 teaspoon salt

Combine evaporated milk, oats, pepper, ground beef, 1 teaspoon salt and onion in bowl; mix well. Shape into 8 patties. Brown patties in hot oil in skillet, turning to brown both sides; drain. Combine remaining ingredients in small bowl; mix well. Pour over patties. Cook, covered, for 10 minutes longer. Yield: 8 servings.

MEXICAN HAMBURGERS

2 tomatoes, seeded,
  chopped
1 small onion, chopped
1 clove of garlic, minced
2 tablespoons chopped
  fresh coriander
  (optional)

1 teaspoon lemon juice
1 1/2 pounds ground beef
2 teaspoons oil
Salt and pepper to taste
4 large rolls, toasted
1 avocado, sliced
1/4 cup sour cream

Combine tomatoes, onion, garlic and coriander in bowl; mix well. Stir in lemon juice. Shape ground beef into 4 patties. Cook patties in hot oil in skillet for 4 minutes on each side or to desired degree of doneness. Sprinkle with salt and pepper. Place patties in rolls. Top each patty with tomato mixture, avocado slices and sour cream. Yield: 4 servings.

TACO CHEESEBURGERS

1 pound ground beef
2 tablespoons taco sauce
1 1/2 teaspoons chili
  powder
1/4 teaspoon salt

4 1-ounce slices
  Monterey Jack cheese
8 taco shells
8 lettuce leaves
1 medium tomato, chopped

Combine ground beef, taco sauce, chili powder and salt in bowl; mix well. Shape into eight 1/2-inch thick patties. Place in 9x13-inch baking pan. Bake at 350 degrees for 15 minutes. Cut cheese slices into halves diagonally. Place cheese triangles on patties. Bake for 1 to 2 minutes longer or until cheese melts. Place patties in taco shells with lettuce leaves and tomato. Serve with additional taco sauce. Yield: 8 servings.

LASAGNA

2 medium cans tomato
sauce
1 small can tomato paste
1 large can tomatoes,
mashed
1 pound ground beef
1 pound hot sausage
3 stalks celery, chopped
2 onions, finely chopped
2 green bell peppers,
finely chopped
Sliced fresh mushrooms
(optional)

1 clove of garlic, crushed
1 1/2 teaspoons basil
1 tablespoon oregano
16 ounces mozzarella
cheese, shredded
12 ounces Swiss cheese,
shredded
4 ounces Parmesan
cheese
1 cup chopped parsley
1 package uncooked
lasagna noodles
1 pound ricotta cheese

Combine tomato sauce, tomato paste and tomatoes in saucepan; mix well. Cook over low heat for 1 hour, stirring frequently. Brown ground beef and sausage in large skillet, stirring until crumbly; drain. Add celery, onions, green peppers and mushrooms. Sauté until vegetables are tender. Add garlic, basil and oregano; mix well. Combine mozzarella, Swiss and Parmesan cheeses in bowl; toss to mix. Add parsley; mix well. Cook lasagna noodles using package directions; drain. Rinse in cold water; drain. Spread thin layer of sauce in large obling baking dish. Layer noodles, sauce, ricotta cheese and Parmesan cheese mixture 1/4 at a time in prepared dish, alternating layers of noodles lengthwise then crosswise and trimming noodles to fit. Bake at 350 degrees for 35 to 45 minutes or until hot and bubbly. May substitute cottage cheese for ricotta cheese. May be frozen uncooked or cooked. Yield: 8 servings.

SPAGHETTI WITH MEAT SAUCE

1/4 cup shortening
1/2 cup chopped onion
1 pound lean ground beef
1 teaspoon garlic salt
1 4-ounce can
mushroom stems and
pieces
1/4 cup chopped parsley
or 2 teaspoons dried
parsley flakes

1 8-ounce can tomato
sauce
2 cups canned tomatoes
1 teaspoon salt
1/2 teaspoon oregano
1/4 teaspoon pepper
Dash of basil
1 bay leaf
8 ounces uncooked thin
spaghetti

Melt shortening in large skillet. Add onion. Sauté for 5 minutes. Add ground beef and garlic salt. Brown ground beef, stirring until crumbly. Add undrained mushrooms, parsley, tomato sauce, tomatoes, salt, oregano, pepper, basil and bay leaf. Simmer, covered, for 1 hour. Simmer, uncovered, for 30 minutes longer or until sauce is of desired consistency, stirring occasionaly. Remove bay leaf. Cook spaghetti using package directions; drain. Serve sauce over hot spaghetti.
Yield: 4 to 5 servings.

CHEESEBURGER PIE

2 pounds ground beef
1 teaspoon salt
1/2 teaspoon oregano
1/4 teaspoon pepper
1/2 cup cracker crumbs
1 8-ounce can tomato
sauce
1/4 cup chopped onion
1/4 cup chopped green
bell pepper

1 unbaked 9-inch pie shell
1 egg, slightly beaten
1/4 cup milk
1/2 teaspoon salt
1/2 teaspoon dry mustard
1/2 teaspoon
Worcestershire sauce
2 cups shredded Cheddar
cheese

Brown ground beef in skillet, stirring until crumbly; drain. Add 1 teaspoon salt, oregano, pepper, cracker crumbs, tomato sauce, onion and green pepper; mix well. Spoon into pie shell. Combine egg, milk, 1/2 teaspoon salt, dry mustard, Worcestershire sauce and cheese; mix well. Spread over ground beef mixture. Bake at 425 degrees for 30 minutes or until golden brown. Yield: 6 servings.

GROUND BEEF AND POTATO PIE

1 to 1½ pounds ground
  beef
1 medium onion, chopped
1 small can peas
1 cup tomatoes
1 cup tomato juice
½ cup catsup

½ cup uncooked
  macaroni
½ teaspoon salt
½ teaspoon pepper
5 potatoes, cooked,
  drained
1 egg

Brown ground beef with onion in medium skillet, stirring frequently; drain. Spoon into 2-quart casserole. Add peas, tomatoes, tomato juice, catsup, macaroni, salt and pepper; mix well. Bake at 350 degrees for 30 minutes. Mash potatoes in mixer bowl until smooth. Add egg; beat well. Spoon over ground beef mixture. Increase oven temperature to 375 degrees. Bake until peaks are golden brown.
Yield: 4 to 6 servings.

TACO PIE

1 pound lean ground beef
1 clove of garlic, crushed
1 large onion, chopped
1 cup mild or hot salsa
1 16-ounce can refried
  beans
2 cups shredded Cheddar
  cheese

1 cup sour cream
1 medium tomato,
  chopped
1 2-ounce can sliced
  black olives, drained
1 avocado, chopped

Crumble ground beef into 2-quart glass casserole. Add garlic and onion. Cover with paper towel. Microwave on High for 4 to 5 minutes or until ground beef is tender, stirring once; drain. Stir in salsa and beans. Spread over bottom of 10-inch deep-dish glass pie plate. Cover with paper towel. Microwave on High for 4 to 5 minutes or until very hot. Sprinkle with cheese. Microwave, uncovered, on Medium for 2 minutes or until cheese melts. Top with sour cream; sprinkle with tomato, olives and avocado. Serve hot with tortilla chips or use as base for tostado salad. Yield: 6 servings.

IMPOSSIBLE TACO PIE

1 pound ground beef
1/2 cup chopped onion
1 envelope taco
  seasoning mix
1 4-ounce can chopped
  green chilies, drained

1¼ cups milk
¾ cup baking mix
3 eggs
2 tomatoes, sliced
1 cup shredded Monterey
  Jack Cheddar cheese

Brown ground beef with onion in medium skillet, stirring frequently; drain. Stir in seasoning mix. Spread in greased 10-inch pie plate. Top with chilies. Beat milk, baking mix and eggs in mixer bowl for 1 minute or until smooth. Pour over ground beef mixture. Bake at 400 degrees for 25 minutes. Top with tomatoes and cheese. Bake for 8 to 10 minutes or until knife inserted between center and edge comes out clean. Cool for 5 minutes. Garnish with sour cream, tomatoes, lettuce and additional cheese. Yield: 6 to 8 servings.

 # LAMB

ARABIAN LAMB AND EGGPLANT

6 small eggplants
1/2 cup olive oil
1 pound ground lamb
1/2 cup pistachios, pine
  nuts or chopped almonds

Salt and pepper to taste
1 10-ounce can tomato
  purée
1 8-ounce can tomato
  sauce

Wash eggplants; trim stem ends. Heat olive oil in skillet. Add eggplants. Fry until all skin is brown. Place in baking dish. Brown ground lamb in skillet, stirring until crumbly; drain. Add pistachios, salt and pepper; mix well. Cut slit in each eggplant; stuff with lamb mixture. Mix tomato purée and tomato sauce in skillet; season with salt and pepper to taste. Cook until heated through, stirring constantly. Pour over eggplants. Bake, covered with foil, at 350 degrees for 1 hour or until eggplant is very tender. Serve on mound of hot cooked rice; spoon sauce over eggplant and rice. If using large eggplants, cut into halves after browning. Yield: 6 servings.

BRAISED LAMB WITH SAUCE

2 pounds boneless leg of
lamb
1 teaspoon salt
1/4 cup chopped whites of
green onions
2 large slices fresh ginger
2 large cloves of garlic,
sliced
3 large Chinese star anise
5 Szechwan peppercorns
1 teaspoon sesame oil

2 tablespoons rice wine
vinegar
2 teaspoons light soy
sauce
1/2 teaspoon salt
4 or 5 red pepper flakes
(optional)
1 tablespoon minced
Chinese parsley
Hot steamed rice

Wash lamb; pat dry. Cut into 2-inch cubes. Place in water to cover in large saucepan. Bring to a boil over low heat. Skim. Add 1/2 cup cold water. Bring to a boil; skim. Repeat 2 times. Add 1 teaspoon salt, green onions, ginger, garlic, star anise and peppercorns; mix well. Bring to a boil; reduce heat. Cook, uncovered, for 1 hour or until lamb is tender. Remove lamb. Cook broth until reduced to about 1 cup. Return lamb to broth. Heat to serving temperature. Combine oil, vinegar, soy sauce, 1/2 teaspoon salt and red pepper flakes in small serving bowl; mix well. Place lamb on heated platter. Spoon small amount of broth over lamb; sprinkle with parsley. Serve with rice and sauce. Yield: 4 servings.

BEYTI KABOBS (Ground Lamb Kabobs)

1 1/2 pounds ground lamb,
beef or veal
1/4 cup chopped parsley
1/4 cup chopped mint
leaves

1 large onion, minced
2 cloves of garlic, minced
Dash of red pepper flakes
1 egg

Combine lamb, parsley, mint, onion, garlic, red pepper flakes and egg in bowl; mix well. Shape by 1/4-cupfuls into 4-inch rolls. Thread 2 or 3 rolls lengthwise through center onto each of six 15-inch skewers. Grill over medium-hot coals to desired degree of doneness, turning to cook all sides. Serve as appetizer, in pita bread or as entrée with rice or potatoes. Yield: 6 servings.

LAMB KABOBS

2 pounds boneless leg of
lamb, cut into 1-inch
cubes
1/4 cup olive oil
1/4 cup red wine vinegar
2 cloves of garlic, minced

1/4 cup chopped parsley
1/4 cup chopped mint
leaves
Dash of red pepper flakes
Salt and pepper to taste

Place lamb in large bowl. Add olive oil, vinegar, garlic, parsley, mint, red pepper flakes, salt and pepper; toss to coat. Marinate in refrigerator for 2 hours or longer. Thread lamb cubes onto long skewers. Grill over medium coals to desired degree of doneness, turning and basting frequently with marinade. May substitute lamb chops for cubes. Thread horizontally through meatiest part of lamb chop. For Grape Leaf-Wrapped Loin Kabobs remove loin portion of lamb chop. Wrap loin medallion in large fresh or preserved grape leaf, using toothpick to secure. Thread 2 to a skewer horizontally. For Lamb Riblet Kabobs, use rib ends of rack of lamb. Yield: 6 servings.

LAMB WITH YOGURT SAUCE

1 pound boneless lamb,
cut into 1 1/2-inch cubes
3 tablespoons melted
butter
1/2 teaspoon marjoram
1 1/2 cups plain yogurt, at
room temperature

1/3 cup toasted slivered
almonds
1 to 2 teaspoons curry
powder
1/2 teaspoon salt
2 cups hot cooked rice

Brush lamb cubes with butter; sprinkle with marjoram. Place on rack in broiler pan. Broil 4 inches from heat source to desired degree of doneness, turning occasionally. Combine yogurt, almonds, curry powder and salt in small bowl; mix well. Spoon rice onto serving plates; top with lamb. Spoon yogurt mixture over lamb and rice. Yield: 4 servings.

# *P*ORK

APRICOT-GLAZED PORK ROAST

1 4 to 5-pound pork
   roast
1 teaspoon salt
1/4 teaspoon pepper

1 18-ounce bottle of
   barbecue sauce
1 18-ounce jar apricot
   preserves

Sprinkle roast with salt and pepper. Place fat side up on rack in roasting pan. Insert meat thermometer in thickest part of roast; do not allow thermometer to touch bone. Roast at 325 degrees for 2 to 3 hours or to 170 degrees on meat thermometer. Combine barbecue sauce and preserves in bowl; mix well. Brush small amount over roast. Roast over low heat for 1 hour longer, basting frequently. Serve with remaining sauce. Yield: 16 to 20 servings.

FARMER'S PORK CHOPS

4 pork chops
1/2 cup flour
Salt and pepper to taste
1 clove of garlic, minced
Oil
4 Irish potatoes, peeled,
   sliced

2 large onions, sliced
11/2 cups sour cream
1/2 teaspoon dry mustard
11/2 teaspoons salt

Dredge pork chops in flour seasoned with salt and pepper to taste. Brown pork chops with garlic in a small amount of oil in skillet, turning to brown both sides. Place potatoes in 3-quart casserole. Arrange pork chops over potatoes; top with onions. Combine sour cream, dry mustard and 11/2 teaspoons salt in small bowl; mix well. Pour over onions. Bake at 350 degrees for 11/2 hours. Yield: 4 servings.

GINGER PORK CHOPS WITH APPLES AND PRUNES

8 pitted prunes, cut into halves
1/4 cup Brandy
4 thick center-cut pork chops, trimmed
Freshly ground pepper to taste
1 to 2 tablespoons corn oil
Coarsely grated rind of 1/2 lemon
2 cloves of garlic, minced
2 slices fresh ginger, minced
1 large apple, thickly sliced
1 cup apple juice
1 cup plain nonfat yogurt
1 tablespoon cornstarch
1 1/4 pounds tiny new potatoes, cooked in skins

Place prunes in small bowl. Pour Brandy over prunes. Sprinkle pork chops with pepper. Heat oil in large skillet. Add lemon rind, garlic and ginger; mix well. Add pork chops. Cook until brown on both sides. Add apple, prune mixture and apple juice. Cook, covered, for 20 to 30 minutes or until pork chops are tender. Mix yogurt with cornstarch in small bowl. Stir into pork chop mixture; reduce heat. Cook just until sauce is thickened and heated through, stirring constantly. Serve with hot cooked new potatoes. Yield: 4 servings.

LEMON AND HERB PORK CHOPS

2 tablespoons white wine Worcestershire sauce
2 tablespoons lemon juice
1/2 teaspoon browning and seasoning sauce
4 3/4-inch thick pork chops
1 teaspoon dried whole rosemary, crushed
1/2 teaspoon lemon pepper
1 tablespoon oil

Combine first 3 ingredients in small bowl; mix well. Drizzle over both sides of pork chops. Sprinkle with mixture of rosemary and lemon pepper. Place 10-inch microwave-safe browning skillet in microwave. Microwave, uncovered, on High for 6 to 8 minutes. Add oil to hot skillet, tilting to coat surface. Add pork chops, placing thickest portions toward outside of skillet. Microwave on High for 1 minute. Turn pork chops. Microwave on High for 1 minute longer. Microwave, covered, on Medium for 8 to 9 minutes longer or until pork chops are tender, turning after 4 minutes. Yield: 4 servings.

SAUCY PORK CHOPS

6 to 8 1/2-inch thick loin
pork chops
2 tablespoons flour
1 teaspoon salt
Dash of pepper
1 can cream of
mushroom soup

3/4 cup water
1/2 teaspoon ginger
1/4 teaspoon crushed
rosemary (optional)
1 3-ounce can French-
fried onions
1/2 cup sour cream

Trim excess fat from pork chops. Render fat in large skillet to obtain 2 tablespoons drippings. Dredge pork chops in flour; sprinkle with salt and pepper. Brown on both sides in hot drippings in skillet. Place in baking dish. Pour mixture of next 4 ingredients over pork chops; sprinkle with 3/4 of the fried onions. Bake, covered, at 350 degrees for 50 minutes or until tender. Sprinkle with remaining onions. Bake, uncovered, for 10 minutes longer. Remove pork chops to serving platter. Stir sour cream into pan juices. Cook until heated through, stirring constantly. Pour over pork chops. Serve with rice. Yield: 6 to 8 servings.

PORK CHOPS WITH SAUERKRAUT

2 1-pound packages
fresh sauerkraut
1 pound new potatoes
1 tablespoon oil
4 1/2-inch thick pork
chops

Salt and pepper to taste
3/4 cup water
1/4 teaspoon salt
1/2 teaspoon pepper
1/2 teaspoon caraway
seeds

Rinse sauerkraut; drain. Cut potatoes into halves. Heat oil in large stainless steel skillet over medium-high heat. Add pork chops. Sprinkle with salt and pepper to taste. Cook for 4 minutes or until brown on both sides, turning once; remove from pan. Brown cut side of potatoes in pan drippings for 2 minutes; remove from pan. Add water, stirring to deglaze. Add sauerkraut, 1/4 teaspoon salt, 1/2 teaspoon pepper and caraway seeds; mix well. Top with pork chops and potatoes; press into sauerkraut. Reduce heat. Simmer, covered, for 40 minutes or until pork chops are tender. Iron or aluminum skillets may react with the acidity in the sauerkraut to affect flavor and color. Yield: 4 servings.

SWEET AND SOUR PORK

1 20-ounce can juice-pack
  pineapple tidbits
1 1/2 pounds lean pork loin,
  cut into 1-inch strips
3/4 cup water
2 tablespoons brown
  sugar
2 tablespoons cornstarch
1/2 teaspoon reduced-
  sodium soy sauce
1/4 teaspoon salt
1/4 teaspoon pepper
1/4 cup vinegar
3/4 cup diagonally sliced
  carrots
3/4 cup green bell pepper
  strips
3/4 cup thinly sliced onion
3 1/2 cups cooked brown
  rice

Drain pineapple, reserving 1 cup juice. Brown pork in large skillet sprayed with nonstick cooking spray over medium heat, stirring constantly. Add water; mix well. Simmer, covered, for 1 hour or until tender. Combine brown sugar, cornstarch, soy sauce, salt, pepper, reserved pineapple juice and vinegar in saucepan; mix well. Cook over low heat until thickened, stirring constantly. Add to pork. Add carrots. Cook, covered, over medium heat for 7 minutes. Add pineapple tidbits, green pepper and onion. Cook, covered, for 2 to 3 minutes longer or until vegetables are tender-crisp. Serve over rice.
Yield: 6 to 8 servings.

DOUBLE-COOKED ORANGE SPARERIBS

2 teaspoons salt
2 teaspoons light soy
  sauce
2 teaspoons sugar
1 1/2 tablespoons
  cornstarch
1 1/2 tablespoons ginger
  juice
1 1/2 pounds pork
  spareribs, cut into bite-
  sized pieces
2 tablespoons finely
  chopped orange rind
2 teaspoons orange
  liqueur
1/2 cup orange juice
1 tablespoon cornstarch
2 teaspoons light soy
  sauce
2 cups peanut oil for
  deep frying
2 teaspoons sesame oil

Combine salt, soy sauce, sugar, cornstarch and ginger juice in medium bowl; mix well. Add spareribs; mix well. Marinate at room temperature for 1½ hours or in refrigerator overnight. Combine orange rind, orange liqueur, orange juice, cornstarch and soy sauce in small bowl; mix well. Heat peanut oil in wok or deep skillet. Deep-fry 4 or 5 spareribs for 10 minutes. Remove with slotted spoon; drain on paper towels. Repeat with remaining spareribs. Reheat oil until very hot. Deep-fry spareribs for 5 minutes longer or until very brown and crisp; drain on paper towels. Drain wok or skillet, reserving 1 tablespoon pan drippings. Combine reserved pan drippings and orange liqueur mixture in wok or skillet; mix well. Bring to a boil. Add spareribs, stirring to coat well. Add sesame oil. Cook for 2 minutes longer. Serve immediately. Yield: 4 servings.

 # *H*AM

ASPARAGUS AND HAM ROLLS

1 can cream of mushroom soup	1 tablespoon melted butter
3/4 cup milk	1 cup chopped ham
1 egg, slightly beaten	Cooked asparagus spears
1 cup buttermilk pancake mix	1/2 cup milk

Mix 1/2 of the soup, 3/4 cup milk and egg in bowl. Add pancake mix; mix well. Stir in butter. Pour 1/4 cup at a time onto hot lightly greased griddle. Bake until brown on both sides, turning once. Place ham and asparagus on hot baked pancakes; roll to enclose filling. Combine remaining soup with remaining 1/2 cup milk in small saucepan. Cook until heated through. Spoon over asparagus rolls. Yield: 4 servings.

FRESH BAKED HAM WITH PINEAPPLE SAUCE

1 15-ounce can juice-pack crushed pineapple
2 tablespoons frozen orange juice concentrate
4 teaspoons soy sauce
2 teaspoons cornstarch
1 teaspoon brown sugar
1/8 teaspoon curry powder
1/8 teaspoon grated gingerroot
1 4 to 5-pound boneless fresh ham
1/2 teaspoon garlic salt

Drain pineapple, reserving juice. Pour reserved juice into medium saucepan. Add orange juice concentrate, soy sauce, cornstarch, brown sugar, curry powder and gingerroot; mix well. Bring to a boil, stirring constantly. Reduce heat. Simmer for 3 to 5 minutes or until thickened, stirring constantly. Reserve 1/2 cup sauce. Add pineapple to remaining sauce. Cook for 3 to 4 minutes longer or until heated through, stirring constantly. Place ham on rack in roasting pan. Sprinkle with garlic salt. Bake at 325 degrees for 2 hours. Brush with reserved 1/2 cup sauce. Bake for 30 minutes longer or to 155 degrees on meat thermometer. Let stand for 10 to 15 minutes before slicing. Serve with pineapple sauce. Yield: 12 to 15 servings.

COUNTRY HAM WITH RED-EYE GRAVY

2 1/4-inch thick slices uncooked country ham
2 tablespoons oil
1 cup strong black coffee
2 tablespoons flour
1/2 teaspoon paprika

Slit fat in several places to but not through ham to prevent ham from curling. Cook ham in oil in heavy skillet over low heat for 3 to 4 minutes on each side or until done to taste. Remove to serving plate; keep warm. Mix coffee and flour in small bowl until smooth. Stir into pan drippings. Cook until thickened, stirring constantly. Add paprika; mix well. Serve with ham. Yield: 2 servings.

EDWARDS' ROASTED COUNTRY HAM

1 10 to 14-pound
   uncooked country ham
1 tablespoon flour
1 quart water

Whole cloves
1 cup soft bread crumbs
1 cup packed brown
   sugar

Place ham in water to cover in large container. Let stand for 24 hours; drain. Scrub with stiff brush; rinse. Place flour in oven cooking bag; shake to coat well. Place in 10x15-inch baking pan. Place ham in bag; add water. Seal bag. Make six 1/2-inch slits in top of bag. Insert meat thermometer through bag into ham; do not allow thermometer to touch bone. Bake at 325 degrees for 2 to 3 hours or to 142 degrees on meat thermometer. Slit bag down center; remove ham. Discard bag and drippings. Place ham in baking dish. Remove skin carefully, leaving fat. Score fat in diamond pattern; stud with cloves. Combine bread crumbs and brown sugar in small bowl; mix well. Press over ham. Increase oven temperature to 425 degrees. Bake for 10 to 15 minutes or until light brown and crusty. Yield: 25 to 35 servings.

HAM PINWHEELS

2 cups ground cooked
   ham
2 tablespoons brown
   sugar
2 teaspoons prepared
   mustard
1/4 cup melted butter

1 teaspoon
   Worcestershire sauce
1 10-count can biscuits
1 can Cheddar cheese
   soup
1/3 cup milk

Combine ham, brown sugar, mustard, butter and Worcestershire sauce in bowl; mix well. Separate biscuits; arrange with sides touching in 2 rows on work surface. Pat 1/4 inch thick into 6x12-inch rectangle. Spread with ham mixture. Roll as for jelly roll. Cut into 8 slices. Place cut side up in shallow baking pan. Bake at 400 degrees for 10 to 15 minutes or until light brown. Combine soup and milk in small saucepan; mix well. Heat to serving temperature, stirring constantly. Serve with pinwheels. Yield: 4 servings.

CHEDDAR-APPLE BREAKFAST LASAGNA

1 cup sour cream
1/3 cup packed brown
  sugar
2 9-ounce packages
  frozen French toast
8 ounces boiled ham,
  sliced

2 cups shredded Cheddar
  cheese
1 21-ounce can apple
  pie filling
1 cup granola with raisins
1/2 cup shredded Cheddar
  cheese

Blend sour cream and brown sugar in small bowl; chill. Prepare French toast using package directions. Arrange 6 French toast slices in greased 9x13-inch baking pan. Layer with ham, 2 cups Cheddar cheese and remaining 6 French toast slices. Spread with apple pie filling; sprinkle with granola. Bake at 350 degrees for 25 minutes. Sprinkle with remaining 1/2 cup Cheddar cheese. Bake for 5 minutes longer or until heated through and cheese is melted. Serve with sour cream mixture. Yield: 6 servings.

SAUSAGE

AUTUMN EVENING SUPPER

1 1/2 quarts chopped
  cooked potatoes
7 slices American
  cheese, chopped
1/4 cup sliced green
  onions
1/4 cup golden blend
  Italian salad dressing

2 tablespoons chopped
  pimento
1 pound smoked
  sausage, cut into 6
  portions
3 slices American
  cheese, cut into halves
  diagonally

Combine potatoes, chopped cheese, green onions, salad dressing and pimento in bowl; mix well. Spoon into 8x12-inch baking dish. Top with sausage. Bake at 350 degrees for 30 minutes or until heated through. Top with cheese triangles. Bake until cheese melts. Yield: 6 servings.

SAUSAGE AND RICE CASSEROLE

1 pound hot pork sausage
1 cup chopped onion
1 cup chopped green bell
  pepper
1 cup chopped celery
1 clove of garlic, chopped

1 cup uncooked minute
  rice
1 can cream of
  mushroom soup
2 cans cream of chicken
  soup

Brown sausage in skillet, stirring until crumbly; drain. Add onion, green pepper, celery and garlic; mix well. Simmer until vegetables are tender. Wash rice; drain. Stir into sausage mixture. Add soups; mix well. Pour into 9x9-inch baking dish. Bake at 350 degrees for 1 1/2 hours, stirring occasionally. Yield: 6 servings.

PASTA WITH SAUSAGE AND PEPPERS

1 tablespoon oil
3/4 pound sweet Italian
  sausage, sliced
1 tablespoon oil
2 onions, sliced
3 green bell peppers, cut
  into strips
2 cloves of garlic, minced

2 16-ounce cans plum
  tomatoes, drained,
  chopped
1/2 teaspoon salt
1/2 teaspoon oregano
1/2 teaspoon pepper
8 ounces uncooked
  spaghetti

Heat 1 tablespoon oil in large skillet. Add sausage. Cook for 10 minutes or until brown on both sides, stirring occasionally. Remove with slotted spoon; drain on paper towels. Add remaining 1 tablespoon oil and onions to pan drippings. Cook for 10 minutes or until golden brown, stirring constantly. Add green peppers. Cook for 5 minutes or until soft, stirring constantly. Add garlic. Cook for 1 minute. Stir in tomatoes, sausage, salt and oregano. Bring to a boil, stirring constantly. Reduce heat. Simmer, covered, for 10 minutes or until green peppers are very soft. Stir in pepper. Simmer, uncovered, for 10 to 15 minutes or until liquid thickens, stirring frequently. Cook spaghetti using package directions; drain. Serve spaghetti with sauce. Yield: 4 servings.

CHICAGO-STYLE WHOLE WHEAT PIZZA

1 envelope dry yeast
1 cup whole wheat flour
1/2 cup yellow cornmeal
1 cup unbleached flour
1 teaspoon salt
1 tablespoon olive or
  vegetable oil
1 tablespoon honey
11/2 cups warm (120 to
  130-degree) water
4 to 8 ounces sausage

2 to 21/2 cups unbleached
  flour
8 to 12 ounces mozzarella
  cheese, shredded
1 cup tomato sauce
1/4 cup chopped broccoli
1/2 cup sliced mushrooms
1/4 cup chopped onion
1/4 cup chopped green
  bell pepper
1/4 cup chopped zucchini

Combine yeast, whole wheat flour, cornmeal, 1 cup unbleached flour, salt, oil and honey in large bowl; mix well. Stir in water. Beat 100 strokes. Let stand until bubbly. Brown sausage in skillet, stirring until crumbly; drain. Add enough remaining unbleached flour to yeast mixture to make stiff dough. Knead on floured surface for 2 to 3 minutes or until smooth and elastic. Divide dough into 2 portions. Roll each portion into 14-inch circle. Press into two 14-inch pizza pans. Brush with additional olive or vegetable oil. Reserve 1 cup cheese. Sprinkle remaining cheese over dough; spread with tomato sauce. Sprinkle with sausage and vegetables. Top with reserved 1 cup cheese. Bake at 450 degrees for 15 to 20 minutes or until hot and bubbly. Let stand for 5 minutes before slicing. Yield: 16 servings.

A Lion Tip

Layer 2 to 3 pounds cooked sausage, 3 cans of sauerkraut, 2 sliced onions, 10 sliced potatoes and 4 sliced apples in electric skillet. Pour 3 cups apple juice over the top and simmer, covered, for 45 minutes. This is an Easy Skillet Meal for 12 people.

Poultry
Seafood
and
Egg Dishes

*P*OULTRY

APPLE AND SAUSAGE-STUFFED CHICKEN BREASTS

4 ounces Italian sausage
1/4 cup thinly sliced green
  onions
1/4 cup finely chopped
  celery
2 cups shredded apple
1/4 cup minced parsley
1/2 teaspoon thyme
2 tablespoons dry bread
  crumbs
3 tablespoons plain
  yogurt or sour cream
4 chicken breasts, boned,
  skinned
1 teaspoon oil

Cook sausage in skillet until brown, stirring until crumbly; drain. Add green onions and celery. Cook for 3 minutes, stirring constantly. Add apple, parsley and thyme. Cook for 1 minute, stirring constantly; remove from heat. Add bread crumbs and yogurt; mix well. Pound chicken to 1/4-inch thickness between 2 sheets moistened plastic wrap. Spoon apple mixture onto chicken; roll to enclose filling. Place seam side down in greased baking dish. Brush with oil. Bake at 350 degrees for 25 minutes. Cut into 1/2-inch slices with serrated knife. Garnish with apple slices. Yield: 4 servings.

BALSAMIC CHICKEN BREASTS

1 small onion, thinly
  sliced
1 tablespoon butter
1 tablespoon corn oil
1/4 cup water
1 clove of garlic, crushed
2 chicken breasts, boned,
  skinned
1/4 cup balsamic vinegar
1/2 cup chicken stock
2 cups sliced fresh
  mushrooms
1/4 cup pine nuts
Salt and freshly ground
  pepper to taste

Sauté onion in butter and corn oil in skillet for 1 minute. Add water. Cook, covered, over high heat for 3 minutes. Cook, uncovered, over medium heat for 2 minutes longer or until water evaporates and onions are golden brown. Add garlic. Flatten chicken with palm of hand. Brown chicken in skillet.

Remove chicken and onion to warm platter. Add vinegar, stirring over medium-high heat to deglaze. Cook until liquid is reduced by 1/2. Add chicken stock. Cook until liquid is reduced by 1/2. Add chicken, onion, mushrooms, pine nuts, salt and pepper. Cook, covered, over low heat for 5 minutes. Serve over hot cooked linguine. Yield: 2 servings.

CHICKEN BREASTS WITH DIJON SAUCE

4 boned chicken breasts, skinned
1 teaspoon salt
1/2 teaspoon lemon pepper
3 tablespoons margarine
1/2 cup chicken broth
1/2 cup half and half
1 tablespoon flour
1 tablespoon Dijon mustard
1 teaspoon honey
1/2 teaspoon grated lemon rind

Sprinkle chicken with salt and lemon pepper. Brown chicken in margarine in skillet over medium heat for 5 minutes on each side; reduce heat. Cook, covered, for 10 minutes or until tender. Remove to warm platter. Add broth to skillet. Blend half and half and flour in bowl; stir into skillet. Cook over medium heat until bubbly, stirring constantly. Add mustard, honey and lemon rind; mix well. Spoon a small amount of sauce over chicken. Serve with remaining sauce. Yield: 4 servings.

CHICKEN BREASTS DIVINE

2 10-ounce packages frozen broccoli
4 to 6 boned chicken breasts, cooked
2 cans cream of chicken soup
1 cup mayonnaise
1 teaspoon lemon juice
1/2 cup bread crumbs
1 teaspoon melted butter
1/2 cup shredded Cheddar cheese

Cook broccoli using package directions; drain. Place in greased baking dish. Arrange chicken on broccoli. Combine soup, mayonnaise and lemon juice in bowl; mix well. Spoon over chicken. Sprinkle with mixture of bread crumbs and butter. Sprinkle cheese over top. Bake at 350 degrees for 20 to 30 minutes or until bubbly. Yield: 4 to 6 servings.

CHICKEN BREASTS WITH DRIED BEEF

1 jar dried beef
4 chicken breasts
4 slices bacon
1 cup sour cream

1 can cream of
    mushroom soup
Paprika to taste

Line 2-quart baking dish with dried beef. Wrap each chicken breast with bacon slice. Place chicken breasts over dried beef. Mix sour cream with soup in bowl; spoon over chicken. Sprinkle with paprika. Bake, covered with foil, at 300 degrees for 2½ hours. Bake, uncovered, for 30 minutes longer or until brown. Serve with hot cooked rice. Yield: 4 servings.

CHICKEN BREASTS WITH GREEN CHILI CREAM SAUCE

4 boned chicken breasts,
    skinned
1 to 2 tablespoons corn
    oil
1 large onion, chopped
1 teaspoon minced garlic
½ cup chicken stock

1 cup canned chopped
    green chilies
1 teaspoon coriander
1 teaspoon cumin
½ cup nonfat plain yogurt
½ cup low-fat ricotta
    cheese

Brown chicken on both sides in corn oil in skillet; set aside. Sauté onion and garlic in pan drippings. Stir in chicken stock, green chilies, coriander and cumin. Cook for 1 to 2 minutes, stirring constantly. Add chicken; spoon sauce over top. Cook, covered, over low heat for 10 minutes or until chicken is tender. Process yogurt and ricotta in blender until smooth. Place chicken on serving platter; spoon sauce over chicken. Top with ricotta cheese mixture; sprinkle with additional fresh coriander. Yield: 4 servings.

CREAMY CHICKEN BREASTS

8 chicken breasts
8 slices Swiss cheese
1 can cream of chicken
    soup

¼ cup white wine
1 cup herb-seasoned
    stuffing mix, crushed

Arrange chicken in baking dish sprayed with nonstick cooking spray. Top with cheese. Combine soup and wine in small bowl; mix well. Spoon over chicken and cheese. Sprinkle with stuffing mix. Bake at 350 degrees for 45 to 55 minutes or until chicken is tender. Yield: 8 servings.

OVEN-BARBECUED CHICKEN BREASTS

1   15-ounce can tomato
   sauce
3/4 cup Cran-Fruit sauce
3 tablespoons brown
   sugar

1 teaspoon chili powder
1 tablespoon
   Worcestershire sauce
1/3 cup vinegar
4 chicken breasts

Combine tomato sauce, Cran-Fruit sauce, brown sugar, chili powder, Worcestershire sauce and vinegar in saucepan. Simmer for 15 minutes, stirring occasionally. Arrange chicken in 9x13-inch baking pan. Bake at 375 degrees for 30 minutes. Brush with sauce. Bake for 30 minutes longer or until tender, basting frequently. Yield: 4 servings.

CHICKEN PARMESAN

6 boned chicken breasts,
   skinned
1/3 cup Parmesan cheese
1/4 teaspoon Italian
   seasoning
1/4 cup sliced green
   onions
2 teaspoons margarine

1 tablespoon flour
1/2 cup skim milk
1/2 10-ounce package
   frozen chopped spinach,
   thawed, drained
1 tablespoon chopped
   pimento

Coat chicken with mixture of cheese and Italian season-ing; reserve remaining cheese mixture. Arrange chicken in 8-inch square baking dish. Sauté green onions in margarine in skillet until tender. Stir in flour. Add milk all at once. Cook until bubbly, stirring constantly. Stir spinach and pimento into sauce. Spoon over chicken. Top with reserved cheese mixture. Bake at 350 degrees for 30 minutes or until tender. Yield: 6 servings.

PINEAPPLE-CHEESE CHICKEN BREASTS

4 boned chicken breasts,
  skinned
3 tablespoons flour
1/2 teaspoon salt
1/8 teaspoon white pepper
1/4 cup margarine
1 8-ounce can pineapple
  slices, drained

1 9-ounce package
  frozen broccoli spears,
  cooked, drained
4 1-ounce slices
  Monterey Jack cheese

Pound chicken breasts between 2 sheets plastic wrap to 1/4-inch thickness. Coat with mixture of flour, salt and pepper. Cook in margarine in skillet for 10 to 12 minutes or until cooked through, turning once. Top each with pineapple slice, well-drained broccoli and cheese slice. Cook, covered, for 1 minute longer or until cheese melts. Yield: 4 servings.

CHICKEN AND BROCCOLI OVER RICE

1 1/2 cups water
1 1/2 cups minute rice
1 pound boned chicken
  breasts
2 tablespoons oil
1 can cream of chicken
  soup
1/2 soup can milk

2 tablespoons Dijon
  mustard
1/2 cup shredded Cheddar
  or Swiss cheese
1 1/2 cups frozen chopped
  broccoli, thawed
2 tablespoons chopped
  pimentos

Bring water to a boil in saucepan. Stir in rice; remove from heat. Let stand, covered, for 5 minutes. Cut chicken into strips. Stir-fry in hot oil in skillet until brown. Add soup, milk, mustard and cheese. Cook until cheese melts, stirring constantly. Add broccoli and pimentos; reduce heat. Simmer for 2 minutes. Serve over rice. Yield: 4 servings.

CRUNCHY ORIENTAL CHICKEN

1/2 cup sliced onions
1 tablespoon corn oil margarine
2 cups chopped cooked chicken breasts
1 cup sliced celery
1 8-ounce can sliced water chestnuts, drained
1 1/2 cups chicken broth
2 tablespoons cornstarch
1/2 teaspoon salt

1/4 cup water
2 tablespoons reduced-sodium soy sauce
1 4-ounce jar chopped pimentos, drained
1 16-ounce can bean sprouts, drained
3 1/2 cups hot cooked rice
2 tablespoons sliced almonds, toasted

Sauté onions in margarine in large skillet. Add chicken, celery, water chestnuts and broth. Bring to a boil. Combine cornstarch and salt in water and soy sauce. Stir into chicken mixture. Cook until thickened, stirring constantly. Stir in pimentos and bean sprouts. Heat to serving temperature. Serve over rice; garnish with almonds. Yield: 7 servings.

HOT CHICKEN SALAD CASSEROLE

2 cups chopped cooked chicken
1 cup chopped celery
1 tablespoon minced onion
1/2 cup slivered almonds
3 hard-boiled eggs, chopped
1 can cream of celery soup

1/2 cup mayonnaise
1 tablespoon lemon juice
1/4 teaspoon salt
1/2 teaspoon pepper
1 cup crushed potato chips
1/2 cup shredded Cheddar cheese

Combine chicken, celery, onion, almonds, eggs, soup, mayonnaise, lemon juice, salt and pepper in bowl; mix gently. Spoon into 9-inch square baking dish. Top with potato chips and cheese. Bake at 400 degrees for 15 to 20 minutes or until bubbly. Yield: 6 servings.

CURRIED CHICKEN CASSEROLE

2 cans cream of chicken
 soup
1 cup mayonnaise
2 teaspoons lemon juice
1 teaspoon curry powder
4 cups chopped cooked
 chicken

1 cup crushed cheese
 crackers
1/2 to 1 cup shredded
 Cheddar cheese
1 cup bread crumbs
1/4 cup melted butter

Combine soup, mayonnaise, lemon juice and curry powder in small bowl; mix well. Layer chicken, cracker crumbs, cheese and soup mixture 1/2 at a time in greased 2-quart baking dish. Combine bread crumbs and melted butter. Sprinkle over top of casserole. Bake at 350 degrees for 50 minutes or until bubbly. Yield: 8 servings.

FIESTA CHICKEN CASSEROLE

1 cup sour cream
1/3 cup milk
1/4 cup chopped onions
1/2 teaspoon garlic salt
1/4 teaspoon cumin
Dash of hot pepper sauce
1 can cream of chicken
 soup
1 9-ounce package
 frozen chopped spinach,
 thawed, drained
1 4-ounce can chopped
 green chilies, drained
1 2-ounce jar chopped
 pimentos, drained

2 to 3 cups chopped
 cooked chicken
1 cup shredded Monterey
 Jack cheese
1/2 cup shredded sharp
 Cheddar cheese
2 egg yolks, beaten
1 cup self-rising flour
1 1/2 teaspoons baking
 powder
3/4 cup milk
1/4 cup margarine,
 softened
2 egg whites, stiffly beaten
Paprika to taste

Combine sour cream, 1/3 cup milk, onions, garlic salt, cumin, hot pepper sauce and soup in bowl; mix well. Add spinach to sour cream mixture with green chilies and pimentos; mix well. Combine chicken and cheeses in bowl; toss lightly. Alternate layers of spinach mixture and chicken mixture in greased 2-quart baking dish until all ingredients are used. Combine egg yolks, flour, baking powder, 3/4 cup milk and margarine in mixer bowl. Beat at low speed until moistened. Beat at high speed for 4 minutes. Fold in stiffly beaten egg whites gently. Spread over chicken mixture. Sprinkle with paprika. Bake at 375 degrees for 30 to 45 minutes or until deep golden brown. Yield: 6 to 8 servings.

MEXICAN CHICKEN CASSEROLE

1 chicken, cooked, chopped
1 large onion, cut into rings
1 large green bell pepper, cut into rings
1 12-ounce package nacho corn chips, crushed
1 cup shredded Cheddar cheese
1 can Ro-Tel tomatoes
1 can cream of celery soup
1 can cream of chicken soup
1 cup chicken broth
1 cup shredded Cheddar cheese

Layer chicken, onion, green pepper, corn chips, 1 cup cheese and tomatoes in large baking dish. Combine soups and broth in bowl; mix well. Pour over layers. Top with remaining 1 cup cheese. Bake at 350 degrees for 30 minutes. Yield: 6 to 8 servings.

POPPY SEED CHICKEN CASSEROLE

2 3-pound chickens, cooked, chopped
1 can cream of chicken soup
1 can cream of mushroom soup
1 cup sour cream
6 ounces spaghetti, cooked
Salt and pepper to taste
Cracker crumbs
Poppy seed
1/2 cup melted margarine

Combine chicken, soups and sour cream in large bowl. Add spaghetti, salt and pepper; mix well. Pour into large baking dish. Cover with cracker crumbs; sprinkle with poppy seed. Drizzle margarine over top. Bake at 350 degrees for 30 minutes or until bubbly. Yield: 8 to 10 servings.

CHICKEN AND VEGETABLE CASSEROLE

2 to 3 cups chopped
cooked chicken
1 3-ounce can French-
fried onions
1 10-ounce package
frozen mixed vegetables,
thawed

1 can cream of
mushroom soup
1/2 cup milk

Combine chicken, half the onions, mixed vegetables, soup and milk in bowl; mix well. Pour into 1 1/2-quart baking dish. Top with remaining onions. Bake, covered, at 375 degrees for 45 minutes. Yield: 6 servings.

TWENTY-MINUTE CHICKEN CACCIATORE

1 pound boneless
chicken strips
1/2 cup chopped onions
1 clove of garlic, minced
2 tablespoons oil
1 28-ounce can
tomatoes, drained
1 8-ounce can tomato
sauce

1 teaspoon salt
1/2 teaspoon oregano
1/2 teaspoon basil
1/8 teaspoon red pepper
1 cup green bell pepper
strips
1 1/2 cups uncooked
minute rice

Brown chicken, onions and garlic in oil in large saucepan. Add tomatoes, tomato sauce, salt, oregano, basil, red pepper and green pepper strips; mix well. Bring to a boil. Stir in rice. Remove from heat. Let stand, covered, for 5 minutes. Stir to mix well. Yield: 4 servings.

A Lion Tip

Buy chicken in quantities and bake or stew. Store meal-sized portions of chopped chicken in plastic bags in freezer — ready for a busy-day meal.

CHICKEN CROQUETTES WITH PECANS

1 5 to 6-pound chicken
2 cups chopped pecans
4 tablespoons flour
4 to 5 teaspoons butter,
  softened
2 cups milk
1/2 teaspoon salt
2 tablespoons grated
  onion

2 tablespoons minced
  parsley
1 egg, beaten
2 tablespoons milk
Cracker crumbs
Oil for deep frying

Cook chicken in salted water to cover in large saucepan. Skin chicken; cut into very small pieces. Combine chicken and pecans. Combine flour, butter, 2 cups milk and salt in saucepan; mix well. Cook over low heat until very thick, stirring constantly. Cool. Stir in onion and parsley. Add to chicken mixture; mix well. Shape into 1-inch balls. Dip into mixture of egg and remaining 2 tablespoons milk. Roll in cracker crumbs. Chill, covered, overnight. Deep-fry in oil in large skillet until golden brown. Yield: 8 servings.

CHICKEN CURRY

2 to 3 tablespoons curry
  powder
1/4 teaspoon oil
1 large onion, peeled,
  chopped
5 cloves of garlic, minced
6 chicken breasts, boned,
  skinned, chopped
1/2 cup chicken broth

1 green papaya, peeled,
  seeded, cut into 1-inch
  pieces
1/4 cup golden raisins
1 cup low-fat yogurt
1/4 cup freshly squeezed
  lemon juice
4 to 5 teaspoons freshly
  ground ginger

Combine curry powder and oil in 9x13-inch microwave-safe baking dish; mix well. Microwave, uncovered, on High for 1 1/2 minutes. Stir in onion and garlic. Microwave, uncovered, on High for 3 minutes. Add chicken pieces, chicken broth, papaya and raisins; mix well. Microwave, covered tightly with plastic wrap, on High for 6 minutes, stirring 2 times. Pierce plastic wrap to release steam. Stir in yogurt, lemon juice and ginger. Serve immediately. Yield: 6 servings.

CHICKEN CUTLETS

1 5-pound chicken
1/4 cup chicken fat
1/4 cup flour
1 cup chicken broth
1/4 teaspoon salt
Pinch of pepper
1 small can chopped
  pimento, drained
1 hard-boiled egg,
  chopped

1/4 cup chopped celery
1/8 teaspoon pepper
1/8 teaspoon paprika
1/4 cup flour
2 eggs, beaten
4 cups cornflake crumbs
  or dry bread crumbs
Oil for deep frying

Cook chicken in salted water to cover in saucepan until tender; drain. Bone and chop chicken. Blend chicken fat and 1/4 cup flour in saucepan. Stir in broth. Cook until thickened, stirring constantly. Add 1/4 teaspoon salt and pinch of pepper. Add chicken, pimento, egg, celery, 1/8 teaspoon pepper and paprika; mix well. Cook over medium heat for 5 to 10 minutes or until very thick, stirring constantly. Spread evenly in shallow pan. Chill for 2 hours. Cut into squares. Dust on all sides with 1/4 cup flour. Dip squares 1 at a time into eggs; coat with crumbs. Repeat egg and crumb coating. Deep-fry in hot oil until golden brown; drain on paper towels. Yield: 8 to 10 servings.

CHICKEN FOR FAJITAS

4 chicken breasts
1 lime, peeled, cut into
  quarters
1 onion, cut into quarters
Freshly ground pepper to
  taste
4 to 5 teaspoons chili
  powder

1/4 cup orange juice
1 teaspoon garlic powder
1/2 teaspoon fresh cilantro
1/4 teaspoon cumin
1/4 teaspoon oregano
Salt to taste
2 tablespoons oil

Place chicken in large saucepan with enough water to cover. Add lime, onion and pepper; mix well. Bring to a boil over medium heat. Simmer, covered, over low heat for 15 minutes. Let stand for 10 minutes. Reserve 2 tablespoons broth. Skin and bone chicken. Cut into 3-inch strips. Combine reserved broth, chili powder, orange juice, garlic powder, cilantro, cumin, oregano and salt in large bowl; mix well. Add chicken. Toss to coat. Chill, covered, for 2 hours. Cook undrained chicken pieces in oil in skillet for 3 minutes or until heated through and golden brown. Yield: 4 servings.

HERB-BAKED CHICKEN FINGERS

2 pounds skinned
  boneless chicken
  breasts
1 1/2 teaspoons instant
  chicken bouillon
1/2 teaspoon dry mustard
1/2 cup boiling water

1 clove of garlic, minced
2 teaspoons
  Worcestershire sauce
1 teaspoon oregano
1/2 teaspoon paprika
2 to 3 drops of Tabasco
  sauce

Cut chicken into 30 strips. Place in 1 1/2-quart baking dish. Dissolve instant bouillon and dry mustard in boiling water in small saucepan. Add garlic, Worcestershire sauce, oregano, paprika and Tabasco sauce; mix well. Pour over chicken. Bake, uncovered, at 350 degrees for 30 to 35 minutes or until chicken is tender; drain. Garnish with additional paprika.
Yield: 5 servings.

CHICKEN YOGURT KABOBS

2 pounds boneless
  chicken breasts
Salt and pepper to taste
1/2 cup yogurt
2 cloves of garlic, minced
1 shallot, minced

Grated rind of 1/2 lemon
2 tablespoons chopped
  parsley
2 tablespoons chopped
  mint
1 tablespoon lemon juice

Rinse chicken breasts; pat dry. Rub with salt and pepper. Combine yogurt, garlic, shallot, lemon rind, parsley, mint and lemon juice in large bowl; mix well. Add chicken. Marinate, covered, for 2 hours. Thread chicken accordion-style onto skewers, shaking off excess marinade. Place on grill over medium coals. Cook until no longer pink, turning and basting with remaining marinade occasionally. Yield: 6 servings.

SPICY CHICKEN KABOBS

2 pounds chicken breast filets

Juice of 2 lemons
2 tablespoons Baharat

Rinse chicken; pat dry. Cut into cubes. Dip into lemon juice; sprinkle with Baharat to coat. Thread onto skewers; place in shallow dish. Chill, covered, for 2 hours. Grill over medium-low coals for 10 to 15 minutes or until cooked through, turning frequently. Yield: 6 servings.

Baharat (Mixed Spice)

1 tablespoon freshly ground pepper
1¹/₂ teaspoons ground coriander
1¹/₂ teaspoons ground cloves
1 tablespoon ground cumin

¹/₄ teaspoon ground cardamom
¹/₄ teaspoon ground nutmeg
Dash of ground cinnamon

Combine pepper, coriander, cloves, cumin, cardamom, nutmeg and cinnamon in small covered jar; shake well to mix. Store unused spice mixture in refrigerator.

CHICKEN LIVER KABOBS

1 pound chicken livers
¹/₄ cup freshly chopped parsley
¹/₂ teaspoon red pepper flakes

1 small onion, thinly sliced
1 clove of garlic, minced
¹/₄ cup ouzo or whiskey
Salt and pepper to taste

Rinse livers; pat dry. Place in bowl. Add parsley, red pepper flakes, onion, garlic and ouzo; toss gently. Marinate in refrigerator for 2 hours to overnight. Drain, reserving marinade. Thread onto skewers; place in shallow dish. Chill, covered, until ready to cook. Grill over medium-hot coals for 10 minutes or until livers are cooked through, turning and basting frequently with reserved marinade. Yield: 4 to 6 servings.

CHICKEN NARANJA

1 3-pound chicken,
cut up
Salt and pepper to taste
1/4 cup butter
1/2 cup slivered blanched
almonds
1/2 cup raisins
2 1/2 cups orange juice

1/4 teaspoon cinnamon
1/8 teaspoon cloves
1/8 teaspoon nutmeg
1 orange, peeled, cut into
1/4-inch slices
1 tablespoon flour
2 tablespoons water

Sprinkle chicken with salt and pepper. Cook in butter in skillet until golden brown. Stir in almonds, raisins, orange juice, cinnamon, cloves and nutmeg. Simmer, covered, for 25 minutes. Cut orange slices into halves; add to skillet. Simmer, covered, for 15 minutes longer. Remove chicken to serving plate. Stir flour and water into pan drippings. Cook for 10 minutes or until thickened, stirring frequently. Serve with chicken. Yield: 4 servings.

CAJUN-STYLE CHICKEN NUGGETS

1 envelope onion or
onion-mushroom soup
mix
1/2 cup dry bread crumbs
1 1/2 teaspoons chili
powder
1 teaspoon cumin

1 teaspoon thyme
1/4 teaspoon red pepper
2 pounds boneless
chicken breasts, cut into
1-inch pieces
2 to 3 tablespoons oil

Combine soup mix, bread crumbs, chili powder, cumin, thyme and red pepper in large bowl; mix well. Add chicken; toss to coat. Place in 9x13-inch microwave-safe baking dish. Drizzle with oil. Microwave, uncovered, on High for 6 minutes or until chicken is tender, rearranging once. Drain on paper towels. Serve with assorted mustards. Yield: 8 servings.

CHICKEN AND POTPIE DUMPLINGS

1 3-pound chicken,
cut up
1 onion, chopped
2 stalks celery, chopped
2 tablespoons parsley

Salt and pepper to taste
4 potatoes, peeled, cut
into quarters
1 recipe 2-crust pie pastry

Combine chicken, onion, celery, parsley, salt and pepper in large saucepan. Fill with water. Bring to a boil over medium heat. Simmer, covered, over low heat for several hours, adding water as necessary. Remove and bone chicken. Return chicken to saucepan. Add potatoes. Return to a boil. Roll pastry into large rectangle on lightly floured surface. Cut into 2½-inch squares. Place squares gently on boiling broth. Dough will sink into broth. Add more squares until all are used. Cook for 15 minutes more or until broth is almost absorbed.
Yield: 6 to 8 servings.

Pie Pastry

2²/₃ cups flour
1 teaspoon salt
1 cup shortening

7 to 8 tablespoons cold
water

Combine flour and salt in bowl; mix well. Cut in shortening until crumbly. Add water 1 tablespoon at a time, mixing with fork until mixture forms ball.

A Lion Tip

For quick chicken and dumplings, tear flour tortillas into simmering canned chicken broth and cook until tender. Add canned chunk chicken.

CHICKEN AND VEGETABLE SPAGHETTI

1/4 cup margarine or butter
1 clove of garlic, minced
2 cups fresh asparagus,
  cut into 2-inch pieces
1 cup thinly sliced carrots
1 6-ounce package
  frozen pea pods, thawed,
  drained
2 cups chopped cooked
  chicken
1/4 cup sliced green
  onions

1 cup water
2 tablespoons dry Sherry
2 teaspoons chicken-
  flavored instant bouillon
1/4 teaspoon tarragon
1 tablespoon cornstarch
1 tablespoon water
4 ounces uncooked
  spaghetti
1/4 cup Parmesan cheese

Melt margarine in large skillet. Sauté garlic for 1 minute. Add asparagus and carrots. Stir-fry for 5 minutes. Add pea pods, chicken, green onions, water, Sherry, bouillon and tarragon. Cook for 3 to 5 minutes or until vegetables are tender-crisp, stirring occasionally. Combine cornstarch and water in small bowl. Add to chicken mixture. Cook until thickened, stirring constantly. Cook spaghetti using package directions; drain. Serve chicken mixture over spaghetti. Sprinkle with Parmesan cheese. Yield: 4 servings.

COUNTRY-STYLE CHICKEN AND GRAVY

3 tablespoons margarine
  or butter
2 pounds chicken legs
  and thighs
1 teaspoon salt

1/8 teaspoon pepper
1/2 cup water
2 tablespoons flour
1/2 cup cold water
1/4 cup sour cream

Melt margarine in large skillet over medium heat. Add chicken. Brown for 5 minutes on each side. Sprinkle with salt and pepper. Add 1/2 cup water; bring to a boil. Simmer, partially covered, over low heat for 30 to 35 minutes or until tender, turning once. Place chicken on warm serving plate. Combine flour and cold water in small tightly-covered jar; shake well. Stir flour mixture into pan drippings gradually. Cook until thickened and bubbly, stirring constantly. Remove from heat. Stir in sour cream. Serve with chicken. Yield: 4 servings.

CREAMY CHICKEN FETTUCINI WITH SNOW PEAS AND WALNUTS

1 tablespoon butter or margarine
1 tablespoon flour
1/2 teaspoon salt
1/2 teaspoon lemon pepper
1 1/2 cups evaporated milk
1/4 cup dry white wine or vermouth
1 pound chicken, boned, skinned
3 tablespoons olive oil
1 clove of garlic, minced
2 cups snow peas
1 cup sliced mushrooms
1 cup thinly sliced carrots
2 tablespoons chopped fresh basil
8 ounces fettucini, cooked
1/4 cup chopped walnuts

Melt butter in medium saucepan. Stir in flour, salt and lemon pepper. Add evaporated milk. Cook over medium heat until thickened, stirring constantly. Stir in wine. Keep warm. Cut chicken into 1/2-inch strips. Sauté in 2 tablespoons olive oil in large skillet until tender and lightly browned. Remove from skillet; keep warm. Heat remaining 1 tablespoon olive oil in separate large skillet. Add garlic, snow peas, mushrooms and carrots. Stir-fry until tender-crisp. Add chicken and wine mixture to vegetables; mix well. Stir in basil. Serve over hot fettucini. Sprinkle with walnuts. Yield: 4 servings.

JAPANESE CHICKEN

2 to 4 tablespoons soy sauce
4 to 6 tablespoons Sake
1 tablespoon brown sugar
1/2 ounce fresh gingerroot, minced
4 lemon slices, coarsely chopped
2 shallots, chopped
1 clove of garlic, coarsely chopped
1 3-pound chicken, cut up
Corn flour
1/4 cup peanut oil or olive oil

Combine first 7 ingredients in large bowl; mix well. Dust chicken with corn flour. Add to soy sauce mixture. Marinate, covered, for 4 hours, turning chicken occasionally. Place chicken in baking dish. Sprinkle with oil. Bake at 325 degrees for 1 hour to 1 hour and 30 minutes or until chicken is tender, basting with pan juices occasionally. Yield: 4 servings.

FANCY CHICKEN WITH HERBS

2 tablespoons oil
1 3-pound chicken,
  cut up
1 onion, chopped
1 clove of garlic, minced
3 cups chopped
  mushrooms
2 tablespoons flour
$^1/_2$ teaspoon basil
$^1/_2$ teaspoon rosemary
Salt and pepper to taste
2 cups chicken broth
1 9-ounce package
  frozen artichoke hearts
1 cup frozen peas

Heat oil in large saucepan. Brown chicken in oil over medium-high heat a few pieces at a time. Remove as browned. Stir in onions and garlic. Cook for 3 minutes, stirring frequently. Add mushrooms. Cook for 5 minutes longer, stirring occasionally. Stir in flour and seasonings. Add chicken broth; mix well. Cook for 1 minute longer. Return chicken to saucepan. Add artichoke hearts; bring to a boil. Simmer, covered, over low heat for 30 minutes or until chicken is tender. Stir in peas. Simmer for 5 minutes longer. Serve over cooked noodles or rice. Yield: 4 to 6 servings.

SWISS CHICKEN QUICHE

1 cup shredded Swiss
  cheese
2 tablespoons flour
1 tablespoon instant
  chicken bouillon
2 cups chopped cooked
  chicken
1 cup milk
$^1/_4$ cup chopped onions
1 baked 9-inch pie shell

Combine cheese, flour and bouillon in large bowl; mix well. Stir in chicken, milk and onions. Pour into pastry-lined pie plate. Bake at 350 degrees for 35 to 40 minutes or until firm. Let stand for 10 minutes. Yield: 6 to 8 servings.

A Lion Tip

Stir a little peanut butter into medium white sauce for a new version of creamed chicken.

ROAST CHICKEN WITH TARRAGON-WINE SAUCE

1　6-ounce package long grain and wild rice
2 tablespoons butter
1 cup chopped onions
1 cup chopped celery
1 cup thinly sliced carrots
1 cup chopped pecans or walnuts
1　3-pound chicken
¼ cup butter
½ cup wine
1 teaspoon tarragon
1 clove of garlic, minced
Salt and pepper to taste
2 cups chicken broth
2 tablespoons cornstarch
½ cup wine

Cook rice using package directions. Melt 2 tablespoons butter in large skillet over medium-high heat. Add onions, celery and carrots. Cook for 10 minutes or until vegetables are tender, stirring occasionally. Stir in pecans. Add rice; mix well. Remove giblets and neck from chicken. Rinse chicken with cold water; pat dry. Spoon stuffing lightly into neck and body cavities. Fasten with skewers. Tuck wings under body. Place chicken breast side up on rack in roasting pan. Melt remaining ¼ cup butter in skillet. Stir in ½ cup wine, tarragon, garlic, salt and pepper. Brush chicken with wine mixture. Bake, uncovered, at 350 degrees for 1½ to 2 hours or to 180 degrees on meat thermometer, basting frequently. Remove chicken to warm serving plate. Skim fat from pan juices. Add chicken broth; mix well. Cook over medium heat, stirring to deglaze. Stir in mixture of cornstarch and remaining ½ cup wine. Bring to a boil. Cook for 1 minute, stirring constantly. Serve with chicken.
Yield: 4 to 6 servings.

A Lion Tip

Baked or roasted chicken has fewer calories than stewed chicken. Remove skin to further reduce calories.

SPINACH CHICKEN

2 3-ounce packages thin
chicken slices
1/2 cup chopped onions
2 tablespoons oil
1 10-ounce packaged
frozen chopped spinach,
thawed, drained

1/3 cup shredded ricotta
cheese
2 eggs, beaten
1/8 teaspoon pepper
4 slices mozzarella
cheese

Divide chicken slices into 4 servings. Place in ungreased 9-inch square baking dish. Sauté onions in oil in medium skillet until tender, stirring frequently. Stir in spinach, ricotta cheese, eggs and pepper. Top each serving with 1/4 of the spinach mixture. Bake at 375 degrees for 15 to 20 minutes or until firm. Top each serving with cheese slice. Bake for 1 minute longer or until cheese is melted. Yield: 4 servings.

STIR-FRIED CHICKEN

4 chicken breasts, boned,
skinned
2 tablespoons oil
3 tablespoons soy sauce
2 tablespoons dry Sherry
1 tablespoon sugar
1/2 teaspoon ginger
1/4 teaspoon garlic powder
1/8 teaspoon pepper

1 16-ounce package
frozen broccoli and
carrots
1 small onion, cut into
rings
1 tablespoon cornstarch
1 tablespoon water
Hot cooked rice
1/3 cup salted peanuts

Cut chicken breasts into 1/2-inch strips. Stir-fry chicken in oil in large skillet or wok for 1 minute. Combine soy sauce, Sherry, sugar, ginger, garlic powder and pepper in bowl; mix well. Pour over chicken. Stir-fry for 2 minutes longer. Stir in frozen vegetables and onion. Simmer, covered, for 6 to 8 minutes or until vegetables are tender-crisp, stirring once. Add mixture of cornstarch and water gradually; mix well. Stir constantly until thickened. Serve over rice. Top with peanuts. Yield: 4 servings.

BROILED CHICKEN THIGHS WITH MUSTARD-MAPLE GLAZE

3 tablespoons maple syrup
2 tablespoons Dijon mustard
1½ teaspoons cider vinegar

1½ teaspoons oil
1 teaspoon low-sodium soy sauce
⅛ teaspoon red pepper
8 chicken thighs, boned, skinned

Combine syrup, mustard, vinegar, oil, soy sauce and pepper in bowl; mix well. Coat chicken with glaze. Place on lightly greased rack in broiler pan. Broil 4 inches from heat source for 7 minutes, basting 1 time. Turn and baste. Broil for 7 minutes, basting 1 time. Yield: 4 servings.

CHEESE-STUFFED CHICKEN THIGHS

10 ounces low-fat Monterey Jack cheese
8 chicken thighs, boned, skinned
1 tablespoon rosemary
1 tablespoon tarragon
1 tablespoon thyme
3 green onions, chopped

Salt and pepper to taste
¼ cup white wine
¼ cup melted reduced-calorie margarine
1 teaspoon rosemary
1 teaspoon tarragon
1 teaspoon thyme

Cut cheese into 8 pieces. Pound chicken to ¼-inch thickness. Sprinkle with mixture of 1 tablespoon each rosemary, tarragon and thyme and green onions. Add salt and pepper. Wrap each chicken piece around cheese piece; secure with toothpicks. Combine wine, margarine and remaining 1 teaspoon each rosemary, tarragon and thyme in bowl; mix well. Grill chicken over medium-hot coals for 10 to 15 minutes on each side or to desired degree of doneness, basting with wine mixture. Yield: 8 servings.

RANCH CHICKEN THIGHS

1 teaspoon salt
1/2 teaspoon pepper
1 teaspoon paprika
8 chicken thighs
1 tablespoon margarine

Flowerets of 1 head
  cauliflower
1 tablespoon margarine
1 cup low-calorie ranch
  salad dressing

Combine salt, pepper and paprika in bowl; mix well. Arrange chicken skin side down around outer edge of rack placed in round microwave-safe baking dish. Sprinkle with half the paprika mixture. Dot with 1 tablespoon margarine. Microwave, uncovered, on High for 10 minutes. Turn chicken. Place cauliflowerets in center of dish. Sprinkle all with remaining paprika mixture. Dot with remaining 1 tablespoon margarine. Cover cauliflowerets loosely with plastic wrap. Microwave on High for 10 minutes longer. Remove plastic. Pour salad dressing over all. Microwave, loosely covered, on High for 10 minutes longer. Spoon pan juices over all. Yield: 4 servings.

HOT AND HONEYED CHICKEN WINGS

3 pounds chicken wings
3/4 cup picante sauce
2/3 cup honey
1/3 cup soy sauce
1/4 cup Dijon mustard

3 tablespoons oil
2 tablespoons grated
  fresh gingerroot
1 1/2 teaspoons grated
  orange rind

Rinse chicken; pat dry. Remove and discard wing tips. Disjoint wings. Place in 9x13-inch baking dish. Combine picante sauce, honey, soy sauce, mustard, oil, gingerroot and orange rind in small bowl; mix well. Pour over chicken. Marinate, covered, in refrigerator for 6 hours to overnight. Drain, reserving marinade. Arrange chicken in single layer in foil-lined 10x15-inch baking pan. Drizzle reserved marinade over chicken. Bake at 400 degrees for 40 to 45 minutes or until brown. Serve hot or at room temperature with additional picante sauce. Yield: 4 to 6 servings.

SPICY CHICKEN WINGS

15 chicken wings
1/2 cup soy sauce
1/2 cup lemon juice
2 tablespoons canola oil
1/4 cup honey

2 cloves of garlic, minced
1/4 teaspoon hot pepper
  sauce
Sweet and Sour Sauce

Rinse chicken; pat dry. Remove and discard wing tips. Disjoint wings. Place in bowl. Combine soy sauce, lemon juice, oil, honey, garlic and hot pepper sauce in small bowl; mix well. Pour over chicken. Marinate, covered, in refrigerator overnight. Drain, reserving marinade. Arrange chicken in single layer in foil-lined baking pan. Pour marinade over chicken. Bake at 450 degrees for 20 minutes or until tender, basting several times with marinade. Drain, reserving marinade for Sweet and Sour Sauce. Serve with Sweet and Sour Sauce.
Yield: 2 to 4 entrée servings or 30 appetizers.

Sweet and Sour Sauce

Reserved marinade
1 8-ounce can pineapple
  cubes, drained
1 green pepper, cut into
  cubes

1/4 cup vinegar
1 cup chicken broth
1/4 cup cornstarch
1 teaspoon ground ginger
1/4 cup pineapple juice

Combine reserved marinade, pineapple, green pepper, vinegar and broth in saucepan. Bring to a boil over low heat. Blend cornstarch, ginger and pineapple juice in small bowl. Stir into hot mixture. Cook for 2 minutes or until thickened and clear, stirring constantly.

PLUM-TERI TURKEY

1/2 cup bottled teriyaki
  glaze
1/4 cup plum jam
1 tablespoon dry Sherry

1 teaspoon cider vinegar
1 clove of garlic, crushed
1 1 1/2-pound boneless
  turkey breast

Combine first 5 ingredients in small bowl. Brush both sides of breast with glaze. Place skin side up in shallow roasting pan. Bake, covered with foil, at 450 degrees for 20 minutes. Reduce temperature to 325 degrees. Turn breast over; brush with glaze. Bake, uncovered, for 40 minutes longer or until juices run clear when turkey is pierced with fork, turning and basting with glaze one time. Yield: 10 servings.

TURKEY CASSEROLE

1 can cream of chicken soup
1/2 cup milk
1 16-ounce package frozen chopped broccoli, thawed
1 tablespoon lemon juice
3 cups cooked cubed turkey
6 slices American cheese
1 3-ounce can French-fried onion rings

Combine soup and milk in bowl; mix well. Place broccoli in 7x12-inch baking dish. Sprinkle with lemon juice. Place turkey cubes and cheese over broccoli. Pour soup mixture over top. Bake, uncovered, at 350 degrees for 30 minutes or until bubbly. Sprinkle with onion rings. Bake for 5 minutes longer. Yield: 6 servings.

TURKEY CORDON BLEU

8 thick slices fresh boned turkey breast
2 tablespoons melted margarine
8 slices turkey ham
8 1-ounce slices Swiss cheese, at room temperature
1/2 cup bread crumbs
1/4 cup flour
2 tablespoons Parmesan cheese
1/2 teaspoon seasoned salt
1/4 teaspoon paprika
1/4 teaspoon basil
1/4 cup milk
1 egg, beaten

Slit each turkey slice lengthwise to within 1/2-inch of opposite side, forming a pocket. Brush insides of pockets with margarine. Roll 1 slice turkey ham and 1 slice Swiss cheese together; place in pocket. Secure with toothpicks. Combine bread crumbs, flour, Parmesan cheese, seasoned salt, paprika and basil in shallow dish. Mix milk with egg in separate shallow dish. Dip turkey into egg mixture; coat with crumbs. Place in lightly greased 9x13-inch baking dish. Bake at 325 degrees for 20 minutes. Turn turkey over. Bake for 20 to 25 minutes longer or until tender. Yield: 8 servings.

TURKEY DRUMSTICK STEAKS WITH APRICOT SAUCE

3 tablespoons flour
1/2 teaspoon salt
11/4 pounds turkey
   drumstick steaks

2 tablespoons margarine
Apricot Sauce

Combine flour and salt in shallow dish; coat turkey steaks with mixture. Melt margarine in large skillet over medium-high heat. Brown steaks in margarine for 5 minutes on each side. Simmer, covered, for 4 to 5 minutes or until no longer pink. Serve with Apricot Sauce. Yield: 4 to 6 servings.

Apricot Sauce

1/2 cup apricot preserves
2 teaspoons prepared
   mustard

1/4 cup applesauce
2 tablespoons water

Combine apricot preserves, mustard, applesauce and water in saucepan. Cook over medium heat until heated through, stirring constantly.

TURKEY CUTLETS AND ZUCCHINI

2 tablespoons tarragon
   vinegar
1 teaspoon basil leaves
2 cloves of garlic, crushed
1 pound turkey cutlets
4 tablespoons margarine

4 cups sliced fresh
   zucchini
11/2 cups sliced fresh
   mushrooms
Salt and pepper to taste

Combine vinegar, basil and garlic in bowl; mix well. Brush on both sides of turkey cutlets. Melt 2 tablespoons margarine in large skillet over medium-high heat. Sauté half the cutlets for 2 minutes on each side or until no longer pink. Repeat with remaining margarine and turkey cutlets. Remove to platter; keep warm. Add zucchini and mushrooms to skillet. Sauté until tender-crisp. Arrange vegetables around cutlets on platter. Yield: 4 to 6 servings.

TURKEY WITH OYSTERS AND SAUSAGE

8 ounces sausage
2 onions, chopped
1 stalk celery, chopped
Sage to taste
1/2 teaspoon salt
1/4 teaspoon pepper
2 tablespoons oil
1 pound firm white bread,
cubed, toasted

1 pint fresh oysters,
drained, cut into halves
2 tablespoons chopped
fresh parsley
1 tablespoon butter
Salt and pepper to taste
1   12 to 14 pound turkey

Shape sausage into 1-inch balls. Brown in skillet over medium-high heat; drain and set aside. Sauté next 5 ingredients in drippings in skillet until vegetables are tender, adding oil if necessary. Add bread cubes, oysters, sausage balls and parsley; mix well. Stuff into neck and body cavities of turkey; truss. Rub with butter and additional salt and pepper. Place in roasting pan; tent with foil. Bake at 325 degrees for 2½ hours for 12-pound turkey or 3¼ hours for 14-pound turkey. Bake, uncovered, for 1 hour longer or until turkey is tender and golden brown. Yield: 8 to 10 servings.

TURKEY SALISBURY STEAK

1   14-ounce can tomatoes
1 pound ground turkey
1/4 cup bread crumbs
3/4 teaspoon thyme
1/4 teaspoon salt

1/8 teaspoon red pepper
2 cups sliced mushrooms
1/4 teaspoon thyme
2 teaspoons cornstarch
1/3 cup water

Drain tomatoes, reserving juice. Combine 1/4 cup reserved juice with next 5 ingredients in bowl; toss lightly with fork. Shape into four 1-inch thick patties. Chop tomatoes and remaining reserved juice in food processor with steel blade. Brown patties on both sides in large skillet sprayed with non-stick cooking spray over low heat. Add tomatoes, mushrooms and remaining 1/4 teaspoon thyme. Bring to a boil; reduce heat. Simmer, covered, for 10 minutes or until patties are no longer pink in center. Transfer patties to warm platter. Add mixture of cornstarch and water to skillet. Cook for 1 minute or until thickened, stirring constantly. Spoon over patties. Yield: 4 servings.

TURKEY SAUTÉ MARENGO

1/4 cup dry white wine
2 teaspoons cornstarch
2 tablespoons oil
1 cup green bell pepper
 strips
1 pound boneless turkey
 breast, cut into 1/2-inch
 strips
8 ounces fresh
 mushrooms, cut into
 quarters

2 14-ounce cans stewed
 tomatoes
1/2 teaspoon thyme
3/4 teaspoon garlic powder
1/2 teaspoon grated
 orange rind
1/2 teaspoon salt
1/4 teaspoon pepper

Combine wine and cornstarch in small bowl; mix until smooth; set aside. Heat oil in large skillet. Add green pepper. Cook over medium-high heat for 2 minutes or until crisp-tender. Add turkey and mushrooms. Stir-fry for 2 to 3 minutes or until turkey is no longer pink. Stir in remaining ingredients. Cook for 2 minutes or until heated through, stirring frequently. Add cornstarch mixture. Cook until thickened, stirring constantly. Serve over steamed rice. Yield: 4 servings.

 # *S*EAFOOD

COMPANY-STYLE COD

4 carrots
4 stalks celery
1 onion, thinly sliced
2 tomatoes, chopped
1/4 cup chopped fresh
 basil
2 pounds North Atlantic
 cod filets

1/2 cup dry white wine
1/4 cup lemon juice
1 teaspoon salt
1/2 teaspoon pepper
2 tablespoons butter

Slice carrots and celery julienne-style. Mix with onion, tomatoes and basil in bowl. Layer half the vegetable mixture, cod filets and remaining vegetable mixture in baking dish. Pour white wine and lemon juice over vegetables. Sprinkle with salt and pepper. Dot with butter. Bake, covered, at 450 degrees for 15 to 20 minutes or until fish flakes easily. Yield: 8 servings.

GRILLED FISH WITH LEMON AND THYME

1/2 cup freshly squeezed
lemon juice
1 teaspoon salt
1/2 teaspoon pepper
1/2 teaspoon thyme

1 1/2 pounds snapper, sole
or cod filets
2 tablespoons melted
butter

Combine lemon juice, salt, pepper and thyme in glass baking dish; mix well. Add fish; turn to coat. Chill, covered, for 1 hour, turning 3 times; drain. Brush with melted butter. Place on rack in broiling pan. Broil for 5 minutes on each side or until fish flakes easily, turning once. Yield: 4 servings.

TANGY GLAZED BROILED FISH

1 1/2 pounds fish steaks or
filets
1/3 cup margarine or butter

1/3 cup packed brown
sugar
3 tablespoons lemon juice

Place fish on lightly greased broiler pan. Combine margarine, brown sugar and lemon juice in small saucepan. Cook over low heat until butter is melted, stirring frequently. Brush glaze on fish. Broil 5 to 6 inches from heat source for 8 to 10 minutes on each side or until fish flakes easily, brushing occasionally with glaze. Spoon any remaining glaze over fish on serving plate. Yield: 6 servings.

 ### A Lion Tip

For an Easy Tartar Sauce, combine 1 cup mayonnaise, 1 teaspoon grated onion, 2 tablespoons minced dill pickle, 1 tablespoon minced parsley and 2 teaspoons chopped pimento.

FLOUNDER EN PAPILLOTE

1 pound flounder, sole or orange roughy filets
2 tablespoons margarine or butter
1/2 cup chopped red bell pepper
1/4 cup sliced green onions
1 4-ounce jar sliced mushrooms, drained
2 tablespoons flour
1/4 teaspoon salt
1/8 teaspoon white pepper
1/3 cup milk
2 tablespoons white wine or Sherry

Cut four 10x12-inch heart-shaped pieces of baking parchment. Place 1/4 of the fish on left half of each piece. Sauté red pepper, onions and mushrooms in margarine in medium saucepan for 2 minutes. Add flour, salt and white pepper. Cook until mixture is bubbly, stirring frequently. Add milk and wine gradually. Cook until mixture boils and is thickened, stirring constantly. Spoon over fish. Fold right side of parchment over left, sealing edges with double folds. Place on ungreased baking sheet. Bake at 425 degrees for 10 to 12 minutes or until paper begins to turn golden brown. Cut X-shaped slit in parchment; tear back to serve. May substitute foil for baking parchment; bake until fish flakes easily. Yield: 4 servings.

POACHED HALIBUT WITH TARRAGON CONFETTI SAUCE

3 cups water
1 cup chopped carrots
1 cup chopped red bell pepper
1 cup chopped celery
1/2 cup sliced onions
1/2 cup dry white wine
4 peppercorns
1 teaspoon tarragon
1 teaspoon salt
4 halibut steaks
1 tablespoon butter or margarine
1 tablespoon flour
1/2 teaspoon tarragon

Combine water, carrots, red pepper, celery, onions, white wine, peppercorns, 1 teaspoon tarragon and salt in large skillet. Bring to a boil over medium heat. Add fish; return to a boil. Simmer, covered, over low heat for 10 minutes per inch of thickness or until fish flakes easily. Transfer fish to serving plate. Strain vegetables, reserving 1 cup cooking liquid; remove peppercorns. Combine butter and flour in skillet; mix well. Sauté vegetables in butter mixture for 1 minute. Stir in reserved liquid and remaining 1/2 teaspoon tarragon. Cook until thickened, stirring frequently. Spoon sauce over fish. Yield: 4 servings.

ORANGE ROUGHY WITH DILL BUTTER

3 tablespoons butter or margarine
1 pound orange roughy filets
1/2 teaspoon dillweed
1/8 teaspoon salt
1/8 teaspoon pepper
1 1/2 teaspoons butter or margarine
2 tablespoons dry bread crumbs

Melt 3 tablespoons butter in 2-quart baking dish. Place fish in baking dish; turn to coat. Sprinkle with dillweed, salt and pepper. Bake at 350 degrees for 15 minutes. Melt remaining 1 1/2 teaspoons butter in small skillet over medium heat. Add bread crumbs. Cook until lightly browned, stirring constantly. Sprinkle over fish. Bake for 3 minutes longer or until fish flakes easily. Yield: 4 servings.

ROASTED MONKFISH WITH LEEKS

1 1/2 pounds monkfish filets
1/8 teaspoon salt
1/8 teaspoon pepper
3 tablespoons butter
1 1/4 pounds chopped leeks
3/4 cup whipping cream
1/8 teaspoon Tabasco sauce
1/2 teaspoon salt

Place monkfish in baking dish. Sprinkle with 1/8 teaspoon each salt and pepper. Bake at 450 degrees for 15 minutes or until fish flakes easily. Melt butter in skillet over medium-low heat. Add leeks. Cook, covered, for 30 minutes, stirring occasionally. Stir in whipping cream. Cook over medium heat for 3 minutes or until thickened, stirring frequently. Stir in Tabasco sauce and remaining 1/2 teaspoon salt. Spoon onto serving plate. Arrange fish over leek sauce. Yield: 4 servings.

SNAPPER WITH SAUTÉED VEGETABLES

8 ounces potatoes,
  peeled, chopped
4 carrots, thinly sliced
2 tablespoons olive oil
2 onions, thinly sliced
8 ounces mushrooms,
  cut into quarters
1/4 teaspoon thyme
1 bay leaf

1 teaspoon salt
1 1/2 pounds red snapper
  filets
1/4 cup flour
1/8 teaspoon salt
1/8 teaspoon pepper
2 tablespoons olive oil
1/4 cup white wine
2 tablespoons water

Parboil potatoes and carrots in separate saucepans for 5 minutes; drain. Brown potatoes in 2 tablespoons olive oil in skillet over high heat. Add carrots, onions, mushrooms, thyme, bay leaf and 1 teaspoon salt; mix well. Cook for 5 minutes, stirring frequently. Remove from skillet; discard bay leaf. Coat snapper with mixture of flour, remaining 1/8 teaspoon salt and pepper. Cook in remaining 2 tablespoons olive oil in skillet for 3 minutes on each side or until lightly browned. Place on serving plate. Stir wine into skillet. Bring to a boil, stirring to deglaze. Add vegetable mixture and water. Cook, covered, for 2 minutes. Spoon around snapper. Yield: 4 servings.

BROILED SALMON

1/4 cup minced onion
1/4 cup minced celery
2 tablespoons minced
  green bell pepper
1 clove of garlic, minced
1 tablespoon oil

1/2 teaspoon salt
1/8 teaspoon pepper
1 cup tomato sauce
1/2 cup Parmesan cheese
4 salmon steaks

Sauté onion, celery, green pepper and garlic in oil in skillet until tender. Add salt, pepper and tomato sauce; mix well. Simmer for 3 minutes. Stir in Parmesan cheese. Place salmon steaks in broiler pan. Broil 2 inches from heat source for 4 minutes; turn salmon over. Broil for 2 minutes longer. Pour sauce over salmon. Broil for 2 minutes longer or until sauce is bubbly and fish flakes easily. Yield: 4 servings.

BRAISED SALMON

1 1¹/₂-pound salmon filet
1 tablespoon dark soy
  sauce
2 tablespoons rice wine
2 tablespoons soy sauce
1 tablespoon sugar
¹/₄ teaspoon salt
1 cup water
¹/₄ cup oil
1 tablespoon bacon
  drippings
2 teaspoons minced
  whites of green onions

2 teaspoons minced
  fresh ginger
¹/₂ cup sliced bamboo
  shoots
¹/₂ cup sliced fresh
  mushrooms
1 tablespoon cornstarch
2 tablespoons cold water
2 teaspoons minced
  cilantro

Score salmon at 2-inch intervals on both sides. Spread with 1 tablespoon soy sauce. Combine rice wine, remaining soy sauce, sugar, salt and 1 cup water water in bowl; mix well. Heat oil in wok over moderate heat. Stir in bacon drippings. Add salmon skin side down. Fry for 8 minutes, turning carefully once. Drain, reserving a small amount of oil. Add green onions, ginger, bamboo shoots, mushrooms and rice wine mixture to skillet. Stir to distribute around and under salmon. Bring to a boil; reduce heat. Cook, uncovered, for 10 minutes. Place salmon on warm serving plate. Bring pan liquids to a boil. Stir in mixture of cornstarch and remaining tablespoon cold water. Cook until thickened, stirring constantly. Pour over salmon. Sprinkle with cilantro. Serve with steamed rice and a dry Riesling. Yield: 2 to 3 servings.

A Lion Tip

Pink salmon is ideal for loaves and patties since it breaks into flakes. Red salmon is better for salads and casseroles because it breaks into larger chunks.

BAKED SALMON CROQUETTES

1 15-ounce can salmon
Milk
1/4 cup margarine
2 tablespoons chopped
  onion

1/3 cup flour
Salt and pepper to taste
1 tablespoon lemon juice
1/2 cup bread crumbs
Crushed potato chips

Drain salmon, reserving liquid. Skin and debone salmon. Add enough milk to reserved liquid to measure 1 cup. Melt margarine in skillet. Add onion. Sauté until tender. Add flour; mix well. Add milk mixture gradually, stirring constantly. Add salt and pepper. Cook until thickened, stirring constantly; remove from heat. Combine salmon, lemon juice, bread crumbs and white sauce in bowl; mix well. Shape into croquettes; roll in potato chip crumbs. Place on lightly greased baking sheet. Bake at 400 degrees for 30 minutes. Yield: 6 servings.

SALMON WITH LEMON AND LIME BUTTER

1/2 teaspoon grated lemon
  rind
1/2 teaspoon grated lime
  rind
2 tablespoons butter,
  softened

1 1 1/2-pound salmon filet
1/3 cup water
1/4 teaspoon salt

Combine lemon rind, lime rind and butter in small bowl; mix well. Place on plastic wrap; roll to form 1-inch cylinder. Chill in refrigerator or freezer until firm. Place salmon in microwave-safe dish with thickest part of salmon toward edge of dish. Pour in water; sprinkle with salt. Cover with plastic wrap; pierce several holes in plastic wrap to vent. Microwave on Medium for 6 minutes; turn salmon over. Microwave for 2 minutes longer. Top each serving with 2 thin lemon slices and lime butter. Serve immediately. Yield: 4 servings.

SALMON TURNOVER

1 cup cubed zucchini
2 tablespoons chopped
  onion
2 tablespoons butter or
  margarine
1 tablespoon flour
1/4 teaspoon marjoram
1/4 teaspoon thyme
1/4 teaspoon salt
1/4 cup milk
1 16-ounce can salmon,
  drained, boned
1/4 cup Parmesan cheese
1 2-ounce can
  mushrooms, drained

2 tablespoons snipped
  parsley
1 egg, beaten
1 recipe 1-crust pie pastry
Sesame seed
1 cucumber, shredded,
  drained
1/2 cup sour cream
1/2 cup mayonnaise or
  mayonnaise-type salad
  dressing
1 teaspoon grated onion
1 teaspoon vinegar
1/8 teaspoon salt
Dash of pepper

Sauté zucchini with chopped onion in butter in skillet until tender. Add flour, marjoram, thyme and 1/4 teaspoon salt; mix well. Stir in milk. Cook until bubbly, stirring constantly; remove from heat. Add salmon, Parmesan cheese, mushrooms and parsley; mix well. Stir in 2 tablespoons egg. Cool. Roll dough into 1/8 inch thick 13-inch circle on floured surface. Place on nonstick baking sheet. Spread salmon mixture over half the dough. Fold dough over; seal edge. Brush with remaining egg; sprinkle with sesame seed. Pierce with fork. Bake at 400 degrees for 25 to 30 minutes or until golden brown. Combine cucumber, sour cream, mayonnaise, grated onion, vinegar, 1/8 teaspoon salt and pepper in bowl; mix well. Pour over turnover. Yield: 4 to 5 servings.

EASY SCALLOPED SALMON

1/2 cup chicken broth
2 eggs, slightly beaten
1/2 cup milk
2 tablespoons parsley
 flakes
1 tablespoon instant
 minced onion
1/2 teaspoon dry mustard

1/4 teaspoon salt
1/8 teaspoon pepper
1 16-ounce can salmon
2 cups herb-seasoned
 stuffing croutons
1 cup shredded Cheddar
 cheese
Vegetable Sauce

Combine first 8 ingredients in bowl. Drain salmon; discard skin and bones. Add to egg mixture; mix well. Add croutons and cheese; mix well. Spoon into greased 9-inch pie plate. Bake at 350 degrees for 35 to 40 minutes or until set. Serve with Vegetable Sauce. Yield: 4 or 5 servings.

Vegetable Sauce

2 tablespoons melted
 butter
2 tablespoons flour
1/4 teaspoon salt

Pepper to taste
1 cup milk
1 cup drained cooked
 peas

Blend butter and flour in saucepan. Add salt and pepper. Stir in milk. Cook until thickened, stirring constantly. Cook for 2 minutes longer, stirring constantly. Stir in peas. Heat to serving temperature.

SALMON PATTIES WITH CREAMED PEAS

1 16-ounce can salmon
1 cup dry potato flakes
1/4 cup chopped onion
1 teaspoon prepared
 mustard
2 tablespoons lemon juice

2 eggs, beaten
1/4 cup dry potato flakes
2 tablespoons margarine
Creamed Peas
 (See page 141)

Drain and flake salmon in large bowl. Add 1 cup potato flakes, onion, mustard, lemon juice and eggs; mix well. Shape into 4 patties; coat with remaining 1/4 cup potato flakes. Melt margarine in skillet over medium heat. Add patties. Fry for 3 to 4 minutes on each side or until brown. Place on serving plate. Spoon Creamed Peas over patties. Yield: 4 servings.

Creamed Peas

1 10-ounce package
  frozen sweet peas in
  butter sauce
1/2 cup mayonnaise

1 egg, beaten
1 tablespoon lemon juice
1/2 teaspoon dillweed

Cook peas using package directions. Combine mayonnaise, egg, lemon juice and dillweed in small saucepan; mix well. Cook over low heat until heated through, stirring constantly; do not boil. Stir in peas.

SOLE WITH MUSHROOM-WALNUT BUTTER

2 tablespoons butter or
  margarine
1 pound frozen sole
  filets, thawed
1/4 cup butter or margarine
1/2 cup sliced fresh
  mushrooms

2 tablespoons coarsely
  chopped walnuts
1/4 teaspoon dry mustard
1/8 teaspoon thyme

Melt 2 tablespoons butter in large skillet over medium heat. Add fish. Cook for 4 to 5 minutes or until fish flakes easily with fork, turning once. Remove to serving platter; keep warm. Add 1/4 cup butter to skillet. Add mushrooms, walnuts, dry mustard and thyme. Sauté for 1 to 2 minutes or until mushrooms are tender. Spoon over fish. May omit butter, arrange fish in 8-inch square microwave-safe dish and microwave, covered with plastic wrap, on High for 4 to 6 minutes or until fish flakes easily; keep warm. Microwave 1/4 cup butter in 4-cup glass measure on High for 30 to 40 seconds or until melted. Add mushrooms; stir to coat. Microwave on High for 2 minutes or until tender. Stir in walnuts, dry mustard and thyme. Microwave on High for 1 minute longer. Pour over fish.
Yield: 4 servings.

GRILLED SWORDFISH WITH SWEET AND SOUR SAUCE

12 ounces swordfish
Vegetable oil
2 tablespoons red-wine
  vinegar
1 tablespoon grated fresh
  ginger
1 tablespoon sugar
1/2 cup water

1 1/2 teaspoons reduced-
  sodium soy sauce
1 cup chopped fresh
  pineapple
2 teaspoons cornstarch
3 tablespoons water
2 or 3 tablespoons fresh
  cilantro leaves

Brush swordfish lightly with oil. Place on rack in broiler pan. Broil 6 inches from heat source for 10 minutes per inch thickness or until fish flakes easily. Combine vinegar, ginger, sugar, 1/2 cup water, soy sauce and pineapple in small saucepan. Bring to a boil; reduce heat. Simmer for 2 minutes.blend cornstarch with 1 tablespoon water in small bowl. Stir in remaining 2 tablespoons water. Add to sauce. Cook just until thickened, stirring constantly. Spoon over swordfish; sprinkle with cilantro leaves. Yield: 2 servings.

SWORDFISH MESSINA

2 tablespoons olive oil
2 cloves of garlic, pressed
1/2 cup chopped parsley
2 tablespoons chopped
  fresh basil
1 cup sliced mushrooms
1   8-ounce can tomato
  sauce
1 tablespoon lemon juice

1 tablespoon water
1 tablespoon capers,
  rinsed
1/4 teaspoon sugar
1/4 teaspoon lemon pepper
1/4 teaspoon salt
2 to 3 pounds swordfish
  or halibut steak

Heat olive oil in small saucepan. Add garlic, parsley, basil and mushrooms. Sauté for 3 to 5 minutes or until just until mushrooms are tender. Stir in tomato sauce and next 6 ingredients. Cook for 5 minutes. Arrange swordfish in greased 9x13-inch baking dish. Pour sauce over swordfish. Bake at 400 degrees for 20 minutes or until fish flakes easily. Yield: 4 to 6 servings.

CRAB CAKES

4 slices firm white bread,
crusts trimmed
1/2 cup olive oil
2 egg yolks
1 teaspoon prepared
mustard
Dash of salt
Dash of paprika

1 1/2 teaspoons
Worcestershire sauce
1 pound back-fin crab
meat
2 egg whites, stiffly
beaten
Butter for frying

Place bread in pan; pour olive oil over top. Let stand for 1 hour; mash. Combine egg yolks, mustard, salt, paprika and Worcestershire sauce in bowl; mix well. Add bread and crab meat; mix well. Fold in egg whites. Shape into small cakes. Brown crab cakes on both sides in butter in skillet over medium heat. Yield: 4 servings.

BAKED SEA SCALLOPS WITH FETA CHEESE

1 tablespoon olive oil
1 1/2 pounds sea scallops
Salt and pepper to taste
1 red bell pepper
2 green bell peppers
3/4 cup sliced onion
2 teaspoons crushed
garlic
2 tablespoons olive oil
1 1/2 cups plum tomatoes,
coarsely chopped

16 pitted black Greek
olives
1 teaspoon oregano
1/2 teaspoon fennel seed
1/2 cup dry white wine
1/8 teaspoon hot red
pepper flakes
Salt and pepper to taste
6 ounces feta cheese,
crumbled

Brush 4 individual ovenproof dishes with 1 tablespoon olive oil. Place 6 ounces scallops in each dish; sprinkle with salt and pepper. Slice red and green peppers into thin 1 1/2-inch strips. Sauté red and green peppers, onion and garlic in 2 tablespoons oil in skillet over medium-high heat until tender-crisp. Add tomatoes, olives, oregano, fennel, wine, pepper flakes, salt and pepper. Bring to a boil. Simmer for 5 minutes. Spoon tomato mixture over scallops. Sprinkle with cheese. Bake at 450 degrees for 15 to 20 minutes or until lightly browned. Yield: 4 servings.

BARBECUED SHRIMP

2 cups margarine
3 bay leaves
1/4 teaspoon black pepper
10 cloves of garlic, minced
10 to 20 drops of liquid smoke
2 tablespoons dried parsley
1 1/2 teaspoons chili powder
1/2 teaspoon salt
3/4 teaspoon red pepper
1 tablespoon paprika
1/4 cup white wine
1/4 cup lemon juice
1 tablespoon brown mustard
4 pounds unpeeled shrimp

Melt margarine in saucepan. Add next 9 seasonings, wine, lemon juice and brown mustard. Simmer for 10 to 15 minutes. discard bay leaves. Rinse shrimp; place in 10x15-inch baking pan. Pour sauce over shrimp. Bake at 350 degrees for 20 to 25 minutes or until shrimp are pink, stirring occasionally. Yield: 8 servings.

SHRIMP CREOLE

1 medium onion, chopped
1 medium green bell pepper, chopped
1/2 cup sliced fresh mushrooms
1 to 3 cloves of garlic, crushed
2 tablespoons melted butter
1 1/2 teaspoons sugar
1 16-ounce can stewed tomatoes
1 6-ounce can tomato paste
1 1/2 teaspoons Creole seasoning
1/2 teaspoon paprika
2 bay leaves
1 1/2 pounds fresh shrimp, peeled
1/2 cup frozen green peas, thawed

Sauté onion, green pepper, mushrooms and garlic in butter in large skillet until tender. Stir in sugar, tomatoes, tomato paste, Creole seasoning, paprika and bay leaves. Bring to a boil, stirring frequently; reduce heat. Simmer for 20 minutes. Add shrimp and peas. Simmer for 10 minutes longer. Discard bay leaves. Serve over rice. Garnish with lemon slices. Yield: 4 servings.

SHRIMP CURRY VERDE

1½ pounds fresh spinach
1 cup loosely packed
 coriander leaves
½ cup loosely packed
 parsley leaves
1 tablespoon oil
2 teaspoons fennel seed
4 teaspoons cumin seed
2 teaspoons whole
 mustard seed
6 cloves of garlic, crushed
1 small onion, chopped
1 medium green bell
 pepper, cut into 1-inch
 pieces

1 large Granny Smith
 apple, cut into 1-inch
 pieces
2 pounds fresh peeled
 shrimp
¾ cup fish or chicken
 broth
1 tablespoon grated fresh
 ginger
5 ounces frozen baby
 lima beans, thawed
1½ teaspoons hot pepper
 sauce
2 tablespoons lime juice
Salt to taste

Stem and wash spinach, coriander and parsley leaves. Place in food processor container. Process with steel blade until finely chopped. Combine oil, fennel seed, cumin seed and mustard seed in 5-quart microwave-safe bowl. Microwave, uncovered, on High for 3 minutes. Stir in garlic and onion. Microwave, tightly covered, on High for 4 minutes. Stir in green pepper and apple. Microwave, tightly covered, on High for 3 minutes. Push vegetables to center of bowl. Place half the spinach mixture around edge of bowl. Arrange shrimp in single layer over spinach; cover with remaining spinach. Pour broth over spinach. Microwave, covered, on High for 6 minutes. Stir in ginger; scatter lima beans over top. Microwave, tightly covered, on High for 3 minutes. Stir in pepper sauce, lime juice and salt. Yield: 8 servings.

A Lion Tip

Barbecue shrimp in a sauce of melted margarine, lemon juice, Italian salad dressing and pepper. Bake at 350 degrees for 30 minutes and then chill until serving time.

CURRIED JUMBO SHRIMP WITH APPLES

2 Golden Delicious apples
24 jumbo shrimp, peeled
2 tablespoons curry
  powder
Salt to taste
1 tablespoon butter
1 tablespoon finely
  chopped shallots

1/4 cup sour cream
1/2 cup plain yogurt
1 tablespoon chopped
  fresh mint or 1 teaspoon
  dried mint

Peel apples; cut into 1/2-inch cubes. Combine apples, shrimp, curry powder and salt in bowl; stir well. Melt butter in nonstick skillet large enough to place shrimp in single layer. Add shrimp mixture and shallots. Cook over high heat for 3 minutes, stirring constantly. Add sour cream and yogurt; mix well. Bring to a boil. Cook for 3 minutes longer, stirring constantly. Add mint. Serve immediately over rice.
Yield: 4 servings.

STIR-FRIED SHRIMP AND VEGETABLES

1 tablespoon dry white
  wine
1 tablespoon water
2 teaspoons reduced-
  sodium soy sauce
1 teaspoon oil
1 pound fresh shrimp,
  peeled
1 teaspoon oil
1/2 cup minced green
  onions
1 teaspoon minced fresh
  gingerroot
1 cup sliced celery

1 medium red bell
  pepper, seeded, cut into
  strips
1 teaspoon minced garlic
Dash of red pepper
1 teaspoon sugar
2 tablespoons water
1/2 teaspoon instant
  chicken bouillon
1 tablespoon cornstarch
1 8-ounce can water
  chestnuts, drained
1/4 teaspoon salt
3 cups hot cooked rice

Combine wine, 1 tablespoon water, soy sauce and 1 teaspoon oil in shallow dish. Add shrimp; toss gently. Coat large skillet or wok with nonstick cooking spray and 1 teaspoon oil. Heat skillet until hot. Add green onions, gingerroot, celery, red pepper strips, garlic, red pepper and sugar. Stir-fry for 1 minute. Add shrimp mixture. Add mixture of remaining 2 tablespoons water, bouillon and cornstarch. Stir-fry for 8 minutes or until shrimp are pink. Add water chestnuts. Stir-fry for 1 minute. Place in serving dish. Garnish with green onion fans. Yield: 6 servings.

SZECHUAN SPICY SHRIMP

2 tablespoons salt
1 pound unpeeled shrimp
2 teaspoons coarse salt
1 teaspoon Szechuan
  peppercorns, roasted,
  ground
1 teaspoon sugar
2 tablespoons finely
  chopped garlic

2 teaspoons minced fresh
  gingerroot
2 tablespoons finely
  chopped scallions
2 fresh red chili peppers,
  coarsely chopped
2 cups peanut oil for
  frying

Fill large bowl with cold water; add 1 tablespoon salt. Wash shrimp in salted water; drain. Repeat, using fresh water and remaining tablespoon salt. Rinse shrimp under cold running water; remove legs. Pat dry with paper towels. Combine coarse salt, peppercorns, sugar, garlic, ginger, scallions, and red chilies in small bowl. Heat wok over high heat; add oil. Heat oil until hot and smoking. Add shrimp. Deep-fry for 1 minute or until shrimp are pink. Remove with slotted spoon; drain well. Pour off all but 1½ tablespoons oil. Heat reserved 1½ tablespoons oil in wok. Add peppercorn mixture. Stir-fry for 10 seconds. Return shrimp to wok. Stir-fry over high heat for 2 minutes or until spices have thoroughly coated outer shells of shrimp. Yield: 2 to 4 servings.

 A Lion Tip

After peeling shrimp, remove the odor from hands by rubbing them with fresh parsley.

SHRIMP KABOBS WITH YOGURT SAUCE

1½ pounds peeled fresh
 shrimp
⅓ cup red wine vinegar
1 small onion, grated
2 cloves of garlic, minced
2 tablespoons chopped
 cilantro
¼ teaspoon pepper

⅛ teaspoon ground
 coriander
⅛ teaspoon cloves
¼ teaspoon cumin
Dash each of cardamom,
 nutmeg and cinnamon
Salt to taste
Yogurt Sauce

Combine shrimp with vinegar, onion, garlic, cilantro, pepper, coriander, cloves, cumin, cardamon, nutmeg, cinnamon and salt in bowl. Marinate for 2 hours. Thread shrimp onto skewers; use 1 or 2 for appetizers or 4 or more for entrée. Grill over medium-hot coals until pink. Serve with Yogurt Sauce. Yield: 6 servings.

Yogurt Sauce

½ cup yogurt
1 clove of garlic, minced

1 teaspoon lemon juice
Salt and pepper to taste

Combine yogurt, garlic, lemon juice, salt and pepper in bowl; mix well.

SHRIMP AND CORN PASTA

1½ pounds shrimp,
 cooked, peeled
1 pound macaroni
1 cup frozen whole kernel
 corn
4 ounces bacon
3 tablespoons olive oil

¾ cup chopped celery
2 or 3 tomatoes, seeded,
 coarsely chopped
3 tablespoons chopped
 parsley
Salt and pepper to taste

Cook pasta in 4 to 5 quarts boiling water for 8 minutes or until tender; drain. Cook corn using package directions for 2 minutes; drain and rinse under cold water. Cook bacon in skillet until crisp; drain, reserving 1 teaspoon drippings. Sauté celery and tomatoes in reserved bacon drippings and olive oil in skillet until celery is tender-crisp. Add corn and shrimp. Cook for 1 minute, stirring constantly. Add pasta, parsley, salt and pepper; toss to mix. Crumble bacon over top. Yield: 4 servings.

EGG DISHES

VEGETABLE CHEESE PIE

3/4 cup all-purpose flour
1/2 cup whole wheat flour
1/3 cup unsalted margarine, softened
3 to 4 tablespoons ice water
1 medium zucchini, sliced
2 cups thinly sliced carrots
1 onion, sliced
1/2 cup dry Sherry
3/4 teaspoon thyme

1/4 teaspoon basil
1/4 teaspoon garlic powder
1/8 teaspoon pepper
3 ounces reduced-cholesterol Muenster cheese, sliced
3 ounces reduced-cholesterol provolone cheese, sliced
1 egg, beaten
1/4 cup skim milk

Mix flours in bowl. Cut in margarine until crumbly. Add water 1 tablespoon at a time, mixing with fork to form ball. Roll into 11-inch circle on lightly floured surface. Fit into 9-inch tart pan; trim edges. Place pie crust weights in shell. Bake at 400 degrees for 10 minutes; remove weights. Bake for 5 minutes longer. Cool. Spray large skillet with nonstick cooking spray. Heat over medium heat. Add zucchini, carrots and onions. Sauté for 5 minutes. Add Sherry, thyme, basil, garlic powder and pepper. Cook, covered, for 10 minutes or until vegetables are tender. Spoon into pie shell. Top with cheeses. Beat egg with milk in bowl. Pour over cheeses. Bake at 400 degrees for 10 minutes. Reduce temperature to 350 degrees. Bake for 15 to 20 minutes longer or until cheese is golden brown. Cool slightly before cutting. Yield: 6 servings.

A Lion Tip

Add chopped meats, vegetables, herbs and cheese to omelets for a quick main dish.

OVERNIGHT BRUNCH CASSEROLE

4 cups hot water
1   16-ounce package
    hashed brown potatoes
5 eggs, beaten
1/2 cup cottage cheese
1 cup shredded Cheddar
    cheese

3 tablespoons minced
    onion
1 teaspoon salt
Dash of pepper
6 slices crisp-fried bacon,
    crumbled

Pour water over hashed browns in bowl. Let stand for 10 minutes; drain. Combine eggs, cottage cheese, Cheddar cheese, onion, salt and pepper in bowl; mix well. Stir in potatoes. Pour into greased 10-inch baking dish. Chill overnight. Place in cold oven. Bake, uncovered, at 350 degrees for 35 minutes or until potatoes are tender and eggs are set. May sprinkle buttered croutons over top before baking if desired. Yield: 6 servings.

CHEDDAR BROCCOLI QUICHE

8 ounces Cheddar
    cheese, shredded
2 tablespoons flour
1 cup milk
3 eggs, beaten
1/2 teaspoon salt
Pepper to taste

Nutmeg to taste
1   10-ounce package
    frozen chopped broccoli,
    cooked, drained
1 unbaked deep-dish pie
    shell

Combine cheese and flour in bowl; add milk, eggs, salt, pepper, nutmeg and broccoli; mix well. Pour into pastry-lined pie plate. Bake at 350 degrees for 1 hour or until set. Yield: 6 servings.

CORN AND CRAB QUICHE

1 cup crab meat
4 eggs, beaten
1 cup half and half
1 cup scraped fresh corn

Salt and pepper to taste
Hot pepper sauce to taste
1 partially baked deep-
dish pie shell

Combine crab meat, eggs, half and half, corn, salt, pepper and hot pepper sauce in bowl; mix well. Pour into pie shell. Bake at 425 degrees for 10 minutes. Reduce temperature to 300 degrees. Bake for 40 minutes or until set. Yield: 6 servings.

QUICHE LORRAINE

1 8-count can
refrigerator crescent
rolls
1 egg, beaten
1 cup evaporated milk
1/2 teaspoon salt
1/2 teaspoon
Worcestershire sauce

1 cup shredded Swiss
cheese
3 1/2-ounce can French-
fried onions
Crisp-fried bacon,
crumbled

Separate dough; press into 9-inch round baking pan to form shell. Combine egg, milk, salt, Worcestershire sauce and cheese in bowl; mix well. Sprinkle half the onions over shell. Pour in egg mixture. Top with remaining onions. Sprinkle bacon over top. Bake at 325 degrees for 45 minutes to 1 hour or until knife inserted near center comes out clean. Yield: 6 servings.

A Lion Tip

To speed up baking time for quiche, bake pie shell for several minutes before filling.

CHEESE PIE IN POTATO CRUST

3 medium potatoes
1 onion, grated
1 egg, beaten
1¼ cups shredded Swiss
  or Cheddar cheese
3 eggs
1¼ cups milk

3 tablespoons chopped
  parsley
¼ teaspoon pepper
¼ teaspoon dry mustard
½ teaspoon paprika
¼ teaspoon cayenne
  pepper

Scrub and shred unpeeled potatoes. Drain potatoes and onion; place in bowl. Add 1 beaten egg; mix well. Butter bottom and side of 9-inch pie plate. Press potato mixture into pie plate to form shell; sprinkle with cheese. Combine remaining 3 eggs, milk, parsley, pepper, dry mustard, paprika and cayenne pepper in bowl; mix well. Pour over cheese. Bake at 375 degrees for 45 minutes or until knife inserted near center comes out clean. Yield: 6 servings.

SAINT STEPHEN'S SCRAMBLED EGGS

6 tomatoes
2 tablespoons oil
6 eggs
6 tablespoons whipping
  cream

Salt and pepper to taste
¼ cup butter
6 large onions, sliced
2 tablespoons oil

Slice tops from tomatoes; scoop out centers, leaving shell. Heat 2 tablespoons oil in skillet. Cook tomatoes cut side down for 1 to 2 minutes; turn over carefully. Cook for 2 minutes. Place tomato shells in greased baking dish. Keep warm in 250-degree oven. Beat eggs and whipping cream in bowl. Add salt and pepper; mix well. Melt butter in large skillet. Add eggs. Scramble eggs just until set; eggs should be moist. Stuff tomato shells with eggs; place in oven to keep warm. Fry onions in remaining 2 tablespoons oil in skillet until lightly browned. Place on serving dish; arrange stuffed tomatoes in center. Serve hot. Yield: 6 servings.

Soups
and
Stews

SOUPS

ONION AND SPINACH BISQUE

1¹/₂ cups chopped sweet
Spanish onions
2 tablespoons butter or
margarine
1   10-ounce package
frozen chopped spinach,
thawed

1¹/₂ cups chicken broth
1 cup milk
Nutmeg, salt and pepper
to taste
Sour cream or yogurt

Sauté onions in butter in saucepan over medium heat for 10 minutes or until golden brown. Reserve ¹/₃ of the onions. Combine remaining onions with undrained spinach and broth in blender container; process until smooth. Combine with milk in saucepan. Heat to the simmering point. Season with nutmeg, salt and pepper. Ladle into warm soup bowls or mugs. Sprinkle with reserved onions. Top with sour cream or yogurt if desired. Yield: 4 servings.

CHILI CON CARNE

2 pounds ground beef
3 medium onions,
chopped
1 medium green bell
pepper, chopped
2 cloves of garlic, minced
1   28-ounce can tomatoes
1   6-ounce can tomato
paste

1 tablespoon sugar
¹/₄ cup chili powder
1 teaspoon oregano
1¹/₂ teaspoons salt
2   16-ounce cans red
kidney beans
Corn chips

Brown ground beef with onions, green pepper and garlic in 5-quart saucepan for 15 minutes, stirring until ground beef is crumbly. Stir in undrained tomatoes, tomato paste, sugar, chili powder, oregano and salt. Bring to a boil over high heat, stirring to break up tomatoes; reduce heat. Simmer, covered, for 45 minutes, stirring occasionally. Add undrained beans. Cook until heated through. Ladle into serving bowls. Serve with corn chips. Yield: 12 servings.

FIREHOUSE CHILI

2¹/₂ pounds ground chuck
3 onions, finely chopped
3   8-ounce cans tomato
   sauce
4 cups water
1 tablespoon vinegar
1 teaspoon cinnamon
1 tablespoon allspice
7 teaspoons chili powder

3 dried chili peppers,
   crushed
3 bay leaves
1 teaspoon garlic salt
1 teaspoon cayenne
   pepper
1¹/₂ pounds spaghetti
Shredded Colby cheese

Brown ground chuck with onions in large saucepan, stirring until ground beef is crumbly. Add tomato sauce, water, vinegar, cinnamon, allspice, chili powder, chili peppers, bay leaves, garlic salt and cayenne pepper; mix well. Simmer for 3 to 4 hours or to desired consistency. Remove bay leaves. Cook spaghetti using package directions. Serve chili over spaghetti. Garnish with cheese. Yield: 8 servings.

WHITE CHILI

1 pound dried Great
   Northern beans
4 cups defatted chicken
   stock
2 medium onions,
   coarsely chopped
3 cloves of garlic, finely
   chopped
1 teaspoon salt

¹/₂ cup canned chopped
   green chilies
2 teaspoons cumin
1¹/₂ teaspoons oregano
1 teaspoon coriander
¹/₄ teaspoon cloves
¹/₄ teaspoon cayenne
   pepper

Soak beans in water to cover in saucepan overnight; drain. Combine with chicken stock, 2 cups onions, garlic and salt in large heavy saucepan. Bring to a boil; reduce heat. Simmer, covered, for 2 hours or until beans are tender, adding additional stock if needed for desired consistency. Add remaining onions, green chilies, cumin, oregano, coriander, cloves and cayenne pepper; mix well. Cook, covered, for 30 minutes. Ladle into serving bowls. May crush oregano in mortar with pestle. Yield: 8 servings.

TURKEY CHILI

1 onion, chopped
2 tablespoons oil
2 cloves of garlic,
  chopped
2 tablespoons chili
  powder
1¹/₂ teaspoons cumin
1 8-ounce can tomato
  sauce

1 16-ounce can plum
  tomatoes
1 teaspoon salt
¹/₄ teaspoon pepper
3 cups chopped cooked
  turkey dark meat
1 16-ounce can black
  beans, drained, rinsed

Sauté onions in oil in large saucepan for 2 minutes or until tender. Add garlic, chili powder and cumin. Cook for 1 minute. Stir in tomato sauce, undrained tomatoes, salt and pepper; crush tomatoes against side of saucepan with spoon. Bring to a boil over medium-high heat; reduce heat. Simmer, covered, for 20 minutes. Add turkey and beans. Simmer for 5 minutes or until heated through. Adjust seasonings if necessary. Serve with shredded cheese, sour cream, chopped scallions and chili peppers if desired. Yield: 4 servings.

BOSTON-STYLE FISH CHOWDER

4 slices bacon, chopped
¹/₂ cup chopped celery
1 5-ounce package
  scalloped potatoes with
  savory onion seasoning
3¹/₂ cups milk
2 cups water

2 tablespoons chopped
  parsley
¹/₄ teaspoon freshly
  ground pepper
1 pound white fish filets,
  cut into 1-inch pieces

Cook bacon in large saucepan until crisp. Remove and drain bacon, reserving drippings. Sauté celery in drippings in saucepan until tender-crisp. Add scalloped potatoes with seasoning mix, milk, water, parsley and pepper; mix well. Bring to a boil; reduce heat. Simmer, covered, for 15 minutes, stirring occasionally. Add fish. Cook for 10 minutes longer or until fish flakes easily, stirring occasionally. Ladle into serving bowls. Sprinkle with bacon. Yield: 4 servings.

NEW ENGLAND CLAM CHOWDER

1 quart clams
3 cups water
4 to 5 ounces salt pork,
  chopped
1 medium onion, chopped
3 medium potatoes,
  peeled, chopped

3 tablespoons butter
1³/₄ cups half and half
Salt and freshly ground
  pepper to taste

Bring undrained clams and water to a boil in 3½-quart saucepan. Drain, reserving broth. Mince clam necks and tougher portions; chop remaining clams. Brown salt pork lightly in saucepan. Add onions. Sauté until tender but not brown. Add reserved clam broth and potatoes. Cook until potatoes are tender. Stir in butter, half and half, clams, salt and pepper. Heat just to serving temperature; do not boil. Ladle into warmed serving bowls. Serve with crackers. Yield: 6 to 8 servings.

HEARTY CORN AND BACON CHOWDER

3 slices bacon, chopped
2 cups milk
1 envelope chicken
  noodle soup mix with
  chopped chicken

1   17-ounce can cream-
  style corn
Freshly ground pepper to
  taste

Cook bacon in medium saucepan until crisp; remove bacon to drain. Add milk, soup mix and corn to saucepan; mix well. Bring to a boil; reduce heat. Simmer for 10 minutes, stirring occasionally. Stir in bacon. Cook until heated through. Ladle into serving bowls. Serve with freshly ground pepper. Yield: 4 servings.

A Lion Tip

Make a quick soup by adding a rounded table-spoon of shredded crab meat for each serving to hot chicken broth and seasoning lightly with soy sauce or dry Sherry and chopped green onion.

HEARTY CORN AND CLAM CHOWDER

4 slices bacon
1/2 cup chopped onion
2 tablespoons flour
1/8 to 1/4 teaspoon pepper
3 cups milk
2 medium potatoes,
  peeled, chopped

1 9-ounce package
  frozen corn
2 7-ounce cans minced
  clams
Salt to taste

Fry bacon in heavy saucepan until crisp. Remove and drain bacon, reserving drippings. Add onion to drippings in saucepan. Sauté until tender. Stir in flour and pepper. Cook until smooth and bubbly. Stir in milk gradually. Cook until thickened, stirring constantly. Add potatoes and corn. Bring to a boil; reduce heat. Simmer for 15 minutes or until potatoes are tender, stirring frequently. Stir in undrained clams. Cook until heated through. Add salt to taste. Ladle into soup bowls. Crumble bacon over servings. Yield: 4 servings.

CORN AND MORE CHOWDER

1 8-inch zucchini
1 medium onion, chopped
1 tablespoon chopped
  fresh parsley
2 tablespoons chopped
  fresh basil
3 tablespoons butter
7 teaspoons flour
Several dashes of hot
  pepper sauce
1/2 teaspoon salt

1 1/2 cups chicken broth
1/2 teaspoon fresh lemon
  juice
1 cup fresh or frozen corn
1 pint light cream
2 medium tomatoes,
  peeled, seeded, chopped
1/2 cup shredded Cheddar
  cheese
2 tablespoons Parmesan
  cheese

Cut zucchini into halves lengthwise; slice. Sauté zucchini, onion, parsley and basil in butter in saucepan for 6 minutes. Stir in flour, hot sauce and salt. Cook over low heat for several minutes, stirring constantly; remove from heat. Stir in chicken broth and lemon juice gradually. Heat to the boiling point, stirring constantly. Add corn. Bring to a boil; reduce heat. Simmer, covered, for 5 minutes. Stir in cream and tomatoes. Heat to serving temperature. Stir in cheeses until melted. Ladle into serving bowls. Garnish with parsley. Yield: 6 servings.

CORNED BEEF AND CABBAGE CHOWDER

1/2 cup chopped leek
2 cloves of garlic, minced
1/4 cup corn oil margarine
3 cups chicken broth
2 cups shredded cabbage
1 cup thinly sliced carrot
4 ounces cooked corned
  beef, chopped

2 tablespoons cornstarch
1 cup milk
1 to 2 tablespoons
  prepared horseradish
Salt and pepper to taste

Sauté leek and garlic in margarine in 4-quart saucepan for 3 minutes or until tender. Add chicken broth, cabbage, carrot and corned beef; cover. Bring to a boil; reduce heat. Simmer for 15 minutes or until vegetables are tender, stirring occasionally. Blend cornstarch and milk in small bowl. Stir in horseradish, salt and pepper. Add to chowder; mix well. Bring to a boil over medium heat, stirring constantly. Cook for 1 minute longer. Ladle into serving bowls. Yield: 6 servings.

SOUTHERN CHICKEN GUMBO

1/2 cup chopped onion
3 cups chopped cooked
  chicken
3 tablespoons margarine
  or butter
1   16-ounce can stewed
  tomatoes, chopped
2 1/2 cups chicken broth

3 cups sliced fresh okra
1/4 cup chopped parsley
2 tablespoons lemon juice
1 clove of garlic, minced
3 drops of hot pepper
  sauce
1/8 teaspoon pepper
1/4 cup uncooked rice

Sauté onion and chicken in margarine in large saucepan over medium heat until onion is tender. Add tomatoes, chicken broth, okra, parsley, lemon juice, garlic, pepper sauce and pepper; mix well. Bring to a boil. Stir in rice; reduce heat. Simmer for 20 minutes or until rice is tender. May use 12-ounce package frozen cooked chicken cubes and 10-ounce package frozen okra if desired. Yield: 4 servings.

PICANTE BLACK BEAN SOUP

4 slices bacon, chopped
1 onion, chopped
1 clove of garlic, minced
2   15-ounce cans black
   beans
1   14-ounce can beef
   broth

1¼ cups water
¾ cup picante sauce
½ teaspoon oregano
½ to 1 teaspoon salt
Sour cream

Cook bacon in 3-quart saucepan until crisp. Remove to paper towel with slotted spoon, reserving drippings. Add onion and garlic to drippings in saucepan. Sauté for 3 minutes. Add undrained beans, beef broth, water, picante sauce, oregano and salt. Simmer, covered, for 20 minutes. Ladle into soup bowls. Top with sour cream. Sprinkle with bacon. Serve with additional picante sauce. Yield: 6 servings.

BROCCOLI CHEESE SOUP

½ cup chopped onion
¼ cup margarine
¼ cup flour
3 cups water
6 cups chopped fresh
   broccoli

4 chicken bouillon cubes
1 teaspoon
   Worcestershire sauce
3 cups shredded Cheddar
   cheese
1 pint half and half

Sauté onion in margarine in large saucepan. Stir in flour. Add water gradually. Add broccoli, bouillon and Worcestershire sauce. Cook over medium heat for 10 minutes or until broccoli is tender, stirring occasionally. Add cheese and half and half. Heat just to serving temperature; do not boil. Ladle into serving bowls. May substitute 2 thawed and drained 10-ounce packages frozen chopped broccoli for fresh broccoli if preferred. Yield: 6 servings.

A Lion Tip

Nuts make an interesting garnish for soups. Try peanuts, almonds, cashews or roasted soybeans.

FRENCH CABBAGE SOUP

1½ pounds lean beef
  chuck roast or steak
2 tablespoons oil
2 onions, chopped
1 clove of garlic, minced
1 jalapeño pepper,
  seeded, chopped
1 16-ounce can
  tomatoes, chopped
3 cups water

2 tablespoons instant
  beef bouillon
3 tablespoons brown
  sugar
1 tablespoon lemon juice
4 potatoes, peeled, cut
  into 1-inch pieces
1 2-pound sweet Texas
  cabbage, coarsely sliced
Salt and pepper to taste

Cut beef into 1-inch pieces. Brown on all sides in oil in heavy saucepan; drain. Add onions, garlic and jalapeño pepper. Cook until onions are tender but not brown. Add undrained tomatoes and next 4 ingredients. Simmer, covered, for 1 hour or until beef is almost tender. Add potatoes. Cook for 10 minutes. Add cabbage. Bring to a boil; reduce heat. Simmer for 4 to 10 minutes or until potatoes are tender. Season to taste. Ladle into serving bowls. Yield: 6 servings.

CANADIAN CHEESE SOUP

1 carrot, finely chopped
1 stalk celery, finely
  chopped
3 scallions or green
  onions with stems, thinly
  sliced
½ cup unbleached flour
10 tablespoons unsalted
  butter
3½ cups chicken stock
  or broth
1½ cups light ale

1 cup freshly grated
  Parmesan cheese
12 ounces Cheddar
  cheese, shredded
5 ounces white Cheddar
  cheese, shredded
1 teaspoon white pepper
2 tablespoons chopped
  green bell pepper
2 tablespoons chopped
  red bell pepper

Cook carrot, celery, scallions and flour in butter in heavy saucepan over low heat for 5 minutes. Add chicken stock and ale. Bring to a simmer, stirring constantly. Whisk in cheeses and white pepper gradually. Simmer for 7 minutes; do not boil. Serve from soup tureen. Sprinkle with green and red peppers. Yield: 6 servings.

LENTIL MINESTRONE

1 medium onion, chopped
1 clove of garlic, minced
1 tablespoon oil
1 medium carrot, sliced
1 stalk celery, sliced
2/3 cup lentils
1/2 10-ounce package
 thawed frozen chopped
 spinach
4 cups water
4 teaspoons instant
 vegetable, chicken or
 beef bouillon
Hot pepper sauce to taste
1 teaspoon oregano
1/4 teaspoon thyme
1 8-ounce can tomatoes
1/2 cup uncooked medium
 pasta such as bows,
 elbows or wagon wheels

Sauté onion and garlic in hot oil in large heavy saucepan over medium-high heat for 5 minutes or until tender. Add carrot, celery, lentils, spinach, water, bouillon, hot pepper sauce, oregano and thyme; mix well. Bring to a boil; reduce heat. Simmer, covered, for 15 minutes. Stir in tomatoes and pasta. Simmer for 10 to 15 minutes longer or just until pasta is tender. Ladle into serving bowls. Yield: 4 servings.

CREAM OF MUSHROOM SOUP

3 tablespoons unbleached
 flour
1 tablespoon corn oil
 margarine
3/4 cup defatted chicken
 stock
1/2 cup skim milk
Garlic powder to taste
1/4 teaspoon salt
Freshly ground pepper to
 taste
1/4 cup finely chopped
 canned or cooked
 mushrooms
Water, chicken stock or
 skim milk

Blend flour into margarine in skillet. Cook over medium heat for 1 minute, stirring constantly; do not brown. Whisk in 3/4 cup chicken stock and 1/2 cup skim milk. Bring to a boil over medium heat, whisking constantly. Add garlic powder, salt, pepper and mushrooms. Cook for 1 minute. Add enough water or additional stock or milk to dilute to desired consistency. Heat to serving temperature. Yield: 2 to 4 servings.

MUSHROOM AND BARLEY SOUP

1 onion, minced
2 shallots, minced
3 cups unsalted defatted
   chicken stock
1/2 cup uncooked barley

1 bay leaf
1/4 teaspoon nutmeg
1 tablespoon thyme
White pepper to taste
4 cups sliced mushrooms

Combine onion and shallots in saucepan sprayed with nonstick cooking spray. Cover saucepan with buttered waxed paper and lid. Cook over low heat until tender. Add chicken stock, barley, bay leaf, nutmeg, thyme and white pepper. Bring to a boil; reduce heat. Simmer for 30 minutes. Add mushrooms. Simmer for 5 minutes. Remove bay leaf. Ladle into soup bowls. Yield: 6 servings.

SPEEDY NACHO SOUP

2 16-ounce cans stewed
   tomatoes, chopped
1 15-ounce can red
   kidney or pinto beans,
   rinsed, drained
1 cup picante sauce
1 cup chicken broth

1/2 teaspoon cumin
16 ounces process
   cheese, cubed
Coarsely crushed tortilla
   chips
Avocado slices
Chopped cilantro

Combine undrained tomatoes, beans, picante sauce, chicken broth and cumin in saucepan. Bring to a boil; reduce heat. Stir in cheese. Cook over medium heat until cheese is melted and soup is of serving temperature, stirring frequently; do not boil. Ladle into serving bowls. Top with tortilla chips, avocado slices and cilantro. Yield: 8 servings.

A Lion Tip

Freeze leftover rice, barley or bulgur in ice cube trays, then store in plastic bags in the freezer. Add a few cubes to thicken and enrich soups.

ONION SOUP WITH GARLIC CROUTONS

2 pounds onions, sliced
  into rings
2 teaspoons oil
3 tablespoons butter
3/4 teaspoon sugar
1/2 teaspoon salt
2 tablespoons flour
5 cups beef broth
1/3 cup dry white wine
6 slices Italian bread,
  crusts trimmed, cubed

1 large clove of garlic,
  crushed
1/4 teaspoon salt
3 tablespoons olive oil
Freshly ground pepper to
  taste
1/2 cup shredded Swiss
  cheese
1/4 cup Parmesan cheese

Cook onions in 2 teaspoons hot oil and butter in large saucepan for 15 minutes, stirring occasionally. Add sugar and 1/2 teaspoon salt. Cook over medium-low heat for 30 minutes or until onions are brown. Sprinkle with flour. Cook for 1 minute. Stir in beef broth and wine. Bring to a boil; reduce heat. Simmer, loosely covered, for 30 minutes. Spread bread cubes on ungreased baking sheet. Brush with mixture of garlic, 1/4 teaspoon salt and 3 tablespoons olive oil. Bake at 350 degrees for 10 to 15 minutes or until light brown. Season soup with pepper. Ladle into oven-proof serving bowls. Sprinkle with croutons. Top with mixture of cheeses. Bake at 425 degrees for 5 minutes or until cheese melts. Yield: 6 servings.

HARVEST ONION SOUP

2 large sweet Spanish
  onions, sliced into rings
1 cup chopped celery
4 ounces mushrooms,
  cut into halves
2 tablespoons oil

1 28-ounce can tomatoes
2 10-ounce cans beef
  broth
1/2 teaspoon basil
1/2 teaspoon salt
1/4 teaspoon pepper

Sauté onions, celery and mushrooms in oil in large saucepan until tender. Add undrained tomatoes, beef broth, basil, salt and pepper. Simmer, covered, for 1 hour. Ladle into serving bowls. Serve with parsley and Parmesan cheese. May substitute 2 pounds chopped fresh tomatoes for canned tomatoes if preferred. Yield: 6 to 8 servings.

CREAMY ONION AND POTATO SOUP

2 medium sweet Spanish
  onions, sliced into rings
3 stalks celery, thinly
  sliced
2 tablespoons butter or
  margarine

3 large potatoes, peeled,
  sliced 1/4 inch thick
5 cups vegetable or
  chicken stock
2 teaspoons dillweed
Salt and pepper to taste

Sauté onions and celery in butter in large saucepan over medium heat for 2 to 3 minutes. Add potatoes, stock and dillweed; cover. Bring to a boil; reduce heat. Simmer for 20 minutes or until potatoes are tender. Process half the soup in blender or food processor until smooth. Stir into soup in saucepan. Add salt and pepper. Heat to serving temperature. Yield: 6 to 8 servings.

RED ONION SOUP

5 large red onions, sliced
  into rings
1 teaspoon salt
3 tablespoons butter
3/4 cup red wine
5 cups chicken stock
3/4 teaspoon thyme
Salt and pepper to taste

4 slices French or Italian
  bread
1 tablespoon butter,
  softened
1/3 cup shredded Swiss
  cheese
1 tablespoon chopped
  fresh parsley

Cook onions with salt in 3 tablespoons butter in large saucepan over medium-low heat for 30 to 40 minutes. Add wine. Cook for 5 minutes. Add chicken stock and thyme. Cook for 15 minutes. Season with salt and pepper. Butter bread on both sides with remaining 1 tablespoon butter. Place on baking sheet; sprinkle with cheese. Bake at 350 degrees for 10 minutes or until golden brown. Stir parsley into soup. Ladle into serving bowls. Top with cheese toast. Yield: 4 servings.

A Lion Tip

Before adding vegetables to soup, sauté them in oil. This seals in their flavor and keeps them firm.

PASTA SOUP ITALIANO

2 ounces uncooked
  whole grain pasta
2 cups chopped peeled
  plum tomatoes
4 cups unsalted defatted
  chicken stock

1 onion, thinly sliced
2 tablespoons Parmesan
  cheese
1 teaspoon basil
1 teaspoon oregano
1/4 teaspoon white pepper

Cook pasta *al dente* in boiling water in saucepan; drain. Rinse in cold water; drain well. Bring tomatoes and chicken stock to a boil in saucepan. Add onion, cheese, basil, oregano and white pepper. Bring to a boil. Cook, covered, for 10 minutes. Stir in pasta just before serving. Yield: 4 servings.

PEA SOUP

1 pound dried green split
  peas
8 cups water
2 stalks celery, coarsely
  chopped
2 large carrots, coarsely
  chopped
1 medium onion, coarsely
  chopped

1 teaspoon thyme
1 teaspoon salt
1/2 teaspoon pepper
1/4 cup chopped fresh
  parsley
4 cups hot cooked brown
  rice

Combine peas, water, celery, carrots, onion, thyme, salt and pepper in heavy saucepan. Bring to a boil; reduce heat. Simmer, covered, for 45 to 60 minutes or until peas are tender. Stir in parsley. Simmer, uncovered, for 45 to 60 minutes or until thickened to desired consistency. Ladle into serving bowls. Top each serving with 1/2 cup rice. Yield: 8 servings.

 ### *A Lion Tip*

Heat leftover vegetables and meat with milk and add snappy cheese for a quick and tasty soup.

OVEN-BAKED SPLIT PEA SOUP

1 pound dried split peas
8 cups water or chicken
  broth
1½ cups sliced celery
1½ cups chopped onions
2 teaspoons thyme

1 teaspoon celery seed
1 bay leaf
Salt and pepper to taste
1 pound kielbasa, sliced,
  cooked

Combine peas, water, celery, onions, thyme, celery seed, bay leaf, salt and pepper in baking dish. Bake, covered, at 350 degrees for 2 hours. Add sausage. Bake for 10 minutes longer. Remove bay leaf. Yield: 8 servings.

EASY CREAM OF POTATO SOUP

½ cup sliced green
  onions
2 tablespoons oil
1 10-ounce can chicken
  broth

1 cup instant potato
  flakes
1 13-ounce can
  evaporated milk
Pepper to taste

Sauté green onions in oil in medium saucepan over medium heat. Add broth. Bring to a boil; remove from heat. Whisk in potato flakes, evaporated milk and pepper. Ladle into serving bowls. Garnish with additional chopped green onions. May serve chilled if preferred. Purée soup in blender or food processor and dilute to desired consistency with a small amount of additional chicken broth or water. Yield: 4 servings.

POTATO SOUP

3 cups chopped potatoes
1 cup water
½ cup chopped celery
½ cup chopped onion
1 teaspoon parsley flakes
½ teaspoon salt

Dash of pepper
1 chicken bouillon cube
1½ cups milk
2 teaspoons flour
1 cup shredded Cheddar
  cheese

Combine potatoes, water, celery, onion, parsley flakes, salt and pepper in saucepan. Cook for 20 minutes. Combine bouillon, milk and flour in bowl. Add to soup. Stir in cheese until melted. Ladle into serving bowls. Yield: 4 servings.

FIESTA TOMATO SOUP

½ cup chopped onion
1 clove of garlic, minced
1 tablespoon oil
1 can tomato soup
1 10¾-ounce can
condensed chicken
broth

1½ soup cans water
Tortilla chips
½ cup shredded
Monterey Jack cheese
Lime slices

Sauté onion and garlic in oil in 2-quart saucepan over medium heat until tender. Stir in soup, chicken broth and water. Cook until heated through. Sprinkle tortilla chips into serving bowls. Ladle soup into bowls. Top with shredded cheese; garnish with lime slices. Yield: 4 servings.

PILGRIMS LANDING SOUP

2 potatoes, finely
chopped
2 large onions, finely
chopped
½ cup finely chopped
carrot
½ cup finely chopped
celery
3 cups water

4 teaspoons instant
chicken bouillon
2 cups shredded Cheddar
cheese
1 cup half and half
6 drops of hot red pepper
sauce
⅛ teaspoon nutmeg
¼ cup chopped parsley

Combine potatoes, onions, carrot and celery with water in 3-quart saucepan. Bring to a boil; reduce heat. Simmer, covered, until vegetables are tender. Stir in chicken bouillon, cheese, half and half, pepper sauce and nutmeg. Heat to serving temperature. Ladle into serving bowls. Sprinkle with parsley. Yield: 4 servings.

OLD-FASHIONED VEGETABLE SOUP

1 pound lean stew beef
1 package medium dried
  lima beans
4 quarts water
1 16-ounce can peas
2 16-ounce cans
  tomatoes
6 medium potatoes,
  chopped

1 large onion, chopped
6 carrots, chopped
5 stalks celery with tops,
  chopped
1/2 head small cabbage,
  chopped
1/3 cup uncooked barley
Salt and pepper to taste

Combine beef, lima beans and water in 8-quart stockpot. Cook over medium heat for 45 minutes. Add peas, tomatoes, potatoes, onion, carrots, celery and cabbage. Cook for 2 1/2 hours over low heat, stirring occasionally. Add barley. Simmer for 30 minutes, stirring frequently. Season to taste. Ladle into serving bowls. Yield: 15 servings.

VEGETABLE AND TORTELINI SOUP

1 large onion, coarsely
  chopped
2 cloves of garlic, minced
1 tablespoon olive oil
3 14-ounce cans beef
  broth
1 16-ounce can stewed
  tomatoes

1/2 to 3/4 cup picante sauce
1 teaspoon basil
1 7-ounce package dried
  cheese-filled tortelini
1 green bell pepper,
  chopped
1 cup Parmesan cheese

Sauté onion and garlic in olive oil for 6 minutes until tender. Add broth, tomatoes, picante sauce and basil. Bring to a boil. Stir in tortelini; reduce heat. Simmer, uncovered, for 15 minutes. Add green pepper. Simmer for 3 to 4 minutes or until tortelini is tender. Ladle into soup bowls; sprinkle with cheese. Yield: 8 servings.

BEEFY HARVEST SOUP

1 pound ½-inch thick
  beef round steak
1 tablespoon oil
2 cans cream of
  mushroom soup
1 soup can water
1 8-ounce can tomatoes,
  chopped
2 carrots, sliced ¼-inch
  thick

2 potatoes, peeled,
  cut into cubes
1 bay leaf
¼ teaspoon thyme
1 8-ounce can French-
  style green beans,
  drained

Freeze steak for 1 hour. Slice into thin 2-inch strips. Brown in hot oil in heavy 5-quart saucepan over high heat. Stir in soup and water gradually. Add undrained tomatoes, carrots, potatoes, bay leaf and thyme. Bring to a boil; reduce heat. Simmer, covered, for 25 minutes. Add green beans. Simmer for 5 minutes longer or until vegetables are tender, stirring occasionally. Remove bay leaf. Ladle into serving bowls. Yield: 6 servings.

CHICKEN POTPIE SOUP

3 cups chicken broth
2 cups milk
½ teaspoon thyme
2 bay leaves
8 ounces chicken breast
  filets
4 tablespoons butter or
  margarine
1⅓ cups sliced fresh
  mushrooms

1 10-ounce package
  frozen mixed vegetables,
  thawed
⅓ cup flour
½ teaspoon salt
¼ teaspoon pepper
¼ cup herb-flavored
  croutons

Bring chicken broth, milk, thyme and bay leaves to a simmer in medium saucepan. Remove from heat; let stand for 10 minutes. Wash chicken and pat dry. Cut into ½-inch pieces. Sauté in 2 tablespoons butter in deep skillet for 2 to 3 minutes. Add remaining 2 tablespoons butter, mushrooms and mixed vegetables. Sprinkle with flour; mix well. Stir in hot chicken broth mixture, salt and pepper. Cook until thickened and vegetables are tender, stirring constantly. Remove bay leaves. Ladle into soup bowls. Serve with croutons. Yield: 4 servings.

ORIENTAL CHICKEN SOUP

1 cup sliced fresh
mushrooms
2 cups shredded Chinese
cabbage
2 10³/₄-ounce cans
condensed chicken
broth

1¹/₂ broth cans water
1 tablespoon honey
1 tablespoon soy sauce
¹/₂ teaspoon hot pepper
sauce
1 cup cooked rice

Combine mushrooms, cabbage, chicken broth, water, honey, soy sauce and pepper sauce in 2-quart saucepan. Bring to a boil over medium heat; reduce heat. Simmer, covered, for 10 minutes or until vegetables are tender, stirring occasionally. Add rice. Cook until heated through. Ladle into soup bowls. Yield: 5 servings.

BEAN AND SAUSAGE SOUP

¹/₄ cup onion flakes
1 tablespoon garlic flakes
¹/₃ cup water
2 tablespoons oil
1 28-ounce can crushed
tomatoes in purée
1 19-ounce can white
kidney beans, drained,
rinsed

1 14-ounce can chicken
broth
8 ounces kielbasa, sliced
¹/₄ inch thick
2 bay leaves
¹/₂ teaspoon caraway seed

Combine onion flakes and garlic flakes with water in cup. Let stand for 10 minutes; drain. Sauté onion flakes and garlic flakes in oil in saucepan for 4 minutes. Add tomatoes, beans, chicken broth, sausage, bay leaves and caraway seed. Simmer for 15 to 20 minutes or to desired consistency. Remove bay leaves. Ladle into serving bowls. Yield: 6 servings.

A Lion Tip

Combine 2 kinds of canned soups such as asparagus and cream of chicken or tomato and clam chowder for a quick supper with a different taste.

HOME-STYLE SAUSAGE SOUP

8 ounces kielbasa or
smoked sausage
1 medium onion, coarsely
chopped
2 cups water
1 5-ounce package
homestyle rice mix with
chicken and vegetables

1 teaspoon flour
2 cups milk
1/3 cup chopped parsley

Slice sausage 1/2 inch thick; cut slices into quarters. Brown lightly in large saucepan for 5 minutes. Add onion. Cook for 2 minutes, stirring constantly. Stir in water and contents of rice and seasoning packets. Bring to a boil; reduce heat. Simmer, covered, for 8 minutes. Blend flour and 1/2 cup milk in cup. Stir into soup. Add remaining 1 1/2 cups milk. Bring to a boil, stirring constantly. Stir in parsley. Ladle into serving bowls. Yield: 6 servings.

SPICY TURKEY AND RICE SOUP

8 ounces ground fresh
turkey
1 egg white
1/4 cup mild salsa or
picante sauce
1/4 cup dry bread crumbs
1/4 teaspoon salt
1 14-ounce can chicken
broth

2 1/2 cups water
1/4 cup mild salsa or
picante sauce
1 4 1/2-ounce package
rice mix with green
beans and almonds
1/4 cup coarsely chopped
cilantro

Combine turkey, egg white, 1/4 cup salsa, bread crumbs and salt in bowl; mix well. Shape into 3/4-inch meatballs. Combine chicken broth, water, remaining 1/4 cup salsa and contents of rice and seasoning packets; reserve almond packet. Bring to a boil. Add meatballs; reduce heat. Simmer, covered, for 8 minutes. Ladle into serving bowls. Sprinkle with cilantro and reserved almonds. Yield: 6 servings.

TURKEY AND VEGETABLE SOUP

1 uncooked meaty turkey breast carcass
2 tablespoons safflower oil
7 cups chicken stock
4 cups water
2 cups fresh green beans, puréed
1/2 large red onion, thinly sliced
1 1/2 pounds potatoes, peeled, cut into cubes
4 large sprigs of parsley, chopped
1/2 teaspoon pepper
1 10-ounce package frozen peas

Chop turkey carcass into 4 or 5 pieces. Brown well in safflower oil in saucepan for 5 minutes. Stir in chicken stock and water. Simmer for 40 minutes, skimming occasionally. Strain, reserving turkey and broth. Remove meat from turkey bones and reserve; discard bones. Chop turkey meat; set aside. Combine green bean purée and onion with reserved broth in saucepan. Bring to a simmer over low heat. Add potatoes. Cook for 5 minutes. Add parsley, pepper and chopped turkey. Simmer until potatoes are tender. Add peas. Heat just to serving temperature. Yield: 8 servings.

HAM AND VEGETABLE SOUP

2 cups shredded cabbage
1 cup chopped onion
1/4 cup butter
1/4 cup flour
1/2 teaspoon paprika
1/2 teaspoon dry mustard
1/4 teaspoon dillweed
1 teaspoon seasoned salt
1/4 teaspoon salt
1/8 teaspoon pepper
2 1/2 cups milk
1 10 3/4-ounce can condensed chicken broth
1 10-ounce package frozen cauliflower, thawed, chopped
1 cup thinly sliced carrots
1 2 1/2-ounce package thinly sliced smoked ham, chopped

Sauté cabbage and onion in butter in 3-quart saucepan for 5 minutes or until tender. Stir in flour and next 6 ingredients. Stir in milk and broth gradually. Bring to a boil over medium heat, stirring constantly. Cook for 1 minute longer. Add cauliflower, carrots and ham. Simmer, covered, for 15 minutes or until vegetables are tender. Yield: 8 servings.

MICROWAVE BACON AND SPINACH SOUP

8 slices bacon
1 cup chopped potato
1 small onion, chopped
1/4 cup water
1 1/2 teaspoons instant
beef bouillon

3/4 cup water
1 cup milk
1/8 teaspoon nutmeg
1 5-ounce package
frozen chopped spinach,
thawed, drained

Microwave bacon between paper towels on High for 6 minutes or until crisp. Drain and crumble, reserving 1 tablespoon drippings. Combine reserved drippings, potato, onion, 1/4 cup water and bouillon in 2-quart glass bowl. Microwave, covered, on High for 4 minutes or until vegetables are tender. Combine with remaining 3/4 cup water, milk and nutmeg in food processor or blender. Process until smooth. Combine with spinach in glass bowl. Microwave on High for 2 minutes or until heated through. Ladle into serving bowls. Top with bacon and cracked pepper. Yield: 2 servings.

VEAL SHANK AND VEGETABLE SOUP

4 pounds veal shanks,
cross cut 1 1/2 inches thick
3 tablespoons olive oil
1 1/2 cups chopped onions
3 cloves of garlic, minced
1 16-ounce can whole
tomatoes
2 1/2 cups water
3/4 cup dry white wine
2 teaspoons basil

2 teaspoons thyme
1 teaspoon salt
1/2 teaspoon coarsely
ground pepper
3 medium carrots, thinly
sliced
1 16-ounce can white
beans, well drained
2 cups lightly packed
shredded fresh spinach

Brown veal shanks on all sides in olive oil in heavy saucepan. Remove veal shanks. Add onions and garlic. Sauté for 5 minutes, stirring to deglaze skillet. Stir in undrained tomatoes, breaking up with spoon. Add water, wine, basil, thyme, salt, pepper and veal shanks. Bring to a boil; reduce heat. Simmer, covered, for 1 hour or until veal is tender. Remove veal shanks. Cut veal from bones; discard bones. Add veal and carrots to soup. Cook, covered, for 5 minutes or until carrots are tender-crisp. Stir in beans and spinach. Cook until heated through. Ladle into serving bowls. Yield: 6 servings.

STEWS

PAUL LYNDE'S BAKED BEEF STEW

2 pounds beef stew meat in 1-inch cubes
1 16-ounce can diced carrots, drained
1 16-ounce can small whole onions, drained
1 16-ounce can whole tomatoes
1 16-ounce can peas, drained
1 16-ounce can cut green beans, drained
1 16-ounce can small whole potatoes, drained
1/2 can beef consommé
1/4 cup quick-cooking tapioca
1 tablespoon brown sugar
1/2 cup fine dry bread crumbs
1 bay leaf
1/2 cup dry white wine
Salt and pepper to taste

Combine stew beef, carrots, onions, tomatoes, peas, green beans with next 7 ingredients in large baking dish. Season with salt and pepper. Bake, covered, at 250 degrees for 6 to 7 hours or to desired consistency. Remove bay leaf. Yield: 8 to 10 servings.

SAVORY BEEF STEW

2 1/2 pounds beef stew meat in 1-inch cubes
3 large cloves of garlic, minced
3 tablespoons olive oil
1 cup dry red wine
2 cups water
1/3 cup tomato paste
1 tablespoon brown sugar
1 teaspoon cumin
2 bay leaves
3 cinnamon sticks
1 teaspoon salt
1 1/2 pounds white boiling onions
1/4 cup golden raisins
4 cups cooked orzo (rice-shaped pasta)

Brown beef with garlic in olive oil in heavy saucepan; drain. Add wine, water, tomato paste, brown sugar, cumin, bay leaves, cinnamon sticks and salt. Simmer, covered, for 1 1/2 hours. Add onions. Cook, covered, for 25 minutes. Stir in raisins. Cook for 5 minutes longer. Discard bay leaves and cinnamon sticks. Serve over pasta. Yield: 8 servings.

HEALTHFUL BEEF STEW

2 pounds lean beef
  chuck, cubed
1/4 cup flour
2 tablespoons oil
1 cup chopped onion
2 cloves of garlic, minced
2/3 cup chopped celery
1/2 cup dry red wine
1 cup water

1/4 cup chopped parsley
1/2 teaspoon rosemary
1/4 teaspoon oregano
1/4 teaspoon thyme
1/2 teaspoon pepper
2 cups chopped tomatoes
4 medium potatoes, cut
  into quarters
4 cups chopped carrots

Coat beef with flour. Brown on all sides in oil in large heavy saucepan. Add onion and garlic. Sauté until tender; drain. Add celery, wine, water, parsley, rosemary, oregano, thyme and pepper. Bring to a boil; reduce heat. Simmer, covered, for 1 hour. Stir in tomatoes, potatoes and carrots. Simmer for 45 minutes or until vegetables are tender. Ladle into serving bowls. Yield: 8 servings.

CHUCK WAGON STEW

3 1/2 pounds boneless
  beef chuck roast, 2 1/2 to
  3 inches thick
2 tablespoons shortening
  or oil
1 can cream of
  mushroom soup
1 can cream of onion
  soup

1/2 cup water
2 tablespoons prepared
  horseradish
1/4 teaspoon pepper
6 medium potatoes,
  peeled, cut into halves
2 cups diagonally sliced
  2-inch carrot pieces

Slice beef cross grain into 8 slices. Brown in shortening in saucepan over medium-high heat; drain. Stir in soups, water, horseradish and pepper. Bring to a boil; reduce heat. Simmer, covered, for 45 minutes. Add potatoes and carrots. Cook for 45 minutes or until beef and vegetables are tender, stirring frequently. Ladle into serving bowls. Yield: 8 servings.

SOUTHWESTERN BEEF AND LENTIL STEW

1 cup dried lentils
1 pound stew beef in
1-inch cubes
2 tablespoons flour
2 tablespoons oil
1/4 cup soy sauce

1   14 1/2-ounce can
stewed tomatoes
1 3/4 cups water
1 tablespoon chopped
jalapeño peppers

Rinse and drain lentils. Coat beef with flour. Brown beef in hot oil in heavy saucepan. Add lentils, soy sauce, tomatoes and water to beef; mix well. Simmer, covered, for 2 hours or until beef and lentils are tender, stirring occasionally. Stir in jalapeño peppers. Ladle into serving bowls. Garnish with sour cream, chopped cilantro and diced red bell pepper if desired. Yield: 6 servings.

QUICK BISTRO BEEF STEW WITH POTATO CRUST

4 medium potatoes
1 pound sirloin steak, cut
into 1-inch cubes
2 tablespoons oil
8 ounces fresh
mushrooms, sliced
1 onion, chopped
1 clove of garlic, minced
1 cup beef bouillon
1 tablespoon tomato
paste

1/2 teaspoon basil
1/2 teaspoon salt
1/4 teaspoon pepper
4 ounces fresh green
beans, cut into halves
1 cup sliced carrots
2 tablespoons cornstarch
1/4 cup dry red wine
1 tablespoon oil

Peel potatoes; slice 1/8 inch thick. Combine with water to cover in saucepan. Cook for 3 to 5 minutes or until tender-crisp. Drain; set aside. Brown steak in hot oil in Dutch oven, stirring frequently. Add mushrooms, onion, and garlic. Cook for 5 minutes. Stir in next 5 ingredients. Bring to a boil. Add green beans and carrots. Cook, covered, for 5 minutes. Combine cornstarch and wine in bowl; mix until smooth. Add to soup. Boil over medium heat for 1 minute, stirring constantly. Remove from heat. Arrange potatoes over top; brush with 1 tablespoon oil. Broil 3 to 5 inches from heat source for 10 minutes or until potatoes are browned. Yield: 4 servings.

BLUE STEW

1 pound carrots
1 pound onions
1 pound potatoes
1/4 cup butter
2 cloves of garlic,
  coarsely sliced

5 cups chicken stock
1/2 teaspoon coarsely
  ground pepper
1 medium cabbage
1 teaspoon salt
9 ounces blue cheese

Peel carrots, onions and potatoes; chop into 2-inch pieces. Melt butter in 4-quart saucepan. Add carrots, onions, potatoes and garlic. Cook, covered, over medium heat for 10 minutes. Add chicken stock and pepper. Simmer, covered, for 20 minutes. Slice cabbage into 8 portions. Add cabbage and salt to stew. Simmer for 10 minutes. Crumble 1 1/2 ounces blue cheese into each serving bowl. Ladle hot stew over cheese in bowls. Yield: 6 servings.

BUBBA'S BRUNSWICK STEW

1 3-pound chicken, cut up
1 3-pound pork roast
3 large onions, chopped
1 cup low-sodium
  chicken broth
2 16-ounce cans
  tomatoes
2 cups catsup
1 cup barbecue sauce
3 tablespoons pepper
2 cups 1-inch potato cubes

1 10-ounce package
  frozen lima beans
3 tablespoons salt
  substitute
2 tablespoons Tabasco
  sauce
1 tablespoon
  Worcestershire sauce
1 10-ounce package
  frozen corn

Cook chicken in water to cover in saucepan until tender. Bone and chop chicken. Cook pork in water in saucepan until tender. Let stand until cool. Chop pork. Cook onions in a small amount of chicken broth in stockpot until tender. Add remaining chicken broth. Bring to a boil. Add chicken, pork, tomatoes, catsup, barbecue sauce and pepper. Bring to a boil over medium-high heat; reduce heat. Simmer for 2 hours, stirring frequently. Add potatoes, lima beans, salt substitute, Tabasco sauce and Worcestershire sauce. Simmer for 1 hour. Add corn. Cook for 15 minutes. Ladle into serving bowls. May be frozen and reheated. Yield: 12 servings.

BRUNSWICK STEW FOR A CROWD

10 pounds beef
20 pounds pork
15 pounds chicken
25 pounds potatoes
15 pounds onions
12 cans tomatoes
1 small can pepper

2 small bottles of
  Worcestershire sauce
2 bottles of hot sauce
1 gallon catsup
10 cans cream-style corn
Salt to taste

Cook meats and chicken in water to cover in stockpot or pressure cooker using manufacturer's directions until very tender. Skin and bone meats and chicken, reserving meat and chicken broths. Cook potatoes and onions in reserved meat and chicken broths. Grind beef, pork, chicken, potatoes, and onions coarsely. Combine with tomatoes, pepper, Worcestershire sauce, hot sauce, catsup, corn and salt in large stockpots; mix well. Cook, uncovered, for 2 hours, stirring frequently. Serve with barbecued pork, coleslaw, pickles and bread. Yield: 150 servings.

MEATBALL STEW

1 pound ground beef
1 egg, beaten
1/2 cup soft bread crumbs
1/2 cup water
1 1/2 teaspoons salt
1/4 teaspoon pepper
1/8 teaspoon cloves
2 tablespoons oil
1   16-ounce can
  tomatoes, chopped

1/2 cup chopped onion
4 carrots, thinly sliced
1/2 cup water
1 clove of garlic
1/2 teaspoon salt
1   10-ounce package
  frozen green beans,
  thawed
1   12-ounce can whole
  kernel corn, drained

Combine ground beef, egg, crumbs, 1/2 cup water, 1 1/2 teaspoons salt, pepper and cloves in bowl; mix well. Shape into 1-inch balls. Brown on all sides in hot oil in saucepan; drain. Add tomatoes, onion, carrots and remaining 1/2 cup water. Mash garlic with remaining 1/2 teaspoon salt; add to stew. Bring to a boil. Add beans; reduce heat. Simmer, covered, for 10 minutes. Add corn. Cook for 5 minutes. Ladle into serving bowls. Yield: 6 servings.

PORK STEW

2 onions, chopped
1/2 teaspoon black pepper
1 teaspoon red pepper
2 tablespoons paprika
1 tablespoon salt
1 drop of garlic juice
4 ounces tomato sauce

1 4-pound pork
  tenderloin, cubed
3/4 cup red or white wine
1/3 cup flour
2 tablespoons sugar
3 tablespoons vinegar
1 cup sour cream

Cook onions in a small amount of water in saucepan until tender. Add next 6 ingredients; mix well. Add pork cubes and wine; mix well. Cook, covered, over medium-high heat for 15 minutes. Reduce heat to medium-low. Cook for 1 1/2 hours or until pork is tender. Mix flour, sugar, vinegar and sour cream in small bowl. Stir a small amount of hot broth into sour cream mixture; stir sour cream mixture into stew. Heat to serving temperature, stirring constantly; do not boil. Yield: 8 servings.

OYSTER STEW

1 1/2 pints fresh oysters
1/3 cup butter or margarine
3 cups milk

3/4 cup half and half
1 teaspoon salt
Dash of pepper

Cook undrained oysters in butter in 2-quart saucepan over low heat until edges curl, stirring constantly. Heat milk and half and half in 3-quart saucepan. Stir in salt, pepper and oysters. Ladle into serving bowls. Yield: 4 servings.

LA COSTA SPA CHICKEN STOCK

1 onion, unpeeled, halved
Uncooked chicken bones
2 cups chopped celery
  with tops

2 carrots, chopped
Fresh parsley
Garlic
2 bay leaves

Roast onion until dark brown. Rinse chicken bones. Place bones in stockpot with cold water to cover. Bring to a simmer over low heat; do not boil. Add remaining ingredients to stockpot. Simmer, uncovered, for 2 to 3 hours, skimming as necessary. Add water if needed for desired consistency. Strain broth. Chill in refrigerator overnight. Skim fat from surface. Ladle into small containers. Freeze until needed. Yield: 8 pints.

Vegetables
and
Side Dishes

VEGETABLES

ELEGANT ASPARAGUS AMANDINE

2 16-ounce cans
asparagus
1 can cream of
mushroom soup
1/2 teaspoon salt
1/4 teaspoon pepper

1 cup shredded cheese
1/4 cup margarine,
softened
1 cup bread crumbs
1/2 cup sliced almonds

Drain asparagus, reserving 1/2 cup liquid. Arrange in casserole. Combine reserved liquid, soup, salt and pepper in bowl; mix well. Pour over asparagus. Sprinkle with shredded cheese. Top with mixture of margarine and bread crumbs. Sprinkle with sliced almonds. Bake at 350 degrees for 30 minutes or until bubbly. Yield: 8 servings.

ASPARAGUS DELICIOUS

2 pounds fresh
asparagus spears,
drained
1 tablespoon butter
1 tablespoon flour
1/4 teaspoon salt

Dash of white pepper
1 cup milk
1/2 cup sharp cheese
1/4 cup slivered blanched
almonds, toasted

Rinse asparagus; trim ends. Cook in a small amount of water in saucepan; drain. Arrange hot asparagus in serving dish; keep warm. Melt butter in saucepan over low heat. Stir in flour, salt and white pepper. Add milk all at once. Bring to a boil over medium heat. Cook until thickened, stirring constantly. Cook for 2 minutes longer, stirring constantly. Add cheese; mix well. Pour over asparagus. Sprinkle with almonds. May substitute two 10-ounce packages frozen asparagus spears for fresh. Yield: 6 servings.

ASPARAGUS-CHEESE CASSEROLE

2 16-ounce cans
asparagus, drained
1 cup shredded American
Cheddar cheese

1 egg, beaten
1/2 cup milk
1/4 teaspoon salt
Dash of pepper

Layer asparagus and cheese 1/2 at a time in shallow baking dish. Combine egg, milk, salt and pepper in bowl; mix well. Pour over asparagus and cheese. Bake for 15 minutes at 350 degrees. Yield: 6 servings.

ASPARAGUS AND EGGS ON TOAST

1 14-ounce can
asparagus spears
Milk
2 tablespoons butter or
margarine

2 tablespoons flour
1/4 teaspoon salt
4 hard-boiled eggs, thinly
sliced
4 to 6 slices toast

Drain asparagus, reserving liquid. Add enough milk to reserved liquid to make 1 cup. Melt butter in saucepan over low heat. Stir in flour and salt. Add milk mixture; mix well. Cook over medium heat until bubbly and thickened, stirring constantly. Stir in asparagus and egg slices. Serve hot on toast.
Yield: 4 servings.

ASPARAGUS AU GRATIN

2 pounds fresh asparagus
6 tablespoons melted
butter
1/4 cup dry white wine

1/4 teaspoon salt
1/8 teaspoon pepper
2 ounces Parmesan
cheese

Rinse asparagus; trim ends. Tie in bunch. Stand upright in boiling salted water in deep saucepan. Steam for 15 minutes. Untie; place in baking dish. Pour mixture of melted butter and wine over asparagus. Sprinkle with salt, pepper and Parmesan cheese. Bake at 425 degrees for 10 minutes or until cheese is lightly browned. Yield: 4 servings.

ASPARAGUS WITH ALMOND-CHEESE SAUCE

1 cup butter cracker
  crumbs
1/2 cup butter or
  margarine
2 10-ounce cans
  asparagus, drained
1/2 cup slivered blanched
  almonds

1/4 cup butter
3 tablespoons flour
11/2 cups milk
1 8-ounce jar Old
  English cheese
1 cup butter cracker
  crumbs

Combine 1 cup cracker crumbs with 1/2 cup butter in bowl; mix well. Press half the crumb mixture over bottom and sides of buttered 11/2-quart casserole. Place asparagus over crumbs. Sprinkle with almonds. Melt remaining 1/4 cup butter in saucepan over medium heat. Blend in flour. Stir in milk. Cook until thickened, stirring constantly. Add cheese; stir until melted. Pour over asparagus. Sprinkle with remaining 1 cup cracker crumbs. Bake at 450 degrees for 15 minutes. Yield: 8 servings.

ASPARAGUS-A-RONI

11/4 cups elbow macaroni
3 tablespoons butter
4 to 5 tablespoons flour
21/2 cups milk
Salt and pepper to taste
1 small can sliced
  mushrooms, drained

8 ounces American
  cheese, shredded
2 cans asparagus spears,
  drained
1 small can chopped
  pimentos, drained
Buttered cracker crumbs

Cook macaroni using package directions; drain well. Melt butter in saucepan. Blend in flour. Stir in milk. Cook until thickened, stirring constantly. Add salt and pepper. Layer macaroni, mushrooms, cheese, asparagus, pimento and white sauce 1/2 at a time in buttered 21/2-quart baking dish. Top with buttered cracker crumbs. Bake at 350 degrees for 40 minutes. Yield: 10 to 12 servings.

MEAN BEANS

3 pounds ground beef
1 large onion, chopped
1 clove of garlic (optional)
Salt and pepper to taste
2 medium potatoes,
  peeled, chopped
1 large head cabbage,
  shredded

1 cup water
1 can corn
2 cans pinto beans
2 cans Great Northern
  beans

Brown ground beef with onion, garlic, salt and pepper in skillet, stirring until ground beef is crumbly; drain. Layer potatoes and cabbage in large saucepan. Add water, salt and pepper. Cook until tender. Add ground beef mixture, corn and beans. Simmer for 15 minutes. May chill and reheat to serve. Yield: 12 servings.

MIXED BAKED BEANS

8 ounces bacon
2 large onions, chopped
1   16-ounce can pork
  and beans, drained
1   16-ounce can kidney
  beans, drained
1   17-ounce can baby
  lima beans, drained

$1/3$ cup packed brown
  sugar
$1/4$ cup vinegar
1 cup catsup
1 tablespoon dry mustard
1 tablespoon
  Worcestershire sauce

Cook bacon in skillet until crisp; drain, reserving drippings. Crumble bacon. Sauté onions in reserved drippings in skillet until tender. Combine crumbled bacon, sautéed onions, beans, brown sugar, vinegar, catsup, dry mustard and Worcestershire sauce in large bowl; mix well. Spoon into lightly greased baking dish. Bake, covered, at 350 degrees for 45 minutes. May sprinkle with favorite grated cheese if desired. Yield: 8 to 10 servings.

GREEN BEANS WITH ALMONDS

2 cups frozen cut green
  beans
1/4 cup sliced celery

2 tablespoons slivered
  almonds
2 tablespoons margarine

Cook beans using package directions; drain. Sauté celery and almonds in margarine in skillet until celery is tender-crisp. Add beans; toss gently to mix. Yield: 4 servings.

BARBECUED GREEN BEANS

5 slices bacon
1/3 cup chopped onion
2 15-ounce cans green
  beans, drained

1/3 cup barbecue sauce
3 tablespoons catsup
1 clove of garlic, minced
Pinch of pepper

Cook bacon in large skillet until crisp; drain, reserving 1 tablespoon drippings. Crumble bacon. Sauté onion in reserved drippings in skillet until tender. Stir in crumbled bacon, green beans, barbecue sauce, catsup, minced garlic and pepper. Cook over medium heat until heated through. Yield: 6 servings.

CHEDDAR GREEN BEANS

2 16-ounce cans French-
  style green beans
1 cup shredded sharp
  Cheddar cheese
1 cup sour cream
1/4 cup butter, softened

1 teaspoon sugar
Dash of Tabasco sauce
Dash of salt
1/2 cup Italian bread
  crumbs

Combine beans, Cheddar cheese, sour cream, butter, sugar, Tabasco sauce and salt in large baking dish. Top with bread crumbs. Bake, covered, at 350 degrees for 20 minutes. Yield: 6 to 8 servings.

GREEN BEAN CASSEROLE CRISP

2 10-ounce packages
frozen French-style
green beans
2 tablespoons butter
2 tablespoons flour
1 cup sour cream

1/2 cup shredded sharp
Cheddar cheese
2 tablespoons melted
butter
1/2 to 1 cup crisp rice
cereal

Cook green beans using package directions until tender-crisp. Melt 2 tablespoons butter in small saucepan. Blend in flour; cool. Add to beans; mix well. Stir in sour cream and cheese. Spoon into shallow baking dish. Combine remaining 2 tablespoons butter with cereal in bowl; mix well. Sprinkle over casserole. Bake at 350 degrees until heated through and bubbly. Yield: 8 servings.

GERMAN-STYLE GREEN BEANS

4 slices bacon
1/3 cup chopped onion
1 16-ounce can French-style green beans

2 tablespoons sugar
1 tablespoon flour
3 tablespoons vinegar

Cook bacon in medium skillet until crisp; drain, reserving drippings. Crumble bacon. Sauté onion in reserved drippings in skillet until tender-crisp. Drain beans, reserving 1/3 cup liquid. Combine reserved liquid, sugar, flour and vinegar with sautéed onion in skillet; mix well. Cook until smooth and thickened, stirring constantly. Stir in beans. Cook until heated through. Top with crumbled bacon. Yield: 3 to 4 servings.

A Lion Tip

A few drops of liquid smoke give a "cook-out" flavor to bean dishes.

GREEN BEAN DELIGHT

2   16-ounce cans French-
style green beans,
drained
2 cans cream of
mushroom soup
1 cup chopped celery
1 cup chopped green bell
pepper
1 cup chopped onion
5 or 6 black olives,
sliced
3/4 cup crushed potato
chips
1/4 cup slivered almonds
5 or 6 pimento-stuffed
olives, sliced

Layer beans, mushroom soup, celery, green pepper and onion 1/2 at a time in greased 2-quart casserole. Top with layer of black olives, potato chips, almonds and stuffed olives. Bake at 325 degrees for 35 to 40 minutes or until heated through. Yield: 8 servings.

GREEN BEANS WITH CELERY AND BACON SAUCE

2   10-ounce packages
frozen green beans
4 slices bacon
1/4 cup chopped onion
1 can cream of celery
soup
1/3 cup milk

Cook beans using package directions; drain. Cook bacon in skillet until crisp; drain, reserving 2 tablespoons drippings. Crumble bacon. Sauté onion in reserved drippings in skillet until tender. Stir in soup and milk. Add beans. Cook over medium heat until heated through, stirring occasionally. Top with crumbled bacon. Yield: 4 servings.

A Lion Tip

Add your favorite dry salad dressing mix to white sauce to give a different flavor to green beans.

GREEN BEANS WITH CHEESE

2 10-ounce packages
  frozen green beans
4 slices bacon
1 onion, chopped
1 16-ounce can chopped
  tomatoes, drained

1/4 teaspoon salt
Dash of pepper
1/4 cup shredded Swiss
  cheese
1/4 cup Parmesan cheese

Cook beans using package directions; drain. Cook bacon in skillet until crisp; drain, reserving 1 tablespoon drippings. Crumble bacon. Cook onion in reserved drippings in skillet until tender, stirring occasionally. Combine beans, bacon, onion, tomatoes, salt and pepper in baking dish. Sprinkle with mixture of Swiss cheese and Parmesan cheese. Bake at 350 degrees for 15 to 20 minutes or until cheese is golden brown. May substitute 1 1/2 pounds fresh green beans and 4 large fresh tomatoes if preferred. Yield: 5 to 6 servings.

PARTY GREEN BEANS

3 10-ounce packages
  frozen French-style
  green beans
2 4-ounce cans
  mushrooms
1/2 cup butter
1/4 to 1/2 cup flour
2 cups warm milk
1 cup half and half
12 ounces shredded
  sharp cheese

2 teaspoons soy sauce
1 teaspoon salt
1 teaspoon MSG
1/8 teaspoon Tabasco
  sauce
1 5-ounce can sliced
  water chestnuts, drained
1/2 cup toasted slivered
  almonds

Cook green beans using package directions; drain. Sauté mushrooms in butter in skillet. Stir in flour. Cook until smooth, stirring frequently. Place mushroom mixture, milk and half and half in double boiler; mix well. Stir in cheese, soy sauce, salt, MSG and Tabasco sauce. Simmer until cheese is melted. Stir in beans and water chestnuts. Pour into 1 1/2-quart casserole. Sprinkle with almonds. Bake at 375 degrees for 20 minutes. Yield: 8 to 10 servings.

SOUR CREAM GREEN BEANS

6 tablespoons minced
  onion
3 tablespoons melted
  butter
3 tablespoons flour
2¼ teaspoons sugar

1 tablespoon salt
2¼ cups sour cream
1 tablespoon vinegar
9 cups cooked green
  beans

Sauté onion in butter in skillet until clear. Add flour, sugar, salt and sour cream; mix well. Cook over low heat until thickened, stirring constantly. Stir in vinegar. Pour over hot beans in casserole. Yield: 12 servings.

GREEN BEANS WITH ALMOND SAUCE

1 16-ounce can French-
  style green beans
¼ cup slivered almonds

¼ cup butter
¼ teaspoon salt
2 teaspoons lemon juice

Cook beans over medium heat until heated through; drain. Place in casserole. Sauté almonds in butter in skillet until golden brown. Stir in salt and lemon juice. Pour over beans. Yield: 4 servings.

GREEN BEANS WITH WATER CHESTNUTS

2 16-ounce cans whole
  green beans
1 8-ounce can sliced
  water chestnuts

2 cans cream of
  mushroom soup
2 cans French-fried onion
  rings

Combine beans and water chestnuts in casserole; mix well. Cover with soup; top with onion rings. Bake at 300 degrees for 20 to 30 minutes or until onion rings are golden brown. Yield: 6 to 8 servings.

A Lion Tip

Cook vegetables in the least amount of water possible to preserve both nutrients and flavor.

ZIPPY GREEN BEAN CASSEROLE

3 16-ounce cans cut
  green beans
2 cloves of garlic
1/4 cup margarine
1/4 cup flour
1 cup milk

1 can cream of
  mushroom soup
8 ounces process
  cheese, shredded
1 tablespoon chili powder

Combine undrained beans with garlic in saucepan. Cook for 20 minutes. Drain, discarding garlic. Melt margarine in saucepan. Blend in flour. Stir in milk. Cook until thickened, stirring constantly. Add soup, cheese and chili powder; stir until cheese melts. Combine with green beans in greased baking dish. Bake at 300 degrees for 30 minutes. Yield: 8 servings.

TASTY LIMAS

1 pound dry lima beans
1 teaspoon salt
1 clove of garlic, minced
1/3 bottle of catsup

2 tablespoons brown
  sugar
1/2 teaspoon dry mustard
1/2 cup chopped onion

Rinse beans; drain. Combine beans, salt, garlic, catsup, brown sugar, dry mustard and onion in large saucepan; mix well. Add enough water to cover. Simmer, covered, for 3 to 4 hours or until tender. Yield: 8 to 10 servings.

BUTTERY LIMA BEANS

2 or 3 10-ounce packages
  frozen lima beans
3/4 cup butter
3/4 cup packed brown
  sugar

1 tablespoon dry mustard
1 tablespoon molasses
1 cup sour cream

Cook beans using package directions; drain. Stir in butter. Mix brown sugar and dry mustard; sprinkle over beans. Stir in molasses; mix well. Fold in sour cream. Spoon into large baking dish. Bake at 350 degrees for 45 minutes. Yield: 8 servings.

LIMA CASSEROLE

2　10-ounce packages
　frozen green lima beans
.　1 can chopped green
　chilies

1 can cream of
　mushroom soup
Shredded sharp Cheddar
　cheese

Cook beans using package directions; drain. Layer beans, green chilies, soup and cheese 1/2 at a time in baking dish. Bake at 375 degrees until cheese melts and casserole is bubbly. Yield: 6 to 8 servings.

LIMA BEANS WITH CHEESE

2　10-ounce packages
　frozen baby lima beans
1/4 cup flour
2 ounces Cheddar
　cheese, shredded
2 ounces Roquefort
　cheese, shredded

1　4-ounce can sliced
　mushrooms, drained
1 teaspoon salt
1/2 teaspoon paprika

Cook beans using package directions; drain, reserving 1 1/2 cups liquid. Combine flour with a small amount of water to make a paste. Stir into reserved liquid in saucepan. Stir in Cheddar cheese, Roquefort cheese, mushrooms, salt and paprika. Cook over low heat until smooth and thickened, stirring frequently. Add beans; mix well. Spoon into baking dish. Bake at 350 degrees until heated through. Yield: 4 to 5 servings.

A Lion Tip

Substitute crushed wheat germ for buttered crumbs for a delicious, nutritious and easy casserole topping. Crushed canned French-fried onions and crushed cereal also add a different taste and texture.

NAVY BEANS WITH SAUSAGE

1½ pounds small navy
  beans
1 large onion, minced
5 slices bacon, chopped

Salt to taste
1 pound mild sausage
Pepper to taste

Rinse beans; drain. Place in saucepan; add enough water to cover. Bring to a boil. Turn off heat. Let stand for 1 hour. Stir in onion, bacon and salt. Cook, covered, until tender, adding water if necessary. Brown sausage in skillet; drain. Stir into beans. Add pepper. Cook on low heat for 30 minutes to 1 hour longer. Serve with corn bread. Yield: 8 servings.

PINEAPPLE PORK AND BEANS

1 16-ounce can pork
  and beans
1 15-ounce can 3-bean
  salad, drained
⅓ cup barbecue sauce

1 8-ounce can crushed
  pineapple
1 tablespoon
  Worcestershire sauce

Combine all ingredients in baking dish; mix well. Bake at 350 degrees for 1 hour. Stir before serving. Yield: 8 servings.

QUICK RED BEANS AND RICE

1 pound Italian sausage
3 stalks celery, coarsely
  chopped
1 large onion, coarsely
  chopped
3 cloves of garlic, minced
2 cups New Orleans red
  beans
½ bean can (about) water

3 bay leaves
1 teaspoon pepper
½ teaspoon cumin
6 drops of Tabasco sauce
Cooked ham, cut into bite-
  sized pieces
Salt to taste
Cooked rice

Brown sausage in skillet; drain. Stir in celery, onion and garlic. Cook until celery is tender, stirring occasionally. Add beans; mix well. Stir in enough water to moisten. Add bay leaves, pepper, cumin, Tabasco sauce, ham and salt; mix well. Cook over low heat for 30 minutes. Remove bay leaves. Serve over rice. Yield: 8 servings.

HARVARD BEETS

1/2 cup sugar
1/2 cup vinegar
1 tablespoon cornstarch

1 medium can sliced or
diced beets, drained
1 tablespoon butter

Mix sugar, vinegar and cornstarch in saucepan. Cook over medium heat for 5 minutes or until mixture thickens and boils, stirring constantly. Add beets; mix gently. Let stand for 30 minutes. Bring to a boil. Stir in butter. Yield: 4 to 5 servings.

HONEY-GLAZED BEETS

1/4 cup honey
2 tablespoons sugar
1 tablespoon butter
1 tablespoon lemon juice
1 teaspoon
  Worcestershire sauce

1 teaspoon cider vinegar
1/4 teaspoon salt
1/8 teaspoon pepper
2 16-ounce cans whole
  beets, drained

Combine honey, sugar, butter, lemon juice, Worcestershire sauce, vinegar, salt and pepper in large skillet; mix well. Bring to a boil. Cook for 1 minute, stirring occasionally; reduce heat. Stir in beets. Simmer for 5 minutes or until beets are glazed and heated through, stirring occasionally. Spoon beets into serving dish. Spoon glaze over beets.
Yield: 4 to 6 servings.

SPICY ORANGE BEETS

2 pounds beets, peeled
1 tablespoon sugar
1/4 cup orange juice

1/8 teaspoon cloves
1 teaspoon salt
2 tablespoons butter

Shred beets or slice very thin with vegetable shredder. Combine with sugar, orange juice, cloves and salt in bowl; mix well. Spoon into 1 quart-baking dish. Dot with butter. Bake, covered, at 375 degrees for 1 hour or until beets are tender. Garnish with grated orange rind if desired. Yield: 6 servings.

ORANGE-GLAZED BEETS

1/4 cup butter
1/2 cup sugar
1/4 teaspoon salt
2 tablespoons grated
  orange rind
1/2 cup orange juice

1 teaspoon cider vinegar
1 tablespoon cornstarch
2 tablespoons water
3 cups chopped canned
  beets, drained

Melt butter in skillet over low heat. Stir in sugar, salt, orange rind, orange juice and vinegar. Add mixture of cornstarch and water; mix well. Cook until clear, stirring occasionally. Stir in beets. Simmer for 10 minutes. Yield: 6 to 8 servings.

SAVORY BEETS

1   16-ounce can sliced
  beets
1 onion, chopped
3 tablespoons margarine
  or butter

2 teaspoons sugar
1/2 teaspoon salt
1/2 teaspoon allspice
1 tablespoon
  Worcestershire sauce

Drain beets, reserving 1/4 cup liquid. Sauté onion in margarine in skillet until tender but not browned. Stir in reserved liquid, beets, sugar, salt, allspice and Worcestershire sauce. Cook until heated through, stirring occasionally. Yield: 4 servings.

 A Lion Tip

When cooking beets, leave 1 inch of stem to prevent bleeding. Serve beets in a Sour Cream Sauce made by heating 1/2 cup sour cream, 2 tablespoons mayonnaise, 2 teaspoons lemon juice and seasonings to taste.

BROCCOLI WITH MUSHROOM SOUP

1 16-ounce package
  frozen broccoli
1 onion, minced
1/4 cup butter
1 can cream of
  mushroom soup

1 8-ounce jar Cheez Whiz
2 cups cooked rice
1 egg, beaten
1/2 to 3/4 cup cracker
  crumbs
1/4 cup butter

Cook broccoli using package directions; drain. Sauté onion in 1/4 cup butter in skillet until tender; do not brown. Combine broccoli, sautéed onion, soup, Cheez Whiz, rice and egg in greased 9x13-inch baking dish. Top with mixture of cracker crumbs and remaining 1/4 cup butter. Bake at 350 degrees for 25 to 30 minutes or until bubbly. Yield: 12 to 15 servings.

BROCCOLI WITH RICE

1 10-ounce package
  frozen chopped broccoli
1 cup cooked rice
1 can cream of
  mushroom soup

1 onion, minced
1 8-ounce jar Cheez
  Whiz
1 can sliced water
  chestnuts

Cook broccoli using package directions; drain. Place in medium saucepan. Stir in rice, mushroom soup and onion. Cook over low heat until bubbly, stirring occasionally. Remove from heat. Stir in Cheez Whiz. Spoon into serving dish. Top with water chestnuts. Yield: 4 servings.

LEMON-GARLIC BROCCOLI

1 bunch fresh broccoli
1 clove of garlic, minced
2 tablespoons olive oil

Juice of 1/2 lemon
Salt and pepper to taste
1/4 cup Parmesan cheese

Cut tops off broccoli; divide into flowerets. Peel and slice stems. Place in boiling salted water in large saucepan. Cook for 8 minutes or until tender; drain. Combine garlic and olive oil in skillet. Cook over medium heat for 2 minutes or until fragrant, stirring occasionally. Add broccoli; toss. Stir in lemon juice, salt and pepper. Sprinkle with Parmesan cheese. Yield: 4 servings.

BROCCOLI AND NOODLES WITH SESAME SAUCE

8 ounces uncooked egg noodles
3 tablespoons Chinese sesame paste
5 tablespoons water
1 teaspoon minced garlic
1/2 teaspoon hot sesame oil
4 teaspoons reduced-sodium soy sauce
1 tablespoon red wine vinegar
2 cups cooked broccoli flowerets, drained
2 scallions, minced

Cook noodles using package directions; drain. Combine sesame paste and water in bowl; mix well. Stir in garlic, sesame oil, soy sauce and vinegar. Stir noodles into sesame mixture. Add broccoli flowerets; mix well. Cut broccoli and noodles into bite-sized pieces. Stir in scallions. Spoon into serving dish. May substitute unsalted peanut butter for sesame paste.
Yield: 2 servings.

BROCCOLI WITH WATER CHESTNUTS

1 10-ounce package frozen chopped broccoli
1 can sliced water chestnuts
1 can sliced mushrooms
2 teaspoons butter
1 can cream of celery soup
1/4 cup shredded cheese

Cook broccoli using package directions; drain. Sauté water chestnuts and mushrooms in butter in skillet until tender. Combine with broccoli and soup in baking dish; mix well. Top with cheese. Bake at 350 degrees for 15 minutes or until bubbly. Yield: Yield: 2 to 3 servings.

A Lion Tip

Chop unused broccoli stems in the food processor and store in a plastic bag in the freezer for use in soups and dips.

SAVORY BROCCOLI

2 10-ounce packages
  frozen chopped broccoli
1 can mushroom soup
1 cup shredded Cheddar
  cheese

1 cup mayonnaise
1 onion, minced
2 eggs, beaten
1 tablespoon savory
Bread crumbs

Cook broccoli using package directions; drain. Combine soup, cheese, mayonnaise, onion, eggs and savory in greased casserole; mix well. Stir in broccoli. Top with bread crumbs. Bake at 350 degrees for 45 minutes. Yield: 4 to 5 servings.

STIR-FRIED ORIENTAL BROCCOLI

2 tablespoons oil
3 cups chopped broccoli
  flowerets
1 small onion, thinly
  sliced
1/4 cup water
1 8-ounce can sliced
  bamboo shoots, drained

1 4-ounce jar whole
  mushrooms, drained
2 tablespoons slivered
  almonds
2 tablespoons soy sauce
1 tablespoon chopped
  pimento

Heat oil in large skillet or wok. Add broccoli and onion; stir to coat. Add water. Stir-fry over high heat for 3 to 5 minutes or until broccoli is tender-crisp. Add bamboo shoots, mushrooms, almonds, soy sauce and pimento. Stir-fry until heated through. Yield: 8 servings.

BRUSSELS SPROUTS WITH BACON

1 pound fresh Brussels
  sprouts

4 slices bacon
1/4 cup red wine vinegar

Trim Brussels sprouts. Cook in boiling salted water in saucepan for 10 minutes or until tender; drain. Cook bacon in skillet until crisp; drain, reserving 2 tablespoons drippings. Crumble bacon. Combine reserved drippings and vinegar in skillet. Cook for 1 minute over medium-high heat, scraping pan frequently. Stir in Brussels sprouts. Toss until heated through. Top with bacon crumbs. May substitute broccoli, cauliflower, spinach or green beans for Brussels sprouts. Yield: 4 servings.

CHINESE CABBAGE

1 head Chinese cabbage
1/2 cup oil

2 tablespoons soy sauce

Cut leaves and stems of cabbage into thin 2-inch long strips. Heat oil in large saucepan. Stir in cabbage. Bring to a boil. Cook for 5 minutes, stirring frequently. Add soy sauce; mix well. Simmer, covered, for 10 minutes. Yield: 4 to 6 servings.

FRENCH-FRIED CAULIFLOWER

1 cup flour
1/4 teaspoon salt
1 egg, slightly beaten
1 cup milk

1 tablespoon oil
1 large head cauliflower, chopped
Oil for deep frying

Combine flour and salt in bowl; mix well. Beat in egg, milk and oil with rotary beater until very smooth. Dip cauliflower pieces into batter with slotted spoon; drain. Deep-fry in 365 to 375-degree oil until tender and golden brown. May substitute okra for cauliflower. Yield: 4 servings.

CARROTS IN ORANGE JUICE

1 pound fresh carrots, thinly sliced
1/2 cup fresh orange juice
1 3/4 cups cold water
2 tablespoons sugar
1/2 teaspoon salt

1/2 cup boiling water
3 tablespoons butter, softened
1 tablespoon flour
Ground ginger to taste

Combine carrots, orange juice, cold water, sugar and salt in medium saucepan; mix well. Bring to a boil, stirring occasionally; skim. Cook until carrots are tender. Stir in boiling water. Blend butter, flour and ginger in small bowl. Stir into carrots. Cook for 2 minutes, stirring constantly.
Yield: 4 servings.

 A Lion Tip

It is easier to slice or shred carrots if you leave an inch or so of the green top to use as a handle.

CELERY WITH ORANGE SAUCE

2¹/₂ pounds celery
¹/₂ cup chopped fresh
orange sections
4¹/₂ teaspoons butter
1 tablespoon cornstarch

³/₄ cup orange juice
2 tablespoons brown
sugar
¹/₂ teaspoon salt
Pepper to taste

Trim celery base; cut celery diagonally into 1-inch pieces. Add to 2 inches boiling water in large saucepan. Simmer, covered, for 5 to 7 minutes or until tender-crisp; drain. Place in serving dish. Stir in orange sections; cover. Melt butter in small saucepan. Add cornstarch. Cook over low heat for 1 minute or until bubbly, stirring constantly. Stir in orange juice, brown sugar, salt and pepper. Cook for 3 to 4 minutes or until thickened, stirring constantly. Pour over celery mixture. Garnish with orange slices and celery leaves. May substitute one drained 11-ounce can mandarin oranges for fresh orange. Yield: 6 servings.

BAKED CORN AND PEAS

1 17-ounce can cream-
style corn
1 16-ounce can whole
kernel corn
1 8-ounce can peas

2 eggs, slightly beaten
¹/₃ cup bread crumbs
³/₄ cup sour cream
¹/₂ teaspoon salt
¹/₂ teaspoon pepper

Combine corn, peas, eggs, bread crumbs, sour cream, salt and pepper in greased casserole; mix well. Bake at 350 degrees for 40 minutes. Yield: 6 to 8 servings.

CORNY-CORN BREAD BAKE

1 can whole kernel corn,
drained
1 can cream-style corn,
drained

1 cup sour cream
¹/₂ cup melted butter
1 envelope Mexican
cornmeal

Combine corn, sour cream, butter and cornmeal in casserole. Bake at 350 degrees for 40 to 50 minutes or until set and golden brown. Yield: 6 to 8 servings.

PICNIC CORN

12 ears of fresh corn
8 cups water
8 cups milk

1 cup butter, softened
Salt and pepper to taste

Remove husks and silks from corn. Bring water and milk to a boil in large saucepan. Add butter, corn, salt and pepper. Cook for 10 to 15 minutes or until tender. Remove from heat; cover. Corn will stay warm for 1 hour. Yield: 12 servings.

EGGPLANT PARMIGIANA

3 tablespoons melted
  butter or margarine
1/2 cup crushed cornflakes
1/4 cup Parmesan cheese
1/2 teaspoon salt
Dash of pepper
1 small eggplant, peeled,
  cut into 3/4-inch thick
  pieces

1 egg, slightly beaten
1 8-ounce can tomato
  sauce
1/2 teaspoon oregano
1/2 teaspoon sugar
Dash of onion salt
2 1-ounce slices
  mozzarella cheese, cut
  int halves diagonally

Pour melted butter into 8x10-inch baking dish. Combine crushed cornflakes, Parmesan cheese, salt and pepper in bowl; mix well. Dip eggplant slices into egg. Coat with cornflake mixture. Arrange in prepared baking dish. Bake at 400 degrees for 20 minutes. Turn slices. Bake for 15 minutes longer. Bring tomato sauce, oregano, sugar and onion salt to a boil in small saucepan, stirring occasionally. Pour over eggplant. Top with mozzarella cheese slices. Bake for 3 minutes or until cheese is melted. Yield: 2 servings.

A Lion Tip

Male eggplants have fewer seeds and are less bitter than female. The grayish indentation on the blossom end of a male eggplant is round; it is oval or oblong on a female eggplant.

CRISPY BAKED EGGPLANT

1¹/₄ pound eggplant
1¹/₂ cups dried bread
  crumbs or cornmeal
1 teaspoon oregano

¹/₄ cup Parmesan cheese
2 tablespoons olive oil
2 eggs, slightly beaten

Peel eggplant if desired. Slice eggplant ¹/₂-inch thick, discarding stem. Combine bread crumbs, oregano and Parmesan cheese in bowl; mix well. Spread oil in baking pan. Dip eggplant slices into beaten eggs; drain. Coat with bread crumb mixture. Place in single layer in prepared baking pan. Bake at 425 degrees for 20 to 24 minutes or until tender-crisp, turning slices once. Yield: 4 to 6 servings.

STUFFED MUSHROOMS

1 to 2 containers fresh
  mushrooms
Mild bulk sausage
1   8-ounce can tomato
  sauce

1 tomato sauce can red
  wine

Clean mushrooms; remove and reserve stems. Stuff uncooked sausage into mushroom caps. Place sausage side up in electric skillet. Combine tomato sauce and wine in bowl. Pour over mushrooms. Add reserved stems. Simmer for 1 to 1¹/₂ hours. Yield: 6 to 12 servings.

A Lion Tip

Stuff 36 mushroom caps with a mixture of 16 ounces softened cream cheese, 1 can of crab meat, 1 teaspoon of lemon juice and garlic powder to taste. Sprinkle with cheese and bake the Crab-Stuffed Mushrooms at 350 degrees until cheese melts.

FRENCH-FRIED ONION RINGS

3 or 4 large Spanish or
  Bermuda onions
2 to 3 cups buttermilk or
  ice water
1 egg, beaten
1 teaspoon salt
1 1/2 teaspoons baking
  powder

2/3 cup water
1 cup flour
1 tablespoon salad oil
1 teaspoon lemon juice
1/4 teaspoon cayenne
  pepper
Oil for frying

Peel onions; slice 3/8-inch thick. Separate into rings. Soak onion rings in buttermilk in shallow pan for 30 minutes. Combine egg, salt, baking powder, water, flour, salad oil, lemon juice and cayenne pepper in bowl; mix well. Dip onion rings into batter. Fry in 375-degree oil until golden brown; drain. Yield: 6 to 8 servings.

CREAMY PEAS AND CORN MEDLEY

1 10-ounce package
  frozen peas in butter
  sauce
1 10-ounce package
  frozen corn niblets in
  butter sauce

1/3 cup sour cream
2 tablespoons minced
  green onions
1 tablespoon chopped
  pimento

Cook peas and corn using package directions. Combine sour cream, green onions and pimento in bowl; mix well. Stir in corn and peas. Yield: 4 to 6 servings.

BRAISED PEAS AND CUCUMBERS

3 cups fresh peas
1/2 cup butter
2 cups coarsely chopped
  cucumbers

Salt and pepper to taste

Braise peas in butter in skillet until tender. Remove from heat; stir in cucumbers. Add salt and pepper. Yield: 8 servings.

CREOLE BLACK-EYED PEAS

4 slices bacon
1 cup chopped onion
1 cup chopped green bell
  pepper
1 cup chopped celery
1 14-ounce can chopped
  tomatoes, drained

1 16-ounce can black-
  eyed peas, drained
2 to 3 teaspoons sugar
1 bay leaf

Cook bacon in skillet until crisp; drain, reserving drippings. Crumble bacon. Sauté onion, green pepper and celery in reserved drippings in skillet until tender. Stir in tomatoes, peas, sugar and bay leaf. Cook over low heat for 10 to 15 minutes or until heated through, stirring occasionally. Remove bay leaf. Top with crumbled bacon. Yield: 6 servings.

STUFFED GREEN PEPPERS

4 large green bell peppers
8 ounces ground beef
4 teaspoons shortening
1 tablespoon minced
  onion
1 teaspoon salt
1/4 teaspoon pepper

1 tablespoon meat sauce
1 cup cooked rice
1 1/4 cups chopped cooked
  tomatoes
1 tablespoon chili powder
1/3 cup bread crumbs

Remove stems and seeds from peppers. Place in saucepan with water to cover. Bring to a boil. Cook for 5 minutes; drain. Brown ground beef with shortening, onion, salt and pepper in skillet, stirring frequently; drain. Stir in meat sauce, rice, tomatoes and chili powder. Stuff peppers with ground beef mixture. Place upright in greased baking dish. Top with bread crumbs. Bake at 375 degrees for 35 minutes. Yield: 4 servings.

BAKED SLICED POTATOES

4 medium baking
  potatoes
1/3 cup melted margarine
1 teaspoon onion salt

1/2 teaspoon lemon pepper
2 tablespoons Parmesan
  cheese

Slice unpeeled potatoes 1/4 inch thick. Arrange in single layer in 10x15-inch baking pan. Combine margarine, onion salt and lemon pepper in bowl; mix well. Pour over potatoes; turn to coat well. Bake at 425 degrees for 15 minutes. Turn slices; sprinkle evenly with cheese. Bake for 15 minutes longer or until potatoes are slightly crisp and brown on edges.
Yield: 4 servings.

BISTRO POTATOES

1/4 cup butter or margarine
2 cups thinly sliced leeks
2 cloves of garlic, minced
1 pound cooked smoked
  ham, cubed
1 cup water
4 carrots, thinly sliced
1 teaspoon thyme
1/2 teaspoon sage
1/2 teaspoon marjoram

1/4 teaspoon pepper
1/8 teaspoon ground
  cloves
1 bay leaf
31/2 cups frozen hashed
  brown potatoes
1 15-ounce can kidney
  beans, drained
1 15-ounce can white
  beans, drained

Melt butter in large saucepan over medium heat. Stir in leeks and minced garlic. Cook for 5 minutes, stirring frequently. Add ham. Cook for 5 minutes longer, stirring occasionally. Add water, carrots, thyme, sage, marjoram, pepper, cloves and bay leaf. Cook, covered, for 10 minutes or until carrots are tender-crisp. Stir in potatoes and beans. Cook, uncovered, for 15 minutes or until liquid is absorbed, stirring occasionally. Remove bay leaf. Yield: 8 to 10 servings.

GERMAN-STYLE POTATOES

4 potatoes	1/2 teaspoon celery seed
6 to 8 slices bacon	1 1/2 teaspoons salt
1 onion, minced	1/4 teaspoon pepper
2 tablespoons flour	6 tablespoons vinegar
2 tablespoons sugar	2/3 cup water

Boil unpeeled potatoes in water to cover in medium saucepan until tender; drain. Cool. Peel; slice thinly. Cook bacon in skillet until crisp; drain, reserving drippings. Crumble bacon. Sauté onion in reserved drippings in skillet until tender. Stir in flour, sugar, celery seed, salt, pepper, vinegar and water. Cook over medium heat until thickened, stirring occasionally. Add potatoes and crumbled bacon; mix well. Yield: 4 servings.

NO-FUSS NATURAL HASHED BROWNS

2 unpeeled potatoes, coarsely chopped	1/2 cup chopped onion
	1/2 teaspoon fines herbes
1/2 tablespoon butter or margarine	2 tablespoons chopped parsley
1/2 tablespoon oil	Salt and pepper to taste

Rinse potatoes. Pat dry between paper towels. Heat butter and oil in nonstick skillet. Stir in potatoes, onion, and fines herbes. Cook over medium-high heat until potatoes are tender and golden brown, stirring occasionally. Add parsley, salt and pepper. Yield: 2 servings.

A Lion Tip

Use leftover vegetables in a cream sauce or cheese sauce as a topping for baked potatoes.

PARMESAN BAKED POTATOES

1/4 cup minced celery
1/4 cup melted margarine
1 teaspoon oregano
1/2 teaspoon salt

1/8 teaspoon garlic powder
1/8 teaspoon pepper
4 baking potatoes
Parmesan cheese

Sauté celery in margarine in skillet until tender. Stir in oregano, salt, garlic powder and pepper. Scrub potatoes. Place on foil squares. Cut diagonal slashes in potatoes 1/2 inch apart. Spread celery mixture over potatoes. Sprinkle with cheese. Wrap foil around potatoes. Bake at 375 degrees for 1 hour or until tender. Yield: 4 servings.

PLEATED POTATOES

6 medium potatoes
2 tablespoons melted margarine

2 tablespoons water
Chives, seasoned salt and pepper to taste

Slice potatoes crosswise at 1/4-inch intervals, slicing to but not through bottom. Place cut side up in greased shallow baking dish. Combine margarine, water, chives, seasoned salt and pepper in bowl; mix well. Brush over potatoes. Bake at 400 degrees for 1 hour or until tender, basting occasionally. Potatoes will fan out as they bake. Yield: 6 servings.

A Lion Tip

Cook small new potatoes in your Crock•Pot on Low for 8 to 10 hours. Serve them with dishes of sour cream, crumbled bacon, butter and chives.

CREAM CHEESE POTATOES

4 cups hot mashed
 potatoes
8 ounces cream cheese,
 softened
1/4 cup chopped pimento

1/3 cup minced onion
1 egg, beaten
1 teaspoon salt
Dash of pepper

Combine potatoes, cream cheese, pimento, onion, egg, salt and pepper in 1-quart casserole; mix well. Bake, covered, at 350 degrees for 30 minutes. Bake, uncovered, for 15 minutes longer. Yield: 6 servings.

POTATO BOATS

3/4 cup water
3 tablespoons margarine
 or butter
Dash of pepper
1/2 cup milk
1 1/2 cups instant potato
 flakes

1 egg yolk, beaten
1/4 cup Parmesan cheese
1 cup frozen peas, thawed
1 tablespoon margarine
 or butter
Paprika

Bring water, 3 tablespoons margarine and pepper to a boil in medium saucepan, stirring occasionally. Remove from heat. Stir in milk, potato flakes, egg yolk and cheese. Place 4 mounds of potato mixture on lightly greased baking sheet. Make indentation in each mound with back of spoon. Fill indentations with 1/4 cup peas. Dot peas with remaining 1 tablespoon margarine. Sprinkle potato edges with paprika. Bake at 350 degrees for 15 minutes or until heated through. May use ice cream scoop to form the potato mounds. Yield: 4 servings.

MUSHROOM SCALLOPED POTATOES

1 can cream of
mushroom soup
1/2 cup shredded
American cheese
1 4-ounce can chopped
mushrooms, drained
1/4 cup chopped pimento

1/2 teaspoon salt
1 5-ounce can
evaporated milk
4 cups thinly sliced
peeled potatoes
1/4 cup shredded
American cheese

Combine soup, 1/2 cup cheese, mushrooms, pimento and salt in large bowl; mix well. Stir in evaporated milk and potatoes gradually. Spoon into greased 1 1/2-quart baking dish. Top with remaining 1/4 cup cheese. Bake at 350 degrees for 1 hour or until potatoes are tender. Yield: 6 servings.

SCALLOPED POTATOES

1/4 cup butter or margarine
1/4 cup flour
1 teaspoon salt
1/4 to 1/2 teaspoon pepper
2 cups milk
4 potatoes, peeled, cut
into 1/8-inch thick pieces

2/3 cup coarsely chopped
onion
2 cups shredded Cheddar
cheese

Melt butter in 1-quart saucepan. Stir in flour, salt and pepper. Cook over medium heat for 1 minute, stirring occasionally. Beat in milk. Cook for 3 to 4 minutes or until smooth and thickened, stirring frequently. Pour 1/4 cup sauce in buttered 2-quart baking dish. Layer potatoes, onion, remaining sauce and cheese 1/2 at a time in prepared dish. Bake, covered with foil, at 350 degrees for 1 hour and 15 minutes or until potatoes are tender. Bake, uncovered, for 5 minutes longer. Yield: 6 servings.

TEXAS-STYLE POTATOES

1 2-pound package
  hashed brown potatoes
1/2 cup melted margarine
1 can cream of chicken
  soup

2 cups sour cream
1 cup chopped onion
8 ounces sharp Cheddar
  cheese, shredded

Combine potatoes, margarine, soup, sour cream and onion in large casserole; mix well. Cook, covered, at 350 degrees for 1 hour. Sprinkle with Cheddar cheese. Bake for 30 minutes longer. Yield: 8 servings.

TWICE-BAKED POTATOES

4 russet potatoes
1 cup cream-style cottage
  cheese
Salt and pepper to taste

2 tablespoons chopped
  chives
1/2 cup shredded Cheddar
  cheese

Scrub potatoes; prick with fork. Bake at 400 degrees for 1 hour or until tender. Remove top third of each potato. Scoop potato from skins, reserving skins. Mash potatoes until smooth. Cream cottage cheese in mixer bowl until light and fluffy. Add potatoes, salt, pepper and chives; mix well. Stir in Cheddar cheese. Spoon into reserved potato skins. Place on baking sheet. Bake at 425 degrees for 15 to 20 minutes or until lightly browned. Yield: 4 servings.

QUICK AND EASY RATATOUILLE

1 large onion, chopped
2 cloves of garlic, minced
2 tablespoons olive oil
1 eggplant, peeled,
  chopped
1/4 teaspoon basil

2 large zucchini, cut into
  bite-sized pieces
1 or 2 green bell peppers,
  chopped
3 to 6 tomatoes, chopped

Sauté onion and garlic in olive oil in skillet until tender-crisp. Stir in eggplant and basil. Cook, covered, over medium heat for 5 minutes, stirring occasionally. Add zucchini and green pepper. Cook, covered, for 5 minutes, stirring occasionally. Add tomatoes. Cook until heated through, stirring frequently. Yield: 6 to 8 servings.

SQUASH STUFFED WITH SPINACH PESTO

4 medium yellow squash
1 10-ounce package
   frozen chopped spinach
1/2 cup shredded low-fat
   mozzarella cheese
1/4 cup Parmesan cheese
1 clove of garlic, minced
2 tablespoons chopped
   onion

1 tablespoon pine nuts
1 teaspoon basil
1/4 teaspoon marjoram
1/8 teaspoon white pepper
2 tablespoons Chablis
1 tablespoon water
1/3 cup low-fat yogurt
1/4 cup shredded low-fat
   mozzarella cheese

Pierce squash with fork. Arrange on paper towels in microwave oven. Microwave, uncovered, on High for 4 minutes, turning once. Let stand for 5 minutes. Halve squash lengthwise. Scoop out and discard pulp, leaving 1/2-inch shells. Place spinach in microwave-safe bowl. Microwave on High for 3 minutes or until thawed. Drain and press between layers of paper towels. Combine spinach, 1/2 cup mozzarella cheese, Parmesan cheese, minced garlic, onion, pine nuts, basil, marjoram, white pepper, Chablis, water and yogurt in blender container. Process at medium speed until smooth. Spoon spinach mixture into squash shells. Sprinkle with remaining 1/4 cup mozzarella cheese. Place in microwave-safe 8x12-inch baking dish. Microwave, loosely covered with plastic wrap, on High for 2 to 4 minutes or until heated through. Yield: 8 servings.

CHEESY SPINACH CRUMBLE FOR TWO

2 cups chopped cooked
   fresh spinach, drained
1/8 teaspoon nutmeg
1/8 teaspoon salt
Dash of pepper

1/2 cup cottage cheese
1/4 cup bread crumbs
1 tablespoon Parmesan
   cheese

Combine spinach, nutmeg, salt and pepper in medium casserole; mix well. Spoon cottage cheese over spinach. Sprinkle with mixture of bread crumbs and Parmesan cheese. Bake at 400 degrees for 15 minutes. Yield: 2 servings.

GOURMET BAKED SPINACH

2 tablespoons minced
  onion
3 tablespoons melted
  butter or margarine
3 tablespoons flour
2 cups milk
2 14-ounce cans
  spinach

3 hard-boiled eggs,
  minced
1 teaspoon salt
1/4 teaspoon pepper
1/2 cup crushed cornflakes
1/2 cup shredded
  American cheese
Paprika

Sauté onion in butter in heavy saucepan until tender. Add flour, stirring until smooth. Cook over medium heat for 1 minute, stirring constantly. Add milk gradually. Cook until thickened and bubbly, stirring constantly. Drain spinach; press between layers of paper towels until barely moist. Stir spinach, eggs, salt and pepper into sauce. Spoon into lightly greased 8-inch square baking dish. Mix cornflakes and cheese. Sprinkle over spinach. Sprinkle lightly with paprika. Bake at 375 degrees for 20 minutes. Yield: 6 servings.

SPINACH MADELEINE

2 10-ounce packages
  frozen chopped spinach
1/4 cup butter
2 tablespoons flour
2 tablespoons chopped
  onion
1/2 cup evaporated milk
1 6-ounce roll jalapeño
  cheese, chopped

1 teaspoon
  Worcestershire sauce
3/4 teaspoon celery salt
3/4 teaspoon garlic salt
1/2 teaspoon black pepper
Salt to taste
Red pepper to taste

Cook spinach using package directions; drain, reserving 1/2 cup liquid. Melt butter in saucepan over low heat. Stir in flour and onion. Cook until onion is tender, stirring frequently. Add evaporated milk and reserved spinach liquid. Stir in cheese and seasonings. Cook until smooth and thickened, stirring occasionally. Add spinach; mix well. Serve at once. May spoon spinach mixture into baking dish and sprinkle with buttered bread crumbs. Bake at 350 degrees for 20 to 30 minutes or until bubbly and heated through. May chill in refrigerator for 24 hours before baking to improve flavor. Yield: 4 to 6 servings.

SPINACH PARMESAN

3 pounds spinach
6 tablespoons Parmesan
  cheese
6 tablespoons minced
  onion
1/4 cup melted butter

6 tablespoons whipping
  cream
1/2 cup cracker crumbs
1 tablespoon melted
  butter

Combine spinach, Parmesan cheese, onion, 1/4 cup melted butter and whipping cream in shallow baking dish; mix well. Top with mixture of cracker crumbs and remaining 1 tablespoon butter. Bake at 350 degrees for 10 to 15 minutes or until crumbs are lightly browned. Yield: 12 servings.

BUTTERNUT SQUASH

2 cups mashed cooked
  butternut squash
1 cup mayonnaise
1 cup shredded cheese
1 cup chopped onion

1 cup cracker crumbs
1/2 cup butter or
  margarine, softened
1 cup chopped nuts

Combine squash, mayonnaise, cheese, onion, cracker crumbs, butter and nuts in large casserole; mix well. Bake at 350 degrees until heated through. Yield: 4 servings.

MEXICAN SQUASH PUFFS

2 cups cooked squash
1/4 cup minced onion
1/4 cup minced green bell
  pepper
2 tablespoons pancake
  mix

1 tablespoon paprika
1 egg
Salt and pepper to taste
Oil for deep frying

Combine squash, onion, green pepper, pancake mix, paprika, egg, salt and pepper in bowl; mix well. Drop by tablespoonfuls into 375-degree oil. Deep-fry until golden brown. Yield: 4 servings.

SQUASH CASSEROLE

1 pound squash, sliced
1 large onion, chopped
1 can cream of
  mushroom soup
3 hard-boiled eggs,
  chopped

½ cup butter, softened
16 saltine crackers,
  crushed
Salt and pepper to taste
2 cups shredded cheese

Combine squash and onion in water to cover in saucepan. Bring to a boil over medium heat. Cook until tender; drain and mash. Combine squash mixture, soup, eggs, butter, half the crushed crackers, salt and pepper in bowl; mix well. Layer half the squash mixture, half the cheese, remaining squash mixture and remaining cracker crumbs in baking dish. Top with remaining cheese. Bake at 350 degrees for 45 minutes. Yield: 4 servings.

COLBY SQUASH AU GRATIN

1 butternut squash
2 tablespoons butter or
  margarine
3 leeks, cut into ¼-inch
  thick slices
½ cup bread crumbs
½ teaspoon thyme

¼ teaspoon pepper
1 cup shredded Colby
  cheese
Salt to taste
⅓ cup milk
½ cup shredded Colby
  cheese

Cut squash into halves; remove seeds. Place cut side down in ½ inch boiling water in shallow baking pan. Bake, covered with foil, at 375 degrees for 35 to 45 minutes or until tender. Melt butter in large skillet. Add leeks. Cook over low heat for 5 to 8 minutes or until wilted, stirring occasionally. Stir in bread crumbs, thyme and pepper. Cook over medium heat for 3 minutes or until lightly browned, stirring occasionally. Remove from heat. Scoop squash from skins; discard skins. Add squash, 1 cup cheese and salt to skillet, stirring to coat. Spoon into greased 2-quart baking dish. Pour milk over squash. Sprinkle with remaining ½ cup cheese. Bake, covered with foil, at 375 degrees for 20 minutes. Bake, uncovered, at 425 degrees for 10 minutes longer. Yield: 6 servings.

CHEDDAR CHEESE SQUASH

4 slices bread, cut into cubes
2 tablespoons melted margarine
6 to 8 squash, chopped
1 small onion, chopped
Salt and pepper to taste
1 cup shredded Cheddar cheese
1 can cream of chicken soup
1 cup sour cream
1 can French-fried onions

Line baking dish with bread cubes. Pour melted margarine over crumbs. Bake at 350 degrees until lightly browned. Combine squash, onion, salt and pepper in medium saucepan. Add water to cover. Cook over medium heat until tender, stirring occasionally. Drain. Stir in cheese, soup and sour cream. Spoon over bread cubes in baking dish. Bake at 350 degrees for 20 minutes. Top with French-fried onions. Bake for 5 minutes longer or until onions are heated through. Yield: 6 to 8 servings.

FRIED TOMATOES WITH GRAVY

4 tomatoes, cut into 1/3-inch slices
1/2 cup flour
6 tablespoons oil
1 tablespoon flour
1 cup whipping cream
2 tablespoons brown sugar
1/2 teaspoon salt
1/8 teaspoon pepper

Coat tomato slices with 1/2 cup flour. Fry tomatoes in hot oil in large skillet over medium heat until golden brown, turning once. Drain, reserving drippings. Arrange tomatoes on warm serving platter. Blend reserved drippings and remaining 1 tablespoon flour in skillet. Cook over medium heat for 1 minute, stirring constantly. Add whipping cream gradually. Cook over medium heat until thickened, stirring constantly. Stir in brown sugar, salt and pepper. Spoon over tomatoes. Yield: 8 servings.

STUFFED PARMESAN TOMATOES

4 large tomatoes
3 cups bread crumbs
3/4 cup melted butter
6 tablespoons Parmesan
  cheese

2 to 3 tablespoons Italian
  salad dressing

Cut tomatoes into halves; place in large casserole. Combine bread crumbs, butter, Parmesan cheese and salad dressing in bowl; mix well. Spoon over tomatoes. Bake at 350 degrees for 15 to 20 minutes or until tomatoes are heated through and crumbs are lightly browned. May broil 2 inches from heat source for 4 to 5 minutes if preferred. Yield: 4 servings.

SPINACH-TOPPED TOMATOES

1 cup water
2 tablespoons margarine
  or butter
1/2 teaspoon salt
1/4 to 1/2 teaspoon oregano
1 1/2 cups instant potato
  flakes

1/2 cup milk
1 egg
1 10-ounce package
  frozen chopped spinach
6 tomato slices
Parmesan cheese

Combine water, margarine, salt and oregano in medium saucepan; mix well. Bring to a boil, stirring occasionally. Remove from heat. Stir in potato flakes, milk and egg. Cook spinach using package directions; drain well, pressing out excess liquid. Fold spinach into potato mixture. Slice tomatoes 1/4 inch thick. Place tomato slices in ungreased 9x13-inch baking dish. Spoon 1/2 cup spinach mixture onto each slice. Sprinkle with Parmesan cheese. Broil 4 to 6 inches from heat source for 5 minutes or until cheese is lightly browned. Yield: 6 servings.

TURNIP AND TOMATO CASSEROLE

1 small turnip	Salt and cracked pepper
2 tablespoons butter	to taste
1 tablespoon oregano	4 winter tomatoes
1/2 cup Parmesan cheese	

Slice 3/4 of turnip into thin rounds; julienne remaining turnip. Spread butter over bottom and sides of deep glass baking dish. Arrange turnip slices to cover bottom and sides of baking dish. Combine oregano, cheese, salt and pepper in small bowl; mix well. Sprinkle 3/4 of the mixture over turnips. Cut cores from tomatoes; arrange in baking dish. Sprinkle with remaining spices; fill with julienne turnips. Bake at 375 degrees for 45 minutes or until turnips are lightly browned. The winter tomatoes will acquire the illusion of taste. Yield: 4 servings.

SWEET POTATO BAKE

2 16-ounce cans sweet potatoes	1 1/2 cups packed brown sugar
2 cups sugar	1 cup flour
1 teaspoon vanilla extract	1/2 cup butter
2 eggs	2 cups chopped pecans
1/2 cup butter, softened	Coconut

Combine sweet potatoes, sugar, vanilla, eggs and 1/2 cup butter in baking dish; mix well. Cover with mixture of brown sugar and flour. Dot with remaining 1/2 cup butter. Top with chopped pecans. Bake at 350 degrees for 30 to 45 minutes or until heated through and bubbly. Sprinkle with coconut. Bake for 5 minutes longer or until coconut is golden brown. Yield: 4 servings.

BROWN SUGAR SWEET POTATOES

3 cups mashed cooked
  sweet potatoes
1 cup sugar
1/2 cup milk
1/4 cup melted margarine
2 eggs, beaten
1/2 teaspoon vanilla
  extract

1/2 teaspoon salt
1 cup packed brown
  sugar
1/2 cup melted margarine
1/3 cup flour
1 cup chopped pecans

Combine sweet potatoes, sugar, milk, 1/4 cup margarine, eggs, vanilla and salt in 9x13-inch baking dish; mix well. Combine brown sugar, remaining 1/2 cup margarine, flour and pecans in small bowl; mix well. Sprinkle over sweet potatoes. Bake at 350 degrees for 35 minutes. Yield: 6 servings.

VEGETABLE BOUQUET

1 1/4 pounds favorite
  vegetables
3 tablespoons butter
1 clove of garlic, minced
1/2 teaspoon lemon juice
1/4 teaspoon hot pepper
  sauce

1/2 cup dry bread crumbs
1 cup shredded Asiago
  cheese
1/4 cup chopped parsley

Trim vegetables as desired. Cook vegetables individually in a small amount of water in saucepan until tender-crisp; drain. Arrange vegetables on ovenproof platter. Melt butter in medium skillet over medium heat. Stir in garlic, lemon juice and hot pepper sauce. Cook over low heat for 2 minutes, stirring frequently. Add bread crumbs. Cook over low heat until lightly browned, stirring frequently; remove from heat. Stir in cheese and parsley. Spoon over vegetables. Bake, covered with foil, at 375 degrees for 20 minutes or until heated through. May use green beans, carrots, Brussels sprouts, broccoli, cauliflower or any combination. Yield: 4 to 6 servings.

INDIAN-STYLE ZUCCHINI

1 tablespoon oil
1 tablespoon mustard
  seed
1 large onion, chopped
2 cloves of garlic, minced
1 teaspoon ginger

³/₄ teaspoon turmeric
¹/₈ teaspoon cayenne
  pepper
2 zucchini, cut into
  ¹/₄-inch strips
³/₄ teaspoon salt

Heat oil in skillet over high heat until very hot. Drop in mustard seed. Cook, covered, over low heat until mustard seed pops. Add onion, garlic, ginger, turmeric and cayenne pepper. Cook, uncovered, over medium heat for 5 minutes or until tender, stirring frequently. Add zucchini and salt. Cook, uncovered, over medium-low heat for 15 minutes or until tender, stirring frequently. May substitute green beans or broccoli for zucchini. Yield: 4 servings.

ZUCCHINI-TOMATO PIE

2 cups chopped zucchini
1 cup chopped tomato
¹/₂ cup chopped onion
¹/₃ cup Parmesan cheese
³/₄ cup baking mix

1¹/₂ cups milk
3 eggs, beaten
¹/₂ teaspoon salt
¹/₄ teaspoon pepper

Combine zucchini, tomato, onion and Parmesan cheese in bowl; mix well. Place in 10-inch pie plate. Combine baking mix, milk, eggs, salt and pepper in bowl; mix well. Pour over vegetables. Bake at 400 degrees for 30 minutes. Yield: 6 to 8 servings.

 ### A Lion Tip

Serve cooked fresh vegetables with Parmesan Butter. Combine ¹/₂ cup melted butter with ¹/₄ cup Parmesan cheese, 1 tablespoon lemon juice and ¹/₂ teaspoon oregano.

STUFFED ZUCCHINI

4 medium zucchini
1 cup canned corn
1 cup shredded low-fat
  Monterey Jack cheese
1 2-ounce jar chopped
  pimento, drained
1/4 cup chopped green
  pepper
2 teaspoons salt-free
  herb and spice blend
1/2 teaspoon onion powder

Pierce zucchini with fork. Arrange on paper towels in microwave oven. Microwave, uncovered, on High for 7 minutes, turning once. Let stand for 5 minutes. Cut in half lengthwise. Scoop out and discard pulp. Combine corn, cheese, pimento, green pepper and seasonings in bowl; mix well. Spoon into zucchini shells. Place in microwave-safe 8x12-inch baking dish. Microwave, loosely covered with plastic wrap, on High for 2 to 3 minutes or until heated through.
Yield: 8 servings.

ZUCCHINI BOATS

4 medium zucchini
1/4 pound pork sausage
1/4 cup chopped onion
1/2 cup fine cracker
  crumbs
1 egg, beaten
1/2 cup Parmesan cheese
1/2 teaspoon MSG
1/4 teaspoon salt
1/4 teaspoon thyme
Dash of garlic salt
Dash of pepper

Cook whole zucchini in boiling salted water in saucepan for 7 to 10 minutes or just until tender; drain. Cut into halves lengthwise. Scoop out pulp, reserving shells; mash pulp in bowl. Sauté sausage and onion in skillet until brown, stirring to crumble sausage; drain. Add sausage mixture, cracker crumbs and egg to mashed zucchini; mix well. Reserve 2 tablespoons cheese. Add remaining cheese, MSG, salt, thyme, garlic salt and pepper to zucchini mixture; mix well. Spoon into zucchini shells. Place in baking dish. Sprinkle with reserved cheese. Bake at 350 degrees for 25 to 30 minutes or until brown.
Yield: 4 servings.

GARDEN VEGETABLE PIE

2 cups chopped broccoli
1 large onion, chopped
1/2 green bell pepper,
  chopped
1 cup shredded sharp
  Cheddar cheese

3 eggs
1 1/2 cups milk
1 teaspoon salt
3/4 cup baking mix

Combine broccoli, onion, green pepper and cheese in 11-inch pie plate. Combine eggs and milk in mixer bowl; beat well. Add salt and baking mix; mix well. Pour over vegetables. Bake at 350 degrees for 40 minutes or until light brown. May substitute sliced zucchini for broccoli. Yield: 6 servings.

JULIENNE VEGETABLES WITH WALNUTS

1 3-ounce package
  walnuts, coarsely
  chopped
8 ounces carrots, cut into
  3-inch julienne strips
1/4 cup water
1/8 teaspoon salt

2 medium zucchini, cut
  into 3-inch julienne strips
1 1/2 tablespoons butter or
  margarine
2 teaspoons chopped
  fresh parsley
1/4 teaspoon nutmeg

Spread walnuts in glass dish. Microwave on High for 4 to 5 minutes or until toasted, stirring every 2 minutes. Combine carrots, water and salt in 2-quart glass casserole. Microwave, tightly covered with plastic wrap, on High for 4 minutes. Add zucchini; mix well. Microwave, covered, on High for 3 or 4 minutes. Let stand, covered, for 3 minutes. Place butter in 1-cup glass measure. Microwave on High for 40 seconds or until melted. Stir in parsley and nutmeg. Drain vegetables. Pour butter mixture over vegetables; toss to coat. Stir in walnuts. Yield: 4 to 6 servings.

SOUTHWEST VEGETABLE MÉLANGE

1 large onion, chopped
1 tablespoon oil
1/2 to 1 jalapeño pepper,
  seeded
2 medium zucchini

3 cups frozen corn
2 medium tomatoes,
  chopped
Salt to taste

Sauté onion in oil in skillet until tender. Mince jalapeño pepper; cut zucchini into quarters, then slice thinly. Add jalapeño and zucchini to skillet. Cook over medium heat for 5 minutes, stirring frequently. Add corn and tomatoes. Cook for 5 minutes longer or until corn is heated through. Add salt. May substitute 4 plum tomatoes or 8 to 10 cherry tomatoes for tomatoes. Yield: 4 servings.

VEGETABLE MEDLEY

1 1/2 cups broccoli
  flowerets
1 1/2 cups sliced zucchini
1/2 cup red bell pepper
  strips
1/2 cup sliced water
  chestnuts

1/4 cup sliced green
  onions
2 teaspoons instant
  chicken bouillon
2 tablespoons butter or
  margarine

Combine broccoli, zucchini, red pepper, water chestnuts and green onions in 2-quart glass casserole. Sprinkle with bouillon; dot with butter. Cover tightly with plastic wrap, turning back 1 corner for steam vent. Microwave on High for 4 minutes, rotating dish 1/2 turn after 2 minutes. Let stand, covered, for 5 minutes. Yield: 4 servings.

A Lion Tip

On refrigerator clean-up day, wash and chop the small amounts of vegetables you find and sauté them in butter for a quick and economical dish. Serve with rice and cheese for a main dish.

WINTER VEGETABLE MEDLEY

4 medium white turnips,
  cubed
2 medium carrots, thickly
  sliced
1 large parsnip, quartered
Flowerets of 1 bunch
  broccoli
1 cup peas
1/2 onion, minced
3 tablespoons butter

3 tablespoons flour
2 1/2 cups hot milk
3/4 teaspoon salt
Freshly ground pepper
  to taste
1/2 teaspoon thyme
1 small bay leaf
Nutmeg to taste
2 scallions, chopped

Cook turnips and carrots in boiling salted water to cover in saucepan for 4 minutes. Add parsnip, broccoli and peas. Cook for 7 minutes longer; drain. Keep warm. Sauté onion in butter in saucepan until tender. Stir in flour until well mixed. Add hot milk gradually, mixing well after each addition. Cook until thickened, stirring constantly. Add seasonings. Cook for 5 minutes, stirring constantly. Remove bay leaf. Place vegetables in serving dish. Add enough sauce to cover, stirring gently to coat vegetables. Sprinkle with scallions.
Yield: 6 to 8 servings.

BROILED VEGETABLE KABOBS

2 small zucchini, cut into
  1-inch slices
8 medium fresh
  mushrooms

8 cherry tomatoes
3 to 4 tablespoons
  Italian salad dressing

Arrange vegetables alternately on 4 skewers; skewer mushrooms through cap rather than stem to prevent splitting. Place kabobs on rack of broiler pan; brush with salad dressing. Broil 4 to 6 inches from hot broiler for 3 to 4 minutes on each side or until vegetables are tender. Brush with dressing. May substitute Caesar or Spicy French dressing for Italian.
Yield: 4 servings.

CORN BREAD DRESSING

1 6-ounce package corn bread mix
1 5-count can refrigerator biscuits
1½ cups chopped onions
1 cup chopped celery
3 tablespoons butter
1 teaspoon salt
1 teaspoon pepper
1 teaspoon rubbed sage
3 cups chicken broth
4 eggs, slightly beaten

Prepare and bake corn bread and biscuits according to package directions. Cool. Crumble into large bowl. Sauté onions and celery in butter in skillet until tender. Stir into corn bread mixture. Add salt, pepper, sage, chicken broth and eggs; mix well. Spoon into lightly greased baking dish. Bake at 350 degrees for 55 minutes or until golden brown. Yield: 8 servings.

EASY PAN DRESSING

1 medium pan corn bread
½ cup chopped celery
½ cup chopped onion
1 cup melted margarine
½ tablespoon poultry seasoning
1 egg, beaten
1 package herb-seasoned stuffing mix
1 can chicken broth
Salt and pepper to taste

Crumble cooled corn bread into large bowl. Combine celery, onion, margarine and poultry seasoning in saucepan; mix well. Bring to a boil, stirring occasionally. Stir into corn bread. Add egg, stuffing mix, chicken broth, salt and pepper; mix well. Spoon into baking dish. Bake at 350 degrees for 15 to 20 minutes or until lightly browned. Yield: 8 servings.

A Lion Tip

Toast stale bread and trimmed crusts for stuffing or breading. Crumble or process in blender or food processor. Store in airtight container.

SAUSAGE DRESSING

1 pound pork sausage
2 cups chopped celery
1½ cups chopped onions
4 teaspoons instant
  chicken bouillon
1¾ cups boiling water
2 8-ounce packages
  herb-seasoned stuffing
  mix

1⅓ cups mincemeat
1 8-ounce can sliced
  water chestnuts, drained,
  chopped
2 teaspoons poultry
  seasoning

Brown sausage in large saucepan, stirring until crumbly; drain. Add celery and onion; mix well. Cook over low heat until tender-crisp, stirring occasionally. Add bouillon and boiling water. Bring to a boil. Stir in stuffing mix, mincemeat, water chestnuts and poultry seasoning. Stuff turkey cavity lightly with 2 cups dressing. Bake using directions for turkey. Spoon remaining dressing into lightly greased baking dish. Bake, covered, at 350 degrees for 45 minutes. Yield: 10 servings.

LIONS TURKEY DRESSING

4 cups dry bread crumbs
½ cup sage
¼ cup chopped onion
½ cup chopped celery

½ cup unpopped popcorn
1 teaspoon salt
5 cups broth
1 teaspoon pepper

Combine all ingredients in bowl; mix well. Stuff turkey. Bake at 400 degrees for 5 hours or until popcorn blows the ass off the turkey.

TURKEY DRESSING

2 large loaves day-old
  bread
1 pound pork sausage
1 onion, chopped

2 stalks celery, chopped
1 large can chicken broth
Sage to taste
Salt and pepper to taste

Crumble bread into large bowl. Brown sausage in skillet, stirring until crumbly; drain. Add onion and celery. Cook over low heat until tender, stirring occasionally. Add to bread crumbs; mix well. Stir in chicken broth gradually. Add sage, salt and pepper. Stuff lightly into turkey cavity. Yield: 8 servings.

CHEESE GRITS

1 cup quick-cooking grits
1/2 cup butter, softened
1 roll garlic cheese
2 eggs, beaten

3/4 cup milk
1 roll garlic cheese, cut
  into pieces

Prepare grits using package directions. Pour into large bowl. Combine butter and 1 roll garlic cheese in saucepan. Cook over low heat until melted, stirring frequently. Stir in eggs and milk. Combine with grits; mix well. Spoon into greased casserole. Dot with garlic cheese pieces. Bake at 350 degrees for 30 minutes. Yield: 4 servings.

GRITS AND CHEESE SOUFFLÉ

3 cups grits
1/2 cup butter, softened
8 ounces Cheddar
  cheese, shredded
1 teaspoon salt

1/4 teaspoon red pepper
4 to 6 eggs, beaten
1/3 cup milk
2 teaspoons baking
  powder

Prepare grits using package directions. Blend in butter, Cheddar cheese, salt and red pepper. Beat eggs and milk in small bowl. Add baking powder; mix well. Stir into grits mixture. Spoon into greased 3-quart casserole. Bake at 375 degrees for 45 minutes to 1 hour or until firm and lightly browned. Will keep for 1 hour in warm oven. Yield: 6 to 8 servings.

JUST PLAIN FANCY CHEESE GRITS

1 cup quick-cooking grits
1/4 cup low-fat margarine,
  softened

1 cup shredded sharp
  Cheddar cheese
3 egg whites

Prepare grits using package directions. Blend in margarine and Cheddar cheese. Cool. Beat in egg whites. Pour into casserole. Bake at 350 degrees for 30 minutes or until lightly browned. Yield: 4 to 6 servings.

BUTTERED NOODLES AND PEAS

8 ounces uncooked thin
  egg noodles
1 cup frozen peas, thawed

¹/₄ cup melted butter or
  margarine
Salt and pepper to taste

Cook noodles using package directions; drain. Rinse with hot water. Combine noodles, peas and butter in large saucepan. Cook over medium heat until noodles are heated through, stirring constantly. Add salt and pepper.
Yield: 4 servings.

PARSLEY BUTTERED NOODLES

8 ounces uncooked wide
  egg noodles
¹/₄ cup margarine or butter
1 tablespoon chopped
  fresh parsley

¹/₂ teaspoon salt
Dash of pepper

Cook noodles using package directions; drain. Melt butter in large saucepan. Stir in noodles, parsley, salt and pepper. Cook over low heat until heated through, stirring constantly.
Yield: 4 servings.

TOMATO PESTO LASAGNA

8 ounces uncooked
  lasagna noodles
1 pound sausage
1 14-ounce can chunky-
  style stewed tomatoes
1 6-ounce can tomato
  paste

³/₄ cup water
8 ounces ricotta cheese
1 4-ounce package
  frozen pesto, thawed
8 ounces mozzarella
  cheese, shredded

Cook noodles using package directions; drain. Brown sausage in skillet, stirring until crumbly; drain. Stir in tomatoes, tomato paste and water. Layer sausage mixture, noodles, ricotta cheese, pesto and mozzarella cheese alternately in 9-inch square baking dish, ending with sausage mixture. Bake at 350 degrees for 30 minutes or until heated through. May prepare in microwave-safe baking dish. Microwave, tightly covered, on High for 10 minutes, turning once.
Yield: 6 servings.

MANICOTTI FLORENTINE

3 eggs
1/4 cup Parmesan cheese
1 tablespoon instant
  minced onion
3/4 teaspoon Italian
  seasoning
1 10-ounce package
  frozen chopped spinach,
  thawed

3 hard-boiled eggs,
  chopped
6 manicotti shells
1 4-ounce can tomato
  sauce
1/2 cup shredded
  mozzarella cheese

Beat eggs in medium bowl. Stir in Parmesan cheese, onion and seasoning. Drain spinach; squeeze dry. Add spinach and hard-boiled eggs; mix well. Cook manicotti using package directions. Spoon 1/2 cup spinach mixture into each manicotti shell. Place in greased 6x10-inch baking dish. Drizzle with tomato sauce. Sprinkle with mozzarella cheese. Bake at 350 degrees for 20 minutes or until heated through.
Yield: 6 servings.

MACARONI AND CHEESE

7 ounces uncooked
  macaroni
1/4 cup margarine
3 tablespoons flour
1 teaspoon salt
1/8 teaspoon pepper
1/2 teaspoon dry mustard

3 cups milk
1 teaspoon
  Worcestershire sauce
1/4 cup minced onion
2 cups shredded cheese
1/4 cup buttered bread
  crumbs

Cook macaroni using package directions; drain. Melt butter in a medium saucepan. Stir in flour, salt, pepper and dry mustard. Cook over low heat for 2 minutes, stirring constantly; do not brown. Add milk, Worcestershire sauce and onion; mix well. Cook until smooth and thickened, stirring constantly. Add cheese. Cook until cheese is melted, stirring frequently. Add macaroni; mix well. Pour into 2 1/2-quart casserole. Top with bread crumbs. Bake at 350 degrees for 30 minutes.
Yield: 4 servings.

BAKED MACARONI AND CHEESE WITH SLICED TOMATOES

8 ounces uncooked
  elbow macaroni
1/4 cup butter or margarine
1/4 cup flour
1/4 teaspoon salt
1/8 teaspoon pepper

2 cups milk
2 cups Cheddar cheese,
  grated
1 large tomato, thickly
  sliced

Cook macaroni using package directions; drain. Melt butter in medium saucepan. Remove from heat. Blend in flour, salt and pepper. Stir in macaroni, milk and cheese. Spoon into baking dish. Top with tomato slices. Bake at 375 degrees for 15 to 20 minutes or until bubbly and heated through. Yield: 4 to 5 servings.

NEWFANGLED MACARONI AND CHEESE

6 ounces uncooked
  tricolor pasta ruffles
2 tablespoons margarine
2 tablespoons cornstarch
2 1/2 cups skim milk
1 cup shredded Fontina
  cheese
3/4 cup shredded sharp
  Cheddar cheese
1/2 cup crumbled
  Gorgonzola cheese

2 tablespoons margarine
1 cup broccoli flowerets
1/2 cup chopped onion
1 cup sliced mushrooms
1 red bell pepper, cut into
  1/2-inch pieces
Freshly ground pepper to
  taste

Cook pasta ruffles using package directions; drain. Melt 2 tablespoons margarine in 3-quart saucepan over medium heat. Blend in cornstarch. Remove from heat. Stir in skim milk gradually. Bring to a boil over medium heat. Boil for 1 minute, stirring constantly. Add cheeses. Cook until cheeses are melted, stirring constantly. Melt remaining 2 tablespoons margarine in medium skillet over medium heat. Sauté broccoli and onion in melted margarine for 2 minutes, stirring frequently. Add mushrooms and red pepper. Sauté for 3 to 4 minutes longer or until tender-crisp, stirring frequently. Add pasta and vegetable mixture to cheese sauce. Bring to a boil over medium heat. Boil for 1 minute, stirring constantly. Add pepper. Yield: 4 servings.

WISCONSIN'S FAVORITE MACARONI AND CHEESE

8 ounces uncooked
  elbow macaroni
Flowerets of 1 bunch
  broccoli
2 tablespoons butter or
  margarine
1/2 cup chopped onion
1 16-ounce package
  Cheddar cheese spread

1/2 cup milk
2 teaspoons prepared
  mustard
1/8 teaspoon pepper
1 tablespoon melted
  butter or margarine
1/3 cup crushed saltine
  crackers

Cook macaroni using package directions; drain. Cook broccoli flowerets in boiling water for 3 minutes; drain. Melt 2 tablespoons butter in 3-quart saucepan over medium heat. Add onion. Cook for 3 minutes, stirring frequently. Stir in cheese spread, milk, prepared mustard and pepper. Cook until cheese is melted, stirring constantly. Add macaroni; mix well. Layer half the macaroni mixture, broccoli and remaining macaroni mixture in greased 3-quart casserole. Top with mixture of remaining 1 tablespoon butter and crushed crackers. Bake at 375 degrees for 25 to 30 minutes or until bubbly and lightly browned. Let stand for 10 minutes. Yield: 4 to 6 servings.

AUSTRIAN RICE WITH PEAS

1/4 cup butter
1 tablespoon parsley
1 cup uncooked rice
4 cups water

2 10-ounce packages
  frozen peas, thawed,
  drained
Pepper to taste

Combine butter, parsley, rice and water in large saucepan. Bring to a boil. Cook over medium heat for 2 minutes, stirring frequently. Stir in peas and pepper. Pour into 2-quart baking dish. Bake, covered, at 350 degrees for 40 minutes. Yield: 4 to 6 servings.

FRIED RICE

1½ cups uncooked long grain rice
8 cups cold water
5 or 6 green onions, chopped
1 onion, chopped

2 tablespoons shortening
2 eggs, scrambled
Bean sprouts
Chopped cooked shrimp, pork or chicken
Soy sauce to taste

Rinse rice in warm water until water remains clear. Combine rice and cold water in large saucepan. Bring to a boil over medium heat. Boil for 10 to 12 minutes or until tender, stirring frequently; drain. Sauté onions in shortening in wok for 3 minutes or until tender. Stir in rice, scrambled eggs, bean sprouts and meat. Simmer for 3 minutes, stirring frequently. Sprinkle with soy sauce. Yield: 4 to 5 servings.

FRIED RICE WITH PINEAPPLE

½ cup ground pork
2 tablespoons peanut oil
1 teaspoon light soy sauce
½ teaspoon salt
1 tablespoon minced fresh ginger

2 tablespoons minced scallions
3 cups cooked rice
2 cups chopped fresh pineapple

Stir-fry pork in hot oil in wok for 2 minutes. Add soy sauce, salt, ginger and scallions. Stir-fry for 1 minute longer. Add rice and pineapple. Stir-fry for 3 minutes longer or until pineapple is heated through. Yield: 4 servings.

A Lion Tip

Make a rice salad of leftover rice by adding artichoke hearts, chives, chutney, canned French-fried onions or curry powder.

LEMON PILAF

2 tablespoons butter or
  margarine
1/2 cup uncooked rice
1/2 cup uncooked
  vermicelli, broken into
  1-inch pieces

13/4 cups chicken broth
1 tablespoon grated
  lemon peel
1 tablespoon chopped
  fresh parsley

Melt butter in medium saucepan. Add rice and vermicelli. Cook over medium heat until golden brown, stirring frequently. Stir in chicken broth. Bring to a boil; reduce heat. Simmer, covered, for 15 to 20 minutes or until rice is tender and liquid is absorbed. Stir in lemon peel and parsley. Yield: 4 servings.

MEXICAN RICE

2/3 cup chopped onion
3 tablespoons bacon
  drippings
1 cup uncooked rice
1 cup chopped green bell
  pepper
1 teaspoon chili powder

1 8-ounce can whole
  tomatoes
2 teaspoons salt
2 cups water
Chopped fresh tomatoes,
  green bell peppers and
  green onions

Sauté onion in bacon drippings in large heavy skillet. Stir in rice, 1 cup green pepper, chili powder, canned tomatoes, salt and water. Bring to a boil; reduce heat. Simmer, covered, for 20 minutes or until rice is tender and liquid is absorbed. Garnish with chopped tomatoes, remaining green peppers, and green onions. Yield: 6 servings.

RICE WITH RAISINS AND PISTACHIOS

1/4 cup minced onion
1 tablespoon melted
  butter
1 cup uncooked rice
1/3 cup raisins

1/4 cup pistachios
1 1/2 cups water
1 bay leaf
Salt and pepper to taste

Combine onion and melted butter in saucepan. Cook over low heat until onion is wilted, stirring frequently. Stir in rice, raisins and pistachios. Add water, bay leaf, salt and pepper; mix well. Bring to a boil; reduce heat. Simmer, covered, for 17 minutes. Remove bay leaf. Fluff rice with fork. Yield: 4 servings.

RICE STUFFING WITH CELERY AND FRUIT

2 14-ounce cans
  chicken broth
1 cup uncooked long
  grain rice
3 cups chopped celery
1/2 cup chopped dried
  apricots

1/2 cup golden raisins
1/4 cup chopped celery
  leaves
1 1/2 teaspoons crushed
  thyme leaves
1/8 teaspoon freshly
  ground pepper

Bring chicken broth to a boil in medium saucepan. Stir in rice. Return to a boil; reduce heat. Simmer, covered, for 7 minutes. Stir in celery, apricots, raisins, celery leaves, thyme leaves and pepper. Simmer, covered, for 5 minutes longer. Spoon into 2-quart casserole. Bake at 350 degrees for 15 minutes or until heated through. May use to stuff small turkey or chicken. Yield: 6 servings.

VEGETABLE CONFETTI RICE

2 cups water
1 tablespoon margarine
  or butter
1 teaspoon instant
  chicken bouillon
3/4 cup uncooked rice

1/2 cup chopped carrot
1/2 cup chopped celery
1 tablespoon minced
  onion
1/2 cup frozen peas,
  thawed, drained

Bring water, margarine and bouillon to a boil in medium saucepan. Stir in rice, carrot, celery and onion. Return to a boil; reduce heat. Simmer, covered, for 20 minutes or until rice is tender and liquid is absorbed. Stir in peas. Simmer for 5 minutes longer, stirring occasionally. Yield: 6 servings.

ALMOND CURRIED FRUIT

1 29-ounce can sliced
   peaches, drained
1 15-ounce can
   pineapple chunks,
   drained
1 16-ounce can pear
   halves, drained
1 6-ounce jar
   maraschino cherries,
   drained

1/2 cup toasted slivered
   almonds
3/4 cup packed brown
   sugar
1/3 cup melted margarine
1/2 teaspoon curry powder

Combine peaches, pineapple, pears and cherries in 9x13-inch baking dish. Sprinkle with almonds. Combine brown sugar, margarine and curry powder in bowl; mix well. Pour over almonds and fruit. Bake at 325 degrees for 1 hour. Yield: 12 servings.

A Lion Tip

Use leftover juice from canned fruit in gelatins and in fruit sauces to serve over cake or ice cream.

CRANBERRIES IN SYRUP

1 cup water
1/2 cup sugar
1 12-ounce package
   frozen cranberries,
   thawed, drained

1/4 cup maple syrup
1/4 cup coarsely chopped
   pecans
1 teaspoon grated lemon
   rind

Combine water and sugar in 2-quart saucepan; mix well. Cook over medium heat until sugar is dissolved; do not stir. Stir in cranberries, maple syrup, pecans and lemon rind. Simmer, uncovered, for 5 minutes or until cranberries begin to pop, stirring occasionally. Yield: 4 to 5 servings.

HOT CURRIED FRUIT

1 29-ounce can fruit
   salad, drained
1 can pitted black
   cherries, drained
1/2 cup maraschino
   cherries, drained
2 bananas, sliced

1/2 cup packed brown
   sugar
2 tablespoons cornstarch
1 tablespoon curry
   powder
1/4 cup melted butter

Combine fruit salad, black cherries, maraschino cherries and bananas in greased 2-quart baking dish. Combine brown sugar, cornstarch, curry powder and melted butter in bowl; mix well. Stir into fruit. Bake at 350 degrees for 40 minutes. Yield: 8 servings.

HOT FRUIT BAKE

1 16-ounce can cling
   peaches, drained
1 16-ounce can pear
   halves, drained
1 20-ounce can sliced
   pineapple, drained

5 maraschino cherries
   and stems
1/3 cup melted butter
3/4 cup packed brown
   sugar
4 teaspoons curry powder

Place fruit in 1 1/2-quart casserole. Combine melted butter, brown sugar and curry powder in bowl; mix well. Spread over fruit. Bake, uncovered, at 325 degrees for 1 hour. May chill and reheat to improve flavor. Yield: 10 servings.

SHERRIED APPLE BUTTER

16 tart apples, cored, cut
  into quarters
4 cups apple cider
1 cup cider vinegar
5 cups sugar
1 cup sweet Sherry

1 lemon, seeded, finely
  ground
1 1/2 teaspoons cinnamon
1/2 teaspoon cloves
1/2 teaspoon allspice

Combine apples, cider and vinegar in large saucepan; mix well. Bring to a boil; reduce heat. Simmer, covered, for 1 hour. Purée apple mixture; yield will be approximately 10 cups. Combine puréed mixture, sugar, Sherry, lemon, cinnamon, cloves and allspice in large saucepan. Bring to a boil; reduce heat. Cook for 1 hour and 30 minutes or until very thick, stirring frequently. Ladle into hot sterilized jars, leaving 1/2-inch headspace; seal with 2-piece lids. Process in boiling water bath for 10 minutes. Remove to rack to cool. Yield: 4 pints.

MILD APPLE CHUTNEY

1 cup water
3 tablespoons vinegar
5 tablespoons sugar
1/2 teaspoon salt
1/2 teaspoon allspice
1 1/4 teaspoons dry
  mustard
1 gingerroot, shaved

6 tart apples, pared,
  chopped
1 green bell pepper,
  chopped
1/2 cup seedless raisins
2 teaspoons
  Worcestershire sauce

Combine water, vinegar, sugar, salt, allspice, dry mustard and gingerroot in large saucepan; mix well. Bring to a boil. Cook for 5 minutes, stirring frequently. Add apples, green pepper, raisins and Worcestershire sauce; Simmer, uncovered, for 45 minutes, stirring occasionally. Spoon into hot sterilized jars, leaving 1/4-inch headspace; seal with 2-piece lids. Store in refrigerator. Yield: 3 cups.

APPLE-PEACH CONSERVE

2 cups chopped unpeeled
  tart apples
2 cups chopped peeled
  peaches

3 cups sugar
1/2 cup lemon juice

Combine apples, peaches, sugar and lemon juice in saucepan. Cook over low heat for 20 minutes or until apples are transparent, stirring frequently. Ladle into hot sterilized 6-ounce jelly jars; seal with 2-piece lids. Yield: 7 jars.

APRICOT JAM

8 ounces dried apricots
1 orange, seeded, finely
  ground

1 8-ounce can crushed
   pineapple, drained
3 cups sugar

Soak apricots overnight in water to cover; do not drain. Cook apricots in soaking liquid in saucepan over low heat until tender, stirring frequently. Mash apricots. Combine with orange and pineapple in saucepan. Bring to a boil, stirring occasionally. Add sugar. Cook over low heat until thickened, stirring constantly. Pour into hot sterilized jars, leaving 1/4-inch headspace; seal with 2-piece lids. Yield: 2 to 3 cups.

TROPICAL FRUIT MARMALADE

2 cups frozen peaches,
  thawed, drained, sliced
1/2 cup canned pineapple
  chunks, drained
1 small orange, seeded,
  cut into quarters

4 teaspoons lemon juice
2 cups sugar
2 tablespoons rum

Combine fruits, lemon juice and sugar in saucepan; mix well. Cook over low heat for 30 to 40 minutes or until thickened, stirring frequently. Stir in rum. Ladle into hot sterilized jars, leaving 1/4-inch headspace; seal with 2-piece lids. Yield: 2 cups.

CHRISTMAS JAM

12 ounces cranberries, coarsely chopped
2 10-ounce packages frozen strawberries, thawed

4 cups sugar
3 ounces pectin

Combine cranberries, strawberries and sugar in saucepan; mix well. Bring to a boil. Simmer for 2 minutes, stirring occasionally. Remove from heat; stir in pectin. Return to a boil. Simmer for 2 minutes, stirring constantly. Remove from heat; skim with metal spoon. Ladle into hot sterilized jars, leaving 1/4-inch headspace; seal with 2-piece lids. Process in boiling water bath for 10 minutes. Yield: 7 cups.

EASY SPICED PEARS

2 16-ounce cans pear halves in light syrup
1/2 cup orange juice
1/4 cup almond liqueur

2 3-inch cinnamon sticks
1 teaspoon allspice
1/2 teaspoon ginger
1/8 teaspoon red pepper

Drain syrup from pears into small saucepan. Place pears in medium bowl. Add orange juice, almond liqueur, cinnamon sticks and allspice to pear syrup. Bring to a boil. Simmer, uncovered, until reduced to 1 3/4 cups, stirring frequently. Stir in ginger and red pepper. Remove cinnamon sticks. Pour over pears. May be frozen in airtight container for 1 month or stored in refrigerator for 4 days. Yield: 3 to 4 cups.

SPICED PLUMS

1 gallon plums
2 cups vinegar
8 cups sugar
2 teaspoons cinnamon

2 teaspoons pickling spices
2 teaspoons cloves

Place plums in water to cover in saucepan. Bring to a boil over medium heat. Simmer for 10 minutes, stirring frequently; drain. Stir in vinegar, sugar and spices. Simmer until thickened, stirring frequently. Ladle into hot sterilized jars, leaving 1/4-inch headspace; seal with 2-piece lids. Process in boiling water bath for 10 minutes. Yield: 10 to 12 pints.

GARLIC AND HERB-MARINATED OLIVES

4 bay leaves
1 tablespoon minced
  garlic
2 teaspoons crushed
  oregano leaves
2 teaspoons crushed
  thyme leaves
1/4 cup red wine vinegar

1   10-ounce jar pimento-
    stuffed green olives,
    drained
2   6-ounce cans pitted
    black olives, drained
2 to 2 1/2 cups olive oil

Combine bay leaves, garlic, oregano and thyme in small cup; mix well. Place half in each of two 3-cup jars. Add 2 tablespoons red wine vinegar to each jar. Place olives in boiling water in large saucepan. Let stand for 1 minute; drain. Place olives in prepared jars. Add olive oil to cover; mix well. Store, covered, in refrigerator for several days, stirring or shaking daily. Bring jars to room temperature before serving; drain. May store in refrigerator for up to 2 months. Yield: 5 cups.

RED HOT OLIVES

2   3-ounce jars almond-
    stuffed olives, drained
1/3 cup oil
1/4 cup water
3 tablespoons lime juice

1 tablespoon fresh
  cilantro
1 tablespoon red pepper
1 teaspoon cumin
1 clove of garlic, minced

Combine olives, oil, water, lime juice, cilantro, red pepper, cumin and garlic in saucepan; mix well. Bring to a boil; reduce heat. Simmer, covered, for 5 minutes. Cool to room temperature. Drain, reserving liquid. Pack olives into hot sterilized jar. Pour reserved liquid into jar. Seal with 2-piece lid. Store in refrigerator for 4 to 7 days before serving. May store for up to 3 weeks. Yield: 1 pint.

A Lion Tip

Add raw cucumber and carrot strips, green beans and cauliflower to the liquid left in a pickle jar. Refrigerate for several days.

SPICY RED PEPPER JELLY

2 large red bell peppers,
  chopped
1 small onion, cut into
  6 pieces
1½ cups apple cider
  vinegar

6½ cups sugar
3 ounces pectin
3 to 4 teaspoons Tabasco
  sauce

Combine red peppers, onion and ¼ cup vinegar in food processor container. Process until very finely ground. Spoon into large nonaluminum saucepan. Stir in remaining 1¼ cups vinegar. Bring to a full rolling boil; reduce heat to low. Simmer for 5 minutes or until slightly thickened, stirring occasionally. Stir in sugar. Bring to a boil. Simmer over high heat for 1 minute, stirring constantly. Remove from heat. Blend in pectin. Skim surface. Stir in Tabasco sauce. Ladle into hot sterilized jars, leaving ¼-inch headspace; seal with 2-piece lids. Process in boiling water bath for 10 minutes. Remove to wire racks to cool. Yield: 7 cups.

HOT PEPPER JELLY

¼ cup chopped red hot
  peppers
¼ cup chopped green
  hot peppers
1½ cups chopped green
  bell pepper

6½ cups sugar
1½ cups vinegar
3 ounces liquid pectin

Combine peppers, sugar and vinegar in large saucepan. Bring to a boil over medium heat. Simmer for 3 minutes, stirring occasionally. Add pectin. Simmer for 1 minute longer. Cool for 5 minutes. Ladle into hot sterilized jars, leaving ¼-inch headspace; seal with 2-piece lids. Process in boiling water bath for 10 minutes. Strain cooked mixture if clear jelly is desired. Yield: 2 to 3 pints.

A Lion Tip

Liquid pectin and powdered pectin cannot be used interchangeably. Always follow recipes using pectin exactly.

DILLY BEANS

Fresh tender green snap beans
2 cups cider vinegar
2 cups water
1/4 cup noniodized salt

1 teaspoon red pepper
2 large cloves of garlic
2 teaspoons dillseed or dillweed

Remove stems from beans. Pack into 2 sterilized 1-pint jars. Combine vinegar, water and salt in saucepan. Bring to a boil. Pour over beans in jars, leaving 1/2 inch headspace. Add 1/2 teaspoon red pepper, 1 clove of garlic and 1 teaspoon dillseed to each jar. Seal with 2-piece lids. Store for 3 weeks before opening. Yield: 2 pints.

GARLIC DILL PICKLES

10 cucumbers
Garlic buds, crushed
Dillseed or dill heads
1 cup sugar

1 cup salt
32 cups water
4 cups white vinegar

Trim ends of cucumbers. Place desired amounts of garlic and dill in two 1-quart jars. Combine with sugar, salt, water and vinegar in large saucepan. Bring to a boil. Pack cucumbers into hot sterilized jars. Add boiling syrup, leaving 1/2-inch headspace; seal with 2-piece lids. Process in boiling water bath for 10 minutes. Yield: 2 quarts.

EASY SWEET PICKLE STICKS

Cucumbers
3 3/4 cups vinegar
3 cups sugar
3 tablespoons salt

4 1/2 teaspoons celery seed
4 1/2 teaspoons turmeric
3/4 teaspoon mustard seed

Cut cucumbers into strips; place in large bowl. Pour boiling water to cover over cucumbers. Let stand for 4 to 5 hours. Combine vinegar, sugar, salt, celery seed, turmeric and mustard seed in saucepan. Bring to a boil. Simmer for 5 minutes, stirring frequently. Drain cucumbers; pack into hot sterilized jars. Add boiling syrup, leaving 1/2-inch headspace; seal with 2-piece lids. Process in boiling water bath for 10 minutes. Yield: 6 pints.

GREEN TOMATO PICKLES

24 small green tomatoes
6 cloves of garlic
6 stalks of celery, cut into
fourths
6 green bell peppers, cut
into fourths

2 quarts water
1 cup salt
1 quart vinegar
Dill

Pack green tomatoes into sterilized jars. Add garlic, celery and green peppers to jars. Combine water, salt, vinegar and dill in saucepan. Boil for 5 minutes. Pour into jars, leaving 1/2 inch headspace. Seal with 2-piece lids. Store for 4 to 6 weeks before serving. Yield: 6 quarts.

HOLIDAY TOMATO PICKLES

1 peck green tomatoes,
sliced
12 onions, sliced
3/4 cup salt
2 tablespoons mixed
pickling spices

4 red bell peppers, finely
chopped
Vinegar
4 cups sugar
1 head cauliflower

Layer tomatoes and onions in large bowl, sprinkling each layer with salt. Let stand overnight. Drain in colander. Tie spices in cheesecloth bag. Combine tomatoes, onions, peppers and spices in saucepan. Add enough vinegar to cover. Cook until vegetables are nearly tender. Add sugar. Cook until tender. Cook cauliflower in salted water in saucepan until tender; drain. Cut cauliflower into small pieces. Spoon tomato mixture into hot sterilized jars, leaving 1/2 inch headspace. Add cauliflower to jars. Seal with 2-piece lids. Yield: 4 to 5 quarts.

SPICY GREEN TOMATO PICKLES

7 pounds sliced green
  tomatoes
3 cups household lime
2 gallons water
5 pounds sugar
8 cups vinegar
1 teaspoon salt

1 teaspoon cloves
1 teaspoon cinnamon
1 teaspoon allspice
1 teaspoon celery seed
1 teaspoon ginger
1 teaspoon mace

Soak tomatoes in brine of household lime dissolved in 2 gallons water for 24 hours. Drain; rinse with cold water. Let stand for 4 hours in cold water, changing water every hour; drain. Combine sugar, vinegar and spices in saucepan. Bring to a boil. Pour boiling syrup over tomatoes. Let stand overnight. Drain, reserving syrup. Bring reserved syrup to a boil. Simmer for 1 hour, stirring frequently. Pack tomatoes into hot sterilized jars. Add boiling syrup, leaving 1/2-inch headspace; seal with 2-piece lids. Process in boiling water bath for 10 minutes. Yield: 3 to 4 quarts.

CRANBERRY RELISH

2 cups cranberries
1 seedless orange
1 cup sugar

2 tablespoons orange
  liqueur

Process cranberries and unpeeled orange in blender or food processor until coarsely chopped. Combine with sugar and orange liqueur in bowl; mix well. Chill, covered, for 1 hour. Yield: 2 cups.

CARROT RELISH

4 large carrots, peeled
1 lemon, thinly sliced

1/2 cup sugar
1/2 teaspoon salt

Grind carrots and lemon together. Combine with sugar and salt in bowl; mix well. Store in refrigerator for several days. Serve with fish or meat. Yield: 4 cups.

UNCOOKED RELISH

8 pounds cabbage
4 green bell peppers
4 red bell peppers
8 large sweet onions
3/4 cup pickling salt
1/4 small container celery
  seed

1/4 small container white
  mustard seed
3 1/2 cups dark vinegar
5 cups sugar

Chop cabbage, peppers and onions in food chopper. Combine with pickling salt in large container; mix well. Let stand for 2 hours. Press moisture from mixture. Rinse and press again. Combine with celery seed, mustard seed, vinegar and sugar in large container. Let stand for 3 days, stirring once each day. Pack in sterilized jars; seal with 2-piece lids.
Yield: 4 to 5 quarts.

A Lion Tip

Relish can be made with chopped fruits preserved with sugar, spices and vinegar. Chutneys are highly seasoned with onion, garlic, ginger and hot peppers.

HOT PEPPER RELISH

24 green bell peppers	3$\frac{1}{2}$ cups sugar
24 red bell peppers	4 cups vinegar
12 to 18 hot peppers	$\frac{1}{4}$ cup salt
24 medium onions	

Grind peppers and onions in food grinder. Combine in large bowl. Add boiling water to cover. Let stand for 5 minutes; drain well. Combine with sugar, vinegar and salt in large saucepan. Bring to a rolling boil. Cook for 10 minutes, stirring frequently. Spoon into hot sterilized jars, leaving $\frac{1}{2}$ inch headspace. Seal with 2-piece lids. Yield: 12 pints.

HOT TOMATO PEPPER RELISH

1 peck green tomatoes	1 cup salt
1 peck green bell peppers	1 gallon vinegar
20 hot peppers with seed	5 pounds sugar
16 medium onions	1 container pickling spice

Grind tomatoes, green peppers, hot peppers and onions in food grinder. Combine with salt in 4 to 5-gallon container; mix well. Let stand for 8 hours to overnight. Drain well. Combine vinegar and sugar in large enamel saucepan. Tie pickling spice in cheesecloth bag. Add to saucepan. Cook over low heat until sugar dissolves, stirring constantly. Add drained vegetables. Bring to a boil; reduce heat. Simmer, covered, for 45 minutes, stirring frequently. Spoon into sterilized pint jars, leaving $\frac{1}{2}$ inch headspace. Seal with 2-piece lids. Yield: 16 to 18 pints.

SUNSHINE PICCALILLI

18 carrots, chopped
6 cucumbers, chopped
2 large green bell
  peppers, chopped
6 onions, chopped
2 sweet red peppers,
  chopped

2 cups white vinegar
3¹/2 cups sugar
1 teaspoon celery seed
1 teaspoon white
  mustard seed

Combine carrots, cucumbers, green peppers, onions, and red peppers in food processor container. Process with medium blade until finely ground. Pour into large saucepan. Stir in vinegar, sugar, celery seed and mustard seed. Bring to a boil over medium heat. Simmer for 15 minutes, stirring frequently. Ladle into hot sterilized jars, leaving ¹/4-inch headspace; seal with 2-piece lids. Process in boiling water bath for 10 minutes. Yield: 5 pints.

HOT DOG RELISH

4 cups coarsely ground
  onions
4 cups coarsely ground
  cabbage
4 cups coarsely ground
  green tomatoes
12 green bell peppers,
  coarsely ground
6 red bell peppers,
  coarsely ground

¹/2 cup salt
6 cups sugar
1 tablespoon celery seed
2 tablespoons mustard
  seed
1¹/2 teaspoons turmeric
4 cups cider vinegar
2 cups water

Combine ground vegetables with salt in large container. Let stand overnight. Rinse and drain well. Combine sugar, celery seed, mustard seed, turmeric, vinegar and water in large saucepan. Add vegetables; mix well. Bring to a boil; reduce heat. Simmer for 3 minutes. Spoon into hot sterilized jars, leaving ¹/2 inch headspace. Seal with 2-piece lids. Yield: 6 to 8 pints.

PICKLED GARDEN RELISH

Flowerets of 1/2 small
cauliflower, sliced
2 carrots, peeled, cut into
2-inch strips
2 stalks celery, cut into
1-inch pieces
1 green bell pepper, cut
into 2-inch strips
1   4-ounce jar chopped
pimentos, drained

1   3-ounce jar pitted
green olives, drained
3/4 cup wine vinegar
1/2 cup olive oil
1/4 cup water
2 tablespoons sugar
1 teaspoon salt
1/2 teaspoon oregano
1/4 teaspoon pepper

Combine cauliflower, carrots, celery, green pepper, pimentos, green olives, vinegar, olive oil, water, sugar and spices in large skillet; mix well. Bring to a boil over medium heat, stirring occasionally. Simmer, covered, for 5 minutes, stirring frequently. Chill, covered, for 24 hours. Drain before serving. Yield: 6 servings.

HAMBURGER RELISH

6 large sweet onions,
chopped
18 large tomatoes,
peeled, chopped
4 cups sugar
1 1/2 cups white vinegar

2 teaspoons salt
1 teaspoon cinnamon
1 teaspoon nutmeg
1/2 teaspoon cloves
1/2 teaspoon allspice

Combine onions, tomatoes, sugar, vinegar and spices in large heavy saucepan; mix well. Bring to a boil over medium heat, stirring occasionally; reduce heat. Simmer for 3 hours, stirring occasionally. Pour into hot sterilized jars, leaving 1/2-inch headspace; seal with 2-piece lids. Process in boiling water bath for 10 minutes. Yield: 3 quarts.

SAUERKRAUT RELISH

1 20-ounce can
sauerkraut
1 cup catsup
1 cup chili sauce
1 cup chopped celery

1 cup chopped onions
1 cup chopped green bell
pepper
1 cup sugar
2 teaspoons paprika

Combine sauerkraut, catsup, chili sauce, celery, onions, green pepper, sugar and paprika in large bowl; mix well. Let stand for 24 hours. Yield: 6 to 8 servings.

SQUASH RELISH

8 cups chopped squash
2 large green bell
peppers, chopped
2 large onions, chopped
1 4-ounce jar chopped
pimentos, drained

2½ cups sugar
2 cups white vinegar
2 teaspoons celery salt
2 teaspoons mustard
seed
2 teaspoons salt

Combine squash, green peppers, onions, pimentos, sugar, vinegar and seasonings in large saucepan; mix well. Let stand for 1 hour. Bring to a boil over medium heat, stirring occasionally. Simmer for 15 minutes, stirring occasionally. Pour into hot sterilized jars, leaving ½-inch headspace; seal with 2-piece lids. Process in boiling water bath for 10 minutes. Yield: 2 quarts.

RIPE TOMATO RELISH

4 cups chopped peeled
ripe tomatoes, drained
1 cup chopped celery
1/2 cup chopped green
bell pepper

1/2 cup chopped onion
1/2 cup sugar
1/2 cup vinegar
1/2 teaspoon salt
1/2 teaspoon dry mustard

Combine tomatoes, celery, green pepper, onion, sugar, vinegar and seasonings in large saucepan. Cook over low heat for 1 hour or until thickened, stirring frequently. Pour into hot sterilized jars, leaving 1/2-inch headspace; seal with 2-piece lids. Process in boiling water bath for 10 minutes. Yield: 1 to 2 quarts.

TART TOMATO RELISH

5 large onions
7 pounds ripe tomatoes,
peeled
7 large apples, peeled,
cored

2 cups vinegar
2 tablespoons salt
2 pounds brown sugar
1 ounce whole mixed
spices

Chop onions, tomatoes and apples in meat chopper. Combine with vinegar and salt in large saucepan. Cook for 1 hour. Add brown sugar and spices tied in cheesecloth. Cook for 1 1/2 hours. Remove spice bag. Cook for 30 minutes longer or until thickened to desired consistency, stirring occasionally. Spoon into hot sterlized jars. Seal with paraffin. Yield: 6 pints.

QUICK MEXICAN HOT SAUCE

1 4-ounce can chopped
green chilies
1 16-ounce can
tomatoes, chopped
1 small onion, chopped

1 teaspoon sugar
2 tablespoons oil
1 tablespoon vinegar
Salt and pepper to taste

Combine green chilies, tomatoes, onion, sugar, oil, vinegar, salt and pepper in large covered jar. Shake to mix well. Chill for 30 minutes before serving. May store in refrigerator for several weeks. Yield: 3 to 4 cups.

QUICK RELISH

1 large can tomatoes
3/4 cup vinegar
1 large onion, chopped
1 tablespoon sugar

1/2 teaspoon cloves
1/2 teaspoon cinnamon
Cayenne pepper to taste
1 teaspoon salt

Combine tomatoes, vinegar, onion, sugar, cloves, cinnamon, cayenne pepper and salt in saucepan. Cook for 15 minutes. Let stand until cool. Store in refrigerator. Yield: 2 cups.

A Lion Tip

Make a Quick Corn Relish of 2 cups drained canned corn, 1/3 cup chopped yellow onion, 1/3 cup chopped red and green bell peppers, 1/4 cup chopped celery and 1/4 cup sweet pickle relish. Add 2 tablespoons each sugar and cider vinegar and 1/2 teaspoon salt. Let stand for 30 minutes.

Breads

 *B*READS

ANGEL BISCUITS

1 envelope dry yeast	1/4 teaspoon soda
5 tablespoons warm water	1/2 teaspoon salt
5 cups flour	2 tablespoons sugar
5 teaspoons baking powder	1 cup shortening
	2 cups buttermilk

Dissolve yeast in warm water in small bowl. Let stand for several minutes. Sift flour, baking powder, soda, salt and sugar into large bowl; mix well. Cut in shortening until crumbly. Add buttermilk and yeast; mix well. Pat dough 1/2 inch thick on floured surface. Cut with biscuit cutter. Place on greased baking sheet. Bake at 350 degrees for 15 to 20 minutes or until golden brown. Yield: 2 dozen.

GOLDEN RAISIN CREAM BISCUITS

2 cups flour	1 cup (about) whipping cream
1 tablespoon baking powder	1 cup golden raisins
2 teaspoons sugar	1 egg, beaten
1 teaspoon salt	Sugar

Combine flour, baking powder, sugar and salt in large bowl; mix well. Stir in 1 cup whipping cream. Shape into ball, adding additional cream if necessary to make soft dough. Knead in raisins on lightly floured surface. Pat into 1/2 inch thick rectangle on floured surface. Cut into 12 squares. Place 1 inch apart on greased baking sheet. Brush with egg; sprinkle with sugar. Bake at 425 degrees for 15 minutes or until light brown. Serve warm with sweet butter and fruit preserves. Yield: 1 dozen.

SOUR CREAM AND CHEDDAR BISCUITS

2 cups flour
1¼ cups shredded
    aged Wisconsin
    Cheddar cheese
1 tablespoon sugar
1 tablespoon baking
    powder
1½ teaspoons dry
    mustard
1 teaspoon salt
¼ teaspoon soda
½ cup sour cream
¼ cup milk
1 egg
¼ cup thinly sliced green
    onions

Combine flour, cheese, sugar, baking powder, dry mustard, salt and soda in large bowl; mix well. Combine sour cream, milk, egg and green onions in small bowl; beat well. Add to cheese mixture; toss with fork to mix well. Shape into ball. Knead on lightly floured surface 10 to 12 times. Pat into 8-inch circle. Cut with 2 to 3-inch biscuit cutter. Place on lightly greased baking sheet. Top with additional cheese. Bake at 425 degrees for 12 to 18 minutes or until light brown. Serve warm. To reheat, place on baking sheet. Bake, loosely covered with foil, at 375 degrees for 5 minutes. Yield: 10 to 14 biscuits.

MEXICAN CORN BREAD

1 cup self-rising cornmeal
2 eggs
1 cup shredded sharp
    Cheddar cheese
1 cup canned cream-style
    corn
1 jalapeño pepper,
    seeded, chopped
½ cup buttermilk
⅓ cup oil

Grease two 6-inch cast-iron skillets with shortening. Heat in 400-degree oven. Combine cornmeal, eggs, cheese, corn, pepper, buttermilk and oil in bowl; mix well. Pour into heated skillets. Bake for 30 minutes. Yield: 8 servings.

SPICY CONFETTI CORN BREAD

3/4 cup flour
1 cup cornmeal
2 tablespoons sugar
2 teaspoons baking
  powder
1/2 teaspoon soda
1/2 teaspoon salt
1/2 teaspoon chili powder

1/4 teaspoon cumin
1/4 cup chopped pimento
  or roasted red pepper
1 cup yogurt
1 egg
3 tablespoons oil
3 tablespoons chopped
  scallions

Sift flour, cornmeal, sugar, baking powder, soda, salt, chili powder and cumin into large bowl; mix well. Add pimento; mix well. Combine yogurt, egg, oil and scallions in bowl; mix well. Stir into flour mixture just until combined. Pour into buttered 8-inch cast-iron skillet. Bake at 400 degrees for 20 to 25 minutes or until toothpick inserted in center comes out clean. Yield: 8 servings.

HUSH PUPPIES

2 cups cornmeal
1/2 teaspoon soda
1 teaspoon salt
1 egg

1 cup buttermilk
1 onion, chopped
2 tablespoons oil
Oil for deep frying

Sift cornmeal, soda and salt into medium bowl. Combine egg, buttermilk, onion and oil in small bowl; beat well. Add to cornmeal mixture; mix well. Drop by spoonfuls into hot oil. Deep-fry until golden brown; drain on paper towels. Yield: 2 dozen.

BANANA NUT BREAD WITH CURRANTS

3 very ripe large bananas
1/2 cup packed brown
 sugar
2 eggs
1/2 cup oil
1 teaspoon vanilla extract

1 1/2 cups flour
3/4 teaspoon salt
1 teaspoon soda
1/2 teaspoon nutmeg
1 cup walnuts
1/2 cup currants

Purée bananas in food processor. Add brown sugar, eggs, oil and vanilla; process just until blended. Add flour, salt, soda and nutmeg; process just until combined. Add walnuts; pulse until chopped. Stir in currants. Pour into buttered 5x9-inch loaf pan. Bake at 325 degrees for 1 hour to 1 hour and 10 minutes or until golden brown. Cool in pan on wire rack for 10 minutes. Remove from pan to wire rack to cool completely. Yield: 20 slices.

HAWAIIAN BANANA BREAD

1 cup butter, softened
2 cups sugar
4 eggs, well beaten
6 to 7 ripe bananas,
 mashed

2 1/2 cups flour
1 teaspoon salt
2 teaspoons soda
1/2 cup chopped
 macadamia nuts

Cream butter and sugar in mixer bowl until light and fluffy. Add eggs and bananas; beat well. Sift flour, salt and soda together. Add to creamed mixture; mix well. Stir in nuts. Pour into 2 greased 5x9-inch loaf pans. Bake at 350 degrees for 50 minutes to 1 hour or until golden brown. Serve hot with cream cheese or butter. Yield: 2 loaves.

TREASURE ISLAND FRUIT CARROT BREAD

4 cups all-purpose flour
1 1/2 cups whole wheat
   flour
5 teaspoons baking
   powder
1 teaspoon soda
1 teaspoon salt
2 teaspoons cinnamon
1/4 cup butter or
   margarine, softened
1 cup honey
2 eggs

2 cups shredded carrots
1 1/2 cups orange juice
1 1/2 cups finely chopped
   glacé red or green
   cherries
1/2 cup confectioners'
   sugar
1 tablespoon orange juice
Glacé whole red or green
   cherries, cut into halves
Glacé pineapple wedges,
   cut into halves

Sift flours, baking powder, soda, salt and cinnamon together. Cream butter and honey in mixer bowl until light and fluffy. Add eggs; beat well. Stir in carrots, 1 1/2 cups orange juice and 1 1/2 cups finely chopped cherries. Add flour mixture, stirring just until moistened. Spoon into 2 lightly greased 5x9-inch loaf pans. Bake at 350 degrees for 50 minutes to 1 hour or until golden brown. Remove to wire racks to cool completely. Mix confectioners' sugar and remaining 1 tablespoon orange juice in small bowl. Drizzle over loaves; top with cherry halves and pineapple. Yield: 2 loaves.

CHERRY BREAD

1 small jar maraschino
   cherries
1 cup sugar
2 eggs

1 teaspoon salt
1 1/2 cups flour
1/2 cup chopped nuts

Drain cherries, reserving juice. Chop cherries. Combine cherries and reserved juice, sugar, eggs, salt, flour and nuts in bowl; mix well. Pour into 2 greased small loaf pans. Bake at 325 degrees for 50 minutes. Remove to wire racks to cool. Yield: 2 small loaves.

CRANBERRY-ORANGE NUT BREAD

2 cups flour
3/4 cup sugar
1 1/2 teaspoons baking
  powder
3/4 teaspoon salt
1/2 teaspoon soda
1/4 cup margarine or
  butter, softened

1 tablespoon grated
  orange rind
3/4 cup orange juice
1 egg
1 cup chopped
  cranberries
1/2 cup chopped nuts

Grease bottom only of 5x9-inch loaf pan. Combine flour, sugar, baking powder, salt and soda in bowl; mix well. Cut in margarine until crumbly. Add orange rind, orange juice and egg, stirring just until moistened. Stir in cranberries and nuts. Pour into prepared pan. Bake at 350 degrees for 55 minutes to 1 hour and 5 minutes or until toothpick inserted in center comes out clean. Loosen sides; remove to wire rack to cool completely. Yield: 1 loaf.

DATE AND HONEY LOAVES

1 1/2 teaspoons soda
3/4 cup boiling water
2 cups coarsely chopped
  pitted dates
2 1/2 cups flour
1 tablespoon baking
  powder

1/2 teaspoon cinnamon
1/2 teaspoon salt
1/2 cup butter, softened
1 cup honey
2 eggs
1 teaspoon vanilla extract

Dissolve soda in boiling water. Pour over dates in bowl. Let stand for 20 minutes or longer. Combine flour, baking powder, cinnamon and salt in bowl; mix well. Cream butter in large mixer bowl until light. Add honey gradually, beating until fluffy. Beat eggs and vanilla in small bowl. Add to creamed mixture; beat well. Add flour mixture gradually, stirring constantly. Stir in date mixture. Pour into 2 greased and floured 5x9-inch loaf pans. Bake at 350 degrees for 1 hour or until toothpick inserted in center comes out clean. Cool in pans for 5 minutes. Remove to wire racks to cool completely. Do not slice until completely cooled. Yield: 2 loaves.

OLD-FASHIONED HARVEST BREAD

1½ cups oats
¾ cup evaporated
  skim milk
¼ cup water
1½ cups flour
1 teaspoon baking
  powder
1 teaspoon soda
¼ teaspoon salt
⅓ cup packed brown
  sugar

1 tablespoon pumpkin
  pie spice
1 egg, beaten
¼ cup molasses
3 tablespoons oil
1 cup chopped green
  cooking apples
¼ cup chopped walnuts
1 tablespoon oats
1 tablespoon chopped
  walnuts

Soak 1½ cups oats in evaporated milk and water in medium bowl for 10 minutes. Combine flour, baking powder, soda, salt, brown sugar and pumpkin pie spice in large bowl; mix well. Add egg, molasses and oil to oat mixture; mix well. Add to flour mixture; mix well. Stir in apples and ¼ cup walnuts. Pour into 5x9-inch loaf pan sprayed with nonstick cooking spray. Sprinkle with remaining 1 tablespoon oats and 1 tablespoon walnuts. Bake at 350 degrees for 40 to 45 minutes or until toothpick inserted in center comes out clean. Cool in pan for 15 minutes. Remove to wire rack to cool completely. Yield: 1 loaf.

RICH MAPLE NUT BREAD

1 cup all-purpose flour
¾ cup whole wheat flour
1 tablespoon baking
  powder
1 teaspoon salt
¼ teaspoon cinnamon
½ cup finely chopped
  walnuts
¼ cup butter or margarine

⅔ cup milk
⅓ cup maple syrup
1 egg
½ teaspoon vanilla
  extract
3 tablespoons finely
  chopped walnuts
2 tablespoons sugar
¼ teaspoon cinnamon

Combine flours, baking powder, salt and ¼ teaspoon cinnamon in medium bowl; mix well. Stir in ½ cup walnuts. Melt butter in 1-quart saucepan; remove from heat. Stir in milk and syrup. Add egg and vanilla; beat well. Add to flour mixture, stirring just until moistened. Spoon into greased 5x9-inch loaf pan. Combine remaining 3 tablespoons walnuts, sugar and 1/4 teaspoon cinnamon in small bowl; mix well. Sprinkle over batter. Bake at 350 degrees for 40 minutes or until bread tests done. Remove to wire rack to cool completely. Wrap tightly in foil. Let stand overnight before slicing. Yield: 1 loaf.

QUICK ORANGE LOAVES

2 cups finely chopped
  orange pulp
1 tablespoon grated
  orange rind
3 cups flour
1/2 teaspoon baking
  powder
1 teaspoon salt

1 teaspoon soda
2 teaspoons cinnamon
1 cup chopped nuts
3 eggs
1 1/2 cups sugar
1 cup salad oil
1 teaspoon vanilla extract

Combine orange pulp and orange rind in small bowl. Combine flour, baking powder, salt, soda, cinnamon and nuts in bowl; mix well. Beat eggs in large mixer bowl. Add sugar and oil; mix well. Stir in vanilla and orange mixture. Add flour mixture; stir just until moistened. Pour into 2 greased and floured 5x9-inch loaf pans. Bake at 350 degrees for 50 minutes to 1 hour or until toothpick inserted in center comes out clean. Cool in pans on wire racks for 10 minutes. Remove to wire racks to cool completely. Let stand in airtight container for 24 hours before slicing. Will keep in refrigerator for up to 1 week. May freeze for longer storage. Yield: 2 loaves.

PEPPER BREAD

2 eggs
1 cup buttermilk
2 cups self-rising
  cornmeal

2/3 cup oil
1/3 cup chopped onion
1/3 cup chopped green
  bell pepper

Combine eggs, buttermilk, cornmeal, oil, onion and green pepper in bowl; mix well. Pour into greased 5x9-inch loaf pan. Bake at 350 degrees for 1 hour. Remove to wire rack to cool. Yield: 1 loaf.

POPPY SEED BREAD

3 cups flour
2½ cups sugar
½ teaspoon salt
½ teaspoon baking
powder
3 eggs
1½ cups milk
1 cup plus 2 tablespoons
oil
1½ tablespoons poppy
seed

¾ cup confectioners'
sugar
¼ cup orange juice
½ teaspoon almond
extract
½ teaspoon vanilla
extract
½ teaspoon butter extract

Combine flour, sugar, salt, baking powder, eggs, milk, oil and poppy seed in bowl; mix well. Pour into 2 greased 5x9-inch loaf pans. Bake at 325 degrees for 1 hour. Cool in pans for 5 minutes. Combine confectioners' sugar, orange juice and flavorings in bowl; mix well. Drizzle over warm loaves. Remove to wire racks to cool completely. Yield: 2 loaves.

PRESIDENTS' BREAD

2 cups flour
¾ cup sugar
1½ teaspoons baking
powder
¾ teaspoon salt
½ teaspoon soda
¼ cup margarine,
softened

1 tablespoon grated
orange rind
¾ cup orange juice
1 egg
1 cup chopped
cranberries
½ cup chopped nuts

Grease bottom only of 5x9-inch loaf pan. Combine flour, sugar, baking powder, salt and soda in bowl; mix well. Cut in margarine until crumbly. Add orange rind, orange juice and egg, stirring just until moistened. Stir in cranberries and nuts. Pour into prepared pan. Bake at 350 degrees for 55 minutes to 1 hour or until toothpick inserted in center comes out clean. Loosen sides; remove to wire rack to cool completely. Yield: 1 loaf.

APRICOT AND PUMPKIN BREAD

1¹/₂ cups canned
   pumpkin purée
1 cup sugar
1 cup oil
3 eggs
2¹/₄ cups flour
1¹/₂ teaspoons soda
1¹/₂ teaspoons baking
   powder
³/₄ teaspoon cinnamon

³/₄ teaspoon nutmeg
³/₄ teaspoon salt
1 4-ounce package
   vanilla pudding and pie
   filling mix
1¹/₂ cups chopped dried
   apricots
1¹/₂ cups chopped
   walnuts

Combine pumpkin, sugar, oil and eggs in large bowl; mix well. Combine next 6 ingredients in bowl; mix well. Add to pumpkin mixture; mix well. Fold in pudding and pie filling mix, apricots and walnuts. Pour into 2 greased 4x8-inch loaf pans. Bake at 350 degrees for 1 hour or until toothpick inserted in center comes out clean. Cool in pans for 10 minutes. Remove to wire racks to cool completely before slicing. May freeze, tightly wrapped, for up to 3 months. Yield: 2 loaves.

SPICED PUMPKIN LOAF

1³/₄ cups flour
1 teaspoon baking
   powder
1 teaspoon soda
¹/₂ teaspoon salt
1 cup canned pumpkin
²/₃ cup sugar
¹/₃ cup sour cream
¹/₃ cup oil

1 egg
3 tablespoons orange
   marmalade
1 teaspoon cinnamon
¹/₂ teaspoon ginger
¹/₄ teaspoon freshly
   grated nutmeg
¹/₈ teaspoon cloves
²/₃ cup chopped walnuts

Sift flour, baking powder, soda and salt together. Combine pumpkin, sugar, sour cream, oil, egg, marmalade, cinnamon, ginger, nutmeg and cloves in mixer bowl. Beat at medium speed until well blended. Add flour mixture gradually, beating at low speed until mixed. Stir in walnuts. Pour into greased and waxed paper-lined 5x9-inch loaf pan. Bake at 350 degrees for 1 hour and 5 minutes or until toothpick inserted in center comes out clean. Cool in pan on wire rack for 10 minutes. Remove to wire rack to cool completely. Yield: 1 loaf.

ZUCCHINI BREAD

3 eggs
1 cup oil
2 cups sugar
2 tablespoons vanilla
extract
3 cups flour
1 tablespoon soda

1 1/2 teaspoons baking
powder
2 tablespoons cinnamon
2 cups puréed zucchini
1 cup chopped walnuts
1 cup raisins

Combine eggs, oil and sugar in large mixer bowl; beat well. Stir in vanilla. Sift flour, soda, baking powder and cinnamon together. Add to egg mixture; mix well. Stir in zucchini, walnuts and raisins. Pour into 2 greased 5x9-inch loaf pans. Bake at 325 degrees for 1 hour. Remove to wire racks to cool completely. Yield: 2 loaves.

CRAN-APPLE STREUSEL BRAIDS

1   1-pound loaf frozen
white or honey wheat
bread dough
1   21-ounce can
cinnamon-apple pie
filling
1 cup fresh or frozen
whole cranberries
1 tablespoon orange juice
1 tablespoon grated
fresh orange rind or 1
teaspoon dried orange
rind
1 teaspoon lemon juice

1 teaspoon apple pie
spice
1/4 cup flour
1/4 cup sugar
2 tablespoons brown
sugar
1/2 teaspoon cinnamon
1/4 cup butter, softened
3/4 cup chopped walnuts
Milk
1/4 cup confectioners'
sugar
1 teaspoon milk

Thaw frozen bread dough until pliable. Combine pie filling, cranberries, orange juice, orange rind, lemon juice and apple pie spice in bowl; mix well. Combine flour, sugar, brown sugar and cinnamon in bowl; mix well. Cut in butter until crumbly. Divide bread dough into 3 portions. Roll each portion into 7x8-inch rectangle on floured surface. Make 2-inch long cuts at 1-inch intervals from outer edge toward center on 7-inch sides. Spread 1 cup cran-apple mixture down center third of each portion. Sprinkle each portion with 1/4 cup walnuts. Fold strips diagonally over filling from alternate sides, overlapping to give braided look. Brush with milk; sprinkle each with ¼ cup brown sugar mixture. Place on baking sheet. Let rise in warm place for 30 minutes. Bake at 350 degrees for 20 minutes. Bake, covered with foil, for 5 to 10 minutes longer or until golden brown. Remove to wire racks to cool. Combine confectioners' sugar and 1 teaspoon milk in small bowl; mix well. Drizzle over braids. Yield: 3 braids.

NEW ENGLAND CRANBERRY NUT BREAD

2½ cups flour
2 envelopes dry yeast
1 cup oats
½ cup sugar
1½ teaspoons salt
1 teaspoon allspice
1 teaspoon mace
1½ cups milk
½ cup water

¼ cup shortening
1 egg
½ cup raisins
½ cup chopped nuts
3 to 3½ cups flour
½ cup sugar
2 cups coarsely chopped
   cranberries

Combine 2½ cups flour, yeast, oats, ½ cup sugar, salt, allspice and mace in large mixer bowl; mix well. Combine milk, water and shortening in saucepan; mix well. Heat to 120 to 130 degrees, stirring constantly; remove from heat. Shortening does not need to melt. Add to flour mixture; mix well. Add egg; beat at low speed until moistened. Beat at medium speed for 3 minutes. Stir in raisins, nuts and enough remaining flour to make a firm dough. Knead on floured surface for 5 to 8 minutes or until smooth and elastic. Place in greased bowl, turning to coat surface. Let rise, covered, in warm place until doubled in bulk. Punch dough down. Divide dough into 2 portions. Pat each portion into 7x14-inch rectangle on lightly floured surface; brush with water. Combine remaining ½ cup sugar and cranberries in bowl; mix well. Spread over dough. Roll as for jelly roll from narrow end, pressing dough tightly with each turn. Seal ends. Place seam side down. Cut diagonally at 1-inch intervals through entire loaf in both directions. Place in 2 greased 5x9-inch loaf pans. Let rise, covered, in warm place until doubled in bulk. Bake at 350 degrees for 40 to 45 minutes or until deep golden brown. Remove to wire racks to cool.
Yield: 2 loaves.

BROCCOLI BREAD

1 10-ounce package
frozen chopped broccoli
2 tablespoons oil
1 loaf frozen bread
dough, thawed
2 cups shredded
provolone cheese

1 package sliced
pepperoni
2 cups shredded
mozzarella cheese

Cook broccoli in oil in skillet just until tender, stirring constantly. Let bread dough rise using package directions. Roll into rectangle. Layer provolone cheese, pepperoni, broccoli and mozzarella cheese over dough. Roll as for jelly roll. Place on oiled baking sheet. Cut 3 vents in top of dough. Bake at 350 degrees for 30 minutes. Yield: 1 loaf.

CHEESE AND SAUSAGE BREAD

1 envelope dry yeast
1/4 cup warm water
1 tablespoon honey
1/2 teaspoon salt
2 1/4 cups flour
2 eggs
1/4 cup chopped fresh
herbs (dill, rosemary,
basil or thyme)

1/4 cup butter or
margarine, softened
1 1/2 cups shredded low-
fat Cheddar cheese
1 pound turkey smoked
sausage, casing removed
1 egg, slightly beaten
1 tablespoon sesame
seed

Dissolve yeast in warm water in large mixer bowl. Stir in honey and salt. Let stand for 5 minutes. Add 1/2 cup flour; beat for 3 minutes or until elastic. Add 2 eggs 1 at a time, beating well after each addition. Add remaining flour gradually, beating until soft dough forms. Add herbs and butter; beat well. Knead in cheese. Place in greased bowl, turning to coat surface. Let rise, covered, in warm place until doubled in bulk. Punch dough down. Pat into 9x12-inch rectangle on floured surface. Place sausage on narrow side of dough. Roll as for jelly roll. Seal ends. Place seam side down in lightly greased 5x9-inch loaf pan. Let rise for 30 minutes or until puffy. Brush with remaining egg; sprinkle with sesame seed. Bake at 350 degrees for 45 to 50 minutes or until golden brown. Cool in pan for 10 minutes. Slice and serve with desired mustards. Yield: 8 servings.

SCRUMPTIOUS CHEESE BREAD

2 cups shredded Cheddar
 cheese
2 cups mayonnaise
1/2 red Bermuda onion,
 chopped

Garlic salt to taste
1 loaf French bread,
 sliced into halves
 lengthwise

Combine cheese, mayonnaise, onion and garlic salt in bowl; mix well. Spread over cut sides of French bread. Place cut side up on foil-lined baking sheet. Bake at 300 degrees for 20 minutes or until bubbly. Yield: 12 servings.

HIGH-PROTEIN HONEY WHEAT BREAD

1/4 cup shortening
2 cups bread flour
2 teaspoons salt
2 envelopes dry yeast
1 cup water
1/2 cup honey
1 cup cream-style cottage
 cheese

1/4 cup margarine or butter
2 eggs
1 cup whole wheat flour
1/2 cup oats
1 cup chopped nuts
2 to 3 cups bread flour
Melted butter (optional)

Grease two 5x9-inch loaf pans generously with 2 table-spoons shortening each. Combine 2 cups bread flour, salt and yeast in large bowl; mix well. Combine water, honey, cottage cheese and margarine in medium saucepan; mix well. Heat to 120 to 130 degrees, stirring constantly. Margarine does not need to melt completely. Add to flour mixture alternately with eggs, beating well after each addition. Add whole wheat flour, oats, nuts and enough remaining bread flour to make soft dough. Knead on floured surface for 10 minutes or until smooth and elastic. Place in greased bowl, turning to coat surface. Let rise, loosely covered with plastic wrap and cloth towel, in warm place until light and doubled in bulk. Punch dough down. Divide dough into 2 portions; shape into balls. Let rest, covered with inverted bowl, for 15 minutes. Shape into 2 loaves. Place in prepared pans. Let rise, covered, in warm place until doubled in bulk. Bake at 375 degrees for 35 to 40 minutes or until loaves sound hollow when lightly tapped. Remove to wire racks to cool. Brush tops of loaves with melted butter for soft crusts. Yield: 2 loaves.

HOLIDAY BREAD WREATH

2 envelopes dry yeast
1/2 cup warm (105 to 115-
degree) water
13/4 cups warm (105 to
115-degree) skim milk
2 tablespoons sugar
1 tablespoon salt

3 tablespoons margarine,
softened
3 egg whites
63/4 to 71/4 cups
unbleached flour
1 egg white
1 tablespoon water

Dissolve yeast in warm water in large bowl. Add warm milk, sugar and salt; mix well. Stir in margarine. Add 3 egg whites and 2 cups flour; mix with wooden spoon. Add 1 cup flour; mix well. Add enough remaining flour to make a smooth, soft dough. Knead on floured surface for 8 to 10 minutes or until elastic. Place in greased bowl, turning to coat surface. Let rise, covered, in warm place until doubled in bulk. Punch dough down. Roll into 12x24-inch rectangle on floured surface. Divide dough into four 3-inch strips. Braid 3 strips together; shape into circle. Place on greased baking sheet; brush with water. Divide remaining strip into thirds; braid. Arrange on top of large braid. Let rise until doubled in bulk. Mix remaining egg white with 1 tablespoon water. Brush over wreath. Bake at 400 degrees until underside is browned and wreath sounds hollow when tapped. Remove to wire rack to cool. Tie with a large red bow. Yield: 1 wreath.

MONKEY BREAD

1 cup milk
1/2 cup butter
1/4 cup sugar
1 teaspoon salt

1 envelope dry yeast
1 egg
31/2 cups flour
1/2 cup melted butter

Heat milk, 1/2 cup butter, sugar and salt in saucepan. Cook until butter melts, stirring constantly. Cool to 105 degrees. Add yeast; mix well. Add egg; mix well. Place flour in large bowl. Add milk mixture; mix well. Let rise, covered, in warm place until doubled in bulk. Shape into 11/2-inch balls; dip in melted butter. Layer in 10-inch bundt pan. Let rise, covered, for 45 minutes. Bake at 375 degrees for 35 minutes. Cool in pan for 5 minutes. Invert onto serving plate. Yield: 12 servings.

PINEAPPLE-CHEESE COFFEE CAKE

2 cups chopped fresh
  pineapple
1 cup sugar
1 tablespoon fresh lemon
  juice
2 teaspoons vanilla
  extract
1/3 cup sugar
16 ounces cream cheese,
  softened
2 eggs
1 tablespoon vanilla
  extract
2 teaspoons lemon juice

1 cup self-rising flour
1/2 cup sugar
1 teaspoon cinnamon
1/2 cup butter or
  margarine, softened
1 cup self-rising flour
1/3 cup sugar
1 teaspoon Rapid-Rise
  dry yeast
1 cup milk
1/4 cup water
1/3 cup unsalted butter
2 eggs
2 cups self-rising flour

Combine pineapple, 1 cup sugar, 1 tablespoon lemon juice and 2 teaspoons vanilla in small saucepan. Cook until syrupy and liquid is reduced to 1 cup, stirring constantly. Set aside to cool. Cream 1/3 cup sugar and cream cheese in mixer bowl until light and fluffy. Add 2 eggs 1 at a time, beating well after each addition. Add 1 tablespoon vanilla and 2 teaspoons lemon juice; beat well. Combine 1 cup self-rising flour, 1/2 cup sugar and cinnamon in bowl; mix well. Cut in 1/2 cup butter until crumbly. Combine 1 cup self-rising flour, 1/3 cup sugar and yeast in large mixer bowl; mix well. Combine milk, water and unsalted butter in saucepan. Heat to 120 degrees, stirring constantly; remove from heat. Pour into yeast mixture. Beat for 3 minutes. Add remaining 2 eggs 1 at a time, beating well after each addition. Add remaining 2 cups flour, stirring to make stiff batter. Spoon 2/3 of the batter into greased 9x13-inch baking pan. Layer cream cheese mixture and pineapple mixture over batter. Top with remaining batter; sprinkle with crumb mixture. Let rise in warm place for 20 minutes. Bake at 375 degrees for 35 to 40 minutes or until coffee cake tests done. Cool. May substitute one 10-ounce jar apricot-pineapple preserves for pineapple mixture. Yield: 15 servings.

TEDDY BEAR BREAD

1 loaf frozen bread
  dough, thawed, or
  homemade dough
1 egg

2 tablespoons water
Poppy seed
Raisins

Divide dough into 1 large ball (body), 1 medium ball (head), 6 small balls (arms, legs and ears) and 1 very small ball (nose). Arrange on greased baking sheet in shape of bear. Let rise, uncovered, in warm place for 2 to 3 hours. Beat egg with water in small mixer bowl until foamy. Brush over dough; sprinkle with poppy seeds. Arrange raisins for eyes, mouth and belly button. Bake at 350 degrees for 30 to 40 minutes or until golden brown. Remove to wire rack to cool completely. Tie a bow around neck for a really festive bear. Yield: 1 bear.

HEALTHFUL WALNUT BREAD

2¾ cups all-purpose flour
2½ cups whole wheat
  flour
1½ cups chopped
  walnuts
½ cup wheat germ
⅓ cup sugar
2 teaspoons salt

2 envelopes Rapid-Rise
  yeast
1½ cups water
¾ cup plain yogurt
¼ cup margarine or
  butter blend
1 cup all-purpose flour

Combine 2¾ cups all-purpose flour, whole wheat flour, walnuts, wheat germ, sugar, salt and yeast in large bowl; mix well. Combine water, yogurt and margarine in small saucepan. Cook over low heat to 125 to 130 degrees, stirring constantly; remove from heat. Stir into flour mixture. Add enough remaining 1 cup all-purpose flour to make stiff dough. Knead on lightly floured surface until smooth and elastic. Let rest, covered, for 10 minutes. Divide dough into 2 portions. Roll each portion into 8x12-inch rectangle. Roll as for jelly roll; seal ends. Place in 2 greased 5x9-inch loaf pans. Let rise, covered, in warm place until doubled in bulk. Bake at 400 degrees for 25 to 30 minutes or until golden brown. Remove to wire racks to cool.
Yield: 2 loaves.

SUGARPLUM TREES

1 1/2 cups flour
2 envelopes dry yeast
3 tablespoons sugar
1 teaspoon salt
3/4 cup sour cream
1/2 cup water
2 tablespoons shortening
1 egg
1 1/2 to 1 3/4 cups flour
1/2 cup finely chopped
   candied fruit
1/4 cup finely chopped
   nuts
2 tablespoons sugar
2 tablespoons butter,
   softened
1 to 2 cups confectioners'
   sugar
2 to 4 tablespoons milk

Combine 1 1/2 cups flour, yeast, 3 tablespoons sugar and salt in large mixer bowl. Combine sour cream, water and shortening in saucepan. Heat until very warm; shortening need not melt. Stir sour cream mixture and egg into flour mixture. Beat at low speed until moistened. Beat at medium speed for 3 minutes. Add enough remaining 1 1/2 to 1 3/4 cups flour gradually to make soft dough, stirring with wooden spoon after each addition. Knead on floured surface for 5 to 8 minutes or until smooth and elastic. Let rest, covered, for 5 minutes. Combine candied fruit, nuts and remaining 2 tablespoons sugar in small bowl; mix well. Divide dough into 2 portions. Roll one portion into 6x12-inch rectangle on lightly floured surface. Spread with half the butter. Sprinkle half the fruit mixture lengthwise over half the dough. Fold dough over to enclose filling; seal edges. Cut into twelve 1-inch strips. Place 2 strips side by side on greased baking sheet to form trunk of tree. Arrange remaining strips diagonally in pyramid pattern to resemble branches. Repeat with remaining dough, butter and fruit mixture. Let rise, covered, in warm place until almost doubled in bulk. Bake at 375 degrees for 15 to 20 minutes or until golden brown. Remove carefully to wire rack. Blend desired amount of confectioners' sugar with enough milk to make of drizzling consistency. Tint with food coloring if desired. Drizzle over trees. Yield: 2 trees.

APPLE SPICE MUFFINS

1¼ cups flour
¾ cup sugar
½ cup chopped walnuts
¼ cup quick-cooking oats
1½ teaspoons baking
  powder
½ teaspoon salt
¾ teaspoon cinnamon

½ teaspoon ginger
½ teaspoon nutmeg
2 eggs
2 cups chopped peeled
  apples
¾ cup oil
1½ tablespoons water

Combine flour, sugar, walnuts, oats, baking powder, salt, cinnamon, ginger and nutmeg in large bowl; mix well. Beat eggs in medium bowl with fork. Stir in apples, oil and water. Pour into flour mixture, stirring just until moistened. Spoon batter into muffin cups sprayed with nonstick cooking spray. Bake at 400 degrees for 20 minutes or until muffins test done. Serve warm or cold. Yield: 1 dozen.

BLUEBERRY AND ORANGE MUFFINS

1⅓ cups flour
1 cup oats
¼ cup packed brown
  sugar
1 tablespoon baking
  powder
½ teaspoon soda
½ teaspoon salt (optional)

¾ cup fresh or frozen
  blueberries
⅔ cup milk
⅓ cup orange juice
¼ cup oil
1 egg, beaten
2 teaspoons grated
  orange rind

Combine flour, oats, brown sugar, baking powder, soda and salt in large bowl; mix well. Stir in blueberries. Combine milk, orange juice, oil, egg and orange rind in bowl; mix well. Add to flour mixture, stirring just until moistened. Fill greased muffin cups ⅔ full. Bake at 400 degrees for 18 to 20 minutes or until golden brown. Serve warm. Yield: 1 dozen.

BRAN MUFFINS

1 15-ounce package
  Raisin Bran
5 cups flour
3 cups sugar
1 tablespoon plus 2
  teaspoons soda

2 teaspoons salt
4 eggs, beaten
1 quart buttermilk
1 cup oil

Combine Raisin Bran, flour, sugar, soda and salt in large bowl; mix well. Make well in center. Add eggs, buttermilk and oil, stirring just until moistened. Chill, covered, until ready to use. Fill greased muffin cups 2/3 full. Bake at 400 degrees for 12 to 15 minutes or until golden brown. May store batter in refrigerator for up to 6 weeks. Yield: 5 1/2 dozen.

MIX-AHEAD BRAN MUFFINS

2 1/2 cups buttermilk
1/2 cup oil
2 eggs, beaten
4 cups bran flake cereal
  with or without raisins

2 cups flour
1 teaspoon salt
2 teaspoons soda
2/3 cup sugar

Combine buttermilk, oil and eggs in large mixer bowl. Beat at low speed until blended. Add cereal, flour, salt, soda and sugar; beat at low speed until moistened. Chill, covered, for 1 hour. Fill paper-lined muffin cups 2/3 full. Bake at 350 degrees for 18 to 22 minutes or until golden brown. Yield: 1 1/2 dozen.

A Lion Tip

Add 1 cup chopped dates, dried apricots, raisins or figs to your favorite muffin recipe.

CRANBERRY OAT BRAN MUFFINS

3 cups oat bran
3/4 cup flour
4 teaspoons baking
powder
1 teaspoon cinnamon
1/2 teaspoon salt
1 cup chopped fresh
cranberries
1 cup raisins

1/2 cup chopped walnuts
or pecans, lightly toasted
1 cup plain yogurt
1/2 cup oil
1/2 cup packed light
brown sugar
2 eggs
1/2 teaspoon vanilla
extract

Combine oat bran, flour, baking powder, cinnamon and salt in large bowl; mix well. Add cranberries, raisins and walnuts; toss to coat. Beat yogurt and oil in bowl with wire whisk. Add brown sugar, eggs and vanilla; stir until blended. Add to oat bran mixture, stirring just until moistened and mixed. Fill lightly buttered muffin cups 2/3 full. Bake at 375 degrees for 20 to 25 minutes or until golden brown. Remove to wire rack to cool. Yield: 1 dozen.

DATE AND OAT BRAN MUFFINS

2 cups flour
1 tablespoon baking
powder
1/4 teaspoon salt
1/2 teaspoon cinnamon
1/3 cup packed light
brown sugar

1/2 cup chopped dates
1 1/2 cups flaked oat bran
cereal
1 1/4 cups milk
3 tablespoons oil
1 egg

Combine flour, baking powder, salt, cinnamon, brown sugar and dates in medium bowl; mix well. Combine cereal, milk, oil and egg in bowl; mix well. Stir into flour mixture until mixed but still lumpy. Fill buttered muffin cups 2/3 full. Bake at 400 degrees for 18 to 20 minutes or until light brown. Yield: 1/2 dozen.

EASTER BREAKFAST MUFFIN BASKETS

1/4 cup packed brown
 sugar
2 tablespoons baking mix
2 tablespoons chopped
 nuts
1/4 teaspoon cinnamon
1 tablespoon butter or
 margarine
2 cups baking mix

1/4 cup sugar
2/3 cup milk
1/4 cup oil
1 egg
1 4-ounce package
 vanilla instant pudding
 mix
Jelly beans
Red string licorice

Combine brown sugar, 2 tablespoons baking mix, nuts and cinnamon in small bowl; mix well. Cut in butter until crumbly. Combine 2 cups baking mix, sugar, milk, oil, egg and pudding mix in mixer bowl. Beat for 30 seconds. Spoon batter evenly into 12 paper-lined muffin cups. Sprinkle with crumb mixture. Bake at 375 degrees for 20 minutes or until golden brown. Cool. Decorate with jelly beans and make handles from red string licorice. For no-cholesterol muffins, use margarine and substitute skim milk for milk and 2 egg whites or 1/4 cup frozen cholesterol-free egg product for the egg. Yield: 1 dozen.

FRENCH TOAST MUFFINS

1 cup sliced strawberries
1 orange, peeled,
 sectioned
2 tablespoons light corn
 syrup
1 egg, slightly beaten
1/4 cup milk

1 tablespoon sugar
1 teaspoon grated orange
 rind
2 honey wheat English
 muffins, split
2 tablespoons margarine

Combine strawberries, orange sections and corn syrup in small bowl. Combine egg, milk, sugar and orange rind in 9-inch pie plate; mix well. Place muffins cut side down in egg mixture. Let stand for 5 minutes to soak; turn to coat other side. Melt margarine in large skillet over medium heat. Add muffins cut side down. Cook until light brown on both sides. Spoon fruit mixture over muffins. Yield: 2 servings.

DOUBLE OAT MUFFINS

2 cups uncooked oat
  bran hot cereal
1/3 cup packed brown
  sugar
1/4 cup flour
2 teaspoons baking
  powder
1/4 teaspoon salt (optional)
1/4 teaspoon nutmeg
  (optional)

1 cup skim milk
2 egg whites, slightly
  beaten
3 tablespoons oil
1 1/2 teaspoons vanilla
  extract
1/4 cup oats
1 tablespoon packed
  brown sugar

Combine oat bran cereal, 1/3 cup brown sugar, flour, baking powder, salt and nutmeg in medium bowl; mix well. Combine skim milk, egg whites, oil and vanilla in bowl; mix well. Add to oat bran mixture, stirring just until moistened. Fill paper-lined muffin cups 3/4 full. Combine oats and remaining 1 tablespoon brown sugar in small bowl; mix well. Sprinkle over batter. Bake at 400 degrees for 20 to 22 minutes or until golden brown. Yield: 1 dozen.

ORANGE MUFFINS

1/2 cup butter, softened
1 cup sugar
2 eggs
Grated rind of 1 orange
2 cups flour
1/4 teaspoon salt

1 teaspoon soda
1 cup buttermilk
3/4 cup chopped pecans
1/4 cup orange juice
1 tablespoon sugar

Cream butter and 1 cup sugar in large mixer bowl until light and fluffy. Add eggs and orange rind; beat well. Stir in flour, salt, soda, buttermilk and pecans; mix well. Spoon batter evenly into 12 greased muffin cups. Bake at 375 degrees for 25 minutes. Brush orange juice over warm muffins; sprinkle with remaining 1 tablespoon sugar. May bake in 6 giant muffin cups instead of 12 regular cups if preferred. Yield: 1 dozen.

PEANUT BUTTER AND BANANA MUFFINS

1 cup flour
3/4 cup oats
1/3 cup packed brown
  sugar
1 tablespoon baking
  powder
1 cup milk
1/2 cup peanut butter
1/2 cup mashed ripe
  banana

1 egg, beaten
2 tablespoons oil
1 teaspoon vanilla extract
1/4 cup oats
1/4 cup flour
2 tablespoons melted
  margarine
2 tablespoons packed
  brown sugar

Combine 1 cup flour, 3/4 cup oats, 1/3 cup brown sugar and baking powder in large bowl; mix well. Mix milk, peanut butter, banana, egg, oil and vanilla in bowl with wire whisk. Add to flour mixture, stirring just until moistened. Fill greased muffin cups 3/4 full. Combine remaining 1/4 cup oats, 1/4 cup flour, melted margarine and 2 tablespoons brown sugar in small bowl. Sprinkle over batter. Bake at 375 degrees for 16 to 18 minutes or until golden brown. Serve warm. Yield: 1 dozen.

PLYMOUTH ROCK MUFFINS

1 egg
1/2 cup milk
1/2 cup canned pumpkin
1/2 cup raisins
1/4 cup melted margarine
  or butter
1 1/2 cups flour

1/2 cup sugar
2 teaspoons baking
  powder
1/2 teaspoon salt
1/2 teaspoon cinnamon
1/2 teaspoon nutmeg
1 tablespoon sugar

Grease bottoms only of 12 medium muffin cups. Beat egg in medium mixer bowl until light. Add milk, pumpkin, raisins and margarine; mix well. Add flour, 1/2 cup sugar, baking powder, salt, cinnamon and nutmeg, stirring just until moistened. Fill prepared muffin cups 2/3 full. Sprinkle remaining sugar. Bake at 400 degrees for 20 minutes or until golden brown. Yield: 1 dozen.

SPICY PUMPKIN MUFFINS

1½ cups flour
6 tablespoons sugar
1 tablespoon baking
  powder
½ teaspoon salt
½ teaspoon cinnamon
½ teaspoon nutmeg

½ cup golden raisins
¼ cup butter or margarine
1 cup fresh or canned
  pumpkin purée
½ cup milk
1 egg

Combine flour, sugar, baking powder, salt, cinnamon and nutmeg in large bowl; mix with fork. Stir in raisins. Melt butter in 1-quart saucepan. Cool slightly. Stir in pumpkin, milk and egg. Add to flour mixture, stirring just until moistened. Batter will be lumpy. Spoon batter evenly into 12 greased muffin cups. Bake at 400 degrees for 15 to 20 minutes or until muffins test done. Remove from cups. Serve warm. Yield: 1 dozen.

SPICED APPLE DOUGHNUTS

1½ cups flour
½ cup sugar
1 tablespoon baking
  powder
1 tablespoon cinnamon
1 teaspoon allspice
½ teaspoon salt
2 eggs
¾ cup milk

2 tablespoons melted
  butter or margarine
¾ cup finely chopped,
  peeled sweet apple
1¾ cups flour
Oil for deep frying
½ cup confectioners'
  sugar
2 teaspoons cinnamon

Combine 1½ cups flour, sugar, baking powder, 1 tablespoon cinnamon, allspice and salt in large mixer bowl; mix well. Add eggs, milk and butter. Beat at medium speed for 2 minutes. Stir in apple and remaining 1¾ cups flour. Shape into ball. Place on well-floured surface; roll to coat with flour. Pat ¼ inch thick; cut with floured 2½-inch doughnut cutter. Heat 2 inches oil in large saucepan. Place 3 or 4 doughnuts in hot oil. Deep-fry for 1 to 1½ minutes on each side or until golden brown; drain on paper towels. Repeat with remaining doughnuts. Roll in mixture of confectioners' sugar and 2 teaspoons cinnamon. Serve warm or at room temperature. Yield: 1½ dozen.

CHEESE ROLLS

8 ounces processed
  American cheese
1 cup chopped celery
1/3 cup minced dill pickle
2 tablespoons chili sauce

3 tablespoons
  mayonnaise
8 frankfurter rolls
1 tablespoon butter,
  softened

Cut cheese into 1/4-inch cubes. Place in bowl. Add celery and pickle. Combine chili sauce and mayonnaise in small bowl; mix well. Pour over cheese mixture; toss to coat. Slit tops of rolls lengthwise halfway through; remove part of center. Fill with cheese mixture; spread top crust with butter. Place in ungreased shallow baking pan. Bake at 350 degrees for 15 to 20 minutes or until rolls are lightly toasted and cheese is melted. Serve hot. Yield: 8 servings.

DESSERT BUTTER ROLLS

1 cup self-rising flour
2 tablespoons shortening
Milk
1/2 cup butter
2 cups sugar

1/2 cup butter
2 cups water or milk
1 tablespoon vanilla
  extract

Place flour in bowl. Cut in shortening until crumbly. Add enough milk to make a firm batter. Chill for several minutes. Pat into large rectangle. Cut 1/2 cup butter into small pieces. Sprinkle over dough; sprinkle with 1 cup sugar. Roll as for jelly roll. Slice into 3/4-inch rolls. Combine remaining 1 cup sugar, 1/2 cup butter, water and vanilla in small saucepan; mix well. Bring to a boil, stirring constantly. Pour into 9x13-inch baking pan. Arrange rolls cut side down in single layer in hot mixture. Bake at 450 degrees for 20 minutes or until golden brown. Serve warm. Yield: 1 dozen.

A Lion Tip

Hot rolls or biscuits will stay hot longer if you place aluminum foil under the napkin in the basket.

EASY DROP ROLLS

³/₄ cup margarine	1 envelope dry yeast
¹/₄ cup sugar	2 cups warm water
1 egg, slightly beaten	4 cups self-rising flour

Melt margarine in large saucepan. Cool. Add sugar, egg, yeast, warm water and flour; mix well. Dough will be soft and sticky. Chill in airtight container for several hours. Spoon into greased muffin cups. Bake at 400 degrees for 20 minutes or until light brown. Dough may be stored in refrigerator for up to 1 week. Yield: 3 dozen large rolls or 6 dozen small rolls.

NEVER-FAIL ROLLS

³/₄ cup shortening	1 cup warm water
¹/₃ cup sugar	2 eggs, well beaten
1 teaspoon salt	3 cups (about) flour
1 envelope dry yeast	¹/₂ cup melted butter

Mix shortening, sugar and salt in large bowl; mix well. Dissolve yeast in warm water. Add to shortening mixture alternately with eggs, mixing well after each addition. Add enough flour to make soft dough. Chill for several hours to overnight. Roll ¹/₂ inch thick on floured surface. Cut with biscuit cutter; place on greased 10x15-inch baking sheet. Let rise in warm place for 2 hours. Brush with melted butter. Fold in half; brush tops with melted butter. Bake at 375 degrees for 10 to 12 minutes or until golden brown. Yield: 1¹/₂ dozen.

A Lion Tip

Reduce yeast bread rising time in half by setting to rise in microwave. Place dough in center of microwave. Place 1 cup hot water in microwave. Microwave on Low (10%) until doubled in bulk.

EASY ORANGE ROLLS

1 16-ounce package hot
   roll mix
2 tablespoons butter or
   margarine
3 tablespoons sugar

1 tablespoon cinnamon
1 cup sifted
   confectioners' sugar
1/4 cup orange marmalade
1/2 teaspoon lemon juice

Prepare and knead roll mix using package directions. Place butter in glass custard cup. Microwave on High for 40 to 50 seconds or until melted. Combine sugar and cinnamon in small bowl; mix well. Roll dough into 12x14-inch rectangle on floured surface. Brush with butter; sprinkle with cinnamon-sugar. Roll as for jelly roll from long side. Pinch seam to seal. Do not seal ends. Cut into 1 1/2-inch slices. Place cut side down in greased shallow 2 1/2-quart glass casserole; cover with plastic wrap. Place in back of microwave; place 1 cup water in glass measure in front of rolls. Microwave on Medium-Low for 1 to 2 minutes. Let stand in microwave for 5 minutes. Repeat 2 to 4 times or until rolls are doubled in bulk. Remove water; uncover rolls. Microwave on Medium-High for 7 to 8 minutes or until tops spring back when lightly touched, turning casserole 3 times. Mix confectioners' sugar, marmalade and lemon juice in bowl. Drizzle over hot rolls. Yield: 9 rolls.

OVERNIGHT ROLLS

1 cup milk
3/4 cup shortening
1/4 cup sugar
1/2 teaspoon salt
1 envelope dry yeast
1/4 cup warm water

2 cups flour
2 eggs, at room
   temperature
2 cups (or less) flour
1/2 cup butter, softened

Heat milk, shortening, sugar and salt in saucepan just until shortening melts, stirring constantly. Remove from heat; cool slightly. Dissolve yeast in warm water in large mixer bowl. Add lukewarm milk mixture; beat well. Add 2 cups flour. Beat at low speed until moistened. Beat at medium speed for 2 minutes. Beat in eggs. Add 1 cup flour gradually, beating at low speed for 2 minutes. Stir in enough remaining flour to make soft dough. Place in greased bowl, turning to coat surface. Let rise, covered, in warm place for 2 hours. Punch dough down; knead.

Divide into 4 portions. Shape into wedges; spread with butter. Place on baking sheet. Bake at 400 degrees for 10 to 12 minutes or until golden brown. Yield: 2 dozen.

POPPY SEED CRESCENTS

1   15-ounce package all
ready pie crusts
8 ounces cream cheese,
softened
1/3 cup confectioners'
sugar

2 tablespoons poppy seed
1 teaspoon grated lemon
rind
1 1/3 cups confectioners'
sugar
3 tablespoons lemon juice

Remove plastic sheets from crusts. Place on lightly floured surface. Cut each crust into 12 wedges. Beat cream cheese, 1/3 cup confectioners' sugar, poppy seed and half the lemon rind in mixer bowl until light and fluffy. Spread 1 1/2 teaspoonfuls on each wedge. Roll up from wide end. Shape into crescents on greased baking sheet. Bake at 350 degrees for 20 to 25 minutes or until light brown. Remove to wire racks to cool. Combine remaining lemon rind, 1 1/3 cups confectioners' sugar and lemon juice in small mixer bowl; mix well. Spread over cooled crescents. Yield: 2 dozen.

QUICK YEAST ROLLS

1/2 cup boiling water
1/2 cup shortening
1 teaspoon salt
1/4 cup sugar
1 envelope dry yeast

1/2 cup warm water
1 egg
3 cups flour
1/2 cup melted butter

Pour 1/2 cup boiling water over shortening in small bowl; mix with wire whisk until smooth. Add salt and sugar; mix well. Dissolve yeast in 1/2 cup warm water. Beat egg in large mixer bowl until frothy. Stir in shortening mixture and yeast. Add flour gradually, stirring until soft dough forms. Place in greased bowl, turning to coat surface. Chill, covered, for 1 hour or longer. Knead on floured surface. Roll 1/2 inch thick; cut with biscuit cutter. Dip in melted butter. Arrange on baking sheet with sides touching. Let rise in warm place for 1 hour. Bake at 425 degrees for 10 to 12 minutes or until golden brown. Yield: 1 1/2 dozen.

Cakes
and
Pies

CAKES

ALMOND CAKE WITH RASPBERRIES

1 cup blanched almonds
1 cup sugar
1 cup flour
8 egg whites
Pinch of salt
1/3 cup sugar
1/2 cup melted butter

2 tablespoons Amaretto
1 10-ounce package
  frozen raspberries,
  thawed, drained
1 1/2 teaspoons
  confectioners' sugar

Butter 9-inch springform pan. Line bottom with buttered waxed paper. Grind almonds and 1 cup sugar to a powder. Combine with flour in bowl; mix well. Beat egg whites with salt in small mixer bowl until soft peaks form. Add remaining 1/3 cup sugar gradually, beating constantly until stiff peaks form. Fold in ground almonds with mixture of melted butter and Amaretto 1/4 at a time. Pour into prepared pan. Press raspberries onto batter. Bake at 350 degrees for 45 minutes or until cake tests done. Cool in pan for 10 minutes. Invert onto serving plate. Dust with confectioners' sugar. Yield: 12 servings.

FRESH APPLE CAKE

2 1/2 cups sifted flour
1 teaspoon salt
1 teaspoon soda
2 teaspoons baking powder
2 cups sugar
3 eggs, beaten
1 1/2 cups oil
1 teaspoon vanilla extract

3 cups chopped peeled
  apples
1 cup chopped walnuts
  or pecans
1 1/2 cups sifted
  confectioners' sugar
3 tablespoons water
2 teaspoons vanilla extract

Sift flour, salt, soda and baking powder together. Beat sugar, eggs and oil in large mixer bowl until smooth. Beat in 1 teaspoon vanilla. Add flour mixture gradually, mixing well. Fold in apples and walnuts gently. Pour into greased waxed paper-lined 10-inch tube pan. Bake at 350 degrees for 1 hour or until cake tests done. Cool in pan for 10 minutes. Invert onto serving plate. Combine remaining ingredients in bowl; mix well. Drizzle over cake. Yield: 16 servings.

APPLE CAKE WITH PECAN-CARAMEL TOPPING

4 eggs
1 2-layer package apple
  cinnamon or applesauce
  spice cake mix
1/2 cup oil
1/3 cup water

1/4 cup apple juice or
  Bourbon
2 cups chopped peeled
  cooking apples
1 cup chopped pecans
Pecan-Caramel Topping

Combine eggs, cake mix, oil, water and apple juice in large mixer bowl. Beat at low speed just until moistened, scraping side of bowl frequently. Beat at medium speed for 2 minutes. Fold in apples and pecans. Pour into greased and floured 10-inch fluted tube pan. Bake at 325 degrees for 1 hour or until cake tests done. Cool in pan on wire rack for 15 minutes. Invert onto serving plate. Serve with Pecan-Caramel Topping and ice cream or frozen yogurt. Yield: 16 servings.

Pecan-Caramel Topping

1/4 cup margarine or
  butter
1/2 cup chopped pecans

1 cup packed brown
  sugar
1 cup whipping cream

Combine margarine and pecans in medium saucepan. Cook over medium heat for 5 minutes or until pecans are toasted and margarine is light brown, stirring constantly. Stir in brown sugar and whipping cream. Bring just to the boiling point over low heat, stirring constantly. Simmer, uncovered, for 2 minutes. Cool slightly.

A Lion Tip

Raisins and nuts coated with flour will not sink to the bottom when added to cake batter.

LAYERED APPLESAUCE CAKE

2¼ cups flour
2¼ teaspoons pumpkin
  pie spice
2 teaspoons soda
¼ teaspoon salt
¾ cup butter, softened
1¼ cups packed light
  brown sugar

3 eggs
1 teaspoon vanilla extract
1½ cups applesauce
⅓ cup milk
½ cup chopped pecans
½ cup golden raisins
Browned Butter Frosting

Mix flour, pumpkin pie spice, soda and salt in bowl. Cream butter and brown sugar in large mixer bowl until light and fluffy. Add eggs 1 at a time, beating well after each addition. Stir in vanilla. Add flour mixture alternately with mixture of applesauce and milk, mixing well after each addition. Fold in pecans and raisins. Pour into 2 greased and floured 8-inch square cake pans. Bake for 30 to 35 minutes or until layers test done. Cool in pans for 15 minutes. Remove to wire racks to cool completely. Spread Browned Butter Frosting between layers and over top and sides of cake. Garnish with fresh apple slices and pecan halves. Yield: 12 servings.

Browned Butter Frosting

½ cup butter
3½ cups confectioners'
  sugar
1 teaspoon vanilla extract

Dash of salt
¼ cup half and half
½ cup confectioners'
  sugar

Heat butter in 1-quart saucepan over medium heat until light amber, stirring frequently. Cool slightly. Combine with 3½ cups confectioners' sugar, vanilla, salt and half and half in small mixer bowl. Beat until smooth, adding, enough remaining ½ cup confectioners' sugar to make of spreading consistency.

BUTTER CAKE

3 cups flour
4 teaspoons baking
 powder
1/2 teaspoon salt
1 cup butter, softened
2 cups sugar

4 egg yolks,well beaten
1 cup milk
1 teaspoon vanilla extract
4 egg whites, beaten
Caramel Icing

Sift flour, baking powder and salt together. Cream butter and sugar in large mixer bowl until light and fluffy. Add egg yolks. Add flour mixture alternately with milk, mixing well after each addition. Stir in vanilla. Fold in egg whites. Pour into 2 greased and floured 9-inch round cake pans. Bake at 350 degrees for 30 minutes. Cool in pans for 10 minutes. Remove to wire racks to cool completely. Spread Caramel Icing between layers and over top and side of cake. Yield: 12 servings.

Caramel Icing

2 cups sugar
1/2 cup butter
1/4 cup light corn syrup

2/3 cup evaporated milk
1/4 teaspoon salt
1 teaspoon vanilla extract

Caramelize 1/4 cup sugar in small cast-iron skillet. Combine 13/4 cups sugar, butter, corn syrup, evaporated milk and salt in heavy saucepan. Cook over low heat until sugar is dissolved, stirring constantly. Bring to a boil. Stir in caramelized sugar. Cook to soft-ball stage, stirring constantly. Remove from heat; beat in vanilla. Cool slightly. Beat until smooth and of spreading consistency.

A Lion Tip

To prevent a soggy or heavy cake, be sure that layers, filling and frosting are completely cool before assembling cake.

CARAMEL CAKE

1 2-layer package butter
cake mix
1 cup sour cream
1/2 cup sugar

4 eggs
1 cup oil
Buttermilk Caramel
Frosting

Combine cake mix, sour cream, sugar, eggs and oil in mixer bowl; beat well. Pour into 2 greased and floured 9-inch round cake pans. Bake at 350 degrees for 25 minutes or until layers test done. Cool in pans for 10 minutes. Remove to wire rack to cool completely. Spread Buttermilk Caramel Frosting between layers and over top and side of cake.
Yield: 12 servings.

Buttermilk Caramel Frosting

2 cups sugar
1/2 cup margarine
1 tablespoon light corn
syrup

1/2 cup buttermilk
1 teaspoon soda
1/8 teaspoon salt

Combine all ingredients in heavy saucepan. Cook over medium heat to soft-ball stage, stirring constantly. Beat by hand until of spreading consistency.

CARROT PUDDING CAKE

1 2-layer package yellow
cake mix
1 4-ounce package vanilla
instant pudding mix
1/2 teaspoon salt
2 teaspoons cinnamon
4 eggs

1/3 cup water
1/4 cup oil
3 cups shredded carrots
1/2 cup finely chopped
raisins
1/2 cup chopped pecans

Combine cake mix, pudding mix, salt, cinnamon, eggs, water and oil in large mixer bowl. Beat at medium speed for 2 minutes, scraping side of bowl frequently. Stir in carrots, raisins and pecans. Pour into 3 greased and floured 9-inch round cake pans. Bake at 350 degrees for 30 to 35 minutes or until layers test done. Cool in pans for 10 minutes. Remove to wire racks to cool completely. Frost with favorite orange frosting. Garnish with pecan halves. Yield: 15 servings.

MOM'S GERMAN CHOCOLATE CAKE

2$\frac{1}{2}$ cups flour
1 teaspoon soda
Pinch of salt
1 cup shortening
2 cups sugar
4 egg yolks, lightly beaten
1 teaspoon vanilla extract

1 cup buttermilk
4 ounces German's
  chocolate, melted
$\frac{1}{2}$ cup boiling water
4 egg whites, stiffly
  beaten
Coconut-Pecan Frosting

Combine flour, soda and salt in bowl; mix well. Cream shortening and sugar in large mixer bowl until light and fluffy. Beat in egg yolks and vanilla. Add flour mixture alternately with buttermilk, mixing well after each addition. Stir in mixture of melted chocolate and water. Fold in stiffly beaten egg whites gently. Pour into 3 greased and floured 8-inch round cake pans. Bake at 350 degrees for 30 to 45 minutes or until layers test done. Cool in pans for 10 minutes. Remove to wire racks to cool completely. Spread Coconut-Pecan Frosting between layers and over top and side of cake. Yield: 16 servings.

Coconut-Pecan Frosting

1 12-ounce can
  evaporated milk
1 cup coconut
3 egg yolks, slightly
  beaten

1 cup chopped pecans
1$\frac{1}{2}$ cups sugar
$\frac{1}{2}$ cup butter
1 tablespoon flour

Combine evaporated milk, coconut, egg yolks, pecans, sugar, butter and flour in saucepan. Cook over medium heat until thickened, stirring constantly.

 A Lion Tip

Place cake pans in the center of the oven, making sure they don't touch each other or sides of oven. Be sure that they are not placed directly under each other as this will restrict heat circulation.

CHOCOLATE SHEET CAKE

2 cups flour
2 cups sugar
1/2 teaspoon salt
2 eggs, beaten
1 teaspoon soda
1/2 cup buttermilk
1 teaspoon vanilla extract

1/2 cup margarine or butter
1 cup water
1/2 cup shortening
3 tablespoons baking cocoa
Chocolate Icing

Sift flour, sugar and salt together. Combine eggs, soda, buttermilk and vanilla in bowl; mix well. Combine margarine, water, shortening and cocoa in saucepan; mix well. Bring to a boil, stirring constantly. Stir into flour mixture. Add egg mixture; mix well. Pour into greased 10x15-inch cake pan. Bake at 350 degrees for 20 minutes. Spread Chocolate Frosting over warm cake. Let cool before cutting. Yield: 16 servings.

Chocolate Icing

1/2 cup margarine or butter
3 tablespoons cocoa
6 tablespoons milk
1 cup chopped nuts

1 1-pound package confectioners' sugar
1 teaspoon vanilla extract

Combine margarine, cocoa and milk in saucepan; mix well. Cook over low heat until margarine is melted, stirring frequently; do not boil. Add nuts, confectioner's sugar and vanilla; mix well.

A Lion Tip

Grease baking pans with the wrappers from butter or margarine.

MINIATURE CHOCOLATE-RASPBERRY LOAF CAKES

1 cup flour
1/3 cup baking cocoa
1/2 teaspoon baking
  powder
3/4 teaspoon soda
1/8 teaspoon salt
1/4 cup butter or
  margarine, softened

1/2 cup sugar
2 eggs
1 teaspoon vanilla extract
1/2 cup buttermilk
1/2 cup seedless red
  raspberry preserves,
  melted
Vanilla Glaze

Combine flour, cocoa, baking powder, soda and salt in bowl; mix well. Cream butter and sugar in mixer bowl until light and fluffy. Add eggs 1 at a time, beating well after each addition. Stir in vanilla. Add flour mixture and buttermilk alternately to creamed mixture, beating well after each addition. Beat at low speed for 2 minutes longer. Blend in preserves. Pour into four 3x5-inch loaf pans sprayed with nonstick cooking spray. Bake at 350 degrees for 25 to 30 minutes or until loaves test done. Cool in pans on wire rack. Drizzle with Vanilla Glaze.
Yield: 16 servings.

Vanilla Glaze

1 tablespoon butter or
  margarine
1 cup confectioners'
  sugar

1 to 2 tablespoons hot
  water
1/4 teaspoon vanilla
  extract

Melt butter in small saucepan over low heat. Add confectioners' sugar alternately with mixture of water and vanilla, beating with wire whisk until smooth.

COCA-COLA CAKE

1 cup butter or
margarine, softened
2 cups flour
1³/₄ cups packed light
brown sugar
3 tablespoons baking
cocoa

1 teaspoon vanilla extract
1 teaspoon soda
2 eggs
¹/₂ cup buttermilk
1 cup Coca-Cola
1¹/₂ cups miniature
marshmallows

Combine butter, flour, brown sugar, cocoa, vanilla, soda, eggs and buttermilk in large mixer bowl. Beat at low speed just until moistened. Beat at medium speed for 1 minute. Stir in Coca-Cola and marshmallows. Pour into greased 9x13-inch cake pan. Bake at 350 degrees for 35 to 40 minutes or until cake tests done. Yield: 15 servings.

FUDGE CAKE

1¹/₂ cups flour
2 cups sugar
6 tablespoons baking
cocoa
1 teaspoon baking
powder
¹/₄ teaspoon salt
1 cup melted butter or
margarine

6 egg yolks, slightly
beaten
1 cup blackberry jam
2 cups chopped pecans
2 teaspoons vanilla
extract
6 egg whites, stiffly
beaten

Combine flour, sugar, cocoa, baking powder and salt in large bowl; mix well. Stir in melted butter, egg yolks, jam, pecans and vanilla. Fold in egg whites. Pour into greased 9x13-inch cake pan. Bake at 350 degrees for 45 minutes or until cake tests done. Yield: 15 servings.

RICH CHOCOLATE MINI-CAKES

2/3 cup flour
1/2 cup sugar
3 tablespoons European-
style cocoa
1/2 teaspoon baking
powder
1/4 teaspoon soda
1/4 teaspoon salt
1/2 cup water
3 tablespoons oil
1 teaspoon vanilla extract

2 tablespoons butter
2 tablespoons European-
style cocoa
2 tablespoons water
1 cup confectioners'
sugar
1/2 teaspoon vanilla
extract
1/2 cup vanilla milk chips
1 tablespoon shortening

Combine flour, sugar, 3 tablespoons cocoa, baking powder, soda and salt in medium mixer bowl; mix well. Add 1/2 cup water, 3 tablespoons oil and 1 teaspoon vanilla. Beat until smooth and well-blended; batter will be thin. Fill lightly greased muffin cups 2/3 full. Bake at 350 degrees for 12 to 14 minutes or until tops spring back when lightly touched. Cool in pans on wire rack for 3 minutes. Invert onto wire racks to cool completely. Melt butter in small saucepan over low heat. Add remaining 2 tablespoons cocoa and 2 tablespoons water. Cook until slightly thickened, stirring frequently; do not boil. Remove from heat. Blend in confectioners' sugar and remaining 1/2 teaspoon vanilla gradually. Dip tops of cakes into chocolate mixture or spread frosting over cakes with spatula. Place on waxed paper-lined tray. Chill until glaze is set. Microwave vanilla chips and remaining 1 tablespoons shortening in small glass bowl on High for 45 seconds to 1 minute or until chips are melted, stirring several times. Drizzle over cakes. Decorate as desired. Yield: 24 servings.

MILK CHOCOLATE BAR SWIRL CAKE

2½ cups flour
¾ teaspoon soda
¼ teaspoon salt
1 cup butter or margarine
2 cups sugar
1 teaspoon vanilla extract
5 eggs
1½ cups sour cream
¼ cup honey or light
   corn syrup
¾ cup chopped pecans
1 8-ounce milk
   chocolate bar
½ cup chocolate syrup

Combine flour, soda and salt in bowl; mix well. Cream butter, sugar and vanilla in large mixer bowl until light and fluffy. Add eggs 1 at a time, beating well after each addition. Add flour mixture and sour cream alternately to creamed mixture, beating well after each addition. Reserve 2 cups batter. Stir honey and pecans into reserved batter; set aside. Melt chocolate bar in chocolate syrup in double boiler over hot water, stirring constantly. Blend into remaining batter. Pour into greased and floured 10-inch tube pan; do not use bundt pan. Spoon reserved pecan mixture over chocolate mixture; do not mix. Bake at 350 degrees for 45 minutes. Reduce oven temperature to 325 degrees; do not open oven door. Bake for 50 to 55 minutes longer or until cake tests done. Cool in pan for 1 hour. Invert onto serving plate to cool completely. Yield: 16 servings.

COCONUT ICEBOX CAKE

1 cup sugar
16 ounces whipped
   topping
2 cups sour cream
1 12-ounce package
   frozen coconut, thawed
1 2-layer package yellow
   cake mix

Combine sugar, whipped topping, sour cream and coconut in bowl; mix well. Chill, covered, overnight. Prepare and bake cake mix using package directions for two 9-inch round cake pans. Cool in pans for 10 minutes. Remove to wire rack to cool completely. Split layers into halves horizontally. Spread chilled coconut mixture between layers and over top and side of cake. Chill until serving time. Yield: 12 servings.

HOLIDAY COCONUT CAKE

7 egg whites
3/4 teaspoon cream of
tartar
2 cups flour
1 1/2 cups sugar
1 tablespoon baking
powder
1 teaspoon salt
1/2 teaspoon nutmeg
7 egg yolks
3/4 cup water
1/2 cup oil
1 teaspoon vanilla extract
1 teaspoon Brandy extract

4 teaspoons sugar
1 envelope unflavored
gelatin
1/3 cup water
3 cups whipping cream
3/4 teaspoon vanilla
extract
3/4 teaspoon Brandy
extract
1 1/3 cups flaked coconut
Red and green glacé
cherries, cut into
quarters (optional)

Beat eggs whites with cream of tartar in large mixer bowl at high speed until stiff but not dry. Combine flour, 1 1/2 cups sugar, baking powder, salt and nutmeg in small mixer bowl. Add egg yolks, 3/4 cup water, oil and 1 teaspoon each vanilla and Brandy extracts. Beat at low speed until thoroughly blended. Fold into egg whites gently. Pour into ungreased 10-inch tube pan. Bake at 325 degrees for 50 minutes to 1 hour or until top springs back when lightly touched. Invert on funnel to cool completely. Loosen cake from side of pan with thin spatula. Invert onto serving plate. Slice cake into 3 layers. Combine remaining 4 teaspoons sugar and gelatin in small saucepan. Add remaining 1/3 cup water; mix well. Let stand for several minutes or until gelatin is softened. Cook over medium heat for 2 minutes or until gelatin is dissolved, stirring constantly. Cool to room temperature. Combine gelatin mixture, whipping cream and remaining 3/4 teaspoon each vanilla and Brandy extracts in large mixer bowl. Beat at high speed until stiff peaks form. Spread frosting between layers and over top and side of cake. Press a small amount of coconut gently onto side of cake. Sprinkle remaining coconut over top. Garnish with cherries. Chill until serving time. Yield: 16 servings.

OLD-FASHIONED COCONUT CAKE

2¼ cups sifted flour
1½ teaspoons baking
  powder
½ teaspoon soda
¾ teaspoon salt
½ cup unsalted butter,
  softened
1¼ cups sugar
3 eggs
½ cup coconut
1¼ cups buttermilk
1½ teaspoons vanilla
  extract
2 egg whites, stiffly
  beaten
½ cup nonalcoholic piña
  colada mix
1½ cups coconut
¼ cup confectioners'
  sugar
Seven-Minute Frosting
Shredded coconut

Sift flour, baking powder, soda and salt together. Cream butter and sugar in large mixer bowl until light and fluffy. Add eggs 1 at a time, beating well after each addition. Add flour mixture alternately with mixture of ½ cup coconut and buttermilk, beating at low speed after each addition. Stir in vanilla. Pour into 2 greased and floured 9-inch round cake pans. Bake at 375 degrees for 25 to 30 minutes or until layers test done. Cool in pans for 10 minutes. Remove to wire racks to cool completely. Combine egg whites, piña colada mix, remaining 1½ cups coconut and confectioners' sugar in bowl; mix gently. Spread between cake layers. Spread Seven-Minute Frosting over top and side of cake. Sprinkle with additional shredded coconut. Yield: 12 servings.

Seven-Minute Frosting

1½ cups sugar
¼ cup water
2 egg whites, slightly
  beaten
2 tablespoons light corn
  syrup
1 teaspoon vanilla extract
¼ teaspoon salt

Combine sugar, water, egg whites, corn syrup, vanilla and salt in top of double boiler; mix well. Place over simmering water. Cook over low heat for 7 minutes, beating constantly with mixer at high speed until mixture triples in volume and holds stiff peaks.

WHITE CHOCOLATE COCONUT CAKE

2½ cups sifted cake flour
1½ teaspoons baking
  powder
½ teaspoon salt
⅓ pound white chocolate
½ cup water
1 cup unsalted butter or
  margarine, softened
1½ cups sugar
4 egg yolks
1 teaspoon vanilla extract
1 cup buttermilk

4 egg whites
½ cup sugar
1 cup chopped almonds
  or pecans
1 3-ounce can flaked
  coconut
2 cups whipping cream
2 tablespoons
  confectioners' sugar
2 teaspoons vanilla
  extract
1 cup flaked coconut

Grease three 9-inch round cake pans. Line bottoms of pans with greased waxed paper. Sift cake flour, baking powder and salt together. Combine white chocolate and water in top of double boiler. Cook over simmering water until chocolate is melted, stirring constantly. Cool slightly. Cream butter and 1½ cups sugar in mixer bowl until light and fluffy. Beat in egg yolks 1 at a time. Add 1 teaspoon vanilla and buttermilk to chocolate. Add to creamed mixture alternately with flour mixture ⅓ at a time, beating well after each addition. Beat egg whites in small mixer bowl until soft peaks form. Add remaining ½ cup sugar gradually, beating constantly at high speed until stiff peaks form. Fold into batter. Fold in almonds and 3 ounces coconut. Pour into prepared pans. Bake at 350 degrees for 30 to 35 minutes or until layers test done. Cool in pans on wire racks for 10 minutes. Remove to wire racks to cool completely. Remove waxed paper. Beat whipping cream in mixer bowl until frothy. Add confectioners' sugar and remaining 2 teaspoons vanilla; beat until soft peaks form. Fold in remaining 1 cup coconut. Spread between layers and over top and side of cake.
Yield: 12 servings.

MINIATURE GLAZED CRANBERRY CAKES

1 cup flour
1/2 teaspoon baking
  powder
1/4 teaspoon soda
1/4 teaspoon salt
1/4 cup butter or
  margarine, softened
1/4 cup sugar
1/4 cup packed light
  brown sugar

1 egg
1 teaspoon vanilla extract
1 cup coarsely chopped
  fresh cranberries
1/2 cup coarsely chopped
  walnuts
1/3 cup vanilla chips
Vanilla Chip Glaze

Combine first 4 ingredients in bowl; mix well. Cream butter, sugar, brown sugar, egg and vanilla in large mixer bowl until light and fluffy. Add flour mixture gradually, mixing well. Stir in cranberries, walnuts and vanilla chips. Fill 36 lightly greased muffin cups 3/4 full. Bake at 350 degrees for 12 to 14 minutes or until cakes test done. Cool in muffin cups for 5 minutes. Remove to wire racks to cool. Drizzle with Vanilla Chip Glaze. Chill for 10 minutes to set glaze. Yield: 36 servings.

Vanilla Chip Glaze

1 cup vanilla chips   2 tablespoons oil

Combine vanilla chips and oil in microwave-safe bowl. Microwave on High for 1 minute or just until chips melt, stir.

DIETETIC CAKE

2 cups raisins
2 cups water
1 cup unsweetened
  applesauce
2 eggs
2 tablespoons artificial
  sweetener

3/4 cup polyunsaturated oil
2 cups flour
1 teaspoon soda
1 1/2 teaspoons cinnamon
1/2 teaspoon nutmeg
1 teaspoon vanilla extract

Cook raisins in water in large saucepan until water has evaporated. Add applesauce, eggs, sweetener and oil; mix well. Stir in remaining ingredients. Pour into greased and floured 8-inch square cake pan. Bake at 350 degrees for 25 minutes or until cake tests done. Yield: 12 servings.

EASY CAKE

1 2-layer package yellow cake mix
2 eggs
1/2 cup butter, softened
1 cup coconut
1/2 cup chopped nuts

1 1-pound package confectioners' sugar
8 ounces cream cheese, softened
1 egg

Combine cake mix, 2 eggs and butter in bowl; mix well. Fold in coconut and nuts. Press into 9x13-inch cake pan. Cream confectioners' sugar, cream cheese and remaining egg in mixer bowl until light and fluffy. Spread over batter. Bake at 350 degrees for 35 to 40 minutes or until cake tests done. Yield: 15 servings.

JAPANESE FRUITCAKE

Juice of 1 orange
Juice of 1 lemon
1 cup sugar
1/3 cup butter or shortening, softened
1 cup sugar
1 egg

2 cups sifted flour
1 cup buttermilk
1 teaspoon soda
Grated rind of 1 orange
Grated rind of 1 lemon
1 cup raisins, ground
1 cup chopped nuts

Mix juices and 1 cup sugar in small bowl; set aside. Cream butter and remaining 1 cup sugar in mixer bowl until light and fluffy. Beat in egg. Add flour and mixture of buttermilk and soda alternately to creamed mixture, mixing well after each addition. Fold in grated rinds, raisins and nuts. Pour into lightly greased and floured 5x9-inch loaf pan. Bake at 350 degrees for 1 hour or until cake tests done. Cool in pan for 5 minutes. Pour reserved juice mixture over cake. Let stand until completely cool before removing from pan. Store, covered, in refrigerator. Yield: 12 servings.

A Lion Tip

Fruitcakes can be store indefinitely. Wrap them in cloths soaked in Brandy or wine and then in foil. Store them in an airtight container in a cool place.

CITRUS CHOCOLATE FRUITCAKE

1 cup flour
2/3 cup sugar
1/2 teaspoon soda
1/4 teaspoon baking
  powder
1/4 teaspoon salt
1/2 cup water
1/2 cup sour cream
1 egg

3 tablespoons butter or
  margarine, softened
2 ounces unsweetened
  chocolate, melted
3/4 cup chopped glacé
  orange rind
1/4 cup lemon juice
1/3 cup sugar
Rich Chocolate Glaze

Combine flour, 2/3 cup sugar, soda, baking powder and salt in large bowl; mix well. Stir in water, sour cream, egg, butter and melted chocolate. Beat at medium speed until blended. Beat at high speed for 3 minutes, scraping bowl occasionally. Fold in orange rind. Pour into greased and floured 8-inch square cake pan. Bake at 350 degrees for 30 minutes or until cake tests done. Cool in pan for 10 minutes. Combine lemon juice and remaining 1/2 cup sugar in saucepan; mix well. Bring just to the boiling point over low heat, stirring until sugar is dissolved. Pierce top of cake with fork. Spoon lemon syrup over warm cake. Cool completely in pan on wire rack; remove cake to rack. Pour Rich Chocolate Glaze over cooled cake. Let stand for 5 minutes. Garnish as desired. Place on serving plate. Chill until serving time. Yield: 10 to 12 servings.

Rich Chocolate Glaze

3 ounces semisweet
  chocolate

1/2 cup whipping cream

Cut chocolate into small pieces. Combine whipping cream and chocolate in saucepan. Cook over low heat until chocolate is melted, stirring frequently. Let stand in cool place until thickened.

ITALIAN CREAM CAKE

½ cup margarine,
  softened
½ cup shortening
2 cups sugar
5 eggs
2 cups self-rising flour

1 teaspoon soda
1 cup buttermilk
1 teaspoon vanilla extract
1 small package frozen
  coconut, thawed
Cream Cheese Frosting

Cream margarine, shortening and sugar in large mixer bowl until light and fluffy. Add eggs 1 at a time, beating well after each addition. Add flour and mixture of soda and buttermilk alternately to creamed mixture, beating well after each addition. Stir in vanilla and coconut. Pour into 3 greased and floured 9-inch round cake pans. Bake at 350 degrees for 40 minutes or until layers test done. Cool in pans for 10 minutes. Remove to wire racks to cool completely. Spread Cream Cheese Frosting between layers and over top and side of cake. Yield: 12 servings.

Cream Cheese Frosting

¼ cup margarine,
  softened
8 ounces cream cheese,
  softened
1 1-pound package
  confectioners' sugar

1 tablespoon vanilla
  extract
1 cup chopped pecans

Cream margarine and cream cheese in mixer bowl until light and fluffy. Add confectioners' sugar and vanilla. Beat until smooth. Fold in pecans.

 A Lion Tip

Cut a hot cake with a thread or dental floss instead of a knife.

MOM LINDBERG'S JAM CAKE

4 cups flour, sifted
2 teaspoons cinnamon
1 teaspoon cloves
1 cup butter, softened
2 cups packed brown
 sugar
3 egg yolks
2 ounces unsweetened
 chocolate, melted

1 teaspoon soda
1 cup buttermilk
1 cup strawberry jam
1 cup raisins or dates
1 cup chopped nuts
3 egg whites, stiffly
 beaten

Combine flour, cinnamon and cloves in bowl; mix well. Cream butter and brown sugar in large mixer bowl until light and fluffy. Stir in egg yolks 1 at a time. Add melted chocolate; mix well. Add flour mixture and mixture of soda and buttermilk alternately to creamed mixture, beginning and ending with flour and beating well after each addition. Stir in jam, raisins and nuts. Fold in egg whites. Pour into greased and floured tube pan. Bake at 350 degrees for 45 minutes or until cake tests done. Cool in pan for 10 minutes. Invert onto serving plate. Yield: 16 servings.

LEMONY RAISIN TEA CAKE

2 cups flour
2 teaspoons baking
 powder
1 teaspoon salt
3/4 cup butter or
 margarine, softened
1 1/2 to 2 tablespoons
 grated lemon rind

1 cup sugar
3 eggs
1/2 cup lemon juice
1 1/2 cups raisins
3/4 cup chopped walnuts
1/2 cup chopped candied
 ginger
Confectioners' sugar

Sift flour, baking powder and salt together. Cream butter, lemon rind and sugar in mixer bowl until light and fluffy. Add eggs 1 at a time, beating well after each addition. Stir in lemon juice. Add flour mixture gradually, mixing well. Fold in raisins, walnuts and ginger. Pour into greased and floured 2-quart tube pan. Bake at 350 degrees for 1 hour to 1 1/4 hours or until cake tests done. Cool in pan for 10 minutes. Invert onto wire rack. Wrap cake in foil while still slightly warm. Store in refrigerator for 24 hours. Dust with confectioners' sugar. Yield: 16 servings.

OATMEAL CAKE

1 cup oats
1 1/2 cups boiling water
1/2 cup margarine,
  softened
1 cup packed brown
  sugar
1 cup sugar

2 eggs
1 1/2 cups flour
1 teaspoon soda
1 teaspoon cinnamon
1 teaspoon vanilla extract
1/2 teaspoon salt
Brown Sugar Frosting

Combine oats and boiling water in bowl; mix well. Let stand, covered, for 20 minutes. Cream margarine, brown sugar and sugar in mixer bowl until light and fluffy. Add eggs 1 at a time, beating well after each addition. Add flour, soda, cinnamon, vanilla and salt; mix well. Stir in oats mixture. Pour into greased and floured 9x13-inch cake pan. Bake at 375 degrees for 20 to 30 minutes or until cake tests done. Cool in pan. Spread with Brown Sugar Frosting. Yield: 15 servings.

Brown Sugar Frosting

1 cup packed brown
  sugar
6 tablespoons butter

1 3-ounce can coconut
1/4 cup cream

Combine brown sugar, butter, coconut and cream in small saucepan; mix well. Bring to a boil. Cook over low heat until light brown, stirring frequently.

A Lion Tip

Cut butter-type cakes easily with a sharp, thin knife. Use a gentle sawing motion with a fine serrated knife to cut angel food, chiffon and sponge cakes. If the frosting sticks, dip the knife in hot water and wipe with a damp paper towel after cutting each slice.

MANDARIN ORANGE CAKE

1   2-layer package butter-
recipe yellow cake mix
1/2 cup oil
4 eggs

1   11-ounce can
mandarin oranges
Pineapple Frosting

Combine cake mix, oil, eggs and undrained oranges in mixer bowl; mix well. Pour into 2 greased and floured 9-inch round cake pans. Bake at 325 degrees for 30 minutes or until layers test done. Remove to wire rack to cool. Spread Pineapple Frosting between layers and over top and side of cake. Chill, covered, until serving time. Yield: 12 servings.

Pineapple Frosting

1   4-ounce package
vanilla instant pudding
mix
8 ounces whipped
topping

1   15-ounce can crushed
pineapple

Combine pudding mix, whipped topping and undrained pineapple in bowl; mix well.

PEANUT BUTTER FUDGE CAKE

3 cups flour
1 1/2 teaspoons soda
3/4 teaspoon salt
3/4 cup butter or
margarine, softened
1 cup peanut butter
2 1/4 cups sugar
3 eggs

1 1/2 teaspoons vanilla
extract
3 ounces unsweetened
chocolate, melted
1 1/2 cups ice water
Peanut Butter Fudge
Frosting (See page 303)

Sift flour, soda and salt together. Cream next 5 ingredients in mixer bowl until light and fluffy. Blend in chocolate. Add flour mixture and water alternately, beginning and ending with flour and mixing well after each addition. Pour into 3 greased 8-inch cake pans. Bake at 350 degrees for 1 hour or until cake tests done. Cool in pan for 5 minutes. Invert onto wire rack to cool completely. Frost with Peanut Butter Fudge Frosting. Yield: 12 servings.

Peanut Butter Fudge Frosting

2 ounces unsweetened
  chocolate
1/2 cup peanut butter

1 cup light cream
2 cups sugar

Melt chocolate and peanut butter in heavy saucepan over low heat, stirring constantly. Stir in cream and sugar. Cook over low heat to soft-ball stage. Cool slightly. Beat until of spreading consistency.

BROWN SUGAR POUND CAKE

1 cup sugar
1   1-pound package light
  brown sugar
1/2 cup butter, softened
1 cup shortening
5 eggs, beaten

1 cup self-rising flour
2 cups all-purpose flour
1 teaspoon vanilla extract
1/2 teaspoon maple extract
1 cup milk
1 cup chopped pecans

Cream sugar, brown sugar, butter, shortening and eggs in mixer bowl. Add flours and mixture of flavorings and milk alternately, mixing well after each addition. Fold in pecans. Pour into greased waxed paper-lined tube pan. Bake at 325 degrees for 1 3/4 hours or until cake tests done; do not open oven during baking time. Cool in pan for 15 minutes. Invert onto serving plate. Yield: 16 servings.

CHOCOLATE CHIP POUND CAKE

1   2-layer package
  German chocolate cake
  mix
1   4-ounce package
  chocolate instant
  pudding mix

1 cup sour cream
1/2 cup oil
1/2 cup warm water
4 eggs
1 cup semisweet
  chocolate chips, melted

Combine cake mix, pudding mix, sour cream, oil, water, eggs and melted chocolate in mixer bowl. Beat until smooth. Pour into greased bundt pan. Bake at 350 degrees for 55 minutes to 1 hour or until cake tests done. Cool in pan for 10 minutes. Invert onto serving plate. Yield: 16 servings.

COCONUT CREAM POUND CAKE

3 cups flour
1/4 teaspoon soda
1/4 teaspoon salt
1/2 cup butter or
   margarine, softened
1/2 cup shortening
8 ounces cream cheese,
   softened

3 cups sugar
6 eggs
1 6-ounce package
   frozen coconut, thawed
1 teaspoon vanilla extract
1 teaspoon coconut
   extract

Combine flour, soda and salt in bowl; mix well. Cream butter, shortening and cream cheese in large mixer bowl until light. Add sugar gradually, beating until fluffy. Add eggs 1 at a time, beating well after each addition. Add flour mixture; mix well. Stir in coconut and flavorings. Pour into greased and floured 10-inch tube pan. Bake at 350 degrees for 1 1/4 hours or until cake tests done. Cool in pan for 15 minutes. Invert onto serving plate. Yield: 16 servings.

KENTUCKY WONDER POUND CAKE

2 1/2 cups sifted self-rising
   flour
2 cups sugar
1 1/2 cups oil
4 egg yolks, slightly
   beaten
2 tablespoons hot water

1 small can crushed
   pineapple
2 1/2 teaspoons cinnamon
1 1/2 teaspoons nutmeg
4 egg whites, stiffly
   beaten
1 cup chopped pecans

Combine flour, sugar, oil, egg yolks, water, undrained pineapple, cinnamon and nutmeg in bowl; mix well. Fold in egg whites and pecans. Pour into greased tube pan. Bake at 350 degrees for 1 hour or until cake tests done. Cool in pan for 15 minutes. Invert onto serving plate. Yield: 16 servings.

MELT-IN-YOUR-MOUTH POUND CAKE

1½ cups butter, softened
1 1-pound package
  confectioners' sugar
3½ cups flour, sifted

6 eggs
1 teaspoon vanilla extract
½ teaspoon almond
  extract

Cream butter and confectioners' sugar in mixer bowl until light and fluffy. Add flour and eggs alternately to creamed mixture, beginning and ending with flour and beating well after each addition. Stir in flavorings. Pour into greased and floured 10-inch tube pan. Bake at 350 degrees for 1 hour or until cake tests done. Cool in pan for 10 minutes. Invert onto serving plate. Slice very thin. Serve with fruit and whipped topping. Yield: 16 servings.

YOGURT POUND CAKE

2½ cups flour
½ teaspoon soda
½ teaspoon salt
1 cup margarine, softened
1½ cups sugar
3 eggs

1 cup peach yogurt
1 teaspoon grated lemon
  rind
1 teaspoon vanilla extract
Confectioners' sugar

Combine flour, soda and salt in bowl; mix well. Cream margarine and sugar in large mixer bowl until light and fluffy. Add eggs 1 at a time, beating well after each addition. Add flour mixture; mix well. Stir in yogurt, lemon rind and vanilla. Pour into greased and floured 10-inch bundt pan. Bake at 350 degrees for 40 minutes or until cake tests done. Cool in pan for 15 minutes. Invert onto serving plate to cool completely. Sprinkle with confectioners' sugar. Yield: 16 servings.

PRUNE PLUM CAKE

1/2 cup butter or
  margarine, softened
1/2 cup sugar
1 egg
1 1/2 cups flour
1/2 teaspoon baking
  powder

2 cups prune plums,
  pitted, cut into quarters
1/4 cup sugar
Streusel Topping

Cream butter and 1/2 cup sugar in mixer bowl until light and fluffy. Beat in egg. Add flour and baking powder gradually, mixing well after each addition. Layer half the batter, prunes, remaining 1/4 cup sugar and remaining batter in lightly greased 9-inch pie plate. Sprinkle with Streusel Topping. Bake at 375 degrees for 45 minutes or until lightly browned. Cool slightly before serving. Yield: 8 to 10 servings.

Streusel Topping

1/2 cup flour
3 tablespoons butter,
  softened

5 tablespoons sugar
1/2 teaspoon cinnamon

Combine flour, butter, sugar and cinnamon in blender container. Process until crumbly.

SEVEN-UP CAKE

1 1/2 cups butter, softened
3 cups sugar
5 eggs
3 cups flour

2 tablespoons lemon
  extract
3/4 cup 7-Up

Cream butter and sugar in mixer bowl until light and fluffy. Add eggs 1 at a time, beating well after each addition. Add flour gradually, beating at medium speed. Stir in lemon extract. Add 7-Up, beating at low speed. Pour into nonstick bundt pan. Bake at 350 degrees for 1 hour and 10 minutes. Cool in pan for 15 minutes. Invert onto serving plate. Yield: 16 servings.

SPICE CAKE

2¹/2 cups sifted cake flour	³/4 teaspoon cloves
1 cup sugar	¹/2 cup shortening
1 teaspoon baking powder	²/3 cup packed brown sugar
1 teaspoon soda	1 cup buttermilk
³/4 teaspoon salt	2 eggs
³/4 teaspoon cinnamon	¹/4 cup buttermilk

Line two 9-inch round cake pans with greased waxed paper. Combine first 7 ingredients in large mixer bowl; mix well. Cut in shortening. Add brown sugar. Add 1 cup buttermilk; mix just until flour mixture is moistened. Beat at medium speed for 2 minutes. Add eggs and remaining ¹/4 cup buttermilk. Beat for 1 minute. Pour into prepared pans. Bake at 375 degrees for 25 minutes or until layers test done. Cool in pans on wire racks for 5 minutes. Remove to wire racks to cool completely. Remove waxed paper. Frost as desired. Yield: 12 servings.

STRAWBERRY CAKE

1 2-layer package white cake mix	¹/2 package frozen strawberries, thawed
6 tablespoons flour	¹/2 cup cold water
1 3-ounce package strawberry gelatin	14 tablespoons oil
4 eggs	Strawberry Frosting

Combine cake mix, flour, gelatin, eggs, strawberries, water and oil in large mixer bowl. Beat at medium speed for 4 minutes, scraping bowl occasionally. Pour into 2 greased and floured 9-inch round cake pans. Bake at 350 degrees for 30 minutes. Cool on wire racks. Spread Strawberry Frosting between layers and over top and side of cake. Yield: 12 servings.

Strawberry Frosting

¹/2 cup butter or margarine, softened	¹/2 package frozen strawberries, thawed
1 1-pound package confectioners' sugar	

Combine all ingredients in large bowl; mix well.

STRAWBERRY CRUNCH CAKE

2 10-ounce packages
frozen sliced
strawberries, thawed
2 cups flour
1 teaspoon baking
powder
1/2 teaspoon soda
1/2 teaspoon salt
1 cup butter or
margarine, softened

1 1/4 cups sugar
2 eggs
1 cup sour cream
1/3 cup packed light
brown sugar
1/2 cup chopped pecans
1 teaspoon cinnamon
4 teaspoons cornstarch
2 teaspoons lemon juice
Whipped cream

Drain strawberries, reserving liquid. Combine flour, baking powder, soda and salt in bowl; mix well. Cream butter and sugar in large mixer bowl until light and fluffy. Add eggs 1 at a time, beating well after each addition. Blend in sour cream. Add flour mixture; mix well. Combine brown sugar, pecans and cinnamon in small bowl; mix well. Layer half the batter, all the strawberries and half the brown sugar mixture in lightly greased 9x13-inch cake pan. Top with remaining batter and brown sugar mixture. Bake at 350 degrees for 30 to 35 minutes or until cake tests done. Cool in pan. Combine reserved strawberry liquid and cornstarch in small saucepan. Cook over medium heat until thickened, stirring constantly. Remove from heat; stir in lemon juice. Cut cake into squares. Top cake squares with warm glaze and whipped cream. Yield: 15 servings.

MILLY'S BLUE-RIBBON YELLOW CAKE

3 cups twice-sifted flour
2 teaspoons baking
powder
1/2 teaspoon salt
1 cup shortening
2 cups sugar

3 eggs
1 teaspoon vanilla extract
1 cup milk
Blue-Ribbon Penuche
Icing (See page 309)

Combine flour, baking powder and salt in bowl; mix well. Cream shortening and sugar in large mixer bowl until light and fluffy. Add eggs 1 at a time, beating well after each addition. Stir in vanilla. Add flour mixture and milk alternately to creamed mixture, mixing well. Pour into 2 greased and floured 9-inch square cake pans. Bake at 350 degrees for 30 to 40 minutes or until layers test done. Cool in pans for 8 minutes. Remove to towel-lined wire racks to cool completely. Spread Blue-Ribbon Penuche Icing between layers and over top and sides of cake. Yield: 12 to 15 servings.

Blue-Ribbon Penuche Icing

2 cups packed light brown sugar
1 cup sugar
1 cup evaporated milk
2 tablespoons butter

2 tablespoons light corn syrup
1/4 teaspoon salt
1 teaspoon vanilla extract

Combine brown sugar, sugar, evaporated milk, butter, corn syrup and salt in saucepan; mix well. Cook to 234 degrees on candy thermometer, stirring constantly. Beat in vanilla.

YUM-YUM CAKE

13/4 cups flour
11/2 teaspoons baking powder
1/4 teaspoon soda
1/4 teaspoon salt
1/2 cup butter or margarine, softened
1 cup sugar
1 teaspoon vanilla extract
1 egg

3/4 cup buttermilk
12 marshmallows, cut into pieces
1/2 cup chocolate chips
2 tablespoons butter or margarine, softened
1/4 cup packed brown sugar
1/2 cup chopped pecans

Combine flour, baking powder, soda and salt in bowl; mix well. Cream 1/2 cup butter, sugar and vanilla in large mixer bowl until light and fluffy. Add egg; mix well. Add flour mixture and buttermilk alternately, beating just until smooth after each addition. Stir in marshmallows and chocolate chips. Pour into greased 9-inch square cake pan. Cream remaining 2 tablespoons butter and brown sugar in mixer bowl until light and fluffy. Mix in pecans. Sprinkle over batter. Bake at 350 degrees for 45 minutes or until cake tests done. Cool on wire rack. Yield: 8 to 12 servings.

*P*IES

MARKET STREET GRILL APPLE PIE

7 Golden Delicious apples, peeled, sliced	Dash of salt 3 tablespoons (rounded)
2 tablespoons lemon juice	cornstarch
1½ cups sugar	½ cup water
1 teaspoon cinnamon	3 tablespoons butter
¼ teaspoon nutmeg	Light Pie Pastry
¼ teaspoon allspice	

Toss apples with lemon juice in bowl. Combine sugar, cinnamon, nutmeg, allspice, salt and cornstarch in large saucepan; mix well. Stir in water and butter. Bring to a boil over medium heat, stirring occasionally. Stir in apples. Pour into pastry-lined pie plate. Top with remaining pastry, fluting edge and cutting vents. Place on foil-lined baking sheet. Bake at 350 degrees for 45 minutes to 1 hour or until crust is golden brown. Yield: 6 to 8 servings.

Light Pie Pastry

2 cups flour	½ cup butter
1 teaspoon sugar	½ cup shortening
1 teaspoon salt	½ cup (scant) cold water
1 teaspoon baking powder	

Combine flour, sugar, salt and baking powder in bowl; mix well. Cut in butter and shortening until crumbly. Add water 1 tablespoon at a time, mixing with fork until mixture forms ball. Chill, wrapped in plastic wrap, for 30 minutes or longer.

A Lion Tip

Fruit, mince and chiffon pies freeze well. Custard and meringue pies do not freeze well.

ANGEL PIE

1 cup sugar
1 1/2 cups water
1/4 cup cornstarch
4 egg whites
4 teaspoons sugar
1/4 teaspoon salt

2 tablespoons vanilla
extract
1 baked 9-inch pie shell
Crushed peppermint
candy

Combine 1 cup sugar and water in saucepan; mix well. Cook over low heat for 5 minutes, stirring constantly. Stir in cornstarch; cool. Beat egg whites in mixer bowl at low speed until foamy. Add remaining 4 teaspoons sugar, salt and vanilla gradually, beating constantly at high speed until stiff peaks form. Fold syrup mixture into egg whites. Pour into pie shell. Chill, covered, until serving time. Sprinkle with crushed peppermint candy. Yield: 6 servings.

BLACKBERRY AND PEACH PIE

2/3 cup sugar
1 1/2 tablespoons quick-
cooking tapioca
1 teaspoon grated orange
rind

Pinch of salt
2 cups sliced fresh
peaches
2 cups fresh blackberries
Cream Cheese Pastry

Combine sugar, tapioca, orange rind and salt in large bowl; mix well. Stir in peaches and blackberries. Pour into pastry-lined pie plate. Cut remaining pastry into 1/2-inch strips. Twist each strip several times. Arrange on top in spiral design. Shape any extra pastry into leaf cutouts; place on outer end of spirals. Bake at 425 degrees for 35 to 40 minutes or until crust is golden brown. Yield: 6 servings.

Cream Cheese Pastry

2 cups flour
1/2 teaspoon salt
1/2 cup shortening

6 ounces cream cheese,
softened
5 tablespoons cold water

Combine flour and salt in bowl; mix well. Cut in shortening and cream cheese until crumbly. Add water 1 tablespoon at a time, mixing with fork until mixture forms ball. Chill, wrapped in plastic wrap, for 30 minutes or longer.

CARAMEL NUT PIE

1 tablespoon unflavored
  gelatin
2 tablespoons cold water
2 cups scalded milk
6 tablespoons sugar
3 egg yolks, slightly
  beaten

1/2 teaspoon salt
1 teaspoon vanilla extract
3 egg whites
10 tablespoons sugar
3/4 cup chopped nuts
1 baked 9-inch pie shell

Soften gelatin in cold water. Add to scalded milk; stir until dissolved. Melt 6 tablespoons sugar in skillet until golden brown, stirring constantly. Blend in gelatin mixture. Pour egg yolks into double boiler. Add sugar mixture gradually. Cook over low heat for 10 to 15 minutes or until mixture coats metal spoon, stirring constantly. Stir in salt and vanilla. Cool. Beat egg whites in mixer bowl until soft peaks form. Add remaining 10 tablespoons sugar gradually, beating until stiff peaks form. Fold into cooled custard. Stir in nuts. Pour into cooled pie shell. Yield: 6 servings.

CHESS PIE

2 eggs or 5 egg yolks,
  slightly beaten
1 1/2 cups sugar
1 tablespoon cornmeal
1 tablespoon flour
1/4 cup milk

1/4 cup melted butter
1/2 teaspoon vinegar
1/2 teaspoon vanilla
  extract
1 unbaked 9-inch pie shell

Combine eggs, sugar, cornmeal and flour in bowl; mix well. Stir in milk and melted butter. Add vinegar and vanilla; mix well. Pour into pie shell. Bake at 325 to 350 degrees for 45 minutes or until set. May substitute brown sugar for 1/3 of the sugar. Yield: 6 servings.

A Lion Tip

Chess pies freeze well for up to 3 months. Freeze, unwrapped, until amost firm. Then wrap well in moisture-proof paper.

LEMON CHESS PIE

2 cups sugar
1 tablespoon flour
1 tablespoon cornmeal
4 eggs, slightly beaten
1/4 cup melted butter

1/4 cup milk
2 tablespoons lemon juice
1/4 teaspoon lemon extract
1 unbaked 9-inch pie shell

Combine sugar, flour and cornmeal in mixer bowl; mix well. Stir in eggs, melted butter, milk, lemon juice and lemon extract. Beat at low speed until smooth. Pour into pie shell. Bake at 375 degrees for 35 to 45 minutes or until golden brown. Cut while warm. Yield: 6 servings.

COCONUT CREAM PIE

14 tablespoons milk
1/2 cup sugar
1/2 teaspoon salt
3 1/2 tablespoons flour
2 tablespoons cornstarch
1 egg, beaten
3 egg yolks, beaten
14 tablespoons milk
1/2 teaspoon vanilla
    extract

1/4 teaspoon almond
    extract
2 tablespoons butter
3/4 cup coconut
1/2 cup whipping cream,
    whipped
1 baked 9-inch pie shell
3 egg whites
1/4 cup sugar
1/4 cup coconut

Scald 14 tablespoons milk in saucepan. Stir in 1/2 cup sugar and salt. Combine flour, cornstarch, egg, egg yolks and remaining 14 tablespoons milk in bowl; beat until smooth. Stir in a small amount of scalded milk mixture. Pour both mixtures into double boiler; mix well. Cook over hot water until thickened, stirring constantly. Remove from heat. Beat in flavorings and butter with wooden spoon until smooth. Stir in 3/4 cup coconut. Fold in whipped cream. Pour into pie shell. Beat egg whites in bowl until soft peaks form. Add remaining 1/4 cup sugar gradually, beating until stiff peaks form. Spread over custard, sealing to edge. Sprinkle with remaining 1/4 cup coconut. Bake at 450 degrees until coconut begins to brown. Yield: 6 to 8 servings.

BUTTERMILK COCONUT PIE

1½ cups sugar
2 tablespoons flour
3 eggs, beaten
½ cup melted margarine
½ cup buttermilk

1 teaspoon vanilla extract
1 3-ounce can flaked
   coconut
1 unbaked 9-inch pie shell

Combine sugar and flour in bowl; mix well. Stir in eggs, melted margarine, buttermilk, vanilla and ⅔ can coconut. Pour into pie shell. Sprinkle with remaining coconut. Bake at 325 degrees for 1 hour or until knife inserted near center comes out clean. Yield: 6 servings.

WHITE CHOCOLATE COCONUT CREAM PIE

2 cups milk
1 vanilla bean, split
   lengthwise
2 eggs, beaten
½ cup sugar
2 tablespoons flour
¼ cup unsalted butter,
   softened

2 cups coconut
1 baked 9-inch pie shell
1½ to 2 cups whipping
   cream
Dash of confectioners'
   sugar
White chocolate curls
Flaked coconut

Combine milk and vanilla bean in saucepan. Bring to a boil; remove from heat. Cool for 5 minutes. Strain. Return milk to a boil. Add sugar and flour to beaten eggs; mix well. Stir a small amount of hot milk into egg mixture. Stir egg mixture into hot milk. Return to a boil, stirring constantly. Stir in butter and 2 cups coconut. Pour into pie shell; cool. Chill, covered, until serving time. Whip cream with confectioners' sugar in small bowl until stiff peaks form. Spread over pie. Sprinkle with white chocolate curls and flaked coconut. Yield: 6 servings.

A Lion Tip

Pies with cream or custard fillings should be cooled to room temperature and then stored in the refrigerator to prevent spoilage.

OLD-TIME EGG CUSTARD PIE

1 unbaked 9-inch pie shell
4 eggs, beaten
1/2 cup sugar
1 teaspoon vanilla extract
Salt to taste
2 1/2 cups scalded milk
Nutmeg
1/4 cup butter

Chill pie shell until baking time. Combine eggs and sugar in bowl; mix well. Stir in vanilla and salt. Add scalded milk gradually, stirring constantly. Pour into chilled pie shell. Sprinkle with nutmeg. Dot with butter. Bake at 400 degrees for 25 minutes or until barely firm. Pie will set when cool. Yield: 6 to 8 servings.

LEMONADE PIES

1 small can frozen
   lemonade concentrate,
   thawed
1 can sweetened
   condensed milk
12 ounces whipped
   topping
2   9-inch graham cracker
   pie shells

Combine lemonade concentrate, condensed milk and whipped topping in bowl; mix well. Pour into 2 pie shells. Chill, covered, until firm. Yield: 12 servings.

LEMON CHIFFON PIE

4 egg yolks, slightly
   beaten
1/2 cup sugar
Juice and grated rind of
   1 lemon
Salt to taste
1 tablespoon unflavored
   gelatin
1/4 cup cold water
4 egg whites
1/2 cup sugar
1 baked 9-inch pie shell

Combine egg yolks, 1/2 cup sugar, lemon juice, lemon rind and salt in double boiler. Cook over low heat until thickened, stirring constantly. Soften gelatin in cold water. Add to hot custard, stirring until gelatin is dissolved. Cool. Beat egg whites in mixer bowl at low speed until foamy. Add remaining 1/2 cup sugar gradually, beating constantly at high speed until stiff peaks form. Fold custard into egg whites. Pour into pie shell. Chill, covered, until serving time. Serve with whipped cream. Yield: 6 servings.

OLD-FASHIONED LEMON PIE

1 cup sugar
2 egg yolks, slightly
  beaten
3 tablespoons butter,
  softened
Juice and grated rind of 1
  lemon

3 tablespoons flour
1 cup milk
2 egg whites, stiffly
  beaten
1 unbaked 9-inch pie shell

Combine sugar, egg yolks and butter in bowl; beat well. Mix in lemon juice, lemon rind and flour. Blend in milk. Fold in egg whites. Pour into pie shell. Bake at 350 degrees for 40 to 45 minutes or until knife inserted near center comes out clean. Yield: 6 servings.

MAPLE DUTCH APPLE PIE

6 cooking apples
1 cup corn syrup
1 unbaked 9-inch pie shell
3 tablespoons sugar
2 teaspoons cornstarch
1 teaspoon cinnamon

1/4 teaspoon nutmeg
1/4 teaspoon salt
1/2 cup half and half
1 recipe favorite crumb or
  streusel topping

Peel, core and quarter apples. Combine with syrup in large covered saucepan. Cook for 10 minutes, turning occasionally. Remove apples to pie shell with slotted spoon. Cook syrup until reduced to 1/2 cup. Pour over apples. Combine sugar, cornstarch, cinnamon, nutmeg and salt in bowl; mix well. Stir in half and half. Spoon over apples. Sprinkle with topping. Bake for 30 to 45 minutes or until golden brown. Serve warm or cold. Yield: 8 servings.

MILLION DOLLAR PIES

8 ounces whipped
topping
1 can sweetened
condensed milk
1 large can crushed
pineapple, drained
1/2 cup coconut

1/2 cup chopped pecans
1/2 teaspoon salt
1/2 teaspoon vanilla
extract
1/3 cup lemon juice
2 9-inch graham cracker
pie shells

Combine whipped topping, condensed milk, pineapple, coconut, pecans, salt, vanilla and lemon juice in bowl; mix well. Pour into pie shells. Chill, covered, until set. Yield: 12 servings.

MINCEMEAT PIE

1 unbaked 9-inch pie shell
2 tablespoons flour
1 18-ounce jar prepared
mincemeat
3 tart apples, peeled, cut
into 1/2-inch wedges
2 tablespoons flour

1/3 cup sugar
1/8 teaspoon salt
1 tablespoon margarine
2 tablespoons red
cinnamon candies
1/4 cup water

Sprinkle 2 tablespoons flour into pie shell. Spread mincemeat in prepared shell. Cover with 2 circles of overlapping apple wedges. Combine remaining 2 tablespoons flour, sugar and salt in bowl; mix well. Cut in margarine until crumbly. Sprinkle over apples. Combine cinnamon candies and water in saucepan. Cook over low heat until candies are dissolved, stirring constantly. Pour over sugar mixture. Cover edge of pie shell with 3-inch strip of foil. Bake at 425 degrees for 25 minutes. Remove foil. Bake for 15 to 20 minutes longer or until crust is golden brown. Yield: 6 servings.

PEACH PRALINE PIE

4 cups sliced fresh
  peaches
1/2 cup sugar
2 tablespoons tapioca
1 teaspoon lemon juice
1/2 cup flour

1/4 cup packed brown
  sugar
1/4 cup butter or
  margarine
1/2 cup chopped pecans
1 unbaked 9-inch pie shell

Combine peaches, sugar, tapioca and lemon juice in bowl; mix well. Let stand for 15 minutes. Combine flour and brown sugar in medium bowl; mix well. Cut in butter until crumbly. Stir in pecans. Sprinkle 1/3 of the flour mixture into pie shell. Spoon peaches into prepared shell. Sprinkle with remaining flour mixture. Bake at 425 degrees for 10 minutes. Reduce oven temperature to 350 degrees. Bake for 20 to 30 minutes longer or until golden brown. Yield: 6 servings.

VIRGINIA DINER PEANUT PIE

3 eggs
1 1/2 cups dark corn syrup
1/4 cup melted butter
1/4 teaspoon salt
1/2 teaspoon vanilla
  extract

1 tablespoon flour
1 1/2 cups coarsely
  chopped, unsalted
  roasted peanuts
1 unbaked 9-inch pie shell

Beat eggs in mixer bowl until foamy. Add corn syrup, melted butter, salt, vanilla and flour; mix well. Stir in peanuts. Pour into pie shell. Bake at 375 degrees for 40 to 45 minutes or until set. Yield: 6 to 8 servings.

A Lion Tip

Always prick the bottom and side of a pie shell which is baked before filling to prevent puffing. Brush the bottom with 1 egg white beaten with 1 tablespoon water just before the shell has finished baking to keep it from becoming soggy when filled.

PEANUT BUTTER PIE

3/4 cup confectioners' sugar
1/2 cup peanut butter
1 baked 9-inch pie shell
1/2 cup sugar
3 tablespoons cornstarch
1 tablespoon flour
1/2 teaspoon salt
3 cups milk

3 egg yolks, slightly beaten
2 tablespoons butter, softened
1 teaspoon vanilla extract
3 egg whites
Pinch of cream of tartar
1/4 cup sugar

Beat confectioners' sugar and peanut butter in mixer bowl until crumbly. Sprinkle 2/3 of the mixture into pie shell. Combine 1/2 cup sugar, cornstarch, flour, salt, milk, egg yolks, butter and vanilla in double boiler; mix well. Cook over medium heat until thickened, stirring constantly. Pour into prepared pie shell. Beat egg whites with cream of tartar in mixer bowl at low speed until foamy. Add 1/4 cup sugar gradually, beating constantly until stiff peaks form. Spread over custard, sealing to edge. Sprinkle with remaining peanut butter mixture. Bake at 350 degrees until golden brown. Yield: 6 to 8 servings.

PEANUT BUTTER MERINGUE PIE

1 cup creamy peanut butter
3/4 cup confectioners' sugar
1 baked 9-inch pie shell
1 cup sugar
2 tablespoons cornstarch
3 egg yolks

1/8 teaspoon salt
11/2 cups milk
1 teaspoon vanilla extract
1 tablespoon butter, softened
3 egg whites
1/4 cup sugar

Cream peanut butter and confectioners' sugar in mixer bowl. Reserve 3 tablespoons peanut butter mixture. Pour remaining mixture into pie shell. Combine 1 cup sugar and next 5 ingredients in saucepan; mix well. Cook until thickened, stirring constantly; remove from heat. Stir in butter and reserved peanut butter mixture. Pour over custard layer. Beat egg whites with remaining 1/4 cup sugar in mixer bowl until stiff peaks form. Spread over top of pie, sealing to edge. Bake at 375 degrees for 10 minutes or until brown. Yield: 6 servings.

BUTTERSCOTCH PECAN PIE

3 eggs, slightly beaten
1 cup light corn syrup
1 cup packed light brown
  sugar
1/8 teaspoon salt
1 teaspoon vanilla extract

2 tablespoons melted
  butter or margarine
1 cup pecan or walnut
  halves
1 unbaked 9-inch pie shell
Whipped cream

Combine eggs, corn syrup, brown sugar, salt, vanilla and butter in bowl; mix well. Stir in nuts. Pour into pie shell. Bake at 400 degrees for 15 minutes. Reduce oven temperature to 350 degrees. Bake for 30 to 35 minutes longer or until outer edge of filling is firm. Cool on wire rack. Decorate edge with rosettes of whipped cream at serving time. Yield: 6 servings.

OLD-FASHIONED PECAN PIE

1 1-pound package
  brown sugar
3/4 cup water
4 eggs, slightly beaten

1/4 cup butter
1 teaspoon vanilla extract
1 cup pecans
1 unbaked 9-inch pie shell

Combine brown sugar and water in saucepan; mix well. Cook until brown sugar dissolves, stirring constantly. Bring to a boil, stirring constantly. Boil for 3 minutes. Stir a small amount of hot mixture into beaten eggs; stir eggs into hot mixture. Stir in butter and vanilla. Pour into pie shell. Arrange pecans over filling. Bake for 1 hour or until set. Yield: 6 servings.

PECAN CHIFFON PIE

4 egg yolks, well beaten
3/4 cup milk
1/2 cup sugar
1 envelope unflavored
   gelatin
2 tablespoons cold water

1 teaspoon vanilla extract
4 egg whites
1/2 cup sugar
1/2 cup toasted pecans
1 baked 9-inch pie shell
Whipped cream (optional)

Combine egg yolks, milk and 1/2 cup sugar in double boiler; mix well. Cook over medium heat to a thin custard, stirring constantly. Cool slightly. Soften gelatin in cold water. Add gelatin and vanilla to custard; mix well. Beat egg whites in mixer bowl until soft peaks form. Add remaining 1/2 cup sugar gradually, beating constantly until stiff peaks form. Fold custard into egg whites. Stir in pecans. Pour into pie shell. Chill, covered, for 2 hours or longer. Top with whipped cream if desired. Yield: 6 servings.

SOUTHERN CHOCOLATE PECAN PIE

4 ounces unsweetened
   chocolate
1/2 cup butter, softened
3 eggs, slightly beaten

1 cup sugar
1 1/2 cups evaporated milk
1 cup chopped pecans
1 unbaked 9-inch pie shell

Melt chocolate and butter in saucepan over low heat, stirring frequently. Cool slightly. Stir in eggs, sugar and evaporated milk. Cook over low heat until sugar is dissolved, stirring constantly. Pour into pie shell. Top with pecans. Bake at 375 degrees for 40 to 45 minutes or until set. Yield: 6 servings.

GOLDEN PECAN PIE

3/4 cup sugar
1 tablespoon flour
Pinch of salt
3 eggs, well beaten
1 cup light corn syrup

1 teaspoon vanilla extract
2 tablespoons margarine,
  softened
1 cup pecan halves
1 unbaked 9-inch pie shell

Combine sugar, flour and salt in large mixer bowl. Add eggs, corn syrup, vanilla and margarine. Beat until smooth. Stir in pecans. Pour into pie shell. Bake at 350 degrees for 55 minutes to 1 hour or until knife inserted near center comes out clean. Yield: 6 servings.

PINEAPPLE-LEMON MERINGUE PIE

1 package lemon pudding
  and pie filling mix
1/2 cup sugar
1/4 cup pineapple juice
2 egg yolks, slightly
  beaten

1 cup pineapple juice
3/4 cup water
1 baked 8-inch pie shell
2 egg whites
1/4 cup sugar

Combine pudding mix, 1/2 cup sugar and 1/4 cup pineapple juice in saucepan; mix well. Add egg yolks; blend well. Stir in remaining 1 cup pineapple juice and water. Cook over medium heat for 5 minutes or until mixture comes to a boil and is thickened, stirring constantly. Remove from heat. Let stand for 5 minutes; stir. Spoon into pie shell. Beat egg whites in mixer bowl until soft peaks form. Add remaining 1/4 cup sugar gradually, beating constantly until stiff peaks form. Spread lightly over filling, sealing to edge. Bake at 425 degrees for 5 to 10 minutes or until meringue is lightly browned. Yield: 6 servings.

TRESSIE'S SOUR CREAM PINEAPPLE PIE

1 cup sugar
1/3 cup flour
1 13-ounce can crushed
  pineapple
1 cup sour cream
1/4 teaspoon salt
1 1/2 tablespoons lemon
  juice

3 egg yolks, slightly
  beaten
1 baked 9-inch pie shell
3 egg whites
6 tablespoons sugar

Combine 1 cup sugar, flour, pineapple, sour cream, salt and lemon juice in saucepan; mix well. Cook over low heat until thickened, stirring constantly. Stir a small amount of hot mixture into egg yolks; stir egg yolks into hot mixture. Cook for 2 minutes longer, stirring constantly. Remove from heat. Stir frequently while cooling. Pour into pie shell. Beat egg whites in mixer bowl until soft peaks form. Add remaining 6 tablespoons sugar gradually, beating constantly until stiff peaks form. Spread lightly over filling, sealing to edge. Bake at 300 degrees for 15 minutes or until lightly browned. Yield: 6 servings.

PINTO BEAN PIE

1/2 cup cooked pinto
  beans
1 1/2 cups sugar
1/2 cup melted margarine

2 eggs, beaten
1/2 cup coconut
1 teaspoon vanilla extract
1 unbaked 9-inch pie shell

Drain and mash beans. Combine with sugar, melted margarine and eggs in bowl; mix well. Stir in coconut and vanilla. Spoon into pie shell. Bake at 350 degrees for 1 hour. Yield: 6 servings.

PRALINE PIE

1/4 cup melted margarine
1/2 cup packed brown
  sugar
2/3 cup chopped pecans
1 unbaked 9-inch deep-
  dish pie shell

2 packages butterscotch
  instant pudding mix
2 cups milk
1 cup whipped topping

Mix melted margarine, brown sugar and pecans in bowl. Pat into pie shell. Bake at 400 degrees until pie shell is lightly browned and praline mixture is bubbly; cool. Combine pie filling mix and milk in bowl; mix until thickened. Fold in whipped topping. Pour into cooled pie shell. Chill, covered, until serving time. Serve with additional whipped topping. Yield: 8 servings.

PUMPKIN PIE

2 eggs, slightly beaten
1 16-ounce can pumpkin
3/4 cup sugar
1/2 teaspoon salt
1 teaspoon cinnamon

1/2 teaspoon ginger
1/4 teaspoon cloves
12/3 cups evaporated milk
1 unbaked 9-inch pie shell

Combine eggs, pumpkin, sugar, salt, cinnamon, ginger, cloves and evaporated milk in bowl; mix well. Pour into pie shell. Bake at 425 degrees for 15 minutes. Reduce oven temperature to 350 degrees. Bake for 45 minutes longer or until knife inserted in center comes out clean. Cool. Serve with sweetened whipped cream if desired. Yield: 6 servings.

A Lion Tip

Dress up your pumpkin pie by adding chopped pecans to the pastry.

PEANUT BUTTER PUMPKIN PIE

1 recipe 2-crust pie pastry
1 egg, beaten
1 teaspoon water
3 eggs, slightly beaten
1 16-ounce can pumpkin
3/4 cup packed light
  brown sugar
1/2 cup peanut butter

1/2 teaspoon pumpkin pie
  spice
1/4 teaspoon salt
1 cup evaporated milk
Bourbon-Flavored
  Whipped Cream
Crushed peanut brittle

Fit half the pastry into 9-inch pie plate. Cut remaining pastry with leaf-shaped cookie cutter. Make veins on leaves with toothpick. Brush edge of pie shell with mixture of 1 egg and water. Apply leaves alternately to inside and outside of edge of pie shell. Chill in freezer for 30 minutes. Combine remaining 3 eggs, pumpkin, brown sugar, peanut butter, pumpkin pie spice, salt and evaporated milk in large mixer bowl; mix well. Pour into pie shell. Bake at 425 degrees for 15 minutes. Reduce oven temperature to 350 degrees. Bake for 40 to 45 minutes longer or until knife inserted near center comes out clean, covering edge of pie crust with foil during last 30 minutes of baking time to prevent overbrowning. Cool. Top with Bourbon-Flavored Whipped Cream; sprinkle with peanut brittle. Yield: 6 servings.

Bourbon-Flavored Whipped Cream

1 cup whipping cream
1/4 cup confectioners'
  sugar

1 tablespoon Bourbon

Combine whipping cream, confectioners' sugar and Bourbon in small mixer bowl. Beat until soft peaks form.

PUMPKIN PECAN PIE

4 eggs, slightly beaten
2 cups mashed cooked
  pumpkin
3/4 cup sugar
1/2 cup dark corn syrup

1 teaspoon cinnamon
1/4 teaspoon salt
1 unbaked 9-inch pie shell
1 cup pecan halves or
  chopped pecans

Combine eggs, pumpkin, sugar, corn syrup, cinnamon and salt in large bowl; mix well. Pour into pie shell. Arrange pecans over filling. Bake at 350 degrees for 45 to 55 minutes or until knife inserted near center comes out clean. Cool in pie plate on wire rack. Yield: 8 servings.

PUFFY PUMPKIN PIE

3 egg yolks
1 cup sugar
1 teaspoon salt
1 1/2 teaspoons cinnamon
1 teaspoon ginger
1/4 teaspoon cloves
1/4 teaspoon nutmeg

2 cups canned pumpkin
1 cup milk
1 teaspoon vanilla extract
3 egg whites, stiffly
  beaten
1 unbaked 9-inch pie shell

Beat egg yolks in large bowl until thick and lemony. Stir in mixture of sugar, salt and spices. Add pumpkin, milk and vanilla; mix well. Fold in egg whites. Pour into pie shell. Bake at 450 degrees for 10 minutes. Reduce oven temperature to 350 degrees. Bake for 25 to 30 minutes longer or until knife inserted near center comes out clean. Yield: 6 servings.

A Lion Tip

Make pies for a crowd with 1/2 gallon softened vanilla ice cream and 12 ounces frozen lemonade concentrate. Spoon into 3 graham cracker pie shells and freeze until firm. Garnish with whipped cream and lemon slices.

BERRY NUTTY PIE

3 egg whites, at room
  temperature
3/4 cup sugar
1/2 teaspoon baking
  powder
10 tablespoons
  semisweet chocolate
  chips, coarsely chopped
6 tablespoons chopped
  pecans, ground
1 cup crushed butter
  crackers
1 teaspoon almond
  extract

1 cup whipping cream
2 tablespoons
  confectioners' sugar
1/2 teaspoon vanilla
  extract
1 1/4 cups sliced
  strawberries
2 tablespoons pecan
  pieces
3/4 cup sliced strawberries
2 tablespoons semisweet
  chocolate chips

Beat egg whites in mixer bowl until soft peaks form. Add mixture of sugar and baking powder gradually, beating until stiff peaks form. Combine chopped chocolate, ground pecans and crushed crackers in small bowl; mix well. Fold into egg whites. Stir in almond extract. Spread in greased 9-inch pie plate. Bake at 350 degrees for 25 minutes. Cool completely. Combine whipping cream, confectioners' sugar and vanilla in mixer bowl. Beat at medium speed until stiff peaks form. Fold in 1 1/4 cups strawberries. Spread over cooled crust. Top with pecan pieces, remaining 3/4 cup strawberries and chocolate chips. Chill, covered, until serving time. Yield: 6 servings.

SWEET POTATO CUSTARD PIE

1 cup mashed cooked
  sweet potatoes
1 1/2 cups sugar
1 2/3 cups milk
3 eggs, slightly beaten

1 teaspoon grated fresh
  orange rind
1/8 teaspoon ginger
1 unbaked 9-inch pie shell
Sweetened whipped cream

Combine sweet potatoes, sugar, milk, eggs, orange rind and ginger in bowl; mix well. Pour into pie shell. Bake at 350 degrees for 1 hour or until knife inserted near center comes out clean. Serve warm with sweetened whipped cream.
Yield: 8 servings.

CHEESY ALMOND TARTLETS

2 tablespoons melted
   butter
1/3 cup almond-flavored
   cookie crumbs
15 ounces low-fat ricotta
   cheese
1/2 cup nonfat dry milk
1/2 cup sugar

3 eggs
3/4 teaspoon almond
   extract
1/4 teaspoon salt
1 cup vanilla low-fat
   yogurt
Sliced strawberries
Almonds

Place foil liners in muffin cups. Brush with melted butter. Sprinkle with cookie crumbs. Combine ricotta cheese, milk powder, sugar, eggs, almond extract and salt in blender container. Process for 45 seconds or until smooth. Spoon into prepared muffin cups. Bake at 325 degrees for 25 minutes or until firm. Spread with yogurt. Bake for 6 to 8 minutes longer or until yogurt is firm. Cool. Chill, covered, until serving time. Garnish with sliced strawberries and almonds.
Yield: 10 servings.

DRIED APRICOT AND CRANBERRY TART

1/3 cup packed light
   brown sugar
1/3 cup light corn syrup
2 eggs, slightly beaten
2 tablespoons melted
   butter or margarine
1 teaspoon vanilla extract
1/4 teaspoon salt

3/4 cup chopped dried
   apricots
1 cup cranberries
1/2 cup chopped walnuts
1 baked 9-inch tart shell
24 dried apricot halves
Corn syrup

Combine brown sugar, 1/3 cup corn syrup, eggs, melted butter, vanilla and salt in bowl. Whisk until smooth. Stir in chopped apricots, cranberries and walnuts. Pour into cooled tart shell. Bake at 400 degrees for 30 minutes. Garnish with apricot halves brushed with additional corn syrup. Cool for 10 minutes. Serve with whipped cream. Yield: 8 servings.

CHOCOLATE AND VANILLA SWIRL TART

2/3 cup semisweet
chocolate chips
1/4 cup milk
2 tablespoons sugar
1/2 teaspoon unflavored
gelatin
1 tablespoon cold water

2/3 cup vanilla chips
1/4 cup milk
1 teaspoon vanilla extract
1 cup chilled whipping
cream, whipped
Tart Shell

Combine chocolate chips, 1/4 cup milk and sugar in small microwave-safe bowl. Microwave on High for 1 minute or until hot. Whisk until smooth. Cool. Soften gelatin in cold water. Combine vanilla chips and remaining 1/4 cup milk in microwave-safe bowl. Microwave on High for 1 minute or until hot. Whisk until smooth. Add gelatin mixture and vanilla. Stir until gelatin is dissolved. Cool. Fold half the whipped cream into each mixture. Spoon chocolate and vanilla mixtures alternately into cooled Tart Shell. Swirl with spatula. Chill until set. Yield: 8 to 10 servings.

Tart Shell

1/2 cup butter or
margarine, softened
2 tablespoons sugar

2 egg yolks, slightly
beaten
1 cup flour

Cream butter and sugar in mixer bowl until light and fluffy. Add egg yolks; mix well. Stir in flour until crumbly. Press into greased 8 or 9-inch fluted tart pan. Prick bottom with fork. Bake at 375 degrees for 8 to 10 minutes or until lightly browned. Cool completely. May sprinkle with 1 tablespoon additional flour before baking if pastry is sticky.

 ### A Lion Tip

Prevent a soggy lower pie crust by brushing it with egg white or melted butter before adding the filling. Be sure that filling is hot also.

GRAPE AND APPLE TART

3 tablespoons vanilla
  cookie crumbs
1 baked 10-inch tart shell
1/3 cup packed brown
  sugar
4 teaspoons lemon juice

2 teaspoons cornstarch
1/2 teaspoon nutmeg
3 Golden Delicious
  apples, peeled, sliced
1 1/2 cups grape halves
1/4 cup orange marmalade

Sprinkle cookie crumbs over bottom of tart shell. Combine brown sugar, lemon juice, cornstarch and nutmeg in bowl; mix well. Stir in apples. Arrange half the apples in spiral layer over cookie crumbs. Sprinkle 1/2 cup grape halves over apples. Arrange remaining apples in second spiral layer around outer half of tart. Fill center of apple ring with remaining 1 cup grape halves. Spoon marmalade over tart. Bake at 400 degrees for 45 minutes or until apples and grapes are tender and pastry is golden brown. Yield: 12 servings.

GOLDEN PECAN TASSIES

1 cup butter, softened
6 ounces cream cheese,
  softened
2 cups sifted flour
2 eggs, beaten
1 1/2 cups packed brown
  sugar

2 tablespoons melted
  butter
Dash of salt
1/2 teaspoon vanilla
  extract
1 cup chopped pecans

Blend butter and cream cheese in bowl. Add flour gradually, mixing until smooth dough forms. Shape into 1 1/4-inch balls. Press each over bottom and side of 1 3/4-inch muffin cup. Beat eggs with brown sugar, butter, salt and vanilla in bowl. Sprinkle half the pecans into pastry-lined muffin cups. Spoon brown sugar mixture over pecans. Top with remaining pecans. Bake at 350 degrees for 15 minutes. Reduce temperature to 250 degrees. Bake for 10 minutes longer. Yield: 3 to 4 dozen.

Candies
and
Cookies

CANDIES

AMARETTO TRUFFLES

6 tablespoons butter,
softened
1 1-pound package
confectioners' sugar
1 egg yolk
2 tablespoons Amaretto
6 1-ounce squares
semisweet chocolate

1 6-ounce package
unsalted whole almonds
5 cups semisweet
chocolate chips
1/2 cup shortening
1 cup semisweet
chocolate chips

Cream butter and confectioners' sugar in bowl until light and fluffy. Add egg yolk and Amaretto; mix well. Process chocolate squares in food processor or blender container until finely chopped. Fold into Amaretto mixture. Chill until firm. Place almonds on baking sheet. Bake at 350 degrees until lightly browned. Cool. Shape a small amount of chocolate mixture around each almond, forming ball. Place on waxed paper. Let stand for 30 minutes or until firm. Melt 5 cups chocolate chips with shortening in top of double boiler over hot water, stirring until smooth. Replace hot water in double boiler with cool water. Stir chocolate mixture until cooled to 88 degrees on candy thermometer. Process remaining 1 cup chocolate chips in food processor or blender container until finely chopped. Stir into chocolate mixture. Dip almond balls into chocolate mixture to coat. Place on waxed paper. Let stand for 48 hours or until firm. Store in airtight container in cool place. Yield: 7 dozen.

AMBER BALLS

2 14-ounce cans
sweetened condensed
milk
2 3-ounce cans coconut

1 pound candy orange
slices, chopped
2 cups chopped pecans
Confectioners' sugar

Combine condensed milk, coconut, candy and pecans in bowl; mix well. Pour into baking dish. Bake at 275 degrees for 30 minutes, stirring occasionally. Cool. Shape into small balls; roll in confectioners' sugar. Yield: 8 dozen.

BUCKEYES

2 cups margarine,
softened
2 1-pound packages
confectioners' sugar
2 pounds peanut butter

1 package graham
cracker crumbs
2 cups semisweet
chocolate chips
3 tablespoons paraffin

Combine margarine, confectioners' sugar, peanut butter and graham cracker crumbs in bowl; mix well. Shape into small balls. Chill overnight. Melt chocolate chips and paraffin in double boiler over boiling water, stirring until smooth. Dip each ball into chocolate, leaving small portion uncoated to represent eye. Place on waxed paper. Let stand until firm. Yield: 8 dozen.

BUTTERMILK CANDY

1 teaspoon soda
1 cup buttermilk
3/4 cup margarine
2 cups sugar
2 tablespoons corn syrup

2 teaspoons vanilla
extract
2 cups coarsely chopped
pecans

Dissolve soda in buttermilk in large saucepan. Add margarine, sugar, and corn syrup; mix well. Cook over medium heat to 234 to 240 degrees on candy thermometer, soft-ball stage. Add vanilla; remove from heat. Beat until thick and creamy. Add pecans; mix well. Drop by spoonfuls onto waxed paper. Cool. Yield: 6 dozen.

BUTTERSCOTCH CLUSTERS

2 cups butterscotch chips
1 8-ounce can peanuts

1 5-ounce can chow
mein noodles

Melt butterscotch chips in saucepan over low heat, stirring constantly. Stir in peanuts and noodles. Drop by spoonfuls onto waxed paper. Let stand until firm. Yield: 2 dozen.

NO-FUSS CARAMEL CORN

3 quarts popped popcorn
1½ cups peanuts
1 cup packed brown
  sugar

½ cup butter
¼ cup light corn syrup
½ teaspoon salt
½ teaspoon soda

    Place popcorn and peanuts in large oven cooking bag; set aside. Combine brown sugar, butter, corn syrup and salt in 2-quart microwave-safe bowl. Microwave on High for 3 to 4 minutes or until mixture comes to a boil, stirring after each minute. Microwave for 2 minutes longer. Stir in soda. Pour syrup over popcorn. Close bag; shake well. Microwave on High for 1½ minutes. Shake bag; pour popcorn into largepan. Let stand until cool. Stir to separate. Yield: 6 quarts.

CARAMEL CORN

1 cup unpopped popcorn
1 cup margarine
2 cups packed light
  brown sugar

½ cup dark corn syrup
⅛ teaspoon cream of
  tartar
1 teaspoon soda

    Pop popcorn as desired. Bring margarine, brown sugar, corn syrup and cream of tartar to a boil in saucepan. Boil for 5 minutes, stirring constantly; remove from heat. Add soda; mix well. Pour over popped popcorn in bowl; mix well. Spread on 2 greased baking sheets. Bake at 225 degrees for 1 hour, stirring occasionally. Cool. Store in airtight container. Yield: 20 cups.

A Lion Tip

It is usually more successful to make 2 recipes of candy than to double the recipe.

CHOCOLATE CARAMELS

2/3 cup butter
1/2 cup baking cocoa
2 cups sugar
1 cup packed brown
  sugar

1 cup half and half
1 cup light corn syrup
2 cups coarsely chopped
  pecans

Line 9-inch square pan with lightly buttered foil. Melt butter in heavy saucepan. Add cocoa; stir until smooth. Remove from heat. Add sugar, brown sugar, half and half and corn syrup; mix well. Cook over medium heat until sugar is completely dissolved, stirring constantly. Cook to 250 degrees on candy thermometer, firm-ball stage, stirring occasionally. Pour candy into prepared pan. Sprinkle pecans evenly over top. Cool until firm. Invert onto wooden board; remove foil. Cut into squares with sharp knife dipped in water. Wrap individually in plastic wrap. Yield: 5 dozen.

CHOCOLATE-COVERED CANDY

2 1-pound packages
   confectioners' sugar,
   sifted
1 14-ounce can
   sweetened condensed
   milk
2 cups chopped pecans

1 8-ounce jar
   maraschino cherries,
   drained, chopped
1 teaspoon vanilla extract
3/4 block paraffin
2 cups semisweet
   chocolate chips

Combine confectioners' sugar, condensed milk, pecans, cherries and vanilla in bowl; mix well. Shape into small balls. Place on waxed paper. Chill until firm. Combine paraffin and chocolate chips in top of double boiler. Heat over boiling water until melted, stirring frequently. Dip balls into chocolate; place on waxed paper. Let stand until cool. Yield: 76 servings.

CHOCOLATE-COVERED CHERRIES

1 1-pound package
confectioners' sugar
1/2 cup butter, softened
1 tablespoon evaporated
milk
1 tablespoon vanilla
extract

1 large jar maraschino
cherries, well drained
1/4 block paraffin
1 cup chocolate chips

Combine confectioners' sugar and butter in bowl; mix well. Add evaporated milk and vanilla; mix well. Chill until firm. Pat cherries dry with paper towels. Shape fondant by spoonfuls around cherries, covering completely. Place on waxed paper-lined tray. Chill in freezer for 20 to 30 minutes. Melt paraffin and chocolate chips in top of double boiler. Dip cherries into chocolate to coat. Place on waxed paper. Let stand until firm. Store in airtight container. Yield: 2 to 3 dozen.

CHOCOLATE-COVERED PEANUTS

2 tablespoons peanut
butter
1 cup chocolate chips

1 cup butterscotch chips
2 cups salted Spanish
peanuts

Melt peanut butter, chocolate chips and butterscotch chips in large saucepan over low heat, stirring constantly. Stir in peanuts. Drop by spoonfuls onto waxed paper. Chill until firm. Yield: 2 dozen.

WHITE CHOCOLATE ALMOND CLUSTERS

3 cups crisp rice cereal
3 cups Captain Crunch
cereal
3 cups dry roasted
peanuts

1 cup slivered almonds
2 1-pound package
vanilla-flavored
Candiquik

Combine cereals, peanuts and almonds in large bowl; mix well. Melt Candiquik in saucepan over low heat; stirring constantly. Add to cereal mixture; mix well. Drop by tablespoonfuls onto waxed paper. Chill until firm. Store in airtight container. Yield: 6 dozen.

DATE NUT BALLS

1/2 cup margarine
1 8-ounce package
  pitted dates, chopped
1 cup chopped pecans
1 cup sugar

1/8 teaspoon salt
1 teaspoon vanilla extract
2 cups crisp rice cereal
2 cups (about)
  confectioners' sugar

Melt margarine in saucepan. Add dates, pecans, sugar and salt. Cook over low heat for 8 minutes, stirring frequently. Add vanilla and cereal; mix well. Cool. Shape into walnut-sized balls. Roll in confectioners' sugar. Store in airtight container. Yield: 3 dozen.

DIVINITY

2 1/2 cups sugar
1/2 cup light corn syrup
1/2 cup water

1/4 teaspoon salt
2 egg whites
1 teaspoon vanilla extract

Combine sugar, corn syrup, water and salt in saucepan; mix well. Cook over low heat until sugar is completely dissolved, stirring constantly. Cook, covered, over medium heat for 2 to 3 minutes or until steam washes sugar crystals from side of pan. Cook, uncovered, over high heat to 234 to 240 degrees on candy thermometer, soft-ball stage, stirring constantly. Beat egg whites in mixer bowl until stiff peaks form. Add hot syrup very gradually, beating constantly. Beat at high speed until very stiff. Stir in vanilla. Drop by spoonfuls onto waxed paper. Let stand until cool. Store in airtight container. Do not make on a rainy day. Yield: 3 dozen.

A Lion Tip

Choose a cool dry day to make candy. Hard candies, divinities, fondants and nougats are especially sensitive to humid conditions.

BUTTERSCOTCH FUDGE

1 cup sugar
1 cup packed brown
  sugar
2/3 cup evaporated milk
1/2 cup margarine

1 7-ounce jar
  marshmallow creme
2 cups butterscotch chips
1/2 cup chopped pecans

Combine sugar, brown sugar, evaporated milk and margarine in heavy 3-quart saucepan; mix well. Bring to the boiling point, stirring constantly. Cook over medium heat to 234 to 240 degrees on candy thermometer, soft-ball stage. Add marshmallow creme; stir until blended. Remove from heat. Stir in butterscotch chips until melted. Add pecans. Beat until mixture thickens and loses its luster. Pour into buttered 9-inch square dish. Let stand until firm. Cut into squares.
Yield: 2 dozen.

MARSHMALLOW CREME FUDGE

4 cups sugar
3/4 cup butter
1 14-ounce can
  evaporated milk
1 7-ounce jar
  marshmallow creme

2 cups semisweet
  chocolate chips
1 teaspoon vanilla extract
1 cup chopped pecans

Bring sugar, butter and evaporated milk to a boil in saucepan; mix well. Cook for 9 minutes, stirring constantly. Remove from heat. Add marshmallow creme, chocolate chips, vanilla and pecans. Stir until chocolate chips are melted. Pour into buttered 9x12-inch dish. Chill until firm. Cut into squares.
Yield: 2 dozen.

MICROWAVE FUDGE

1 1-pound package
   confectioners' sugar
1/2 cup baking cocoa
1/4 teaspoon salt

1 teaspoon vanilla extract
1/4 cup milk
1/2 cup margarine
1/2 cup pecans

Combine confectioners' sugar, cocoa, salt, vanilla and milk in microwave-safe bowl; mix well. Add margarine. Cover with waxed paper. Microwave on High for 2 minutes. Stir until thick and creamy. Stir in pecans. Pour into buttered dish. Chill in refrigerator for 1 hour. Cut into squares. Yield: 2 dozen.

PEANUT BUTTER FUDGE

1 1-pound package
   confectioners' sugar
1/2 cup peanut butter
1/2 cup baking cocoa

2 teaspoons vanilla
   extract
1/8 teaspoon salt

Combine confectioners' sugar, peanut butter, cocoa, vanilla and salt in bowl; mix well. Spread in 9-inch square dish. Let stand until firm. Cut into squares. Yield: 2 dozen.

SODA CRACKER FUDGE

2 cups sugar
3/4 cup milk
6 tablespoons peanut
   butter

2 tablespoons butter
28 soda crackers, crushed
1 teaspoon vanilla extract

Combine sugar, milk, peanut butter and butter in saucepan; mix well. Bring to a boil, stirring constantly. Boil for 3 minutes. Remove from heat. Add crushed crackers and vanilla; mix well. Press into 9-inch square dish. Let stand until firm. Cut into squares. Yield: 2 dozen.

HEAVENLY HASH

2 cups chocolate chips
1 14-ounce can
  sweetened condensed
  milk
3 tablespoons melted
  butter

3 cups chopped pecans
1 10-ounce package
  miniature marshmallows

    Melt chocolate chips in saucepan over low heat, stirring constantly. Add condensed milk, butter, pecans and marshmallows; mix well. Pour into buttered 9x12-inch dish. Let stand at room temperature for 6 hours. Cut into squares.
Yield: 3 dozen.

HONEY BALLS

1 cup honey
1 cup peanut butter

2 cups nonfat dry milk
1 cup cornflakes, crushed

    Cream honey and peanut butter in bowl. Add dry milk; mix well. Shape into small balls. Roll in crushed cornflake.
Yield: 2 dozen.

MARTHA WASHINGTON CANDY

8 ounces milk chocolate
1 package paraffin
2 1-pound packages
  confectioners' sugar
1 tablespoon vanilla
  extract

1 14-ounce can
  sweetened condensed
  milk
1/2 cup butter
4 cups chopped pecans

    Melt chocolate and paraffin in top of double boiler over hot water, stirring until smooth. Combine confectioners' sugar, vanilla, condensed milk and butter in bowl; mix well. Add pecans; mix well. Shape into small balls. Dip into chocolate, coating well. Place on waxed paper; let stand until firm.
Yield: 3 to 4 dozen.

MOLASSES WHEAT GERM CANDY

1/2 cup honey
1/4 cup molasses
1 cup raisins
1 1/2 cups peanut butter

1 cup nonfat dry milk
2 1/2 cups toasted wheat
germ

Combine, honey, molasses, raisins, peanut butter, dry milk and wheat germ in bowl; mix well. Press into 9-inch square dish. Cut into squares. Yield: 2 dozen.

CHOCOLATE PEANUT CLUSTERS

6 ounces sweet chocolate
1/4 block paraffin
2/3 cup sweetened
condensed milk

1 cup peanuts

Melt chocolate and paraffin in top of double boiler over hot water, stirring until smooth. Remove from heat. Stir in milk. Add peanuts; stir until coated with chocolate. Drop by teaspoonfuls onto greased baking sheet. Chill in refrigerator for 3 hours or until firm. Yield: 1 dozen.

PEANUT BUTTER BALLS

1 cup melted margarine
1 cup graham cracker
crumbs
1 teaspoon vanilla extract

1 teaspoon crunchy
peanut butter
1 1-pound package
confectioners' sugar

Combine margarine, graham cracker crumbs, vanilla, peanut butter and confectioners' sugar in bowl; mix well. Chill until firm. Shape into small balls. May coat with confectioners' sugar, coconut or mixture of 1 cup chocolate chips melted with 1/4 block paraffin. Yield: 4 dozen.

NEVER-FAIL PEANUT BRITTLE

2 cups sugar
3/4 cup light corn syrup
1/4 cup water
1/8 teaspoon salt
2 cups raw peanuts

4 teaspoons soda
4 teaspoons vanilla
extract
1 tablespoon margarine

Combine sugar, corn syrup, water, salt and peanuts in saucepan. Cook over high heat to 300 to 310 degrees on candy thermometer, hard-crack stage, stirring constantly. Remove from heat. Stir in soda, vanilla and margarine. Beat vigorously. Spread on 2 buttered baking sheets. Let stand until cool enough to handle. Stretch as thin as possible. Break into pieces. Yield: 1 1/2 pounds.

PECAN LOG

1 16-ounce package
vanilla wafers, crushed
1 cup chopped pecans
1 14-ounce sweetened
condensed milk

1/2 cup maraschino
cherries, drained,
chopped
1 1/2 cups confectioners'
sugar

Combine vanilla wafer crumbs, pecans, condensed milk, cherries and 3/4 cup confectioners' sugar in bowl; mix well. Shape into log. Roll in remaining 3/4 cup confectioners' sugar. Wrap in waxed paper. Chill until firm. Yield: 2 pounds.

PECAN CLUSTERS

5 cups sugar
1 12-ounce can
evaporated milk
1/2 cup butter
1/2 teaspoon salt

4 cups chopped pecans
1 1/2 pounds chocolate
kisses
1 9-ounce jar
marshmallow creme

Combine sugar, evaporated milk, butter, and salt in saucepan; mix well. Bring to a boil. Cook for 7 minutes, stirring constantly. Remove from heat. Add pecans, chocolate kisses and marshmallow creme; mix well. Drop by spoonfuls onto waxed paper. Let stand until firm. Yield: 6 pounds.

POTATO CANDY

½ cup mashed cooked
potatoes
1 teaspoon vanilla extract
2 1-pound packages
confectioners' sugar

1 12-ounce jar peanut
butter

Combine potatoes and vanilla in bowl; mix well. Sift in confectioners' sugar; mix well. Roll a small amount of dough at a time on waxed paper. Spread with peanut butter. Roll as for jelly roll. Chill in refrigerator for 1 hour. Slice into small pieces. Yield: 2 to 3 dozen.

PRALINES

1½ cups margarine
1 1-pound package
brown sugar
3 cups sugar

1 14-ounce can
evaporated milk
1 teaspoon vanilla extract
3 cups chopped pecans

Combine margarine, brown sugar, sugar and evaporated milk in saucepan; mix well. Bring to a boil, stirring constantly. Cook over medium heat to 234 to 240 degrees on candy thermometer, soft-ball stage, stirring constantly. Add vanilla and pecans. Beat until mixture thickens and loses it luster. Drop by spoonfuls on waxed paper. Let stand until firm. Yield: 2 pounds.

PRALINE CRUNCH

½ cup margarine
1 cup packed brown
sugar

½ cup chopped pecans
2½ cups cornflakes

Melt margarine and brown sugar in saucepan. Bring to a boil, stirring constantly. Remove from heat. Add pecans and cornflakes. Mix with a fork to coat thoroughly. Spread on waxed paper. Cool. Store in airtight container. Yield: 2 pounds.

QUICK CANDY

2 cups miniature
marshmallows
2¹/₂ cups Captain Crunch
cereal

2 cups crisp rice cereal
2 cups dry-roasted
peanuts
2 pounds white chocolate

Combine marshmallows, cereals and peanuts in bowl; mix well. Melt white chocolate in saucepan over low heat, stirring constantly. Pour over cereal mixture; mix well. Drop by spoonfuls onto waxed paper. Let stand until cool. Yield: 6 dozen.

ROCKY ROAD SQUARES

2 cups semisweet
chocolate chips
1 14-ounce can
sweetened condensed
milk

1 tablespoon butter
2 cups dry roasted
peanuts
1 10-ounce package
miniature marshmallows

Combine chocolate chips, condensed milk and butter in top of double boiler. Heat over boiling water until chocolate chips are melted, stirring constantly. Remove from heat. Combine peanuts and marshmallows in bowl; mix well. Stir in chocolate mixture. Spread in waxed paper-lined 9x13-inch pan. Chill for 2 hours or until firm. Invert onto wooden board; remove foil. Cut into squares. Store in airtight container. Yield: 3 pounds.

RUM BALLS

1 cup pecans
¹/₂ 16-ounce package
vanilla wafers
2 cups chocolate chips

2 teaspoons baking cocoa
¹/₂ cup light corn syrup
¹/₂ cup rum
Confectioners' sugar

Combine pecans, vanilla wafers and chocolate chips in blender container. Process at high speed until finely chopped. Combine with cocoa, corn syrup and rum in large bowl; mix well. Shape into small balls; roll in confectioners' sugar. Store in airtight container. Yield: 2 to 3 dozen.

STRAWBERRY CANDIES

1 6-ounce package strawberry gelatin	1/2 teaspoon vanilla extract
1 cup pecans, chopped	Red sugar crystals
1 cup coconut	Slivered almonds
3/4 cup sweetened condensed milk	Several drops of green food coloring

Combine dry gelatin, pecans, coconut, condensed milk and vanilla in bowl; mix well. Shape into strawberries; roll in sugar crystals. Toss almonds with green food coloring in bowl. Use for stems and leaves of strawberries. Yield: 24 servings.

TURTLES

78 caramels	2 cups pecan halves
2 tablespoons margarine	4 cups milk chocolate chips
2 tablespoons evaporated milk	1/4 block paraffin

Combine caramels, margarine and evaporated milk in top of double boiler. Cook for 5 minutes or until mixture is smooth, stirring constantly. Stir in pecans. Drop by spoonfuls onto buttered baking sheets. Chill until firm. Combine chocolate chips and paraffin in top of double boiler. Heat until melted, stirring constantly. Dip cooled caramels into warm chocolate. Place on waxed paper-lined baking sheets. Cool until firm. Store in airtight container. Yield: 3 dozen.

A Lion Tip

Make candy in a saucepan with 3 or 4 times the volume of the combined ingredients so the candy can boil freely without boiling over. Use a saucepan with a heavy bottom and a wooden spoon for stirring.

DEE-LICIOUS TOFFEE

2 tablespoons butter
2 cups finely chopped
  pecans

2 cups chocolate chips
2 cups butter
2 cups sugar

Grease 15x18-inch pan with 2 tablespoons butter. Sprinkle half the pecans and half the chocolate chips evenly in pan. Melt butter in 3-quart saucepan over low heat. Add sugar. Cook over medium heat to 300 degrees on candy thermometer, firm-ball stage, stirring constantly. Remove from heat. Spoon over chocolate chips and pecans. Sprinkle with remaining chocolate chips, spreading evenly until melted. Sprinkle remaining pecans over top. Chill until firm. Break into pieces. May substitute walnuts or macadamia nuts for pecans. Yield: 50 to 60 pieces.

 # COOKIES

APPLE AND RAISIN RUM COOKIES

2/3 cup chopped dried
  apples
1 cup raisins
2 teaspoons lemon juice
1/3 cup rum
1 1/4 cups all-purpose flour
1 cup whole wheat flour
1 cup (heaping) oats
1 teaspoon soda
1/2 teaspoon baking
  powder
1/4 teaspoon salt
1 1/2 teaspoons cinnamon

1/2 teaspoon mace
1/2 teaspoon cloves
1 cup butter, softened
1 1/4 cups packed brown
  sugar
1 egg
1 egg yolk
1 1/2 teaspoons vanilla
  extract
1/4 teaspoon grated lemon
  rind
1 1/4 cups chopped
  walnuts

Combine apples, raisins, lemon juice and rum in small bowl; mix well. Let stand for 15 to 20 minutes. Combine all-purpose flour, whole wheat flour, oats, soda, baking powder, salt, cinnamon, mace and cloves in bowl; mix well. Cream butter and brown sugar in large mixer bowl until light and fluffy. Add egg, egg yolk, vanilla and lemon rind; mix well. Add half the flour mixture; beat well. Stir in apple mixture. Add remaining flour mixture; mix well. Shape into 1¼-inch balls. Dip tops of balls in walnuts. Place 2½ inches apart on buttered cookie sheets. Bake at 350 degrees for 9 to 12 minutes or until edges are brown. Cool on cookie sheets for 3 to 4 minutes. Remove to wire racks to cool completely. Yield: 3½ dozen.

LOW-CALORIE APPLESAUCE COOKIES

1¾ cups cake flour
½ teaspoon salt
1 teaspoon cinnamon
½ teaspoon nutmeg
½ teaspoon cloves
1 teaspoon soda
½ cup butter, softened

2 tablespoons Sucaryl
2 eggs
2 cups dietetic
   applesauce
1 cup chopped dates
1½ cups All-Bran

Sift cake flour, salt, cinnamon, nutmeg, cloves and soda into bowl. Beat butter, Sucaryl and eggs in large mixer bowl until light and fluffy. Add cake flour mixture alternately with applesauce, mixing well after each addition. Fold in dates and All-Bran. Drop by teaspoonfuls 1 inch apart onto greased cookie sheets. Bake at 375 degrees for 20 minutes. Remove to wire racks to cool completely. Yield: 2 dozen.

NO-BAKE BANANA PEANUT BUTTER FUDGE BARS

⅔ cup butter
2 teaspoons vanilla
   extract
2½ cups oats
½ cup packed brown
   sugar

1¼ cups finely chopped
   bananas
1 cup semisweet
   chocolate chips
½ cup peanut butter

Melt butter in large skillet over medium heat. Add vanilla, oats and brown sugar; mix well. Cook for 5 minutes, stirring constantly. Reserve ¾ cup mixture. Press remaining mixture into 9-inch square baking pan. Sprinkle with bananas. Melt chocolate chips and peanut butter in small saucepan over low heat, stirring constantly. Pour over bananas. Sprinkle with reserved oat mixture, pressing lightly into chocolate mixture. Chill for 2 hours. Cut into bars. Store in refrigerator. Yield: 2 dozen.

OLD-FASHIONED BUTTER COOKIES

2 cups butter, softened
2 cups sugar
4 egg yolks
2 teaspoons vanilla
  extract

6 cups flour, sifted
2 teaspoons baking
  powder
2 teaspoons salt
1/4 cup milk

Cream butter and sugar in mixer bowl until light and fluffy. Add egg yolks 1 at a time, beating well after each addition. Add vanilla; beat well. Sift flour, baking powder and salt together. Add to creamed mixture alternately with milk, beating well after each addition. Chill for 10 minutes. Press through cookie press onto greased cookie sheets. Bake at 375 degrees for 8 to 10 minutes or until edges are light brown. Remove to wire racks to cool. May substitute cream for milk. Yield: 6 dozen.

CARAMEL BROWNIES

1 1/2 cups flour
2 teaspoons baking
  powder
1 teaspoon salt
1/2 cup shortening, melted
2 cups packed brown
  sugar

2 eggs, slightly beaten
2 teaspoons vanilla
  extract
1 cup chopped pecans

Sift flour, baking powder and salt together. Combine shortening, brown sugar, eggs and vanilla in large bowl; mix well. Add flour mixture; mix well. Fold in pecans. Spread into greased 10x15-inch baking pan. Bake at 350 degrees for 30 minutes. Cool. Cut into squares. Yield: 2 dozen.

A Lion Tip

Always place cookie dough on a cool cookie sheet; it will spread on a hot one.

CHOCOLATE SYRUP BROWNIES

1 cup butter, softened
2 cups sugar
2 teaspoons vanilla
  extract
4 eggs

2¹/₂ cups flour
¹/₂ teaspoon soda
1¹/₂ cups chocolate syrup
1¹/₂ cups chopped pecans

Cream butter and sugar in large mixer bowl until light and fluffy. Stir in vanilla. Add eggs 1 at a time, beating well after each addition. Add mixture of flour and soda alternately with chocolate syrup, beating well after each addition. Stir in pecans. Pour into 2 greased 9-inch square baking pans. Bake at 350 degrees for 40 to 45 minutes or until firm. Cool on wire racks. Cut into squares. Yield: 2³/₄ dozen.

CHOCOLATE SNOWBALL COOKIES

¹/₄ cup butter, softened
¹/₂ cup sugar
1 egg
1 ounce unsweetened
  chocolate, melted
1 teaspoon vanilla extract
¹/₂ teaspoon baking
  powder

1¹/₂ cups flour
¹/₄ teaspoon salt
1 cup sifted
  confectioners' sugar
¹/₂ teaspoon vanilla
  extract
5 teaspoons milk

Cream butter in large mixer bowl until light. Add sugar gradually, beating until fluffy. Add egg, chocolate and 1 teaspoon vanilla; beat well. Combine baking powder, flour and salt in bowl; mix well. Add to creamed mixture gradually, mixing just until smooth. Chill for 1 to 2 hours or until firm. Shape into 1-inch balls. Place on greased cookie sheets. Bake at 350 degrees for 12 minutes. Remove to wire racks to cool completely. Combine confectioners' sugar, remaining ¹/₂ teaspoon vanilla and milk in small mixer bowl; beat until smooth. Dip tops of cookies in glaze. Store in airtight container. Yield: 3 dozen.

FILLED SLICE AND BAKE CHOCOLATE COOKIES

3/4 cup butter, softened
1 cup sugar
1 egg
1 teaspoon vanilla extract
13/4 cups flour
2/3 cup baking cocoa

1 teaspoon baking powder
1/2 teaspoon soda
1/2 teaspoon salt
3 tablespoons milk
Creamy Filling

Cream butter and sugar in large mixer bowl until light and fluffy. Add egg and vanilla; mix well. Combine flour, baking cocoa, baking powder, soda and salt in bowl; mix well. Add to creamed mixture alternately with milk, mixing well after each addition. Chill, covered, for 1 hour or until firm enough to handle. Divide dough into 2 portions. Shape each portion into 7½-inch log on lightly floured surface. Freeze, wrapped in foil, for 8 hours. Cut into 1/8-inch slices. Place 1 inch apart on lightly greased cookie sheets. Bake at 325 degrees for 9 to 10 minutes or until firm. Let stand on cookie sheets for 1 minute. Remove to wire racks to cool completely. Spread 1/2 of the cookies with Creamy Filling; top with remaining cookies to form sandwiches. Yield: 4 dozen.

Creamy Filling

3 ounces cream cheese, softened
1 tablespoon butter, softened
1 teaspoon milk
2¼ cups confectioners' sugar

1/2 teaspoon vanilla extract
4 to 5 drops of red food coloring
1/8 teaspoon peppermint extract

Beat cream cheese and butter in medium mixer bowl until blended. Beat in milk. Add confectioners' sugar gradually, beating until smooth. Stir in vanilla, food coloring and peppermint extract. Yield: 1¼ cups.

COCOA SANDIES

1 cup butter, softened
1¼ cups confectioners' sugar
1½ teaspoons vanilla extract
½ cup baking cocoa
1¾ cups flour
1½ cups confectioners' sugar
2 tablespoons baking cocoa
¼ cup milk

Cream butter, 1¼ cups confectioners' sugar and vanilla in mixer bowl until light and fluffy. Add ½ cup baking cocoa; beat well. Add flour gradually, beating until smooth. Roll dough to ½-inch thickness on lightly floured surface. Cut with 2½-inch heart or star-shaped cutters. Place on ungreased cookie sheets. Bake at 300 degrees for 20 minutes or just until firm. Cool slightly on cookie sheets. Remove to wire racks to cool. Combine remaining 1½ cups confectioners' sugar and 2 tablespoons baking cocoa in small bowl; mix well. Stir in enough milk to make of glaze consistency. Dip half of each cookie into glaze. Place on wire racks until glaze is set. Yield: 2 dozen.

WHITE CHRISTMAS CRINKLES

4 ounces white chocolate
2 cups flour
½ teaspoon soda
¼ teaspoon salt
⅓ cup margarine, softened
1 cup sugar
1 egg
¼ cup buttermilk
1 teaspoon vanilla extract
½ cup sugar
½ cup semisweet chocolate chips
2 teaspoons shortening
Round striped peppermint candies, coarsely crushed

Melt white chocolate in saucepan over low heat. Combine flour, soda and salt in bowl. Beat margarine in mixer bowl for 30 seconds. Add 1 cup sugar; beat until light and fluffy. Add white chocolate, egg, buttermilk and vanilla; mix well. Add flour mixture; mix well. Chill, covered, for 1 hour. Shape into 1-inch balls; roll in remaining ½ cup sugar. Place 2 inches apart on ungreased cookie sheets. Bake at 375 degrees for 10 minutes or until bottoms are lightly browned. Remove to wire racks to cool. Melt chocolate chips and shortening in small saucepan over low heat, stirring constantly. Drizzle over cookies; sprinkle with peppermint. Yield: 4 dozen.

CONTEMPORARY CHIP COOKIES

1/3 cup butter, softened
3/4 cup sugar
1/2 cup packed brown
 sugar
1 egg
1 teaspoon vanilla extract
2 1/2 cups flour
1 teaspoon soda

1/2 teaspoon baking
 powder
1/2 teaspoon salt
1/2 cup buttermilk
1 cup vanilla milk chips
1 cup semisweet
 chocolate chips

Cream butter, sugar and brown sugar in mixer bowl until light and fluffy. Add egg and vanilla; beat until smooth. Combine next 4 dry ingredients in bowl; mix well. Add to creamed mixture alternately with buttermilk, beating well after each addition. Stir in vanilla chips and chocolate chips. Drop by 1/4 cupfuls onto ungreased cookie sheets. Bake at 350 degrees for 12 to 14 minutes or until light brown. Cool slightly on cookie sheets. Remove to wire racks to cool completely. Yield: 2 dozen.

CINNAMON STARS

2 1/2 cups blanched
 almonds
1/3 cup egg whites,
 at room temperature
Pinch of salt
1/8 teaspoon lemon juice
3 cups confectioners'
 sugar

1 tablespoon cinnamon
1 1/2 teaspoons grated
 lemon rind
2/3 cup confectioners'
 sugar
2 teaspoons lemon juice

Grind almonds very fine in food processor container with steel blade. Beat egg whites and salt in mixer bowl until frothy. Add 1/8 teaspoon lemon juice. Beat until soft peaks form. Add 3 cups confectioners' sugar gradually, beating until stiff peaks form. Reserve 1/2 cup mixture. Add ground almonds, cinnamon and lemon rind to remaining egg white mixture. Add enough remaining 2/3 cup confectioners' sugar to make soft dough. Roll dough to 1/8-inch thickness on surface sprinkled with confectioners' sugar. Cut with 2 1/2-inch star-shaped cookie cutter. Place 1 1/4 inches apart on buttered and floured cookie sheets.

Add enough remaining 2 teaspoons lemon juice to reserved egg white mixture to make of spreading consistency. Spread thin layer over each cookie. Bake at 250 degrees for 20 to 25 minutes or just until brown and crisp on the outside and chewy on the inside. Remove to wire racks to cool completely. Yield: 4 dozen.

CREAM CHEESE BARS

1 cup butter, softened
1/2 cup sugar
1/2 cup packed brown
  sugar
1 teaspoon vanilla extract
8 ounces cream cheese,
  softened

1 egg
2 cups flour
1/4 cup butter, softened
1/4 cup confectioners'
  sugar

Cream 1 cup butter, sugar and brown sugar in mixer bowl until light and fluffy. Add vanilla, 3 tablespoons of the cream cheese, egg and flour; mix well. Spread on lightly greased baking sheet. Bake at 350 degrees for 15 minutes or until light golden brown. Cool slightly. Cream remaining cream cheese, 1/4 cup butter and confectioners' sugar in small mixer bowl until light and fluffy. Spread on warm baked layers; cool. Cut into bars. Yield: 15 servings.

CORNMEAL COOKIES

3/4 cup butter, softened
2/3 cup sugar
2 egg yolks
1 1/4 teaspoons vanilla
  extract

1/2 cup white or yellow
  cornmeal
2 cups flour
3 tablespoons pine nuts

Cream butter and sugar in mixer bowl until light and fluffy. Add egg yolks and vanilla; mix well. Add cornmeal; mix well. Let stand for 2 minutes. Add 1 3/4 cups flour; mix well. Let stand for 5 minutes. Add enough remaining flour to make stiff dough. Shape into 1-inch balls. Place on buttered cookie sheets. Flatten with glass. Press 3 pine nuts into each cookie. Bake at 350 degrees for 10 minutes or until edges are brown. Remove to wire racks to cool completely. Yield: 3 dozen.

CHINESE CHEWS

1 cup flour
1 cup sugar
1 cup chopped dates
1 cup chopped nuts

1 egg
1 teaspoon vanilla extract
1/2 cup melted butter

Combine flour, sugar, dates, nuts, egg, vanilla and melted butter in bowl; mix well. Spread in greased baking pan. Bake at 325 degrees for 20 to 30 minutes or until firm. Cool. Cut into squares. Yield: 8 servings.

JUNE BUGS

1/2 cup butter, softened
1 cup shredded cheese
1 1/2 cups flour

Red pepper to taste
Paprika to taste
24 pitted dates

Combine butter and cheese in mixer bowl; mix well. Add flour; mix well. Stir in red pepper and paprika. Divide dough into 3 portions. Roll each portion 1/8 inch thick on lightly floured surface. Cut with small round biscuit cutter. Place date in center of half the cookies. Top with remaining cookies; seal edges. Bake at 400 degrees for 15 to 20 minutes or until browned. Yield: 2 dozen.

ICEBOX COOKIES

1 cup butter, softened
2 cups packed brown
 sugar
2 eggs
3 1/2 cups sifted flour

1 teaspoon soda
1/2 teaspoon salt
1 teaspoon vanilla extract
1 to 2 cups chopped
 pecans

Cream butter in mixer bowl until light and fluffy. Add brown sugar, eggs, flour, soda, salt, vanilla and pecans; mix well. Shape into 4 logs. Chill until firm. Slice and bake as needed. Yield: 4 dozen.

IRRESISTIBLE FINGERS

1 cup corn oil margarine, softened
1/2 cup sugar
2 cups flour
1 teaspoon vanilla extract
1/2 cup finely chopped pecans
2 cups confectioners' sugar

Cream margarine and sugar in mixer bowl until light and fluffy. Add flour 1/2 cup at a time, beating well after each addition. Add vanilla. Fold in pecans. Shape into log. Chill for 1 hour. Shape dough into finger-sized pieces. Place on ungreased cookie sheet. Bake at 300 degrees for 30 to 35 minutes or until lightly browned. Cool. Roll in confectioners' sugar. Store in covered container. May be prepared ahead and frozen. Yield: 6 dozen.

FORTY-NINERS

1 1-pound package light brown sugar
2 cups baking mix
4 eggs, beaten
2 cups chopped pecans
Confectioners' sugar

Combine brown sugar, baking mix, eggs and pecans in bowl; mix well. Spread in greased and floured 9x13-inch baking pan. Bake at 325 degrees for 30 to 35 minutes or until firm. Cool. Cut into bars. Sprinkle with confectioners' sugar. Yield: 4 dozen.

A Lion Tip

Pack homemade refrigerator cookie dough into clean 6-ounce frozen juice cans. Freeze until needed. Thaw for about 15 minutes, remove bottom of can and push dough up, using the top edge as a cutting guide.

REFRIGERATOR FRUIT COOKIES

1 cup butter, softened
1 cup shortening
1 cup packed brown
  sugar
1 cup sugar
3 eggs

5^1/$_2$ cups flour
1 teaspoon soda
1 cup chopped pecans
1 pound mixed candied
  fruits, finely chopped

Cream butter, shortening, brown sugar and sugar in mixer bowl until light and fluffy. Add eggs 1 at a time, beating well after each addition. Sift flour and soda together. Add to creamed mixture; beat well. Fold in pecans and candied fruits. Shape into logs. Chill, wrapped in waxed paper, for several hours to overnight. Cut into thin slices. Place on greased cookie sheets. Bake at 350 degrees for 10 minutes or until brown. Remove to wire racks to cool completely. Store in airtight containers. Yield: 4 to 5 dozen.

OLD-FASHIONED GINGERSNAPS

2^3/$_4$ cups self-rising flour
1 teaspoon soda
1 teaspoon cinnamon
1 teaspoon ginger
^{1}/$_4$ teaspoon cloves

1 cup packed brown sugar
^{3}/$_4$ cup butter, softened
1 egg
^{1}/$_4$ cup light molasses
^{1}/$_2$ cup sugar

Combine flour, soda, cinnamon, ginger and cloves in bowl; mix well. Cream brown sugar and butter in large mixer bowl until light and fluffy. Add egg and molasses; beat well. Stir in flour mixture. Chill in refrigerator. Shape into ^{3}/$_4$-inch balls; roll in sugar. Place 2 inches apart on greased cookie sheets. Flatten with glass dipped in additional sugar. Bake at 375 degrees for 8 to 10 minutes or until cookies are set. Remove to wire racks to cool completely.
Yield: 8 dozen.

A Lion Tip

Use gingersnaps, chocolate wafers, vanilla wafers or sugar cookies to make a crumb pie crust.

GRAHAM CRACKER COOKIES

1/2 cup margarine	1 package graham
1/2 cup butter	crackers
1/2 cup sugar	1 cup chopped pecans

Bring margarine, butter and sugar to a boil in saucepan, stirring constantly. Boil for 2 minutes, stirring constantly. Break crackers into halves. Arrange in single layer on cookie sheet. Pour hot syrup over crackers; sprinkle with pecans. Bake at 325 degrees for 10 minutes. Remove to waxed paper to cool. Store in airtight container. May substitute almonds for pecans. Yield: 2 1/2 dozen.

GRANOLA BARS

3 cups oats	1 1/2 teaspoons cinnamon
1 cup chopped blanched	1 14-ounce can
peanuts	sweetened condensed
1 cup raisins	milk
1 cup sunflower seed	1/4 cup melted butter

Combine all ingredients in large bowl; mix well. Press into greased 10x15-inch baking sheet. Bake at 325 degrees for 25 to 30 minutes or until firm. Cool slightly. Cut into bars. Invert onto waxed paper to cool completely. Store, loosely covered, at room temperature. Yield: 2 dozen.

HAZELNUT SUGAR DUSTIES

2/3 cup hazelnuts	1/8 teaspoon salt
3/4 cup butter, softened	1 3/4 cups flour
1/3 cup sugar	1/3 cup confectioners'
1 egg yolk	sugar

Place hazelnuts on baking sheet. Roast at 325 degrees for 7 minutes. Cool. Rub with rough towel to remove skin. Grind very fine in food processor container. Cream butter and sugar in mixer bowl until light and fluffy. Add egg yolk and salt; beat well. Stir in ground hazelnuts. Add flour gradually, mixing until stiff dough forms. Shape into 1-inch balls. Place 1 inch apart on buttered baking sheets. Bake at 325 degrees for 15 to 17 minutes or until edges are lightly browned. Remove to wire racks to cool completely. Roll in confectioners' sugar. Yield: 4 dozen.

ICED CHRISTMAS TREE COOKIES

3 cups sifted flour
1/2 teaspoon soda
1 teaspoon salt
1 cup shortening
1 cup sugar
2 eggs
2 teaspoons vanilla
    extract

2 egg whites, beaten
1/2 teaspoon vanilla
    extract
4 cups (about)
    confectioners' sugar
Green food coloring

Sift flour, soda and salt together. Combine shortening, sugar, eggs and 2 teaspoons vanilla in large bowl; mix well. Stir in flour mixture. Divide dough into halves. Shape into logs; wrap in waxed paper. Mold logs into triangular shapes. Chill until firm. Slice into triangles. Place on nonstick cookie sheet. Bake at 375 degrees for 8 to 10 minutes or until lightly browned. Combine egg whites and remaining 1/2 teaspoon vanilla in bowl; mix well. Add enough confectioners' sugar to make of desired consistency. Divide frosting into 2 portions. Add food coloring to 1 portion. Spread cookies with green and white frostings. Decorate with candy sprinkles if desired. Yield: 8 dozen.

HOP SCOTCHES

1 16-ounce package
    butterscotch chips
1/2 cup peanut butter

1 3-ounce can chow
    mein noodles

Melt butterscotch chips in double boiler over hot water. Stir in peanut butter. Combine with noodles in large bowl; mix well. Drop by heaping teaspoonfuls onto waxed paper-lined cookie sheets. Chill until firm. Yield: 2 dozen.

HAWAIIAN KISSES

1 cup confectioners' sugar
1 cup margarine
2 teaspoons vanilla extract
1/2 teaspoon salt
2 cups flour
1 1/2 cups finely chopped macadamia nuts
16 ounces cream cheese with pineapple, softened
Toasted flaked coconut

Cream confectioners' sugar and margarine in mixer bowl until light and fluffy. Add vanilla and salt; beat well. Add flour. Beat at low speed until blended. Shape by teaspoonfuls into balls; roll in macadamia nuts. Place on greased baking sheets. Make indentation in each cookie with thumb. Bake at 350 degrees for 10 to 12 minutes or until edges are light brown. Remove to wire racks to cool completely. Fill indentations with cream cheese; sprinkle with coconut. May store dough in refrigerator for up to 1 week, rolling in macadamia nuts just before baking. Yield: 6 dozen.

CORNFLAKE KISSES

2 egg whites
1/4 teaspoon salt
2/3 cup sugar
1/2 cup peanuts
1 1/2 cups crisp cornflakes

Beat egg whites and salt in mixer bowl just until soft peaks form. Add sugar gradually, beating until stiff peaks form. Stir in peanuts with fork. Fold in cornflakes. Drop by teaspoonfuls onto parchment-lined baking sheets. Bake at 300 degrees for 30 minutes. Remove to wire racks to cool completely. May substitute chopped walnuts for peanuts. Yield: 3 dozen.

FORGOTTEN COOKIES

2/3 cup sugar
2 egg whites
1 teaspoon vanilla extract

1 cup chopped pecans
1 cup chocolate chips

Preheat oven to 350 degrees. Beat sugar and egg whites in mixer bowl on low speed until stiff peaks form. Stir in vanilla. Fold in pecans and chocolate chips. Drop by spoonfuls onto greased cookie sheets. Place cookie sheets in oven. Turn off oven. Let stand in oven overnight. Yield: 2 dozen.

KAHLUA HOLIDAY MERINGUE KISSES

3/4 teaspoon instant coffee
1/3 cup water
1 cup sugar
1/4 cup Kahlua
3 egg whites, at room
  temperature

1/4 teaspoon cream of
  tartar
Dash of salt
2 tablespoons sugar

Dissolve coffee in water in 2-quart saucepan. Add 1 cup sugar. Cook over low heat until sugar dissolves, stirring constantly. Do not boil. Stir in Kahlua. Brush down side of pan frequently with pastry brush dipped in cold water. Bring to a boil over medium heat, stirring constantly. Cook to 240 to 242 degrees on candy thermometer, firm-ball stage, stirring constantly; remove from heat. Mixture will be very thick. Beat egg whites, cream of tartar and salt in mixer bowl until soft peaks form. Add remaining 2 tablespoons sugar; beat until stiff peaks form. Add Kahlua mixture 1/3 at a time, beating well after each addition. Beat for 4 to 5 minutes or until meringue is very thick and firm. Cool slightly. Line baking sheet with foil, placing shiny side down. Pipe meringue into 1 1/2-inch kisses on prepared baking sheet. Bake at 200 degrees for 4 hours. Turn off oven. Let stand in oven for 2 hours or until crisp. Remove from oven to cool completely. Store in airtight container for up to 1 week. Yield: 2 1/2 dozen.

LUSCIOUS LEMON BARS

2 cups flour
1/2 cup confectioners'
  sugar
1 cup butter, softened
4 eggs
2 cups sugar
6 tablespoons fresh
  lemon juice

Dash of salt
1/4 cup flour
1 teaspoon baking
  powder
1/4 cup confectioners'
  sugar

Combine 2 cups flour, 1/2 cup confectioners' sugar and butter in bowl; mix well. Press into ungreased 9x13-inch baking pan. Bake at 350 degrees for 20 minutes. Combine eggs, sugar, lemon juice and salt in bowl; mix well. Add mixture of remaining 1/4 cup flour and baking powder; mix well. Pour over baked layer. Bake for 25 minutes longer. Cool. Sprinkle with remaining 1/4 cup confectioners' sugar. Do not use a substitute for butter or fresh lemon juice. Yield: 15 servings.

NEIMAN'S $250 COOKIE

2 cups butter, softened
2 cups packed brown
  sugar
2 cups sugar
4 eggs
2 teaspoons vanilla
  extract
5 cups oats
4 cups flour

1 teaspoon salt
2 teaspoons soda
2 teaspoons baking
  powder
4 cups chocolate chips
3 cups chopped pecans
1 8-ounce chocolate
  candy bar, grated

Cream butter, brown sugar and sugar in large mixer bowl until light and fluffy. Add eggs and vanilla; beat well. Process oats in blender container until very fine. Combine oats, flour, salt, soda and baking powder in large bowl. Add to creamed mixture; mix well. Stir in chocolate chips, pecans and grated chocolate. Shape into balls. Place 2 inches apart on greased cookie sheets. Bake at 375 degrees for 6 minutes. Remove to wire racks to cool completely. Yield: 9 dozen.

NUT CRESCENTS

1 cup butter, softened	1 teaspoon vanilla extract
2/3 cup confectioners' sugar	2 1/3 cups flour
	1 cup chopped pecans
1/2 teaspoon almond extract	1/2 cup confectioners' sugar

Cream butter and 2/3 cup confectioners' sugar in mixer bowl until light and fluffy. Stir in almond and vanilla extracts. Add flour and pecans; mix well. Knead slightly. Shape into crescents. Bake at 350 degrees for 15 to 20 minutes or until light brown. Roll in remaining 1/2 cup confectioners' sugar. Place on wire racks to cool completely. Yield: 2 dozen.

AMISH OATMEAL COOKIES

1 1/2 cups raisins	1 1/2 cups shortening
1 cup salted peanuts	3 cups sugar
6 cups sifted flour	2 cups oats
1 tablespoon baking powder	1 tablespoon soda
	1 cup buttermilk
1 teaspoon salt	1/2 cup dark molasses
1 teaspoon nutmeg	3 eggs
1 teaspoon cinnamon	1 egg, beaten

Grind raisins and peanuts in food grinder using medium blade. Sift flour, baking powder, salt, nutmeg and cinnamon into large bowl. Cut in shortening until crumbly. Add raisin mixture, sugar and oats; mix well. Dissolve soda in buttermilk in small mixer bowl. Add molasses and 3 eggs; mix well. Add to flour mixture; mix well. Drop by tablespoonfuls 3 inches apart on greased cookie sheets. Flatten with glass dipped in additional flour. Brush cookies with remaining egg. Bake at 375 degrees for 8 to 10 minutes or until golden brown. Remove to wire racks to cool completely. Yield: 6 dozen.

DATE AND OATMEAL COOKIES

1½ cups whole wheat
flour
3 tablespoons wheat germ
1 teaspoon soda
1 teaspoon cinnamon
½ teaspoon salt
¼ teaspoon nutmeg

2 eggs
¾ cup packed brown
sugar
¼ cup orange honey
1 cup margarine, softened
3 cups oats
1 cup chopped dates

Combine whole wheat flour, wheat germ, soda, cinnamon, salt and nutmeg in large bowl; mix well. Combine eggs, brown sugar, honey and margarine in food processor container. Process until smooth. Add to flour mixture, stirring until soft dough forms. Add oats and dates; mix well. Drop by teaspoonfuls 2 inches apart on buttered cookie sheets. Bake at 350 degrees for 8 to 10 minutes or until golden brown. Remove to wire racks to cool completely. Store in covered container. Yield: 4½ dozen.

OATMEAL CARMELITAS

2 cups flour
2 cups oats
1½ cups packed brown
sugar
1 teaspoon soda
1¼ cups margarine,
softened

½ teaspoon salt
1 cup semisweet
chocolate chips
½ cup chopped pecans
1   12-ounce jar caramel
ice cream topping
3 tablespoons flour

Combine 2 cups flour, oats, brown sugar, soda, margarine and salt in large mixer bowl; mix well. Beat at low speed until crumbly. Press half the mixture into greased 9x13-inch baking pan. Bake at 350 degrees for 10 minutes. Sprinkle chocolate chips and pecans evenly over baked layer. Combine caramel topping and remaining 3 tablespoons flour in small bowl; mix well. Pour over chocolate chips and pecans; sprinkle with remaining crumb mixture. Bake for 18 to 22 minutes or until golden brown. Cool completely. Cut into bars. May refrigerate for easier cutting. Yield: 3 dozen.

OATMEAL AND RASPBERRY BARS

1/2 cup butter, softened
1/2 cup packed light
  brown sugar
1 cup flour
1/4 teaspoon soda

1/8 teaspoon salt
1 cup oats
3/4 cup seedless
  raspberry jam

Butter 8-inch square baking pan. Line with buttered foil. Combine butter, brown sugar, flour, soda, salt and oats in bowl; mix until crumbly. Press 2 cups mixture into prepared pan. Spread with jam, leaving 1/4-inch edges. Sprinkle with remaining crumb mixture, pressing lightly into jam. Bake at 350 degrees for 35 to 40 minutes or until light brown. Cool in pan on wire rack. Cut into bars. Yield: 2 dozen.

OATMEAL SPICE COOKIES

1 cup sifted flour
1 teaspoon baking
  powder
3/4 teaspoon salt
1 teaspoon cinnamon
3/4 teaspoon nutmeg
Dash of ground cloves

3/4 cup shortening
1 cup packed brown
  sugar
2 eggs
1/3 cup milk
1 cup raisins
3 cups oats

Sift flour, baking powder, salt, cinnamon, nutmeg and cloves into large mixer bowl. Add shortening, brown sugar, eggs and milk; beat until smooth. Fold in raisins and oats. Drop by spoonfuls onto greased cookie sheet. Bake at 375 degrees for 12 to 15 minutes or until light brown. Remove to wire racks to cool completely. Yield: 1 dozen.

SPICY OATMEAL COOKIES

1¾ cups flour
2 teaspoons baking
powder
1 teaspoon salt
1 teaspoon cinnamon
1 teaspoon nutmeg
¼ teaspoon soda
1 cup shortening

1½ cups packed brown
sugar
2 eggs
½ cup milk
3 cups quick-cooking
oats
1 cup raisins
½ cup chopped walnuts

Combine flour, baking powder, salt, cinnamon, nutmeg and soda in bowl; mix well. Beat shortening in large mixer bowl for 30 seconds. Add brown sugar; beat until light and fluffy. Beat in eggs. Add flour mixture and milk alternately to creamed mixture, beating well after each addition. Stir in oats, raisins and walnuts. Drop by tablespoonfuls 2 inches apart on ungreased cookie sheet. Bake at 400 degrees for 8 minutes or until set. Remove to wire rack to cool. Yield: 5 dozen.

PEANUT BUTTER AND JELLY THUMBPRINT COOKIES

1 cup light corn syrup
1 cup creamy peanut
butter

2 quarts popped popcorn
3 tablespoons fruit jam

Bring corn syrup to a boil over medium-high heat in medium saucepan. Cook for 3 minutes. Remove from heat. Stir in peanut butter. Pour quickly over popcorn in large bowl. Toss to coat. Let stand for 10 minutes. Roll into eighteen 2-inch balls. Make indentation in center of each with thumb. Place ½ teaspoon jam in indentations. Store in airtight containers. Yield: 1½ dozen.

GIANT PEANUT BUTTER AND APPLE COOKIES

3/4 cup peanut butter
3 tablespoons margarine,
  softened
1 cup packed brown
  sugar
1/2 cup whole wheat flour
2 egg whites

2 tablespoons skim milk
1/2 teaspoon soda
1/2 cup whole wheat flour
3/4 cup oats
1 medium apple, peeled,
  finely chopped

Beat peanut butter and margarine in small mixer bowl at medium speed for 30 seconds or until smooth. Add brown sugar, 1/2 cup flour, egg whites, skim milk and soda; mix well. Stir in remaining flour, oats and apple. Drop by well-rounded tablespoonfuls onto ungreased cookie sheet. Flatten with glass. Bake at 350 degrees for 12 to 14 minutes or until golden brown. Remove to wire rack to cool completely. Store in airtight container. May freeze for up to 6 months. Yield: 1 1/2 dozen.

PEANUT BUTTER KISS COOKIES

1 2/3 cups flour
1/3 cup cornstarch
1/2 teaspoon baking
  powder
1/2 teaspoon soda
1/2 cup butter, softened
1/3 cup peanut butter
2/3 cup confectioners'
  sugar

1/3 cup packed brown
  sugar
1 egg
2 teaspoons vanilla
  extract
1   6-ounce package
  chocolate candy kisses

Combine flour, cornstarch, baking powder and soda in bowl; mix well. Beat butter and peanut butter in mixer bowl until light. Add confectioners' sugar and brown sugar; beat until fluffy. Add egg and vanilla; beat well. Add flour mixture gradually, beating until smooth. Shape into 1 1/4-inch balls. Press chocolate kiss into each cookie, shaping dough up side of kiss until only point is visible. Place 2 inches apart on buttered cookie sheets. Bake at 350 degrees for 10 minutes or until edges are light brown and top begins to brown. Remove to wire racks to cool completely. Yield: 3 dozen.

CRISPY PEANUT BUTTER COOKIES

3 cups flour
1 teaspoon baking
  powder
1 teaspoon soda
1 teaspoon salt
1 cup shortening
1 cup sugar

1 cup packed brown sugar
2 eggs
1 cup peanut butter
1/2 cup chopped salted
  peanuts
1 tablespoon cold water
1 teaspoon vanilla extract

Sift flour, baking powder, soda and salt together. Beat shortening in mixer bowl until light. Add sugar, brown sugar and eggs; beat until fluffy. Add peanut butter; beat well. Add flour mixture gradually, beating until smooth. Stir in peanuts, water and vanilla. Shape by teaspoonfuls into balls. Place on greased cookie sheet. Flatten each cookie with fork dipped in cold water. Bake at 350 degrees for 15 minutes. Remove to wire racks to cool completely. May flatten cookies with fork dipped in melted chocolate if desired. Yield: 3 dozen.

PEANUT BUTTER FINGERS

2 cups flour
1 teaspoon salt
1 teaspoon soda
1 cup butter, softened
1 cup sugar
1 1/4 cups packed brown
  sugar
2 eggs
2/3 cup peanut butter

1 teaspoon vanilla extract
2 cups oats
1   1-pound package
  confectioners' sugar
1 cup peanut butter
1/4 cup baking cocoa
1/2 teaspoon vanilla
  extract
Milk

Sift flour, salt and soda together. Cream butter, sugar and brown sugar in large mixer bowl until light and fluffy. Add eggs and 2/3 cup peanut butter; beat well. Add flour mixture gradually, beating until smooth. Stir in 1 teaspoon vanilla. Fold in oats. Spread on greased baking sheet. Bake at 300 degrees until light brown. Cool. Combine confectioners' sugar, remaining 1 cup peanut butter, baking cocoa and remaining 1/2 teaspoon vanilla in mixer bowl; mix well. Add enough milk to make of smooth consistency. Spread over cooled baked layer. Cut into bars. Yield: 2 1/2 to 3 1/2 dozen.

PEANUT BUTTER OATMEAL FUDGE COOKIES

2 cups sugar
1/2 cup baking cocoa
1/2 cup margarine,
  softened

1/2 cup milk
1 teaspoon vanilla extract
1/2 cup peanut butter
3 cups oats

Combine sugar, cocoa, margarine and milk in saucepan; mix well. Bring to a boil over medium heat, stirring constantly. Boil for 1 minute, stirring constantly; remove from heat. Add vanilla and peanut butter, stirring until smooth. Add oats 1 cup at a time, mixing well after each addition. Drop by spoonfuls onto waxed paper. Let stand until firm. Yield: 5 dozen.

PECAN BUTTER BALLS

2 cups sifted flour
1/4 cup sugar
1/2 teaspoon salt
1 cup butter, softened

2 teaspoons vanilla
  extract
3 cups finely chopped
  pecans

Sift flour, sugar and salt into bowl. Cut in butter until crumbly. Stir in vanilla. Add 2 cups pecans; mix well. Shape into 1-inch balls. Roll in remaining 1 cup pecans. Place on nonstick cookie sheet. Bake at 325 degrees for 25 minutes. Remove to wire rack to cool. Yield: 5 dozen.

PECAN DROPS

3/4 cup shortening
1/4 cup butter, softened
1/2 cup confectioners'
  sugar
2 tablespoons vanilla
  extract

1 teaspoon salt
2 cups flour
1 cup chopped nuts
Confectioners' sugar

Cream shortening, butter and 3/4 cup confectioners' sugar in mixer bowl until light and fluffy. Add vanilla and salt; mix well. Add flour and nuts; mix well. Shape into small balls. Place on nonstick cookie sheet. Press gently. Bake at 325 degrees for 20 to 25 minutes or just until light brown. Do not overbrown. Remove to wire rack to cool. Roll in additional confectioners' sugar. Yield: 2 dozen.

CHOCOLATE PECAN PIE BARS

1¹/₃ cups flour
2 tablespoons light
  brown sugar
¹/₂ cup butter, softened
2 eggs
¹/₂ cup light corn syrup
¹/₂ cup packed brown
  sugar

¹/₄ cup baking cocoa
2 tablespoons melted
  butter
1 teaspoon vanilla extract
¹/₈ teaspoon salt
1 cup coarsely chopped
  pecans

Combine flour and 2 tablespoons brown sugar in bowl; mix well. Cut in ¹/₂ cup butter until crumbly. Press over bottom and 1 inch up sides of 9-inch square baking pan. Bake at 350 degrees for 10 to 12 minutes or until firm. Press crust lightly into corners and against sides of pan with back of spoon. Beat eggs, corn syrup, remaining ¹/₂ cup brown sugar, baking cocoa, 2 tablespoons butter, vanilla and salt in mixer bowl until smooth. Stir in pecans. Pour over baked layer. Bake for 25 minutes or until set. Cool. Cut into bars. Yield: 16 bars.

PINE CONE COOKIES

2 cups flour
¹/₂ teaspoon baking
  powder
¹/₂ teaspoon salt
¹/₄ teaspoon soda
6 tablespoons butter,
  softened

¹/₃ cup European-style
  cocoa
1 cup sugar
2 eggs
1 teaspoon vanilla extract
Light corn syrup
Sliced almonds

Combine flour, baking powder, salt and soda in bowl; mix well. Melt butter in small saucepan; remove from heat. Add cocoa; stir until smooth. Beat sugar, eggs and vanilla in large mixer bowl until smooth. Stir in cocoa mixture. Add flour mixture; mix until smooth. Chill for 1 hour or until firm. Roll to ¹/₈-inch thickness between waxed paper. Cut into pine cone shapes with 2 or 2¹/₂-inch oval cookie cutter. Place on lightly greased cookie sheet. Brush lightly with corn syrup. Arrange almonds over dough in pine cone fashion. Brush almonds with corn syrup. Bake at 350 degrees for 7 to 8 minutes or until set. Remove to wire racks to cool completely. Yield: 4 dozen.

RAISIN DROP COOKIES

2½ cups seedless raisins
1 cup water
4 cups sifted flour
½ teaspoon soda
2½ teaspoons baking
  powder
1 teaspoon salt

1 teaspoon cinnamon
¼ teaspoon nutmeg
¼ teaspoon allspice
1 cup shortening
1½ cups sugar
3 eggs
1 teaspoon vanilla extract

Rinse raisins; drain. Combine raisins and water in saucepan. Bring to a boil. Boil for 5 minutes. Cool. Sift flour, soda, baking powder, salt, cinnamon, nutmeg and allspice into bowl. Cream shortening and sugar in large mixer bowl until light and fluffy. Add eggs and vanilla; beat well. Add flour mixture gradually, mixing until smooth. Fold in raisins. Drop by tablespoonfuls 3 inches apart on greased cookie sheets. Bake at 375 degrees for 10 minutes or until brown on bottom. Remove to wire racks to cool completely. Yield: 4 dozen.

REFRIGERATOR COOKIES

3½ cups flour
1 teaspoon soda
1 teaspoon baking
  powder
2 eggs

1 cup shortening
2 cups packed brown
  sugar
1 teaspoon vanilla extract
1 cup chopped pecans

Combine flour, soda and baking powder in bowl; mix well. Add eggs; mix well. Cream shortening and brown sugar in mixer bowl until light and fluffy. Add flour mixture; mix well. Stir in vanilla and pecans. Shape into log. Chill overnight. Cut into slices. Place on greased cookie sheets. Bake at 425 degrees for 5 to 8 minutes or until light brown. Remove to wire racks to cool completely. Yield: 4 to 6 dozen.

RUSSIAN TEA COOKIES

3/4 cup shortening
1/4 cup margarine,
  softened
1/2 cup confectioners'
  sugar
1 teaspoon salt

2 tablespoons vanilla
  extract
2 cups flour
1 cup chopped pecans
Confectioners' sugar

Cream shortening, margarine, 1/2 cup confectioners' sugar and salt in mixer bowl until light and fluffy. Stir in vanilla. Add flour; mix well. Stir in pecans. Drop by spoonfuls onto greased cookie sheet. Bake at 325 degrees for 25 minutes. Remove to wire rack to cool completely. Roll in additional confectioners' sugar. Yield: 2 dozen.

SAND TARTS

1 cup butter, softened
5 tablespoons
  confectioners' sugar
2 cups flour

1 teaspoon vanilla extract
1 1/2 cups chopped
  pecans
Confectioners' sugar

Cream butter and 5 tablespoons confectioners' sugar in mixer bowl until light and fluffy. Add flour, vanilla and pecans; mix well. Shape into small balls. Place on nonstick baking sheet. Bake at 350 degrees for 30 minutes or until slightly brown. Remove to wire rack to cool. Roll in additional confectioners' sugar. Yield: 2 dozen.

A Lion Tip

Cool cookies completely in a single layer on a wire rack before storing. Store soft and chewy cookies in an airtight container and crisp cookies in a jar with a loose-fitting lid.

ROLL-OUT SUGAR COOKIES

3 cups sifted
confectioners' sugar
2 cups margarine,
softened
2 eggs
2 teaspoons vanilla
extract
1 teaspoon almond
extract

5 cups sifted flour
2 teaspoons soda
2 teaspoons cream of
tartar
2 cups sifted
confectioners' sugar
1/2 teaspoon salt
1 teaspoon vanilla extract

Cream 3 cups confectioners' sugar and margarine in mixer bowl until light and fluffy. Add eggs, 2 teaspoons vanilla and almond extract; beat well. Combine flour, soda and cream of tartar in bowl; mix well. Add to creamed mixture; mix well. Chill for 2 to 3 hours or until firm. Roll dough to 1/4-inch thickness on floured surface. Cut with cookie cutters. Place on greased cookie sheets. Bake at 375 degrees for 7 to 8 minutes or until light brown. Remove to wire racks to cool completely. Combine remaining 2 cups sifted confectioners' sugar, salt and remaining 1 teaspoon vanilla in small mixer bowl; mix well. Add enough water to make of desired consistency. Pipe over cooled cookies. May tint frosting with food coloring if desired.
Yield: 5 dozen.

SIMPLE SESAMES

2 cups butter, softened
1 1/2 cups sugar
3 cups flour

1 cup sesame seed
2 cups coconut
1/2 cup chopped pecans

Cream butter in mixer bowl until light. Add sugar; beat until fluffy. Add flour; mix just until blended. Stir in sesame seed, coconut and pecans. Divide dough into 3 portions. Shape each portion into logs 2 inches in diameter. Chill, wrapped in waxed paper, until firm. Cut into 1/4-inch slices. Place on ungreased cookie sheet. Bake at 300 degrees for 30 minutes or until light brown. Remove to wire racks to cool. Yield: 3 dozen.

SHADOW COOKIES

3 egg whites
Pinch of salt
1 cup sugar

1 teaspoon vanilla extract
1 cup chopped nuts

Combine egg whites and salt in mixer bowl. Beat at high speed until soft peaks form. Add sugar gradually, beating constantly until stiff peaks form. Fold in vanilla and nuts gently. Drop by teaspoonfuls onto ungreased cookie sheet. Bake at 250 degrees for 1 hour. Remove immediately to wire rack to cool. Yield: 4 dozen.

BUTTER SUGAR COOKIES

2¹/₂ cups butter, softened
1¹/₄ cups sugar
2 eggs
3 cups flour

1¹/₂ teaspoons salt
2 teaspoons baking
powder
1 teaspoon vanilla extract

Cream butter and sugar in mixer bowl until light and fluffy. Add eggs; beat until light and foamy. Sift flour, salt and baking powder together. Add to egg mixture; mix well. Mix in vanilla. Chill until firm. Roll to ¹/₄-inch thickness on lightly floured surface. Cut with cookie cutter. Sprinkle with additional sugar. Place on nonstick cookie sheet. Bake at 350 degrees for 12 to 15 minutes or until light brown. Remove to wire rack to cool completely. Yield: 5 dozen.

SEA ISLAND BARS

¹/₂ cup butter, softened
¹/₂ cup sugar
¹/₃ cup packed brown
sugar
2 tablespoons water
1 cup self-rising flour

1 egg
1 teaspoon vanilla extract
¹/₂ cup chopped pecans
¹/₂ cup coconut
1 cup semisweet
chocolate chips

Melt butter in 2-quart saucepan over very low heat; remove from heat. Add sugar, brown sugar and water; stir until sugars dissolve. Add flour; mix until smooth. Add egg and vanilla; mix well. Fold in remaining ingredients. Pour into greased 9-inch square baking pan. Bake at 350 degrees for 30 minutes. Cool in pan. Cut into bars. Yield: 16 bars.

SNICKERDOODLES

1 cup margarine, softened
1¹/2 cups sugar
2 eggs
2³/4 cups flour
2 teaspoons cream of
  tartar

1 teaspoon soda
¹/4 teaspoon salt
¹/4 cup flour
3 tablespoons sugar
3 tablespoons cinnamon

Cream margarine and 1¹/2 cups sugar in mixer bowl until light and fluffy. Add eggs; beat well. Combine 2³/4 cups flour, cream of tartar, soda and salt in bowl; mix well. Add to creamed mixture; mix well. Add enough remaining ¹/4 cup flour to make stiff dough. Shape into small balls. Roll in mixture of remaining 3 tablespoons sugar and cinnamon. Place 2 inches apart on ungreased cookie sheet. Bake at 400 degrees for 8 to 10 minutes or until light brown. Remove to wire racks to cool completely. May chill dough before shaping. Yield: 4 dozen.

ENGLISH TOFFEE SQUARES

1 cup butter
1 cup sugar
2 cups sifted flour
1 egg yolk

1 teaspoon vanilla extract
1 egg white, lightly beaten
2 cups finely chopped
  walnuts

Melt butter in large saucepan. Add sugar, flour, egg yolk and vanilla; mix well. Spread in 9x13-inch baking pan. Spread egg white over dough; sprinkle with walnuts. Bake at 350 degrees for 20 minutes or until light brown. Cool in pan for 3 to 4 minutes. Cut into squares. Let stand until cool. May substitute pecans for walnuts. Yield: 2 dozen.

A Lion Tip

For an easy no-bake cookie, combine ¹/2 cup softened margarine, 4 cups confectioners' sugar, ¹/2 cup chopped pecans, 6 ounces orange juice concentrate and 4 cups vanilla wafer crumbs. Shape into balls and coat with additional crumbs.

Desserts

DESSERTS

CINNAMON APPLE CREAM

3 medium apples, peeled,
  sliced
Lemon juice
1/4 cup sugar
3/4 teaspoon cinnamon
1/8 teaspoon nutmeg
2 tablespoons butter
1/2 cup sugar

3 tablespoons cornstarch
1/4 teaspoon salt
4 egg yolks, slightly
  beaten
2 cups milk
1 1/2 teaspoons vanilla
  extract
12 baked meringue shells

Dip apples in lemon juice. Cook apples, 1/4 cup sugar, cinnamon and nutmeg in butter in large skillet for 5 minutes or until apples are slightly soft. Combine 1/2 cup sugar, cornstarch and salt in medium saucepan; set aside. Blend egg yolks and milk in small bowl. Add to cornstarch mixture very gradually, blending well. Cook over medium heat until thickened and bubbly, stirring constantly. Boil for 1 minute, stirring constantly; remove from heat. Stir in vanilla. Cool saucepan in bowl of ice water for several minutes. Spoon 1 tablespoon apple mixture into each meringue shell. Spoon custard over apples. Top with remaining apples. Chill, covered, in refrigerator. May serve in baked pastry shell if preferred. Yield: 12 servings.

APPLE DUMPLINGS

2 cups flour
2 teaspoons baking
  powder
1 teaspoon salt
3/4 cup butter, chilled
1/2 cup milk
2 cups sugar
2 cups water
1/4 teaspoon cinnamon

1/4 teaspoon nutmeg
1/4 cup butter
6 to 8 small apples
1/2 cup packed brown
  sugar
1/2 cup granola
1 teaspoon cinnamon
3 to 4 teaspoons butter
1 cup sour cream

Sift flour, baking powder and salt into bowl. Cut in 3/4 cup butter until crumbly. Add milk; mix just until mixture forms

dough. Roll 1/4 inch thick on floured surface. Let rest for 30 minutes or longer. Bring sugar, water, 1/4 teaspoon cinnamon and nutmeg to a boil in saucepan; reduce heat. Simmer for 5 minutes; remove from heat. Stir in 1/4 cup butter. Peel and partially core apples, leaving base intact. Cut pastry into 5x5-inch squares. Place 1 apple on each square. Fill cavities with mixture of brown sugar, granola and 1 teaspoon cinnamon. Dot with 1/2 teaspoon butter. Pull up corners of pastry to enclose apples, sealing edges. Place 1 inch apart in greased 10x15-inch baking pan. Pour syrup over dumplings. Bake at 275 degrees for 35 minutes. Serve with sour cream.
Yield: 6 to 8 servings.

APPLE FRITTERS

1 egg
1/2 cup milk
2 tablespoons oil
1/2 cup flour
2 tablespoons sugar
1/2 teaspoon baking
  powder
1 1/2 teaspoons cinnamon

1/4 teaspoon nutmeg
1/4 teaspoon salt
4 cups sliced peeled
  apples
2 tablespoons lemon juice
Oil for frying
Cinnamon-sugar

Beat egg with whisk in large bowl. Stir in milk and 2 tablespoons oil. Combine flour, sugar, baking powder, cinnamon, nutmeg and salt. Add to egg mixture. Beat for 2 minutes or until smooth. Toss apples with lemon juice in medium bowl. Heat 1 1/2 inches oil to 365 degrees in heavy skillet. Dip apple slices into batter with fork or tongs, allowing excess to drip into bowl. Brown on both sides in hot oil. Drain in single layer on paper towel. Coat with cinnamon-sugar. May make as much as 2 hours ahead and reheat in 450-degree oven for 6 minutes or until crisp; roll in cinnamon-sugar. Oil is correct temperature for frying when 1-inch bread cube browns in 1 minute.
Yield: 4 dozen.

APRICOT RASPBERRY COMPOTE

1/2 cup sugar
1/2 cup water
1 tablespoon Bourbon
6 to 7 apricots, cut into
   halves

1 cup raspberries
1/2 cup vanilla yogurt
1/8 teaspoon nutmeg

Microwave sugar and water on High in glass bowl for 2 minutes or until sugar is dissolved and mixture is hot. Stir in Bourbon. Let stand until cool. Combine with apricots and raspberries in bowl; toss gently to mix well. Spoon into serving dishes. Top with mixture of yogurt and nutmeg. Yield: 4 servings.

APRICOT FOLDOVERS

1/4 cup orange juice
6 tablespoons sugar
1 cup chopped dried
   apricots
1 1/4 cups flour
6 tablespoons sugar
Pinch of salt
1 tablespoon sour cream

4 ounces cream cheese,
   softened
1/2 cup butter or
   margarine, softened
1 cup confectioners'
   sugar
1 tablespoon water

Combine orange juice, 6 tablespoons sugar and apricots in small saucepan. Bring to a boil; reduce heat. Simmer, covered, for 10 minutes. Simmer, uncovered, for 10 minutes longer or until most of the liquid is absorbed. Mix flour, 6 tablespoons sugar and salt in bowl. Add sour cream, cream cheese and butter; mix to form dough. Chill for 1 hour. Roll dough on floured surface. Cut into squares. Place 1/2 teaspoon filling on each square. Fold dough over to enclose filling; press edges to seal. Place on baking sheet. Bake at 325 degrees for 12 to 15 minutes or until golden brown. Cool slightly. Drizzle with mixture of confectioners' sugar and water. Yield: 3 dozen.

BANANA SPLIT DESSERT

½ cup margarine
2 cups graham cracker
crumbs
2 eggs
2 cups confectioners'
sugar
1 cup margarine, softened

4 to 6 bananas, sliced
1 large can crushed
pineapple, drained
9 ounces whipped
topping
Pecans
Chopped cherries

Melt ½ cup margarine in 9x13-inch dish. Mix in cracker crumbs; press evenly over bottom of dish. Combine eggs, confectioners' sugar and 1 cup margarine in bowl. Beat for 10 minutes. Pour into prepared dish. Layer bananas, pineapple and whipped topping over creamed mixture. Top with pecans and cherries. Chill for several hours to overnight.
Yield: 20 to 25 servings.

EASY MICROWAVE BLUEBERRY DESSERT

1 recipe blueberry sauce
or 1 21-ounce can
blueberry pie filling
1 9-ounce package
yellow cake mix

¼ cup butter, thinly sliced
¼ cup chopped pecans
1 teaspoon cinnamon

Spoon hot blueberry sauce into lightly greased 8x8-inch glass dish. Sprinkle dry cake mix evenly into prepared dish. Dot with butter. Top with mixture of pecans and cinnamon. Microwave on High for 12 to 13 minutes or until cake is firm, turning dish ¼ turn every 5 minutes. Serve warm with ice cream. Yield: 6 to 8 servings.

 A Lion Tip

Create a quick dessert with fresh fruit slices, a dollop of sour cream or yogurt and a sprinkle of brown sugar or coconut.

BLACK FOREST CHEESECAKE

1 cup chocolate wafer
  crumbs
3 tablespoons melted
  butter
32 ounces cream cheese,
  softened
1⅓ cups sugar
¼ cup flour
1 tablespoon cherry
  Brandy
1 teaspoon vanilla extract

6 eggs
1 10-ounce jar
  maraschino cherries,
  drained, chopped
¾ cup semisweet
  chocolate chips, melted
1 cup sour cream
2 tablespoons sugar
2 tablespoons cherry
  juice
Chocolate curls

Mix cookie crumbs and butter in bowl. Press over bottom of lightly greased 9-inch springform pan. Combine cream cheese, 1⅓ cups sugar, flour, Brandy and vanilla in bowl; beat until fluffy. Add eggs 1 at a time, beating well after each addition. Reserve ⅓ of the batter in small bowl. Add cherries to remaining batter; mix well. Pour half the cherry batter into prepared pan. Add chocolate to reserved batter; mix well. Spoon over cherry batter in pan. Top with remaining cherry batter. Cut through gently with knife to marbleize. Bake at 350 degrees for 1 hour and 20 minutes or until knife inserted near center comes out clean. Cool on wire rack for 10 minutes. Blend sour cream, 2 tablespoons sugar and cherry juice in small bowl. Spread evenly on cheesecake. Bake for 5 minutes longer. Cool on wire rack for 1 hour. Chill for 8 hours or longer. Place on serving plate; remove side of pan. Garnish with chocolate curls. Yield: 12 servings.

CHOCOLATE CHEESECAKES

24 vanilla wafers
16 ounces cream cheese,
  softened
1 cup sour cream
1¼ cups sugar
⅓ cup baking cocoa
2 tablespoons flour

3 eggs
1 teaspoon vanilla extract
1 cup sour cream
2 tablespoons sugar
1 teaspoon vanilla extract
1 21-ounce can cherry
  pie filling

Place 1 vanilla wafer in each of 24 paper-lined 2½-inch muffin cups. Blend cream cheese and 1 cup sour cream in mixer bowl. Add 1¼ cups sugar, cocoa and flour; mix until smooth. Add eggs and vanilla; mix well. Spoon into prepared muffin cups. Bake at 350 degrees for 15 to 20 minutes or just until set. Combine 1 cup sour cream, 2 tablespoons sugar and 1 teaspoon vanilla in bowl; mix until sugar is dissolved. Spoon onto cheesecakes. Cool completely. Chill in refrigerator. Spoon chilled pie filling on cheesecakes at serving time. Yield: 2 dozen.

CHOCOLATE MINI CHEESECAKES

12 cream-filled chocolate
  cookies
16 ounces cream cheese,
  softened
⅔ cup sugar
1 tablespoon flour
2 eggs
2 tablespoons coffee
  liqueur

½ cup miniature
  semisweet chocolate
  chips, melted
½ cup miniature
  semisweet chocolate
  chips

Place 1 cookie in each of 12 paper-lined muffin cups. Beat cream cheese, sugar and flour at medium speed in mixer bowl until smooth. Add eggs 1 at a time, mixing well after each addition. Blend in liqueur and melted chocolate. Stir in chocolate chips. Spoon into prepared muffin cups. Bake at 325 degrees for 25 to 30 minutes or until set. Cool in pans. Remove to serving plate. Chill until serving time. Garnish with whipped topping and chocolate-covered coffee beans or additional miniature chocolate chips. Yield: 1 dozen.

 ### A Lion Tip

Chocolate should be melted over low heat as it burns very easily. Bring water to a simmer in bottom of double boiler and remove from heat. Place chocolate in top of double boiler over heated water and stir with rubber spatula until melted.

PUMPKIN-ORANGE CHEESECAKE

32 gingersnaps, crushed
1/4 cup melted margarine
  or butter
24 ounces cream cheese,
  softened
1 16-ounce can pumpkin
2 eggs

1 14-ounce can
  sweetened condensed
  milk
3 tablespoons orange
  liqueur or orange juice
1/4 teaspoon salt

    Mix cookie crumbs and margarine in bowl. Press firmly over bottom and halfway up side of 9-inch springform pan. Beat cream cheese in mixer bowl until smooth. Add pumpkin, eggs, condensed milk, liqueur and salt; mix well. Spoon into prepared pan. Bake at 300 degrees for 1 1/4 hours or until cheesecake springs back when lightly touched. Center will be slightly soft. Cool to room temperature. Chill in refrigerator. Place on serving plate; remove side of pan. Serve with whipped topping. Yield: 12 servings.

APPLE CRISP

4 cups sliced cooking
  apples
1 tablespoon lemon juice
1/3 cup sifted flour
1/2 cup packed brown
  sugar

1 cup oats
1 teaspoon cinnamon
1/2 teaspoon salt
1/3 cup melted butter or
  margarine

    Place apples in greased baking dish; sprinkle with lemon juice. Combine flour, brown sugar, oats, cinnamon and salt in bowl. Add margarine; mix until crumbly. Sprinkle over apples. Bake at 375 degrees for 30 minutes or until apples are tender. Serve warm or cold with cream. May sprinkle apples with sugar if they are very tart. Yield: 6 servings.

HOME-STYLE APPLE AND RAISIN CRISP

4 cups thinly sliced
  peeled apples
1/4 cup raisins
2 teaspoons lemon juice
1 tablespoon brown sugar
1/2 teaspoon cinnamon
1/4 teaspoon nutmeg

1/4 cup quick-cooking oats
2 tablespoons flour
1 tablespoon brown sugar
1/2 teaspoon cinnamon
2 tablespoons margarine
1 pint vanilla ice milk or
  frozen yogurt

Toss apples and raisins with lemon juice in bowl. Mix 1 tablespoon brown sugar, 1/2 teaspoon cinnamon and nutmeg in bowl. Sprinkle over apples; toss gently to coat well. Spoon into 1-quart baking dish. Bake, covered, at 375 degrees for 25 minutes. Combine oats, flour, 1 tablespoon brown sugar and 1/2 teaspoon cinnamon in bowl; mix well. Cut in margarine until crumbly. Sprinkle over apples. Bake, uncovered, for 15 to 20 minutes longer or until apples are tender. Serve warm with ice milk or yogurt. Yield: 4 servings.

CHERRY AND RHUBARB CRISP

1 cup chopped fresh or
  frozen rhubarb
1 21-ounce can cherry
  pie filling
1/2 cup all-purpose or
  unbleached flour

1/2 cup oats
1/2 cup packed brown
  sugar
1/3 cup butter or margarine
1/2 teaspoon cinnamon
1/2 teaspoon nutmeg

Layer rhubarb and pie filling in 8x8-inch baking pan. Combine flour, oats, brown sugar, butter, cinnamon and nutmeg in bowl; mix until crumbly. Sprinkle over layers. Bake at 375 degrees for 25 to 35 minutes or until golden brown. Serve warm with vanilla ice cream. Yield: 6 servings.

JUICY BLACKBERRY COBBLER

1½ cups flour
¾ teaspoon salt
½ cup shortening
5 tablespoons cold water
4 cups fresh blackberries
or 2 16-ounce packages
frozen blackberries

1 cup sugar
½ cup water
2 tablespoons melted
butter
2 tablespoons sugar

Combine flour and salt in bowl. Cut in shortening with pastry blender until mixture is crumbly. Sprinkle evenly with cold water 1 tablespoon at a time, stirring with fork until moistened. Shape into ball. Chill in refrigerator. Roll to ⅛-inch thickness on lightly floured surface. Cut into 1-inch strips. Combine blackberries, 1 cup sugar and ½ cup water in saucepan. Cook over medium heat for 10 minutes, stirring gently. Pour half the berry mixture into greased 8x12-inch baking dish. Arrange half the pastry strips over berries. Brush with 1 tablespoon melted butter; sprinkle with 1 tablespoon sugar. Bake at 375 degrees for 10 to 12 minutes or until pastry is light brown. Top with remaining berries and pastry. Brush with remaining 1 tablespoon butter; sprinkle with remaining 1 tablespoon sugar. Bake for 20 to 25 minutes longer or until pastry is golden brown. Yield: 6 servings.

STOVE-TOP BLUEBERRY COBBLER

2 cups fresh blueberries
¾ cup water
¼ to ⅓ cup sugar
1 tablespoon cornstarch
Salt to taste

2 tablespoons water
2 tablespoons margarine
1 cup baking mix
⅓ cup evaporated milk
2 tablespoons sugar

Combine blueberries, ¾ cup water and ¼ to ⅓ cup sugar in skillet. Blend cornstarch, salt and 2 tablespoons water in cup. Stir into berries. Bring to a boil. Cook for 1 minute or until thickened, stirring constantly. Dot with margarine. Combine baking mix, evaporated milk and 2 tablespoons sugar in bowl; mix to form soft dough. Drop into 6 dumplings on berry mixture. Cook, covered, over low heat for 15 minutes or until dumplings test done. Yield: 6 servings.

COLOSSAL CHERRY COBBLER

1/2 cup butter or margarine
1 cup self-rising flour
1 cup sugar
1 cup milk

3/4 teaspoon almond
extract
4 cups fresh sweet
cherries, pitted

Melt butter in 8x12-inch baking dish. Combine flour and sugar in bowl. Add milk and almond extract; mix well. Spoon into butter in dish; do not stir. Spoon cherries over batter; do not stir. Bake at 375 degrees for 35 minutes or until golden brown. Yield: 8 servings.

CHERRY DELIGHT

1 cup sour cream
2 cups milk
1   6-ounce package vanilla
instant pudding mix

30 graham cracker
squares
1   21-ounce can cherry
pie filling

Combine sour cream and milk in bowl. Beat with rotary beater until smooth. Add pudding mix. Beat for 2 minutes or until smooth and thickened. Layer graham crackers and pudding mixture 1/2 at a time in dish. Top with pie filling. Chill, covered, for 3 hours. Cut into squares. Yield: 12 servings.

CRUSTY STRIPS COBBLER

2 cups flour
1 teaspoon salt
2/3 cup shortening
5 to 6 tablespoons water
Melted butter

1 cup sugar
2 tablespoons cornstarch
3 cups fruit or berries
1 tablespoon butter

Combine flour and salt in bowl. Cut in shortening with pastry blender until crumbly. Add water a small amount at a time, mixing to form dough. Roll on floured surface; cut into 1x11/2-inch pieces. Place on baking sheet. Brush generously with melted butter. Bake at 450 degrees for 10 to 12 minutes or until golden brown. Mix sugar and cornstarch in saucepan. Add fruit; mix well. Cook over low to medium heat until thickened, stirring constantly. Stir in 1 tablespoon butter. Alternate layers of pastry and filling in dish until all ingredients are used, beginning and ending with pastry. Yield: 6 servings.

EASY HOLIDAY CUSTARD

2 quarts milk
1 pint half and half
2 small packages vanilla
instant pudding mix

1 cup sugar
2 teaspoons vanilla
extract

Combine milk, half and half, pudding mix, sugar and vanilla in mixer bowl; mix until smooth. Yield: 12 servings.

DATE ROLL

3 cups sugar
1 cup milk
1 medium bottle of
cherries, drained,
chopped

1 package pitted dates,
chopped
2 tablespoons butter
1 cup chopped nuts

Mix sugar and milk in saucepan. Bring to a boil. Add cherries and dates. Cook over low heat to 240 degrees on candy thermometer, soft-ball stage; remove from heat. Stir in butter. Place saucepan in pan of cold water; let stand until almost cool. Beat until thickened. Add nuts. Pour onto damp cloth; shape into roll. Chill until serving time. Slice to serve. Yield: 12 servings.

MINT DAZZLER

2 cups vanilla wafer
crumbs
1/4 cup melted butter
1 1/2 cups sifted
confectioners' sugar
1/2 cup butter, softened
3 eggs, slightly beaten

3 ounces unsweetened
chocolate, melted
1 1/2 cups whipping cream
8 ounces miniature
marshmallows
1/2 cup crushed
peppermint candy

Mix cookie crumbs and 1/4 cup melted butter in bowl. Press firmly over bottom of greased 8x8-inch dish. Cream confectioners' sugar and 1/2 cup butter in mixer bowl until light. Add eggs and chocolate; beat until fluffy. Spoon into prepared dish. Chill in freezer. Whip cream in mixer bowl until soft peaks form. Fold in marshmallows gently. Spread over chocolate layer. Sprinkle with candy. Freeze until serving time. Garnish with additional whipped cream. Yield: 12 to 15 servings.

INSTANT CHOCOLATE MOUSSE

1 cup semisweet
  chocolate chips
1 teaspoon instant coffee
1/2 cup hot water
1 tablespoon sugar
3 eggs

2 tablespoons rum
  (optional)
1/4 teaspoon salt
1/2 cup whipping cream,
  whipped, sweetened

    Combine chocolate chips, instant coffee powder and hot water in blender container. Blend for 1 minute or until smooth. Add sugar, eggs, rum and salt. Blend for 1 minute or until smooth. Pour into individual serving dishes. Chill until serving time. Serve with whipped cream. Yield: 6 servings.

MOUSSE DELUXE

1/2 cup milk
1 cup vanilla milk chips
1 teaspoon vanilla extract
2 egg whites

1 tablespoon sugar
1 cup whipping cream,
  chilled

    Microwave milk on High in small glass bowl for 1 minute or until hot. Whisk in vanilla milk chips until melted and smooth. Stir in vanilla. Cool to room temperature. Beat egg whites in mixer bowl until foamy. Add sugar. Beat just until stiff peaks form. Fold in vanilla mixture gradually. Beat whipping cream in bowl until soft peaks form. Fold mousse in gently. Spoon into individual serving dishes. Chill for several hours.
Yield: 6 servings.

A Lion Tip

Prevent a "skin" from forming on custards and puddings by placing a piece of plastic wrap directly on the surface after removing from heat.

RICE AND PEACHES AND CREAM

1 cup uncooked brown
  rice
1 16-ounce can
  freestone sliced peaches
1/3 cup packed brown
  sugar

2 tablespoons margarine
1 teaspoon lemon juice
1/4 teaspoon cinnamon
1/4 teaspoon nutmeg
1/2 cup whipped topping

Cook rice using package directions. Drain peaches, reserving 1/2 cup liquid and 12 peach slices. Chop remaining peaches. Combine chopped peaches, reserved liquid, brown sugar, margarine, lemon juice, cinnamon and nutmeg with hot rice in saucepan; mix well. Simmer for 5 minutes. Spoon into buttered 1 1/2-quart baking dish. Spread whipped topping over top. Top with reserved peach slices. Bake at 450 degrees for 15 minutes. Yield: 6 servings.

SNAPPY PEACH TREATS

1 1/2 cups gingersnap
  crumbs
1/4 cup sugar
1/4 cup melted margarine
16 ounces cream cheese,
  softened
1/2 cup sugar

2 tablespoons flour
2 eggs
1 teaspoon vanilla extract
1 16-ounce can sliced
  peaches, drained,
  coarsely chopped

Combine cookie crumbs, 1/4 cup sugar and margarine in bowl; mix well. Reserve 1/4 cup mixture. Press remaining mixture into 9x9-inch baking pan. Bake at 325 degrees for 7 minutes. Combine cream cheese, 1/2 cup sugar and flour in mixer bowl. Beat at medium speed until smooth. Add eggs 1 at a time, mixing well after each addition. Blend in vanilla. Fold in peaches. Spoon into prepared pan. Bake for 40 to 45 minutes or until set. Sprinkle with reserved crumb mixture. Chill until serving time. Garnish with marzipan peaches if desired. Yield: 12 servings.

PEAR PECAN CUPS

1 16-ounce can pear
halves, drained, sliced
¹/₄ cup coarsely chopped
pecans

¹/₂ cup apricot preserves
¹/₂ cup whipping cream,
whipped

Toss pears with pecans in bowl. Spoon into individual serving dishes. Melt preserves in small saucepan over low heat. Spoon over pears. Top with whipped cream. Garnish with pecan halves. Yield: 4 servings.

PINEAPPLE BISQUE

1 8-ounce package
vanilla wafers, crushed
1 cup butter, softened
3 cups confectioners'
sugar
4 egg yolks
1 teaspoon vanilla extract
4 egg whites, stiffly
beaten

1 20-ounce can crushed
pineapple
1 4-ounce bottle of
cherries, drained,
chopped
Whipped cream
1 cup chopped nuts

Sprinkle half the cookie crumbs in 14x16-inch pan. Cream butter and confectioners' sugar in mixer bowl until light and fluffy. Add egg yolks and vanilla; mix well. Fold in stiffly beaten egg whites. Spoon evenly into prepared pan. Layer half the pineapple, cherries and remaining pineapple over top. Add layers of whipped cream, nuts and remaining cookie crumbs. Chill for 12 hours. Yield: 12 servings.

 A Lion Tip

Make a party sundae by arranging scoops of different flavors of ice cream in a large bowl. Serve with crushed pineapple, coconut, mandarin oranges, chocolate syrup, strawberry preserves and chopped nuts.

CREAMY BANANA PUDDING

1 cup sugar
3 tablespoons cornstarch
3 cups milk
3 egg yolks, slightly
 beaten
1/2 cup sour cream

2 teaspoons vanilla
 extract
Vanilla wafers
4 medium bananas, sliced
2 cups whipped topping

Mix sugar and cornstarch in 2-quart glass bowl. Stir in milk gradually. Microwave on High for 9 minutes or until thickened, stirring every 3 minutes. Stir a small amount of hot mixture into egg yolks; stir egg yolks into hot mixture. Microwave on High for 1 to 2 minutes or until thickened, stirring twice. Fold in sour cream and vanilla. Line bottom and sides of 2-quart bowl with vanilla wafers. Layer half the bananas and custard in prepared bowl. Repeat layers of vanilla wafers, bananas and custard. Chill until serving time. Spread with whipped topping. Yield: 8 servings.

EASY BANANA PUDDING

1 3-ounce package
 vanilla instant pudding
 mix
2 cups low-fat milk
1 cup low-fat sour cream
1 drop of yellow food
 coloring (optional)

6 ounces whipped
 topping
1 package vanilla wafers
4 medium bananas, sliced

Combine pudding mix, milk, sour cream and food coloring in bowl; mix until smooth. Fold in whipped topping. Line bottom and side of large baking dish with vanilla wafers. Layer half the bananas and pudding in prepared dish. Repeat layers of vanilla wafers, bananas and pudding. Crush several vanilla wafers; sprinkle over top. Chill until serving time.
Yield: 12 servings.

BREAD PUDDING

2 cups fine stale bread
  crumbs
1 quart milk
4 egg yolks
1¹/₂ cups sugar
Juice and grated rind of 1
  lemon

¹/₄ cup melted butter
4 egg whites
¹/₄ teaspoon salt
¹/₄ cup sugar
1 teaspoon vanilla extract
  or almond extract
1 cup fruit preserves

Combine bread crumbs with milk in bowl. Let stand for several minutes. Beat egg yolks in mixer bowl until thick and lemon-colored. Add 1¹/₂ cups sugar, lemon juice, lemon rind and melted butter; mix well. Stir in bread crumbs. Spoon into 1¹/₂-quart baking dish. Bake at 350 degrees for 30 to 40 minutes or until set. Reduce oven temperature to 300 degrees. Beat egg whites with salt in mixer bowl until foamy. Beat in remaining ¹/₄ cup sugar gradually. Add vanilla. Beat for 3 to 4 minutes or until smooth. Spread preserves evenly over pudding. Spread meringue over preserves, sealing to edge. Bake for 15 to 20 minutes or until golden brown. Yield: 8 servings.

MICROWAVE BREAD PUDDING

1 slice bread, cubed
2 tablespoons raisins
1 egg, beaten
¹/₂ cup evaporated milk

3 tablespoons water
2 tablespoons sugar
¹/₂ teaspoon cinnamon
¹/₄ teaspoon nutmeg

Sprinkle bread cubes in 2 lightly greased 6-ounce custard cups. Sprinkle with raisins. Combine egg, evaporated milk and water in bowl; mix well. Pour into prepared cups. Mix sugar, cinnamon and nutmeg in bowl. Sprinkle 1 tablespoon over each pudding. Microwave, covered, on Medium for 3 minutes; stir. Sprinkle with remaining sugar mixture. Microwave on medium for 3 to 4 minutes longer or until set. Yield: 2 servings.

OLD-FASHIONED BROWN PUDDING

1 cup packed brown
sugar
1 tablespoon shortening
1/2 cup milk
2 teaspoons baking
powder
1 teaspoon cinnamon

1/2 cup raisins
1 1/2 cups flour
1 1/2 cups packed brown
sugar
2 cups hot water
1 teaspoon (heaping)
butter

Combine 1 cup brown sugar, shortening, milk, baking powder, cinnamon, raisins and flour in order listed in mixer bowl, mixing well after each addition; set aside. Combine 1 1/2 cups brown sugar, hot water and butter in saucepan. Bring to a rolling boil. Pour into baking pan. Drop batter into syrup. Bake at 350 degrees for 25 to 30 minutes or until pudding tests done. Yield: 6 to 8 servings.

CHOCOLATE PUDDING

2 ounces unsweetened
baking chocolate
1 cup sugar
1 tablespoon flour
Salt to taste

1 cup milk
3 egg yolks, beaten
1/2 teaspoon vanilla
extract

Melt chocolate in heavy saucepan over very low heat. Combine sugar, flour and salt in double boiler. Stir in milk. Heat just to the simmering point. Add to chocolate; mix well. Stir a small amount of hot mixture into egg yolks; stir egg yolks into hot mixture. Cook over hot water until thickened; do not boil. Remove from heat. Stir in vanilla. Chill until serving time. Yield: 4 servings.

A Lion Tip

For a delicious topping for puddings, mix 1 cup sour cream and 1/2 cup packed brown sugar. Chill for 1 hour or longer and mix well before serving.

FROZEN LEMON PUDDING

2 egg yolks
6 tablespoons sugar
1/2 teaspoon grated lemon
  rind
2 tablespoons lemon juice
2 egg whites

1/4 cup sugar
1 cup evaporated milk,
  well chilled
3 tablespoons lemon juice
1 cup graham cracker
  crumbs

Combine egg yolks, 6 tablespoons sugar, lemon rind and 2 tablespoons lemon juice in large bowl; mix well. Beat egg whites in mixer bowl until stiff peaks form. Beat in 1/4 cup sugar. Fold into egg yolk mixture. Whip evaporated milk in bowl with rotary beater until fluffy. Add 3 tablespoons lemon juice; beat until stiff. Fold into pudding. Sprinkle half the cracker crumbs into 2 ice trays. Spoon pudding into prepared trays. Top with remaining crumbs. Freeze at coldest temperature; do not stir. Cut into squares; serve on chilled plates. Garnish with whipped topping. Yield: 8 servings.

FRUIT SHERBET

1 cup sugar
2 cups water
1 cup orange juice

Juice of 3 lemons
1 cup crushed pineapple

Bring sugar and water to a boil in saucepan, stirring to dissolve sugar. Let stand until cool. Add orange juice, lemon juice and pineapple. Spoon into freezer pan. Freeze until firm, stirring occasionally. Yield: 6 servings.

LEMON MILK SHERBET

Juice of 3 lemons
1 1/2 cups sugar
1 tablespoon unflavored
  gelatin

4 cups milk

Combine lemon juice and sugar in bowl, stirring until sugar is dissolved. Soften gelatin in 1/4 cup milk in saucepan. Add remaining 3 3/4 cups milk. Heat until gelatin is dissolved, stirring constantly. Add lemon mixture very gradually, stirring constantly. Pour into ice cream freezer. Freeze using manufacturer's directions. Yield: 6 servings.

LIME JELL-O SHERBET

1 large package lime
   gelatin
1½ cups boiling water
1½ cups sugar
Juice of 2 lemons

1 large can evaporated
   milk
1 evaporated milk can
   water

Dissolve gelatin in hot water in bowl. Stir in sugar until dissolved. Add lemon juice, evaporated milk and water; mix well. Spoon into freezer trays. Freeze until firm.
Yield: 10 servings.

PUMPKIN FREEZE

1¼ cups graham cracker
   crumbs
¼ cup melted margarine
   or butter
1 cup mashed cooked
   pumpkin
½ cup packed brown
   sugar

½ teaspoon cinnamon
½ teaspoon ginger
¼ teaspoon nutmeg
½ teaspoon salt
1 quart vanilla ice cream,
   softened

Mix cracker crumbs and margarine in bowl. Reserve 3 tablespoons crumb mixture; press remaining crumb mixture into pan. Combine pumpkin, brown sugar, cinnamon, ginger, nutmeg and salt in bowl; mix well. Stir in ice cream. Spoon into prepared pan. Sprinkle with reserved crumbs. Freeze for 4 hours or until firm. Let stand at room temperature for 10 to 15 minutes before serving. Yield: 8 servings.

A Lion Tip

A current trend which you can pick up on to fill the dessert gap is fancy and flavored coffees. Serve them with a selection of toppings such as whipped cream, shaved chocolate, grated orange rind, cinnamon sticks and grated nutmeg.

STRAWBERRY ANGEL

2 tablespoons unflavored
gelatin
1/2 cup cold water
1/2 cup sugar
1/2 cup boiling water
1/4 teaspoon salt
2 pints frozen
strawberries, thawed

2 cups whipping cream
1/2 cup sifted
confectioners' sugar
2 or 3 drops of red food
coloring
1 angel food cake, torn
into bite-sized pieces

Soften gelatin in cold water in cup. Combine with sugar, boiling water and salt in bowl; mix until gelatin is dissolved. Chill until thickened. Stir in strawberries. Whip cream in bowl until soft peaks form. Add confectioners' sugar and food coloring gradually. Fold in strawberry mixture. Spread enough strawberry mixture in 10-inch tube pan to cover bottom. Layer cake and remaining strawberry mixture 1/2 at a time in prepared pan. Chill until set. Unmold onto serving plate. May wrap with plastic wrap and freeze if desired. Yield: 12 servings.

HOT STRAWBERRY DUFF

2 pints strawberries
1 cup sugar
1 tablespoon cornstarch
1/4 cup melted butter
2 cups flour
3 tablespoons sugar

1 tablespoon baking
powder
1/2 teaspoon salt
1/2 cup very cold butter,
sliced
1/3 cup milk

Cut large strawberries into quarters. Combine with 1 cup sugar and cornstarch in saucepan. Heat until juicy. Spoon into shallow baking dish. Drizzle with melted butter. Combine flour, 3 tablespoons sugar, baking powder and salt in food processor container. Pulse several times to mix. Add cold butter. Pulse until mixture resembles coarse crumbs. Combine with milk in bowl; mix with spoon. Drop by spoonfuls onto strawberry mixture. Bake at 425 degrees for 20 minutes, covering loosely with foil if necessary to prevent overbrowning. Serve hot or warm with cream or whipped cream. Yield: 6 to 8 servings.

STRAWBERRY TAPIOCA DESSERTS

1 3-ounce package
   tapioca pudding mix
1³/₄ cups milk
½ teaspoon grated lemon
   rind

½ cup strawberry
   preserves or red currant
   jelly
1 pint fresh strawberries
   cut into halves, chilled

Combine tapioca pudding mix, milk and lemon rind in medium saucepan. Bring to a boil over medium heat, stirring constantly. Place saucepan in pan of cold water. Let stand for 10 minutes or until thickened, stirring occasionally. Spoon into individual dessert dishes. Melt preserves in medium saucepan over low heat; remove from heat. Add strawberries; mix lightly. Spoon over pudding. Chill until serving time. Yield: 4 servings.

ALMOND TORTE

1½ cups ground
   blanched almonds
6 tablespoons flour
6 egg whites
6 tablespoons sugar
6 egg yolks
³/₄ cup sugar

Juice and grated rind of 1
   lemon
¼ teaspoon almond
   extract
1½ cups whipping cream
3 tablespoons sugar

Mix almonds and flour in bowl; set aside. Beat egg whites in bowl until soft peaks form. Add 6 tablespoons sugar gradually, beating until stiff and glossy. Beat egg yolks and ³/₄ sugar in mixer bowl until thick and lemon-colored. Beat in lemon juice, lemon rind and almond extract. Fold egg whites into egg yolks mixture alternately with almond mixture, mixing until still streaked. Spoon into 3 buttered and floured 9-inch baking pans. Bake at 350 degrees for 15 to 20 minutes or until layers pull from sides of pans. Remove to wire rack to cool. Beat cream with 3 tablespoons sugar in mixer bowl until soft peaks form. Spoon ½ cup whipped cream into pastry bag fitted with star tip. Spread remaining whipped cream between layers of torte. Decorate top with rosettes of whipped cream. Yield: 8 to 10 servings.

CHOCOLATE-RASPBERRY TORTE

1¹/₃ cups flour
¹/₂ cup sugar
1¹/₂ teaspoons baking
  powder
¹/₂ teaspoon salt
2 egg whites
¹/₄ cup sugar
1 cup whipping cream
2 egg yolks
¹/₄ cup sugar

¹/₂ teaspoon almond
  extract
1 recipe chocolate
  frosting
¹/₂ cup sliced almonds
¹/₄ cup seedless
  raspberry preserves
¹/₂ cup sweetened
  whipped cream

Combine flour, ¹/₂ cup sugar, baking powder and salt in bowl; set aside. Beat egg whites in small mixer bowl until foamy. Add ¹/₄ cup sugar gradually, beating until stiff peaks form. Beat 1 cup whipping cream in mixer bowl until soft peaks form. Fold into egg whites. Beat egg yolks, ¹/₄ cup sugar and almond extract in mixer bowl for 3 minutes or until thick and lemon-colored. Fold gently into egg white mixture. Fold in flour mixture just until moistened. Spoon into 2 greased and floured 8 or 9-inch baking pans. Bake at 350 degrees for 25 to 30 minutes or until layers spring back when lightly touched in center. Cool in pans for 5 minutes. Remove to wire rack to cool completely. Split cake layers into halves horizontally. Spread 3 layers with chocolate frosting; sprinkle each layer with 1 tablespoon almonds. Stack layers on serving plate. Spread top with raspberry preserves. Frost side of torte with remaining chocolate frosting. Pipe ¹/₂ cup sweetened whipped cream around top edge; sprinkle edge and center with remaining almonds. Chill until serving time. Yield: 16 servings.

 ### A Lion Tip

Layer a mixture of 4 cups chopped peaches, 2 tablespoons sugar and a large package of dry peach gelatin with pound cake cubes, prepared vanilla instant pudding and whipped topping for an easy Peach Delight.

MOCHA TORTE WITH FRENCH CREAM FILLING

6 egg whites
1¹/2 cups sifted
  confectioners' sugar
¹/4 teaspoon cream of
  tartar
1¹/2 cups chopped nuts
¹/2 cup margarine,
  softened

1¹/2 cups sifted
  confectioners' sugar
1 tablespoon instant
  coffee
1 teaspoon vanilla extract
4 egg yolks

Beat egg whites in mixer bowl until soft peaks form. Add 1¹/2 cups confectioners' sugar and cream of tartar gradually, beating until very stiff peaks form. Fold in nuts quickly. Spread into four 8 or 9-inch rounds on greased and floured baking sheets. Bake at 270 degrees for 1 hour. Cool on baking sheets. Cream margarine in mixer bowl until light. Add 1¹/2 cups confectioners' sugar, instant coffee and vanilla; mix well. Beat in egg yolks 1 at a time. Spread between layers and over top of torte just before serving. May bake layers in cookie size for individual tortes. May flavor with vanilla, chocolate or almond extract instead of coffee. Yield: 8 servings.

ORANGE AND CRANBERRY TORTE

2¹/4 cups flour
1 cup sugar
1 teaspoon baking
  powder
1 teaspoon soda
¹/4 teaspoon salt
1 cup chopped nuts
1 cup chopped dates

1 cup fresh cranberries
Grated rind of 2 oranges
2 eggs, beaten
1 cup buttermilk
³/4 cup oil
1 cup orange juice
1 cup sugar

Sift flour, 1 cup sugar, baking powder, soda and salt into bowl. Add nuts, dates, cranberries and orange rind; mix well. Mix eggs, buttermilk and oil in small bowl. Add to fruit mixture; mix well. Spoon into greased 10-inch tube pan. Bake at 350 degrees for 1 hour. Cool in pan until lukewarm. Remove to wire rack over wide bowl. Combine orange juice and 1 cup sugar in bowl. Pour over cake, allowing excess to drip into bowl. Pour excess over torte again. Place in deep bowl. Wrap with heavy-

duty foil. Chill for 24 hours. Serve with whipped cream. May store in refrigerator for 2 weeks or longer.
Yield: 12 to 15 servings.

PARTY TORTE

8 egg whites
1/4 teaspoon cream of
  tartar
1 teaspoon vinegar
2 cups sugar
2 cups whipping cream

1 cup drained crushed
  pineapple
1 small bottle of cherries,
  drained, chopped
12 miniature
  marshmallows

Beat egg whites with cream of tartar and vinegar in mixer bowl until stiff but not dry peaks form. Add sugar 1 tablespoon at a time, beating until stiff peaks form. Spoon into two 8-inch baking pans lined with baking parchment. Bake at 350 degrees for 30 minutes. Reduce oven temperature to 275 degrees. Bake for 1 hour longer. Remove to wire rack to cool. Whip cream in mixer bowl until soft peaks form. Add pineapple, cherries and marshmallows; mix well. Spread between layers and over top and side of torte. Garnish with additional cherries. Chill overnight. Slice to serve. Yield: 10 to 12 servings.

HOLIDAY TRIFLE

1　3-ounce package
  vanilla pudding and pie
  filling mix
2 cups milk
1 cup whipping cream,
  whipped

1　8-inch raspberry-filled
  cake roll
1/4 cup orange liqueur
Crushed peppermint
  candy
Green candied pineapple

Prepare pudding and pie filling mix with milk, using package directions. Let stand until cool. Fold in half the whipped cream. Cut cake into 10 slices. Brush with orange liqueur. Arrange 7 slices over bottom and side of 2 1/2-quart glass bowl. Spoon half the pudding mixture into prepared bowl. Top with remaining 3 slices cake and remaining pudding. Spoon remaining whipped cream into pastry bag fitted with large star tip. Pipe onto top of trifle. Chill for up to 4 hours. Garnish with candy and pineapple just before serving.
Yield: 8 to 10 servings.

TIRAMISU

24 ladyfingers
1/3 cup Bourbon
1 cup strong coffee
4 egg yolks
1 cup sugar

12 ounces Mascarpone
 cheese
4 egg whites
3/4 ounce bittersweet
 chocolate, grated

Arrange 2/3 of the ladyfingers over bottom and side of 2-quart bowl. Mix Bourbon and coffee in small bowl. Sprinkle 2/3 of the mixture over ladyfingers in bowl. Beat egg yolks with sugar in mixer bowl until smooth. Add cheese; mix well. Beat egg whites in bowl until stiff peaks form. Fold into cheese mixture gently. Spoon half the cheese mixture over ladyfingers. Top with remaining ladyfingers. Sprinkle with remaining coffee mixture and half the chocolate. Top with remaining cheese mixture and chocolate. Chill for 2 hours or longer. May substitute 30 vanilla wafers for ladyfingers. Yield: 8 servings.

A Lion Tip

Try an easy no-cook dessert:

- Serve a plate of assorted fruits and cheeses with individual knives for paring and slicing for a very continental dessert.

- Shape scoops of lemon or orange sherbet into balls and roll in flaked coconut and freeze until firm. Serve with sliced strawberries or peaches.

- Serve melon balls in wine, liqueur or champagne in a fancy compote.

- Make quick dessert sundaes by topping ice cream with mashed fruit, preserves, crushed peppermint, chocolate chips, chopped nuts or crushed candy bars.

SUBSTITUTION CHART

	Instead of	Use
Baking	1 teaspoon baking powder	1/4 teaspoon soda plus 1/2 teaspoon cream of tartar
	1 tablespoon cornstarch (for thickening)	2 tablespoons flour or 1 tablespoon tapioca
	1 cup sifted all-purpose flour	1 cup plus 2 tablespoons sifted cake flour
	1 cup sifted cake flour	1 cup minus 2 tablespoons sifted all-purpose flour
	1 cup dry bread crumbs	3/4 cup cracker crumbs
Dairy	1 cup buttermilk	1 cup sour milk or 1 cup yogurt
	1 cup heavy cream	3/4 cup skim milk plus 1/3 cup butter
	1 cup light cream	7/8 cup skim milk plus 3 tablespoons butter
	1 cup sour cream	7/8 cup sour milk plus 3 tablespoons butter
	1 cup sour milk	1 cup milk plus 1 tablespoon vinegar or lemon juice or 1 cup buttermilk
Seasoning	1 teaspoon allspice	1/2 teaspoon cinnamon plus 1/8 teaspoon cloves
	1 cup catsup	1 cup tomato sauce plus 1/2 cup sugar plus 2 tablespoons vinegar
	1 clove of garlic	1/8 teaspoon garlic powder or 1/8 teaspoon instant minced garlic or 3/4 teaspoon garlic salt or 5 drops of liquid garlic
	1 teaspoon Italian spice	1/4 teaspoon each oregano, basil, thyme, rosemary plus dash of cayenne
	1 teaspoon lemon juice	1/2 teaspoon vinegar
	1 tablespoon mustard	1 teaspoon dry mustard
	1 medium onion	1 tablespoon dried minced onion or 1 teaspoon onion powder
Sweet	1 1-ounce square chocolate	1/4 cup cocoa plus 1 teaspoon shortening
	1 2/3 ounces semisweet chocolate	1 ounce unsweetened chocolate plus 4 teaspoons granulated sugar
	1 cup honey	1 to 1 1/4 cups sugar plus 1/4 cup liquid or 1 cup corn syrup or molasses
	1 cup granulated sugar	1 cup packed brown sugar or 1 cup corn syrup, molasses or honey minus 1/4 cup liquid

EQUIVALENT CHART

	When the recipe calls for	Use
Baking	½ cup butter 2 cups butter 4 cups all-purpose flour 4½ to 5 cups sifted cake flour 1 square chocolate 1 cup semisweet chocolate chips 4 cups marshmallows 2¼ cups packed brown sugar 4 cups confectioners' sugar 2 cups granulated sugar	4 ounces 1 pound 1 pound 1 pound 1 ounce 6 ounces 1 pound 1 pound 1 pound 1 pound
Cereal – Bread	1 cup fine dry bread crumbs 1 cup soft bread crumbs 1 cup small bread cubes 1 cup fine cracker crumbs 1 cup fine graham cracker crumbs 1 cup vanilla wafer crumbs 1 cup crushed cornflakes 4 cups cooked macaroni 3½ cups cooked rice	4 to 5 slices 2 slices 2 slices 28 saltines 15 crackers 22 wafers 3 cups uncrushed 8 ounces uncooked 1 cup uncooked
Dairy	1 cup shredded cheese 1 cup cottage cheese 1 cup sour cream 1 cup whipped cream ⅔ cup evaporated milk 1⅔ cups evaporated milk	4 ounces 8 ounces 8 ounces ½ cup heavy cream 1 small can 1 13-ounce can

Fruit	4 cups sliced or chopped apples
	1 cup mashed bananas
	2 cups pitted cherries
	3 cups shredded coconut
	4 cups cranberries
	1 cup pitted dates
	1 cup candied fruit
	3 to 4 tablespoons lemon juice plus
	  1 tablespoon grated lemon rind
	⅓ cup orange juice plus 2 teaspoons
	  grated orange rind
	4 cups sliced peaches
	2 cups pitted prunes
	3 cups raisins
		4 medium
		3 medium
		4 cups unpitted
		8 ounces
		1 pound
		1 8-ounce package
		1 8-ounce package
		1 lemon
		
		1 orange
		
		8 medium
		1 12-ounce package
		1 15-ounce package

When the recipe calls for	Use
Meats 4 cups chopped cooked chicken 3 cups chopped cooked meat 2 cups cooked ground meat	1 5-pound chicken 1 pound, cooked 1 pound, cooked
Nuts 1 cup chopped nuts	4 ounces shelled 1 pound unshelled
Vegetables 2 cups cooked green beans 2½ cups lima beans or red beans 4 cups shredded cabbage 1 cup grated carrot 8 ounces fresh mushrooms 1 cup chopped onion 4 cups sliced or chopped potatoes 2 cups canned tomatoes	½ pound fresh or 1 16-ounce can 1 cup dried, cooked 1 pound 1 large 1 4-ounce can 1 large 4 medium 1 16-ounce can

Measurement Equivalents

1 tablespoon = 3 teaspoons 2 tablespoons = 1 ounce 4 tablespoons = ¼ cup 5⅓ tablespoons = ⅓ cup 8 tablespoons = ½ cup 12 tablespoons = ¾ cup 16 tablespoons = 1 cup 1 cup = 8 ounces or ½ pint 4 cups = 1 quart 4 quarts = 1 gallon	1 6½ to 8-ounce can = 1 cup 1 10½ to 12-ounce can = 1¼ cups 1 14 to 16-ounce can = 1¾ cups 1 16 to 17-ounce can = 2 cups 1 18 to 20-ounce can = 2½ cups 1 20-ounce can = 3½ cups 1 46 to 51-ounce can = 5¾ cups 1 6½ to 7½-pound can or Number 10 = 12 to 13 cups

Metric Equivalents

Liquid	Dry
1 teaspoon = 5 milliliters 1 tablespoon = 15 milliliters 1 fluid ounce = 30 milliliters 1 cup = 250 milliliters 1 pint = 500 milliliters	1 quart = 1 liter 1 ounce = 30 grams 1 pound = 450 grams 2.2 pounds = 1 kilogram

NOTE: The metric measures are approximate benchmarks for purposes of home food preparation.

INDEX

This Cookbook is a perfect gift for Holidays, Weddings, Anniversaries and Birthdays.

★ ★ ★ ★ ★ ★ ★ ★ ★

You may order as many of our *Lions in the Kitchen* Cookbooks as you wish for the price of $8.00 each, plus $2.00 postage and handling per book ordered and mailed within the U.S.A. Mail to:

Huntsville Lions Club
P. O. Box 162
Huntsville, Alabama 35804

Make check payable to the order of: Huntsville Lions Club.

★ ★ ★ ★ ★ ★ ★ ★ ★

Please indicate:

Total books ordered _____   Amount enclosed_____

Ship to:

NAME _____

ADDRESS_____

CITY_____   STATE ____   ZIP _____